OFFICE FOR
NATIONAL STATISTICS

Regional Trends 32

1997 edition

Editor :	John Pullinger
Associate Editor :	Alison Holding
Production team :	Jan Kiernan
	Andy Corris
	Max Bonini
	Mario Alemanno
	Martin Smith
	Elizabeth Ankamah
	Louise Pickering
Design & artwork :	Richard Lloyd
Maps :	Annette McArthur
	Alan Smith

London: The Stationery Office

9708089

Contents

HM16
REF ONLY

Contents

Contents

* Indicates related data available in the sub-regional tables in Chapters 14 to 17.

Introduction

R egional Trends provides a unique description of the regions of the United Kingdom. In 17 chapters it covers a wide range of demographic, social, industrial and economic statistics, taking a look at most aspects of life. The chapters fall broadly into four sections: regional profiles (Chapter 1), the European Union (Chapter 2), the main topic areas (Chapters 3 to 13) and sub-regional statistics (Chapters 14 to 17). To make it easy to understand the differences between regions, information is given in simple and clear tables, maps and charts.

Regional statistics are essential for a wide range of people: for example, policy-makers and planners in both the public and private sectors; marketing professionals; researchers; students and teachers; journalists; and anyone with general regional interests. *Regional Trends* brings together data from diverse sources and, for many topics, is the only place where data for the whole of the United Kingdom are available in one table.

Recent changes in regional statistics

For more than 30 years, regional statistics for England have been presented on the basis of the Standard Statistical Regions (SSRs). In 1994, new Government Offices for the Regions were established based on the functions of the then four departments of Environment, Transport, Employment (now Education and Employment), and Trade and Industry. The Government Offices work in partnership with local people to maximise competitiveness, prosperity and quality of life in each region. Following public consultation, the decision was taken that with effect from April 1997 the primary classification for the presentation of regional statistics should be the Government Office Regions (GORs). This is the first edition of *Regional Trends* to use the GOR classification for England, although there are a few cases where the transition has not yet been made. A table showing the relationship between the GORs and the SSRs is included on page 10.

The effect of the change to the regional classification is that it has not always been possible to provide historic data for comparison/long-term trend analysis, although short-term trends are given where possible. For those users who need SSR data for continuity, the equivalent of most of the GOR tables can be obtained from the Regional Reporting Branch at the address overleaf.

Although Merseyside has its own Government Office, for statistical purposes it has not been adopted as a region in its own right because of the difficulties associated with obtaining the full range of data for a relatively small area. Wherever possible, however, figures for the two components of the North West and Merseyside region are given separately.

A second major change to this edition is the presentation of the sub-regional statistics following the recent local government reorganisations in England, Wales and Scotland: there is now one sub-regional chapter for each of the four countries of the United Kingdom. Chapter 15 on Wales and Chapter 16 on Scotland present data for the Unitary Authorities (UAs) and the New Councils respectively which replaced the former two-tier systems on 1 April 1996. Chapter 17 on Northern Ireland continues to give figures at Board or district level as available.

The local government reorganisation in England has been more complex than in Wales and Scotland and is being introduced over a period of four years. The first phase was in April 1995 when the Isle of Wight became a UA. In April 1996 three counties - Avon, Cleveland and Humberside - were abolished altogether in favour of UAs. In the case of Cleveland, the districts simply became UAs (one with a change of name), but in Avon and Humberside there were reductions in the number of UAs compared with the former districts. North Yorkshire was the one other county where local government was reorganised in April 1996: an extended York became a UA, while the rest of the county retained its two-tier system.

Throughout *Regional Trends 32*, maps and tables at county or district level, notably in Chapter 14 on the sub-regions, continue to present statistics for the local government structure in place prior to 1 April 1996. In Chapter 14, however, where available, figures for the new structures are given at the end of each table. The third phase of the local government reorganisation in England came into effect on 1 April 1997, but statistics reflecting these changes are not included in this edition.

The *Gazetteer* accompanying this edition of *Regional Trends* has been prepared to assist users adapt to the GORs and the new structure of local government - notably in England where there is the mixture of UAs and two-tier systems. Although the local government structure in Northern Ireland has not been reorganised, the *Gazetteer* covers the United Kingdom for completeness. It lists every area in the old/new geographies (in alphabetical order of the old district geography within each of the four countries) giving its status and which (former/new) county, SSR and GOR it is in.

Regional boundaries

Apart from the GORs which are used as far as is possible throughout, there are a number of other regional classifications used in *Regional Trends 32*. Maps of these non-standard regions are given on pages 214 and 215 of the Technical notes (known as the Appendix notes in previous editions). Maps of the statistical regions of the United Kingdom and the sub-regions in each of the four countries are given in Chapters 1 and 14 to 17. The United Kingdom comprises Great Britain and Northern Ireland; Great Britain consists of England, Wales and Scotland. The Isle of Man and the Channel Isles are not part of the United Kingdom. The Scilly Isles are included as part of Cornwall throughout.

Coverage and definitions

Due to variations in coverage and definitions, some care may be needed when comparing data from more than one source. Readers should consult the Technical notes as well as reading the footnotes relevant to each table and chart for help in analysing trends or comparing different sources.

Sources

The source of the data is given at the foot of each table, map and chart. Much of the information included in the Population and Households and the Labour market chapters of *Regional Trends* can be found on NOMIS, the online database run by Durham University under contract to the Office for National Statistics (ONS). It contains government statistics down to the smallest available geographic area which may be unpublished elsewhere. The ONS' publication *Social Trends* (The Stationery Office) contains further details on many of the topics covered in this book, generally at national level only.

Availability on electronic media

The data contained in this edition of *Regional Trends* are available electronically either via the Internet or on a diskette. Customers who take out a Standing Order for future editions of *Regional Trends* will be given the data electronically free of charge (see enclosed Order form). Those customers who would like the data electronically, but who do not wish to place a Standing Order can obtain the data by calling the ONS Sales Desk on 0171 533 5678. (Please contact the Regional Reporting Branch for data for the SSRs.)

The first 30 editions of *Regional Trends* are available on CD-ROM, price £99 + VAT (£49 + VAT for public libraries and academia). To order a copy, please ring the ONS Sales Desk.

Contributors

The Editor and Associate Editor wish to thank all their colleagues in the ONS and the rest of the Government Statistical Service and all contributors in other organisations without whose help this publication would not be possible. A special thank you goes to Richard Lloyd in the Onsdesign and to Annette McArthur, Alan Smith, Philip Sharland and Gordon Elliott in the Geographic Information Systems Unit.

Regional Reporting Branch
Office for National Statistics
1 Drummond Gate
London
SW1V 2QQ

Telephone number for enquiries: 0171 533 5796/5797

STANDARD STATISTICAL REGION	COUNTY*	GOVERNMENT OFFICE REGION
NORTH	Cleveland* Durham Northumberland Tyne and Wear	NORTH EAST
	Cumbria	NORTH WEST
NORTH WEST	Cheshire Greater Manchester Lancashire	NORTH WEST
	Merseyside	MERSEYSIDE
YORKSHIRE AND HUMBERSIDE	Humberside* North Yorkshire* South Yorkshire West Yorkshire	YORKSHIRE AND THE HUMBER
EAST MIDLANDS	Derbyshire Leicestershire Lincolnshire Northamptonshire Nottinghamshire	EAST MIDLANDS
WEST MIDLANDS	Hereford and Worcester Shropshire Staffordshire Warwickshire West Midlands	WEST MIDLANDS
SOUTH WEST	Avon* Cornwall Devon Dorset Gloucestershire Somerset Wiltshire	SOUTH WEST
EAST ANGLIA	Cambridgeshire Norfolk Suffolk	EASTERN
	Bedfordshire Essex Hertfordshire	EASTERN
	Greater London	LONDON
SOUTH EAST	Berkshire Buckinghamshire East Sussex Hampshire Isle of Wight* Kent Oxfordshire Surrey West Sussex	SOUTH EAST

* Counties prior to local government reorganisation.

1 Regional profiles

Statistical regions of the United Kingdom

ENGLAND

——————— Government
Office Region
boundary

SCOTLAND

NORTHERN
IRELAND

NORTH
EAST

NORTH
WEST

YORKSHIRE
AND THE
HUMBER

MERSEYSIDE

EAST
MIDLANDS

WEST
MIDLANDS

WALES

EASTERN

LONDON

SOUTH WEST

SOUTH EAST

North East

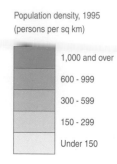

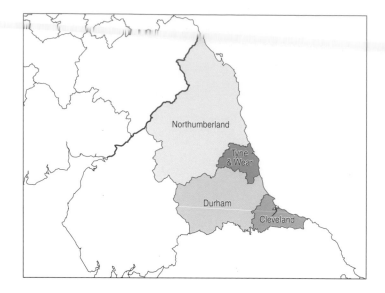

Population density, 1995
(persons per sq km)

	1,000 and over
	600 - 999
	300 - 599
	150 - 299
	Under 150

Northumberland

Tyne & Wear

Durham

Cleveland

Population
The population of the North East fell by just over 1 per cent between 1981 and 1995 compared with growth of 4 per cent in the United Kingdom as a whole.

(Tables 3.1 and 14.1)

Education
The North East has the highest proportion of three and four year olds in school, but the lowest proportion of 16 year olds in post-compulsory education.

(Tables 4.4 and 4.5)

Higher education students from the North East were more likely than those from any other region in 1995/96 to be studying mathematics or a physical science.

(Table 4.11)

Labour market
The North East lost 88 days per 1,000 employees due to labour disputes in 1996, the joint highest with London.

(Chart 5.11)

Average earnings in the North East in April 1996, at £348 for men and £252 for women, were among the lowest in the United Kingdom.

(Tables 5.16 and 5.17)

Housing
Two fifths of households in the North East in 1995-96 lived in semi-detached houses, while a further third lived in terraced houses.

(Table 6.5)

Lifestyles
Twenty seven per cent of households in the North East were on Family Credit or Income Support in 1995-96, a higher proportion than in any other region of Great Britain.

(Table 8.7)

Households in the North East are the most likely to have central heating, together with those in Northern Ireland, but are the least likely to own a dishwasher.

(Table 8.12)

Crime
The North East had the highest recorded crime rate in England and Wales in 1995.

(Table 9.1)

Transport
People in the North East were less likely than those in any other region to be involved in a fatal or serious road accident in 1995.

(Table 10.6)

Industry
On average, factories in the North East are larger than those in any other region.

(Table 13.2)

North West (GOR) and Merseyside

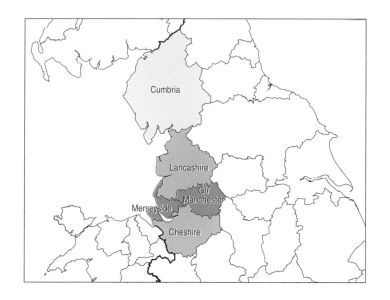

Population density, 1995
(persons per sq km)

	1,000 and over
	600 - 999
	300 - 599
	150 - 299
	Under 150

Population

The population of Merseyside fell by more than 6 per cent between 1981 and 1995 compared with growth of 1 per cent in North West and of 4 per cent for the United Kingdom.

(Tables 3.1 and 14.1)

Education

The average A/AS level point score in 1994/95 was higher in the North West than in any other region in England and Wales.

(Table 4.6)

Higher education students from Merseyside were more likely than those from any other region in 1995/96 to be studying medicine or dentistry.

(Table 4.11)

Labour market

The economic activity rate in the North West in Spring 1996 was nearly 62 per cent (slightly below the UK average) compared with less than 56 per cent in Merseyside, the lowest proportion in the United Kingdom.

(Tables 5.1 and 5.3)

Men in the North West earned an average of £369 a week in April 1996 compared with £362 for men in Merseyside; but among women those in the North West earned less than those in Merseyside, at £262 and £271 respectively.

(Tables 5.16 and 5.17)

Housing

House prices in Merseyside rose by an average of 10 per cent between 1995 and 1996, the greatest increase of all the UK regions, while those in the North West were static.

(Table 6.10)

Health

In 1994, adults in the North West Regional Health Authority area were less likely than those in any other RHA in England to eat vegetables or salad or fruit on at least five days a week.

(Table 7.10)

Lifestyles

On average, households in the North West and Merseyside spent more per week on alcohol and tobacco in 1995-96 than households in any other region.

(Table 8.9)

Crime

The recorded crime rate in the North West fell by 3 per cent between 1994 and 1995 but it rose by 13 per cent in Merseyside.

(Table 9.1)

Environment

The North West is the wettest English region with average rainfall almost half as much again as the average for England.

(Table 11.1)

Industry

Over a quarter of gross value added in manufacturing in the North West and Merseyside was from factories of 1,000 or more employees, a higher proportion than in any other region.

(Table 13.5)

Yorkshire and the Humber

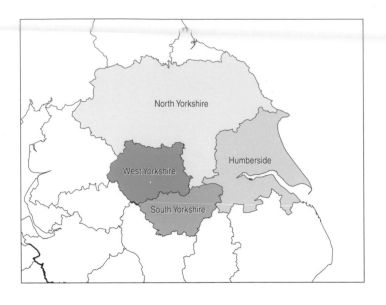

North Yorkshire

West Yorkshire

Humberside

South Yorkshire

Population
The population of the Yorkshire and Humber region grew by just over 2 per cent between 1981 and 1995, compared with growth of 4 per cent in the United Kingdom as a whole.
(Tables 3.1 and 14.1)

Education and training
Non-manual employees in the Yorkshire and Humber region were more likely than those in any other region to receive some form of job-related training in Spring 1996.
(Table 4.15)

Labour market
Almost half of female employees in the Yorkshire and Humber region work part-time; only the South West has a higher proportion.
(Table 5.6)

Yorkshire and the Humber is the only region where the ILO unemployment rate fell every year between 1992 and 1996.
(Table 5.21)

Housing
The average local authority rent in the Yorkshire and Humber region in April 1996 was £31 per week, (jointly with that in Scotland) the lowest in the United Kingdom.
(Table 6.8)

Health
One in six women in the Yorkshire and Humber region has a hearing difficulty, a higher proportion than in any other region.
(Table 7.6)

Lifestyles
In 1995-96, 77 per cent of households in the Yorkshire and Humber region were in receipt of some form of Social Security Benefit compared with the GB average of 75 per cent.
(Table 8.7)

Crime
The recorded crime rate in the Yorkshire and Humber region during 1995 was the second highest in England and Wales, and the region had the lowest clear-up rate.
(Tables 9.1 and 9.3)

Transport
On average people living in the Yorkshire and Humber region travel a shorter distance to work than those in any other region of Great Britain.
(Chart 10.9)

Environment
A fifth of the land area of the Yorkshire and Humber region is designated as National Park.
(Table 11.12)

Agriculture
The Yorkshire and Humber region had the second highest yields of wheat and barley in England and Wales during 1995.
(Table 13.17)

East Midlands

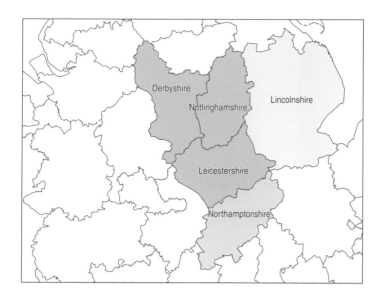

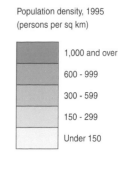

Population density, 1995
(persons per sq km)

1,000 and over
600 - 999
300 - 599
150 - 299
Under 150

Population

The East Midlands is one of the faster growing regions with population growth of 7 per cent between 1981 and 1995, compared with 4 per cent in the United Kingdom as a whole.

(Tables 3.1 and 14.1)

Education and training

Employees in the East Midlands were less likely than those in any other region of Great Britain to receive job-related training in Spring 1996.

(Table 4.15)

Labour market

Over 17 per cent of female employees in the East Midlands worked in manufacturing in 1995, the highest proportion in the United Kingdom.

(Table 5.8)

Excluding unpaid overtime, on average, women in the East Midlands work the longest hours for the lowest pay.

(Table 5.17)

Claimant unemployment in the East Midlands in January 1997 ranged from 4.4 per cent in Northamptonshire and 4.5 per cent in Leicestershire to 8.0 per cent in Nottinghamshire.

(Chart 5.22)

Housing

Just over seven in every ten dwellings in the East Midlands are owner-occupied, one of the highest proportions.

(Table 6.2)

Among the English regions, the East Midlands had the highest rate of new homes completed by local authorities in 1995 and (jointly with the Eastern region) by private developers.

(Table 6.4)

Health

The Trent Regional Health Authority area had a better record for cervical screening in 1995-96 than any other RHA in England.

(Table 7.14)

Lifestyles

On average, households in the East Midlands spent a sixth of their total expenditure on motoring and fares in 1995-96, a higher proportion than in any other region.

(Table 8.9)

Crime

The recorded crime rate in the East Midlands fell by 3 per cent between 1994 and 1995 despite rises of 4 per cent in the rate for offences of violence against the person and of 13 per cent in robberies.

(Table 9.1)

Transport

People in the East Midlands travel less distance by public transport in a year than those in any other English region.

(Table 10.10)

West Midlands

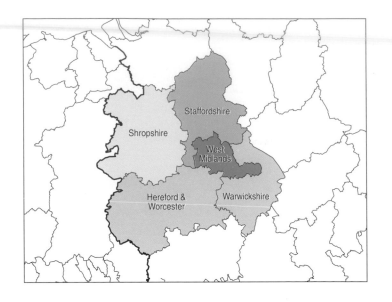

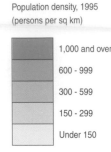

Population density, 1995
(persons per sq km)

	1,000 and over
	600 - 999
	300 - 599
	150 - 299
	Under 150

Population

The population of the West Midlands rose by just over 2 per cent between 1981 and 1995, about half the increase in the United Kingdom as a whole.

(Tables 3.1 and 14.1)

Eight per cent of the population in the West Midlands is from an ethnic minority group, the highest proportion apart from London.

(Table 3.15)

Education and training

Fifty-six per cent of the Youth Training participants in the West Midlands in 1995-96 gained a qualification, the highest proportion in England and Wales.

(Table 4.17)

Labour market

In 1995, 38 per cent of male employees in the West Midlands worked in manufacturing, a higher proportion than any other region.

(Table 5.8)

Claimant unemployment in the West Midlands in January 1997 ranged from 4.1 per cent in Shropshire to 8.1 per cent in the West Midlands Metropolitan County.

(Chart 5.22)

Housing

The average private sector rent in the West Midlands in 1995-96 was £58 per week compared with an average of £76 for England as a whole.

(Table 6.8)

Health

In 1994, adults in the West Midlands Regional Health Authority area were less likely to eat wholemeal bread and more likely to take sugar in their tea or coffee or to add salt in their cooking than those in any other RHA in England.

(Table 7.10)

Lifestyles

Nearly three quarters of households in the West Midlands participated in the National Lottery in 1995-96 compared with two thirds in the United Kingdom as a whole.

(Table 8.15)

Crime

The recorded crime rate in the West Midlands fell by 2 per cent overall between 1994 and 1995, even though the robbery rate increased by 12 per cent.

(Table 9.1)

Transport

New registrations in 1995 accounted for more than 12 per cent of cars licensed to addresses in the West Midlands, a higher proportion than in any other region of Great Britain.

(Table 10.1)

Industry

Production accounted for a higher proportion of gross domestic product in the West Midlands in 1995 than in any other region.

(Chart 13.1)

Eastern

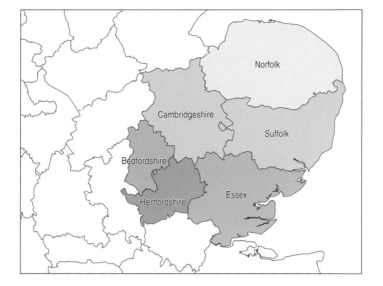

Population density, 1995
(persons per sq km)

■	1,000 and over
■	600 - 999
■	300 - 599
■	150 - 299
■	Under 150

Population

The Eastern region is one of the fastest growing regions with population growth of over 8 per cent between 1981 and 1995, more than double the growth in the United Kingdom as a whole.

(Tables 3.1 and 14.1)

Education and training

Proportionately more pupils in the Eastern region than in any other region of Great Britain are in grant-maintained schools.

(Table 4.1)

Manual employees in the Eastern region were more likely than those in any other region to receive some form of job-related training in Spring 1996.

(Table 4.15)

Labour market

Including unpaid overtime, full-time employees in the Eastern region worked almost 45 hours a week on average in Spring 1996, a longer working week than in any other region.

(Table 5.15)

One in five of the ILO unemployed of working age in the Eastern region in 1995/96 was aged 50 or over, a higher proportion than in any other region.

(Table 5.25)

Housing

In 1995 private developers built more new homes per head of population in the Eastern region (jointly with the East Midlands) than in any other English region.

(Table 6.4)

Health

The infant mortality rate in the Eastern region in 1995 was lower than in any other region.

(Table 7.2)

Lifestyles

In 1995-96, 26 per cent of households in the Eastern region owned stocks and shares and 37 per cent had Premium Bonds, proportions second only to the South East (GOR).

(Table 8.4)

Crime

The Eastern region had the lowest recorded crime rate of all the regions in England and Wales in 1995.

(Table 9.1)

Transport

People in the Eastern region cycle an average of 60 miles a year, the furthest in Great Britain.

(Table 10.10)

Industry

Expenditure on Research and Development in the Eastern region in 1995 accounted for nearly 4 per cent of gross domestic product, a higher proportion than in any other region.

(Table 13.11)

London

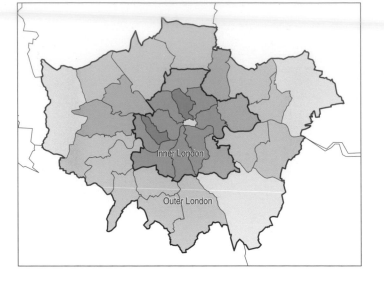

Population density, 1995
(persons per sq km)

▮	10,000 and over
▮	7,500 - 9,999
▮	5,000 - 7,499
▮	2,500 - 4,999
▮	Under 2,500

Population

London has the highest birth rate among women aged 35 or over.

(Table 3.8)

Nearly one in four of the population in London belongs to an ethnic minority group, by far the highest proportion.

(Table 3.15)

Labour market

London has the joint highest proportion of part-time workers among its male employees, yet the lowest proportion among women.

(Table 5.6)

With 23 per cent of the economically active population possessing a degree or equivalent at Spring 1996, London has the most qualified labour force.

(Table 5.10)

Long-term unemployment is more of a problem in London than in any other region except Northern Ireland.

(Table 5.23)

Housing

Fifty seven per cent of dwellings in London are owner-occupied, a lower proportion than in any other region.

(Table 6.2)

Health

Adults in London are less likely to have a regular dental check-up than those in any other region.

(Table 7.5)

Lifestyles

Nearly 4 per cent of people in London had a personal income of £50,000 or more in 1994-95, a higher proportion than in any other region.

(Table 8.5)

Crime

Recorded offences of violence against the person per head of population fell by 15 per cent in London between 1994 and 1995, the greatest fall of any region in England and Wales (although they remain well above the national average).

(Table 9.1)

Transport

Londoners walk further each year and travel further on public transport than people in any other region of Great Britain.

(Table 10.10)

Industry

At nearly £33,500, London had the highest level of gross value added per employee in manufacturing in 1994.

(Table 13.4)

South East (GOR)

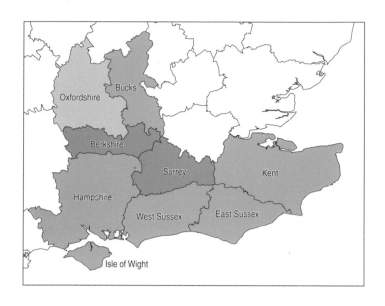

Population density, 1995
(persons per sq km)

1,000 and over

600 - 999

300 - 599

150 - 299

Under 150

Population	The South East is one of the fastest growing regions, with population growth of over 8 per cent between 1981 and 1991, more than double the growth in the United Kingdom as a whole.
	(Tables 3.1 and 14.1)
Education	One in three boys and nearly two in five girls in the South East achieved 2 or more A levels (or equivalent) in 1994/95, the highest proportions in Great Britain.
	(Table 4.6)
Labour market	The South East has the highest economic activity rate for both males and females.
	(Table 5.3)
	Claimant unemployment in the South East in January 1997 ranged from 2.7 per cent in Surrey and 2.9 per cent in Oxfordshire to 11.7 per cent on the Isle of Wight.
	(Chart 5.22)
Housing	Nearly three quarters of dwellings in the South East are owner-occupied, the highest proportion.
	(Table 6.2)
Health	Fifteen per cent of the population in the South East - 35 per cent among the elderly - have a limiting long-standing illness, the lowest proportions of all the regions.
	(Table 7.4)
Lifestyles	Nearly one in five of people in the South East is covered by private medical insurance, by far the highest proportion.
	(Table 7.7)
	Average weekly household income and also expenditure in the South East in 1995-96 were second only to those in London.
	(Tables 8.1, 8.2 and 8.9)
Crime	The South East had the second lowest recorded crime rate of all the regions in England and Wales during 1995.
	(Table 9.1)
Transport	Four in every five households in the South East have at least one car and one in three has two or more, higher proportions than in any other region.
	(Table 10.2)
Industry	At nearly £32,300, the South East had the second highest level of gross value added per employee in manufacturing in 1994.
	(Table 13.4)

South West

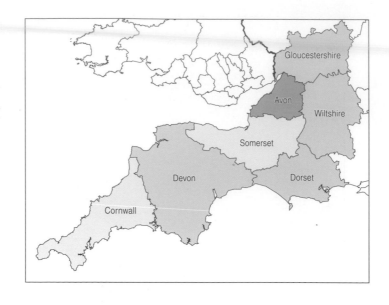

Population density, 1995
(persons per sq km)

1,000 and over
600 - 999
300 - 599
150 - 299
Under 150

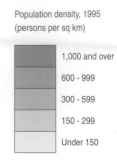

Population

The South West has the fastest growing population of all the regions with growth of 10 per cent between 1981 and 1995.

(Tables 3.1 and 14.1)

The South West has the oldest population: more than one person in five is a pensioner with more than one in 20 aged 80 or over.

(Table 3.3)

Education

Almost half of pupils in their last year of compulsory schooling in the South West in 1994/95 achieved 5 or more GCSEs Grades A*-C and only one in 20 achieved no graded result, together with the South East (GOR) the best record among the English regions.

(Table 4.6)

Labour market

Half of female employees in the South West work part-time, a higher proportion than in any other region.

(Table 5.6)

Housing

Seventy two per cent of dwellings in the South West are owner-occupied, a proportion second only to the South East (GOR).

(Table 6.2)

Health

Allowing for the age structure of the population, overall the South and West Regional Health Authority area had lower death rates in 1995 than any other region.

(Table 7.16)

Lifestyles

People in the South West were less likely than those in any other region of Great Britain to have taken a holiday in 1996.

(Table 8.14)

Crime

The recorded crime rate in the South West fell by 7 per cent overall between 1994 and 1995, the greatest fall of any region in England and Wales.

(Table 9.1)

Transport

There were nearly 60 per cent fewer fatal and serious road accidents in the South West in 1995 than the average for 1981-1985, a better record than in any other region of Great Britain.

(Table 10.6)

Environment

Almost a third of land in the South West is designated as Areas of Outstanding Natural Beauty.

(Table 11.12)

Industry

Over a sixth of spending by UK tourists in 1995 was in the West Country.

(Table 13.12)

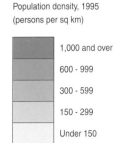

Wales

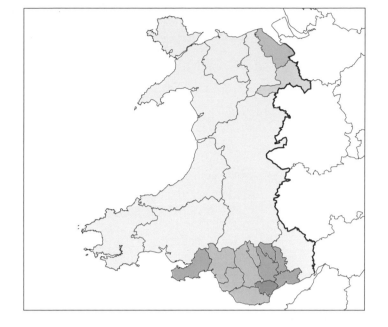

Population density, 1995
(persons per sq km)

- 1,000 and over
- 600 - 999
- 300 - 599
- 150 - 299
- Under 150

N.B. The map shows Unitary Authorities in Wales which came into effect from 1 April 1996.
See map on page 198 for names.

Population	Wales has the second highest proportion of people of pensionable age among its population and the lowest proportion of 16 to 44 year olds. *(Table 3.3)*
Education	Almost three quarters of three and four year olds in Wales are in education; only the North East and Merseyside have higher proportions. *(Table 4.4)*
Labour market	Except for Merseyside, Wales had the lowest economic activity rate in the United Kingdom in Spring 1996. *(Tables 5.1 and 5.3)*
	Average earnings in Wales for both males and females in April 1996 were the second lowest in the United Kingdom. *(Tables 5.16 and 5.17)*
Housing	More than seven in ten dwellings in Wales are owner-occupied; only the South East (GOR) and the South West have a higher proportion. *(Table 6.2)*
Health	The number of prescription items dispensed per person in 1995 was higher in Wales than in any other region. *(Table 7.19)*
Lifestyles	Almost a quarter of households in Wales were in receipt of Incapacity or Disablement Benefit in 1995-96, a higher proportion than in any other region of Great Britain. *(Table 8.7)*
Crime	The recorded crime rate in Wales fell by 6 per cent between 1994 and 1995; within England only the South West had a greater fall. *(Table 9.1)*
	The clear-up rate for recorded crime in Wales is higher than in any English region. *(Table 9.3)*
Environment	Almost a fifth of the land area of Wales is designated as National Park. *(Table 11.12)*
Industry	Wales had one of the highest levels of gross value added per employee in manufacturing in 1994 at £31,600. *(Table 13.4)*

Scotland

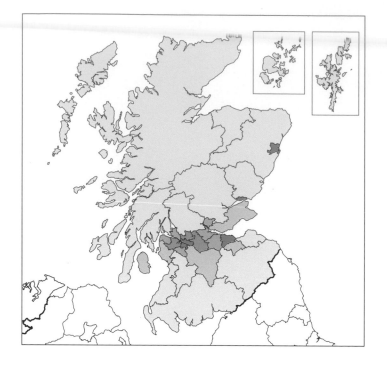

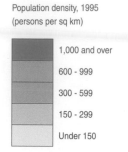

Population density, 1995
(persons per sq km)

	1,000 and over
	600 - 999
	300 - 599
	150 - 299
	Under 150

N.B. The map shows New Council A
in Scotland which came into eff
from 1 April 96.
See map on page 204 for name

Population

Scotland is the most sparsely populated region in the United Kingdom, but Glasgow City is one of the most densely populated local government areas.

(Tables 14-17.1)

Households

Just over 30 per cent of households in Scotland consist of one person living alone, the highest proportion after London.

(Table 3.20)

Education

Nearly three in ten boys and four in ten girls in their last year of compulsory schooling in 1994/95 achieved the equivalent of Grades A*-C in English, maths, a modern language and a science, a better record than elsewhere in Great Britain.

(Table 4.7)

Labour market

After London, Scotland has the most highly qualified labour force, with 42 per cent qualified to at least Higher standard or equivalent.

(Table 5.10)

Housing

The average local authority rent in Scotland in April 1996 was £31 per week, (jointly with that in the Yorkshire and Humber region) the lowest in the United Kingdom.

(Table 6.8)

Health

Allowing for the age structure of the population, Scotland has the highest death rates of all regions from circulatory diseases and from cancer.

(Table 7.16)

Lifestyles

Twenty-eight per cent of households in Scotland in 1995-96 were in receipt of Housing Benefit, a higher proportion than in any other region of Great Britain.

(Table 8.7)

Crime

The recorded crime rate in Scotland fell by 5 per cent between 1994 and 1995.

(Table 9.1)

Transport

Total road casualties in Scotland in 1995 were 18 per cent lower than the average for 1981-1985, a greater reduction than in any other region in Great Britain.

(Table 10.7)

Environment

Scotland is the wettest region with average rainfall a third higher than the UK average.

(Table 11.1)

Northern Ireland

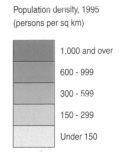

Population density, 1995
(persons per sq km)

	1,000 and over
	600 - 999
	300 - 599
	150 - 299
	Under 150

Population

Northern Ireland has the youngest population with proportionately more children and fewer pensioners than any other region.

(Table 3.3)

Education

Over half of pupils in their last year of compulsory schooling in Northern Ireland in 1994/95 achieved 5 or more A*-C Grades and less than one in 20 achieved no graded result, a better record than elsewhere in the United Kingdom.

(Table 4.6)

Labour market

In 1996 Northern Ireland lost 35 days per 1,000 employees due to labour disputes, a better record than in any other region.

(Chart 5.11)

Claimant unemployment in Northern Ireland in January 1997 ranged from 6.5 per cent in Ballymena to 14.5 per cent in Strabane.

(Chart 5.22)

Housing

Dwelling prices in Northern Ireland rose by 25 per cent between 1993 and 1996, two and a half times the increase in any other region, although on average they remained the lowest.

(Table 6.10)

Health

Northern Ireland has the highest proportion of teetotallers and the lowest proportion of heavy drinkers of all the regions.

(Table 7.9)

Lifestyles

On average over a fifth of the income of households in Northern Ireland comes from social security benefits, a higher proportion than in any other region.

(Table 8.1)

Households in Northern Ireland spend, on average, less on housing and more on food, on fuel, light and power and on clothing and footwear than those elsewhere in United Kingdom.

(Table 8.9)

Crime

The recorded crime rate in Northern Ireland rose by 1 per cent between 1994 and 1995.

(Table 9.1)

Industry

At £23,800, Northern Ireland had the lowest level of gross value added per employee in manufacturing during 1994.

(Table 13.4)

In terms of registrations and deregistration rates, the business population is more stable in Northern Ireland than elsewhere in the United Kingdom.

(Table 13.9)

2 European Union regional statistics[*]

Population

The North West, (SSR) 24 with around 870 people per square kilometre, is one of the most densely populated regions in the EU; only the major city regions of Brussels, Ile de France, Berlin, Bremen, Hamburg and Attiki have a greater density.

(Table 2.1)

The South West, with 18.6 per cent, has the fourth highest proportion of its population aged 65 or over; only the Nord Ovest, the Emilia-Romagna, and the Centro regions of Italy have higher proportions.

(Table 2.1)

Births

Northern Ireland had the second highest birth rate of any EU region in 1994 with 14.9 births per thousand population, more than three times the rate in Brandenburg, Mecklenburg-Vorpommer and Sachsen in Germany.

(Table 2.1)

Deaths

The infant mortality rate in East Anglia in 1994 at 5.2 deaths per thousand live births was among the lowest of all the EU regions.

(Table 2.1)

Transport

The North, Scotland and Northern Ireland have some of the lowest rates of car ownership in the EU.

(Table 2.2)

Labour market

More than three quarters of the workforce in the South East (SSR) is in the service sector; only Brussels and Ile de France have higher proportions.

(Table 2.3)

Just under a third of the unemployed in the East Midlands in 1995 had been out of work for 12 months or longer, one of the lowest proportions among the EU regions.

(Table 2.3)

Gross domestic product

The South East (SSR) is the only region in the United Kingdom where GDP per head in 1994 was above the EU average.

(Table 2.3)

Agriculture

Three quarters of Northern Ireland's total land area is agricultural land, the second highest proportion of any EU region; only Sicilia (Italy) has a higher proportion.

(Table 2.4)

The average yields of wheat and barley in Yorkshire and Humberside are among the highest across the regions of the EU.

(Table 2.4)

---

[*] The UK regional classification currently used for European purposes is the Standard Statistical Region classification. This means that London is excluded from the comparisons above as it forms part of the South East (SSR).

European Union Regions

NETHERLANDS
1 Noord-Nederland
2 Oost-Nederland
3 Zuid-Nederland
4 West-Nederland

BELGIUM
5 Vlaams Gewest
6 Region Wallonne
7 Bruxelles-Brussels

8 LUXEMBOURG

GERMANY
9 Saarland
10 Rheinland-Pfalz
11 Baden-Wuerttemberg
12 Mecklenburg-Vorpommern
13 Hamburg
14 Schleswig-Holstein

2.1 Population and vital statistics, 1994

	Area (sq km)	Popu-lation (thousands)	Persons per sq km	Percentage of population Aged under 15	Aged 65 or over	Births (per 1,000 population)	Deaths (per 1,000 population)	Infant mortality (per 1,000 births)[1]
EUR 15	**3,192,173**	**371,007.1**	**116.2**	*17.6*	*15.4*	**10.9**	**9.9**	..
Austria	**83,859**	**8,030.1**	**95.8**	*17.6*	*15.0*	**11.5**	**10.0**	**6.3**
Ostosterreich	23,554	3,381.0	143.5	*16.1*	*16.4*	10.8	11.6	6.6
Sudosterreich	25,921	1,763.7	68.0	*17.7*	*15.4*	10.9	9.8	4.7
Westosterreich	34,384	2,885.4	83.9	*19.3*	*13.0*	12.8	8.4	6.8
Belgium	**30,518**	**10,115.6**	**331.5**	*18.1*	*15.6*	**11.4**	**10.2**	**8.0**
Vlaams Gewest	13,512	5,856.6	433.4	*17.8*	*15.1*	11.1	9.6	8.1
Region Wallonne	16,844	3,308.7	196.4	*18.8*	*15.9*	11.4	11.0	9.2
Bruxelles-Brussels	161	950.3	5,887.9	*17.5*	*17.4*	13.2	11.5	3.9
Denmark	**43,080**	**5,205.0**	**120.8**	*17.1*	*15.4*	**13.4**	**11.7**	**5.7**
Finland	**338,147**	**5,088.3**	**15.1**	*19.1*	*13.9*	**12.8**	**9.4**	**4.7**
Manner-Suomi	336,595	5,063.2	15.0	*19.1*	*13.9*	12.8	9.4	4.7
Ahvenanmaa/Aland	1,552	25.1	16.2	*18.7*	*16.3*	11.9	12.0	0.0
France[2]	**543,965**	**57,899.6**	**106.4**	*19.8*	*14.7*	**12.3**	**9.0**	**7.2**
Ile de France	12,012	10,960.6	912.5	*20.3*	*11.1*	14.7	7.0	8.9
Bassin Parisien	145,645	10,430.5	71.6	*20.5*	*15.0*	12.0	9.3	7.1
Nord-Pas-de-Calais	12,414	3,991.5	321.5	*22.9*	*12.7*	13.6	8.9	9.4
Est	48,030	5,111.2	106.4	*20.3*	*13.5*	12.2	8.6	7.7
Ouest	85,099	7,603.7	89.4	*19.5*	*16.3*	11.2	9.4	5.8
Sud-Ouest	103,599	6,064.7	58.5	*17.0*	*18.4*	10.1	10.6	5.9
Centre-Est	69,711	6,864.8	98.5	*19.8*	*14.4*	12.0	8.7	6.7
Mediterranee	67,455	6,872.6	101.9	*18.4*	*17.6*	10.6	9.4	5.8
Germany	**356,718**	**81,438.3**	**228.3**	*16.4*	*15.2*	**9.4**	**10.9**	**5.6**
Baden-Wuerttemberg	35,751	10,253.0	286.8	*16.8*	*14.4*	11.1	9.4	5.1
Bayern	70,554	11,892.6	168.6	*16.4*	*15.2*	10.8	10.2	5.4
Berlin	889	3,473.7	3,906.9	*15.6*	*13.7*	8.2	11.7	5.4
Brandenburg	29,480	2,537.2	86.1	*18.6*	*12.7*	4.9	11.2	5.5
Bremen	404	681.6	1,686.2	*13.7*	*17.5*	9.2	11.9	6.7
Hamburg	755	1,704.4	2,256.6	*13.2*	*17.1*	9.5	11.9	5.3
Hessen	21,114	5,974.0	282.9	*15.3*	*15.5*	10.1	10.6	5.4
Mecklenburg-Vorpommern	23,171	1,837.9	79.3	*19.7*	*11.7*	4.8	10.8	7.5
Niedersachsen	47,348	7,681.7	162.2	*16.1*	*15.9*	10.6	11.2	5.6
Nordrhein-Westfalin	34,072	17,787.7	522.1	*16.1*	*15.5*	10.5	10.8	6.0
Rheinland-Pfalz	19,846	3,938.7	198.5	*16.4*	*16.1*	10.3	10.9	5.5
Saarland	2,570	1,084.4	421.9	*15.3*	*16.2*	9.2	11.7	5.6
Sachsen	18,412	4,596.0	249.6	*16.9*	*16.3*	4.9	12.7	5.9
Sachsen-Anhalt	20,446	2,768.6	135.4	*17.4*	*14.8*	5.2	12.2	6.4
Schleswig-Holstein	15,732	2,701.6	171.7	*15.4*	*15.9*	10.2	11.4	5.0
Thueringen	16,174	2,525.3	156.1	*17.9*	*14.4*	5.0	11.4	6.7
Greece	**131,625**	**10,426.3**	**79.2**	*17.6*	*15.0*	**10.0**	**9.4**	**7.9**
Voreia Ellade	56,457	3,363.4	59.6	*17.8*	*14.1*	10.3	9.3	7.9
Kentriki Ellade	53,902	2,575.5	47.8	*17.5*	*16.8*	8.3	9.7	7.4
Attiki	3,808	3,486.2	915.5	*17.0*	*14.1*	10.5	9.0	8.7
Nisia Aigaiou, Kriti	17,458	1,001.2	57.4	*19.2*	*16.5*	11.2	10.1	6.5
Ireland	**68,895**	**3,587.4**	**52.1**	*25.3*	*11.4*	**13.4**	**8.6**	**7.9**

2.1 *(continued)*

	Area (sq km)	Popu-lation (thousands)	Persons per sq km	Percentage of population		Births (per 1,000 population)	Deaths (per 1,000 population)	Infant mortality (per 1,000 births)[1]
				Aged under 15	Aged 65 or over			
Italy	**301,316**	**57,203.5**	**189.8**	*15.2*	*16.0*	**9.4**	**9.8**	**7.1**
Nord Ovest	34,081	6,083.8	178.5	*11.6*	*19.4*	7.3	12.2	8.8
Lombardia	23,872	8,905.7	373.1	*13.3*	*15.4*	8.4	9.5	5.0
Nord Est	39,816	6,517.2	163.7	*13.4*	*16.7*	8.5	10.0	5.1
Emilia-Romagna	22,124	3,923.5	177.3	*10.9*	*20.5*	7.0	11.4	5.7
Centro	41,142	5,787.6	140.7	*12.4*	*20.1*	7.4	11.2	6.4
Lazio	17,227	5,189.3	301.2	*14.7*	*14.9*	9.4	9.0	7.2
Campania	15,232	1,597.4	104.9	*15.9*	*17.7*	9.4	10.3	6.9
Abruzzi-Molise	13,595	5,727.2	421.3	*20.8*	*11.7*	13.2	8.1	9.1
Sud	44,430	6,759.5	152.1	*19.4*	*13.5*	11.4	8.2	8.4
Sicilia	25,707	5,054.0	196.6	*19.6*	*14.2*	12.1	9.2	8.1
Sardegna	24,090	1,658.4	68.8	*17.1*	*13.1*	8.8	8.4	4.3
Luxembourg	**2,586**	**403.8**	**156.1**	*18.1*	*13.8*	**13.5**	**9.4**	**5.3**
Netherlands[3]	**41,029**	**15,382.2**	**374.9**	*18.4*	*13.1*	**12.7**	**8.7**	**5.6**
Noord-Nederland	11,388	1,618.7	142.1	*18.2*	*14.2*	11.9	9.4	6.0
Oost-Nederland	10,495	3,163.4	301.4	*19.4*	*12.7*	13.3	8.4	6.0
West-Nederland	11,854	7,204.1	607.7	*18.1*	*13.5*	12.9	8.9	5.6
Zuid-Nederland	7,292	3,395.3	465.6	*18.1*	*12.1*	12.3	8.0	5.1
Portugal	**91,906**	**9,902.2**	**107.7**	*18.4*	*14.2*	**11.0**	**10.0**	**8.9**
Continente	88,798	9,406.3	105.9	*18.2*	*14.3*	10.9	10.0	8.5
Acores	2,330	239.9	103.0	*24.9*	*12.3*	15.4	10.8	12.5
Maderia	779	256.0	328.7	*22.6*	*11.8*	12.9	9.8	11.7
Spain[4]	**504,790**	**39,149.5**	**77.6**	*17.4*	*14.8*	**9.4**	**8.6**	**6.0**
Noroeste	45,297	4,338.2	95.8	*15.4*	*17.4*	7.0	10.1	7.1
Noreste	70,366	4,053.5	57.6	*14.8*	*16.0*	7.8	8.8	5.8
Madrid	7,995	5,001.1	625.5	*16.9*	*12.9*	9.5	7.1	6.3
Centro	215,025	5,271.1	24.5	*17.0*	*18.0*	9.0	9.6	6.1
Este	60,249	10,684.5	177.3	*16.8*	*14.9*	9.3	8.8	5.1
Sur	98,616	8,265.7	83.8	*20.9*	*12.4*	11.6	7.9	6.7
Canarias	7,242	1,535.3	212.0	*20.3*	*10.2*	11.1	6.8	5.3
Sweden	**410,934**	**8,780.8**	**21.4**	*18.7*	*17.6*	**12.8**	**10.5**	**4.7**
United Kingdom	**242,804**	**58,394.6**	**240.5**	*19.4*	*15.8*	**12.9**	**10.7**	**6.2**
North	15,415	3,099.8	201.1	*19.4*	*16.0*	11.9	11.6	6.3
North West (SSR)	7,342	6,412.0	873.4	*20.2*	*15.6*	12.8	11.4	6.2
Yorkshire & Humberside	15,411	5,025.0	326.1	*19.6*	*15.9*	12.7	10.9	7.7
East Midlands	15,627	4,102.2	262.5	*19.3*	*15.8*	12.5	10.5	6.9
West Midlands	13,004	5,294.9	407.2	*19.9*	*15.4*	13.0	10.5	7.2
East Anglia	12,570	2,104.9	167.5	*18.7*	*17.2*	12.2	10.7	5.2
South East (SSR)	27,224	17,870.2	656.4	*19.1*	*15.1*	13.7	9.9	5.5
South West	23,829	4,798.4	201.3	*18.2*	*18.6*	11.7	11.4	5.3
Wales	20,766	2,913.0	140.3	*19.6*	*17.3*	12.2	11.6	6.2
Scotland	78,133	5,132.4	65.7	*19.0*	*15.1*	12.0	11.6	6.2
Northern Ireland	13,576	1,641.7	121.8	*24.1*	*12.7*	14.9	9.2	6.1

1 1993 data for Belgium and Italy.
2 The regional data are estimates.
3 Including 'centraal persoons register'.
4 The regional birth and death rates are estimates.

Source: Eurostat

2.2 Social statistics

	Depen-dency rate[1] 1995	Proportion of 16-18 year olds in education or training[2] (percentages) 1994/95	Causes of death 1994[3] (rate per 100,000 population)				Transport	
			Circulatory system	Cancer (all neoplasms)	All accidents	Road traffic accidents	Length of motorways (km) per 1,000 sq km 1994[4]	Private cars per 1,000 population 1993[5]
EUR 15	1.2	..	..	..	..	..	..	..
Austria	**1.1**	*81*	**544**	**244**	**40**	**15**	**19**	..
Ostosterreich	1.0	..	660	271	44	15	18	..
Sudosterreich	1.2	..	516	250	37	15	20	..
Westosterreich	1.0	..	426	210	36	15	19	..
Belgium	**1.4**	*97*	**399**	**270**	**42**	**18**	**55**	**408**
Vlaams Gewest	1.4	..	386	263	38	17	61	414
Region Wallonne	1.5	..	419	273	48	23	49	386
Bruxelles-Brussels	1.5	..	409	302	44	12	68	441
Denmark	**0.9**	*82*	**514**	**276**	**47**	**11**	**18**	**312**
Finland	**1.0**	*88*	**449**	**197**	**51**	**9**	..	**370**
Manner-Suomi	1.0	..	449	197	51	9	..	369
Ahvenanmaa/Aland	0.9	..	450	307	36	8	..	507
France	**1.3**	*91*	**301**	**247**	**53**	**15**	**17**	**413**
Ile de France	1.0	*91*	210	201	39	9	42	361
Bassin Parisien	1.3	*90*	312	260	59	18	14	424
Nord-Pas-de-Calais	1.5	*89*	304	258	46	10	44	345
Est	1.3	*91*	307	243	51	15	17	406
Ouest	1.3	*94*	318	263	57	15	8	441
Sud-Ouest	1.3	*92*	381	269	63	18	8	466
Centre-Est	1.2	*91*	291	238	56	14	20	436 .
Mediterranee	1.5	*88*	340	266	60	17	17	425
Germany	**1.1**	*92*	**543**	**263**	**33**	**12**	**31**	**402**
Baden-Wuerttemberg	1.0	*91*	444	236	30	10	29	516
Bayern	1.0	*91*	508	248	33	14	31	517
Berlin	0.9	*90*	576	253	24	8	69	235
Brandenburg	1.0	*90*	583	245	54	25	26	..
Bremen	1.2	*107*	571	327	35	8	114	422
Hamburg	1.0	*96*	502	302	45	8	107	418
Hessen	1.1	*92*	479	270	37	10	45	528
Mecklenburg-Vorpommern	0.9	*89*	504	223	60	24	10	..
Niedersachsen	1.1	*91*	542	267	35	14	28	500
Nordrhein-Westfalin	1.3	*95*	553	281	21	8	63	484
Rheinland-Pfalz	1.2	*87*	558	267	23	12	41	520
Saarland	1.4	*93*	626	283	24	8	88	520
Sachsen	1.0	*92*	702	281	56	15	23	..
Sachsen-Anhalt	0.9	*89*	648	277	47	18	10	..
Schleswig-Holstein	1.0	*92*	580	273	32	10	28	499
Thueringen	1.0	*89*	650	237	34	15	16	..
Greece	**1.4**	*61*	**460**	**202**	**36**	**19**	**2**	**189**
Voreia Ellade	1.4	..	465	208	33	18	1	152
Kentriki Ellade	1.4	..	483	191	35	19	3	98
Attiki	1.5	..	428	209	40	21	18	304
Nisia Aigaiou, Kriti	1.4	..	496	189	34	17	0	140
Ireland	**1.5**	*78*	**402**	**212**	**28**	**11**	**1**	**242**

2.2 *(continued)*

	Depen-dency rate[1] 1995	Proportion of 16-18 year olds in education or training[2] (percentages) 1994/95	Causes of death 1994[3] (rate per 100,000 population)				Transport	
			Circulatory system	Cancer (all neoplasms)	All accidents	Road traffic accidents	Length of motorways (km) per 1,000 sq km 1994[4]	Private cars per 1,000 population 1993[5]
Italy	**1.5**	..	**422**	**264**	**38**	**14**	**21**	**517**
Nord Ovest	1.3	..	532	326	50	15	36	582
Lombardia	1.3	..	385	307	38	16	23	583
Nord Est	1.3	..	416	298	43	18	22	542
Emilia-Romagna	1.2	..	483	341	45	21	28	609
Centro	1.4	..	501	313	45	16	16	591
Lazio	1.5	..	373	250	39	14	28	585
Campania	1.6	..	470	236	43	12	24	472
Abruzzi-Molise	1.9	..	368	185	24	9	33	377
Sud	1.9	..	359	179	31	12	14	370
Sicilia	2.0	..	431	194	29	9	22	452
Sardegna	1.7	..	339	209	41	14	0	444
Luxembourg	**1.4**	..	**417**	**255**	**49**	**20**	**47**	**548**
Netherlands	**1.1**	*91*	**336**	**237**	**22**	**8**	**54**	**376**
Noord-Nederland	1.2	..	369	257	25	10	27	369
Oost-Nederland	1.1	..	333	229	23	10	56	377
West-Nederland	1.1	..	340	244	22	6	62	364
Zuid-Nederland	1.1	..	315	222	21	10	80	405
Portugal	**1.1**	*65*	**430**	**193**	**38**	**22**	**6**	..
Continente	1.0	..	430	194	38	22	7	351
Acores	1.5	..	509	208	30	13	0	..
Maderia	1.3	..	355	157	39	19	0	..
Spain	**1.5**	*71*	**342**	**212**	**32**	**15**	**13**	**359**
Noroeste	1.5	*74*	408	250	40	22	9	326
Noreste	1.4	*82*	326	231	32	16	14	321
Madrid	1.5	*76*	252	182	27	10	59	415
Centro	1.7	*70*	408	235	33	16	8	297
Este	1.3	*69*	352	222	35	16	26	442
Sur	1.7	*66*	331	183	26	15	13	292
Canarias	1.4	*71*	264	170	31	8	23	369
Sweden	**1.0**	*94*	**517**	**230**	**33**	**6**	**3**	..
United Kingdom	**1.0**	*70*	**472**	**275**	**21**	**7**	**14**	**365**
North	1.2	*68*	523	306	22	7	11	300
North West (SSR)	1.2	*68*	511	287	21	6	66	339
Yorkshire & Humberside	1.0	*75*	478	279	19	7	21	325
East Midlands	1.0	*66*	459	268	23	8	12	349
West Midlands	1.0	*72*	465	271	22	7	29	391
East Anglia	0.9	*64*	463	274	25	9	2	409
South East (SSR)	0.9	*70*	418	254	17	5	34	384
South West	1.0	*68*	514	287	20	6	13	409
Wales	1.2	*65*	524	302	23	5	6	335
Scotland	1.0	*71*	529	300	28	7	4	307
Northern Ireland	1.3	*79*	427	223	26	10	9	307

1 Dependency rates are calculated as the number of non-active persons (total population *less* labour force) expressed as a percentage of those active. 1993 for Austria and Iceland.
2 Participation rates are calculated by dividing the number of pupils enrolled in a region by the resident population in that region. As some young people may be resident in one region and in education in another, this inter-regional movement may influence the results. Data for Belgium, France, Portugal and United Kingdom are for 1993/94. The UK data exclude Open University, independent and special schools in Wales, and Youth Training with employers, all of which are not available by region and age. For all countries, age is taken at 1 January except for the UK where it is on 31 August (ie the start of the academic year).
3 Unadjusted death rates using 1994 population estimates. 1990 for Belgium and 1993 for Denmark, Germany, Greece, Spain, France, Ireland, Italy, Luxembourg and Austria.
4 1992 for Greece and 1993 for Italy.
5 1992 for Italy.

Source: Eurostat

2.3 Economic statistics

	Persons in employment[1], 1995 (thousands)	Employment[1], 1995[2] percentage in			Unemployment rate[1] (percentages) 1995	Long-term unemployed[1] as a percentage of the unemployed, 1995	Gross domestic product per head (PPS)[3] (EUR 15=100) 1994	Percentage of GDP in 1994[4] derived from		
		Agriculture	Industry	Services				Agriculture	Industry	Services
EUR 15	**148,409.6**	*5.3*	*30.2*	*64.3*	*10.7*	..	100	..	..	..
Austria	**3,674.3**	*7.3*	*32.1*	*60.6*	..	..	110	*2.4*	*39.0*	*58.7*
Ostosterreich	1,562.6	*6.1*	*28.7*	*65.2*	..	..	122	..	..	..
Sudosterreich	756.9	*9.9*	*33.3*	*56.9*	..	..	87	..	..	..
Westosterreich	1,354.8	*7.4*	*35.3*	*57.3*	..	..	110	..	..	..
Belgium	**3,792.6**	*2.7*	*28.3*	*69.1*	*9.4*	*61.8*	114	*1.7*	*29.2*	*69.1*
Vlaams Gewest	2,341.6	*3.0*	*31.4*	*65.6*	*6.9*	*46.7*	91	*2.2*	*27.6*	*70.2*
Region Wallonne	1,132.3	*2.8*	*25.2*	*72.0*	*12.9*	*71.3*	183	-	*19.2*	*80.8*
Bruxelles-Brussels	318.7	*0.1*	*15.8*	*84.1*	*13.3*	*81.5*	115	*1.9*	*32.6*	*65.5*
Denmark	**2,600.7**	*4.4*	*27.0*	*68.4*	*7.1*	*28.2*	114	*3.7*	*27.0*	*69.3*
Finland	**2,015.7**	*7.8*	*27.6*	*64.6*	*18.1*	*29.9*	91	*6.2*	*32.5*	*61.3*
Manner-Suomi	2,004.3	*7.7*	*27.6*	*64.6*	*18.2*	*30.0*	91	*6.2*	*32.6*	*61.2*
Ahvenanmaa/Aland	11.4	*9.6*	*20.7*	*69.7*	*6.2*	..	126	*6.8*	*16.1*	*77.2*
France	**22,056.6**	*4.9*	*27.0*	*68.1*	*11.2*	*42.6*	108	*3.3*	*28.5*	*68.2*
Ile de France	4,714.1	*0.5*	*20.8*	*78.5*	*10.0*	*45.7*	161	*0.3*	*25.0*	*74.8*
Bassin Parisien	3,841.4	*6.2*	*31.3*	*62.5*	*11.9*	*38.0*	98	*5.9*	*32.8*	*61.3*
Nord-Pas-de-Calais	1,236.6	*3.3*	*29.5*	*67.2*	*15.3*	*53.7*	87	*1.8*	*31.6*	*66.6*
Est	1,942.4	*3.0*	*35.1*	*61.8*	*8.7*	*40.5*	100	*3.0*	*35.9*	*61.1*
Ouest	2,991.6	*8.9*	*29.2*	*61.9*	*10.5*	*33.0*	91	*6.7*	*28.6*	*64.7*
Sud-Ouest	2,293.1	*8.6*	*24.4*	*66.9*	*11.0*	*40.9*	93	*6.1*	*25.9*	*68.0*
Centre-Est	2,740.4	*5.2*	*30.8*	*64.0*	*10.2*	*43.2*	102	*2.5*	*33.6*	*63.9*
Mediterranee	2,297.0	*4.8*	*19.1*	*76.1*	*14.7*	*48.0*	91	*3.3*	*20.8*	*75.9*
Germany	**35,782.1**	*3.2*	*36.0*	*60.8*	*8.2*	*47.8*	110	*1.1*	*34.5*	*64.4*
Baden-Wuerttemberg	4,738.0	*2.5*	*43.4*	*54.1*	*5.5*	*44.3*	126	*1.0*	*40.5*	*58.6*
Bayern	5,726.5	*4.9*	*37.5*	*57.5*	*4.9*	*39.6*	128	*1.1*	*34.7*	*64.2*
Berlin	1,596.4	*0.8*	*24.8*	*74.4*	*11.2*	*53.2*	104	..	..	..
Brandenburg	1,094.2	*4.4*	*35.6*	*60.0*	*15.1*	*51.3*	64	..	..	..
Bremen	283.1	*0.7*	*28.4*	*70.9*	*10.6*	*44.7*	156	*0.3*	*29.8*	*69.9*
Hamburg	789.2	*1.1*	*24.9*	*74.1*	*7.6*	*45.9*	196	*0.3*	*23.2*	*76.5*
Hessen	2,647.5	*2.4*	*33.8*	*63.8*	*6.3*	*51.4*	152	*0.5*	*26.7*	*72.8*
Mecklenburg-Vorpommern	803.6	*7.1*	*29.6*	*63.3*	*11.9*	*60.9*	57	..	..	..
Niedersachsen	3,277.0	*4.4*	*34.0*	*61.5*	*7.9*	*46.2*	105	*2.8*	*33.2*	*64.0*
Nordrhein-Westfalin	7,297.0	*1.9*	*36.0*	*62.1*	*8.2*	*37.1*	112	*0.7*	*36.3*	*63.0*
Rheinland-Pfalz	1,691.9	*3.3*	*36.9*	*59.7*	*6.2*	*45.5*	100	*1.5*	*37.8*	*60.7*
Saarland	416.4	*1.0*	*35.1*	*63.9*	*9.1*	*39.1*	106	*0.3*	*34.4*	*65.2*
Sachsen	1,938.9	*2.6*	*39.8*	*57.6*	*13.8*	*58.5*	60	..	..	..
Sachsen-Anhalt	1,171.8	*4.8*	*37.2*	*57.9*	*16.7*	*56.2*	60	..	..	..
Schleswig-Holstein	1,217.7	*4.4*	*28.9*	*66.7*	*6.5*	*52.6*	106	*2.2*	*29.6*	*68.2*
Thueringen	1,092.7	*3.6*	*37.7*	*58.7*	*11.9*	*63.2*	60	..	..	..
Greece	**3,820.4**	*20.4*	*23.2*	*56.4*	*9.1*	*50.9*	65	*14.8*	*26.3*	*59.0*
Voreia Ellade	1,268.9	*28.9*	*23.2*	*47.9*	*9.2*	*45.7*	62	*21.6*	*30.4*	*47.9*
Kentriki Ellade	786.4	*38.2*	*19.5*	*42.3*	*7.4*	*63.3*	57	*24.5*	*28.7*	*46.8*
Attiki	1,401.4	*1.1*	*26.9*	*72.0*	*11.0*	*50.2*	73	*2.2*	*25.6*	*72.2*
Nisia Aigaiou, Kriti	363.7	*26.9*	*16.9*	*56.2*	*4.5*	*50.7*	67	*23.5*	*15.4*	*61.1*
Ireland	**1,262.0**	*12.0*	*27.7*	*60.0*	*14.3*	*51.1*	88	*7.5*	*34.3*	*58.2*

Regional Trends 32, © Crown copyright 1997

2.3 *(continued)*

	Persons in employment[1], 1995 (thousands)	Employment[1], 1995[2] percentage in			Unemployment rate[1] (percentages) 1995	Long-term unemployed[1] as a percentage of the unemployed, 1995	Gross domestic product per head (PPS)[3] (EUR 15=100) 1994	Percentage of GDP in 1994[4] derived from		
		Agriculture	Industry	Services				Agriculture	Industry	Services
Italy	**19,943.4**	*7.5*	*32.1*	*60.4*	*12.0*	*61.5*	102	*3.6*	*29.2*	*67.2*
Nord Ovest	2,329.5	*4.8*	*36.9*	58.3	8.7	63.2	116	2.6	31.8	65.6
Lombardia	3,647.3	*3.5*	*41.8*	54.7	6.1	50.1	131	1.9	37.6	60.6
Nord Est	2,620.6	*6.3*	*37.2*	56.5	6.0	43.8	119	3.7	33.0	63.3
Emilia-Romagna	1,645.6	*8.4*	*35.0*	56.5	6.3	35.1	128	4.6	33.3	62.1
Centro	2,225.4	*5.5*	*35.6*	58.9	8.0	60.4	107	3.1	31.2	65.6
Lazio	1,794.0	*4.6*	*20.5*	74.8	12.8	62.4	119	1.8	19.0	79.2
Campania	553.1	*9.7*	*31.3*	59.0	10.8	61.6	69	3.8	20.3	76.0
Abruzzi-Molise	1,472.7	*10.2*	*23.3*	66.6	25.9	72.8	87	5.0	29.1	65.9
Sud	1,870.9	*15.7*	*23.2*	61.2	18.8	62.8	68	7.2	19.8	72.9
Sicilia	1,298.8	*13.2*	*18.4*	68.4	23.3	65.9	70	6.7	20.2	73.1
Sardegna	485.4	*15.3*	*24.6*	60.1	20.8	62.4	78	5.4	25.8	68.7
Luxembourg	**161.9**	*3.8*	*25.1*	*70.5*	*2.7*	*24.0*	169	*1.5*	*31.0*	*67.5*
Netherlands	**6,785.1**	*3.7*	*22.6*	*70.6*	*7.3*	*44.4*	106	*3.3*	*27.3*	*69.4*
Noord-Nederland	663.6	*4.8*	*25.5*	66.7	8.9	47.4	102	4.7	40.2	55.1
Oost-Nederland	1,395.6	*5.0*	*25.3*	66.2	7.1	42.9	93	4.2	27.6	68.2
West-Nederland	3,212.3	*2.8*	*18.6*	75.8	7.3	43.4	113	2.9	21.1	76.1
Zuid-Nederland	1,510.1	*4.0*	*27.6*	65.3	6.9	46.4	101	3.1	32.9	64.0
Portugal	**4,416.8**	*11.5*	*32.2*	*56.3*	*7.1*	*48.7*	67	*4.3*	*33.5*	*62.2*
Continente	4,228.0	*11.2*	*32.4*	56.4	7.1	48.1	68	4.1	34.1	61.8
Acores	86.2	*21.0*	*23.3*	55.6	7.8	60.0	48	11.9	19.6	68.4
Maderia	102.6	*13.8*	*31.6*	54.7	4.6	67.2	52	4.4	18.4	77.1
Spain	**12,027.5**	*9.3*	*30.2*	*60.5*	*22.7*	*54.4*	76	*3.4*	*31.3*	*65.3*
Noroeste	1,387.5	*23.1*	*26.9*	50.0	18.5	63.0	64	5.8	33.3	61.0
Noreste	1,335.9	*6.6*	*37.2*	56.2	19.3	58.6	89	2.8	40.1	57.0
Madrid	1,601.6	*0.0*	*25.4*	70.7	20.7	62.1	95	0.2	24.9	74.9
Centro	1,481.1	*15.5*	*29.6*	54.9	22.4	49.3	65	6.8	34.0	59.2
Este	3,638.6	*4.7*	*36.5*	58.8	20.3	53.0	86	1.8	33.4	64.8
Sur	2,106.9	*12.5*	*23.6*	64.0	31.8	51.0	58	6.8	27.0	66.3
Canarias	475.9	*7.0*	*18.7*	74.3	23.7	51.7	75	2.8	18.6	78.6
Sweden	**4,134.3**	*3.3*	*25.8*	*70.9*	*9.1*	..	98	*2.2*	*28.7*	*69.1*
United Kingdom	**25,936.2**	*2.1*	*27.3*	*70.2*	*8.8*	*43.1*	99	*1.9*	*29.2*	*68.9*
North	1,262.9	*1.8*	*31.1*	66.2	11.0	44.3	85	2.2	34.2	63.5
North West (SSR)	2,668.5	*1.1*	*29.4*	69.0	9.2	45.8	88	1.0	32.9	66.1
Yorkshire & Humberside	2,222.5	*2.2*	*30.0*	67.5	9.1	38.3	87	2.1	33.4	64.6
East Midlands	1,894.5	*2.4*	*35.3*	62.1	7.8	32.5	93	2.9	37.5	59.6
West Midlands	2,344.5	*2.2*	*34.2*	63.2	8.8	51.3	90	2.2	36.6	61.2
East Anglia	1,002.6	*3.8*	*27.4*	68.4	6.7	35.2	100	4.9	28.6	66.5
South East (SSR)	8,265.0	*0.9*	*21.9*	76.7	8.6	44.1	117	0.7	20.6	78.7
South West	2,187.6	*3.7*	*25.8*	70.3	7.6	43.9	95	3.7	27.6	68.7
Wales	1,185.8	*3.6*	*30.0*	65.6	8.7	37.3	81	2.3	33.7	63.9
Scotland	2,281.1	*2.7*	*26.1*	70.6	8.8	40.5	98	2.9	30.1	67.0
Northern Ireland	621.3	*5.8*	*26.1*	67.5	13.0	51.6	80	4.8	26.3	68.9

1 The definitions of employment and unemployment differ from those used in UK tables. See Technical notes.
2 1994 for Ireland and Austria.
3 Purchasing Power Standard; see Technical notes.
4 1992 for France and Portugal and 1993 for Belgium, Germany, Italy, the Netherlands and Sweden.

Source: Eurostat

2.4 Agricultural statistics

	Agricultural land as a percentage of total land area 1994[1]	Economic value of farms(SGM)[2] EUR 12=100 1993	Agricultural holdings by economic size, 1993 (percentages)			Average yield		All cattle per 1,000 ha of utilised agricultural land 1994[5]
			Less than 8 ESU[3]	8 to 39 ESU[3]	40 or more ESU[3]	Wheat 100kg/ha 1994[4]	Barley 100kg/ha 1994[4]	
EUR 12	53.9	100.0	68	23	9	54	38	622
Austria	41.1	..	..	..	..	52	47	675
Ostosterreich	49.5	..	..	..	..	52	48	512
Sudosterreich	32.8	..	..	..	..	46	41	709
Westosterreich	41.7	..	..	..	..	55	47	788
Belgium	44.7	273.0	30	34	36	72	59	2,316
Vlaams Gewest	45.6	279.0	..	..	..	71	60	2,736
Region Wallonne	44.4	261.3	31	33	36	72	59	1,971
Bruxelles-Brussels	3.1	..	28	35	36	60	40	1,000
Denmark	62.5	340.6	20	42	38	65	49	774
Finland	7.7	..	..	..	..	38	37	455
Manner-Suomi	..	..	..	..	..	..	..	..
Ahvenanmaa/Aland	..	..	..	..	..	..	..	..
France	54.9	203.9	37	39	23	67	54	681
Ile de France	49.1	493.2	15	27	58	77	62	..
Bassin Parisien	65.2	278.8	34	32	34	71	60	593
Nord-Pas-de-Calais	72.3	276.2	24	37	39	82	66	858
Est	47.1	177.3	42	35	23	61	51	827
Ouest	69.8	207.9	34	41	25	64	52	1,025
Sud-Ouest	49.2	148.6	40	47	13	49	39	629
Centre-Est	46.9	134.2	44	44	12	56	45	750
Mediterranee	34.1	194.4	43	37	20	35	36	..
Germany	48.5	183.9	45	37	18	68	53	922
Baden-Wuerttemberg	41.5	105.6	56	34	10	60	48	951
Bayern	48.2	118.5	44	47	9	64	51	1,264
Berlin	2.0	319.3	32	37	32	..	..	671
Brandenburg	44.3	706.2	54	21	25	53	49	535
Bremen	24.3	..	..	..	..	..	..	1,367
Hamburg	19.5	..	..	..	..	78	60	618
Hessen	37.3	123.1	52	35	13	68	52	762
Mecklenburg-Vorpommern	56.1	965.2	44	17	39	59	54	479
Niedersachsen	57.6	250.4	33	32	35	77	53	1,103
Nordrhein-Westfalin	46.1	199.5	41	33	26	77	54	1,133
Rheinland-Pfalz	36.4	149.1	45	38	17	62	46	675
Saarland	28.9	134.5	54	30	16	52	41	843
Sachsen	48.9	475.9	61	22	17	62	55	725
Sachsen-Anhalt	55.9	1,099.1	38	21	41	71	61	389
Schleswig-Holstein	67.2	299.3	35	24	41	78	64	1,320
Thueringen	48.9	801.0	58	19	22	68	57	596
Greece	30.1	43.7	75	24	1	27	25	153
Voreia Ellade	33.9	46.6	73	26	1	27	28	227
Kentriki Ellade	26.5	45.7	74	26	1	27	23	84
Attiki	25.8	34.7	83	15	1	16	13	83
Nisia Aigaiou, Kriti	30.0	33.6	84	16	1	14	13	84
Ireland	63.2	105.0	53	38	9	71	50	1,442

2.4 *(continued)*

	Agricultural land as a percentage of total land area 1994[1]	Economic value of farms(SGM)[2] EUR 12=100 1993	Agricultural holdings by economic size, 1993 (percentages)			Average yield		All cattle per 1,000 ha of utilised agricultural land 1994[5]
			Less than 8 ESU[3]	8 to 39 ESU[3]	40 or more ESU[3]	Wheat 100kg/ha 1994[4]	Barley 100kg/ha 1994[4]	
Italy	*58.3*	*53.3*	*81*	*15*	*3*	35	37	414
Nord Ovest	*44.9*	66.4	*76*	*18*	*6*	46	47	644
Lombardia	*50.1*	130.4	*68*	*20*	*12*	58	52	1,481
Nord Est	*44.1*	65.0	*76*	*20*	*5*	56	51	797
Emilia-Romagna	*62.8*	110.4	*62*	*30*	*9*	57	52	566
Centro	*52.0*	58.7	*81*	*16*	*4*	41	39	141
Lazio	*59.1*	42.8	*86*	*12*	*2*	33	31	316
Campania	*59.1*	35.5	*85*	*14*	*1*	30	35	189
Abruzzi-Molise	*63.8*	38.8	*86*	*12*	*2*	32	32	431
Sud	*69.9*	36.5	*86*	*12*	*2*	26	28	135
Sicilia	*77.5*	38.0	*85*	*13*	*2*	22	21	221
Sardegna	*69.7*	42.1	*81*	*17*	*2*	20	19	180
Luxembourg	*49.0*	*203.1*	*34*	*34*	*33*	50	45	1,561
Netherlands	*47.4*	*483.2*	*12*	*32*	*57*	81	52	2,392
Noord-Nederland	*48.3*	486.9	*11*	*30*	*59*	71	51	1,867
Oost-Nederland	*50.9*	384.8	*15*	*34*	*51*	82	54	3,297
West-Nederland	*40.5*	596.3	*9*	*30*	*61*	86	54	1,468
Zuid-Nederland	*52.2*	482.9	*11*	*31*	*57*	83	52	2,991
Portugal	*43.4*	*34.9*	*88*	*11*	*1*	20	18	333
Continente	*43.5*	36.2	*87*	*11*	*2*	20	18	291
Acores	*52.8*	30.6	*86*	*13*	*1*	..	..	1,602
Maderia	*11.5*	13.3	*98*	*2*	*0*	12	..	1,111
Spain	*53.4*	*57.9*	*76*	*21*	*3*	25	21	195
Noroeste	*31.0*	41.8	*77*	*22*	*1*	20	18	1,168
Noreste	*54.1*	75.1	*67*	*29*	*4*	28	25	140
Madrid	*50.7*	51.5	*80*	*17*	*3*	17	20	187
Centro	*60.3*	61.6	*74*	*22*	*4*	20	20	134
Este	*43.8*	56.3	*78*	*19*	*4*	38	30	250
Sur	*56.4*	57.3	*80*	*17*	*3*	31	16	108
Canarias	*21.7*	69.3	*76*	*21*	*3*	16	14	92
Sweden	*7.5*	*..*	*..*	*..*	*..*	53	35	543
United Kingdom	*69.9*	*265.6*	*43*	*30*	*27*	74	54	695
North	*64.4*	287.8	*31*	*31*	*37*	76	54	898
North West (SSR)	*58.0*	254.3	*46*	*25*	*30*	69	51	1,441
Yorkshire & Humberside	*64.4*	337.8	*36*	*29*	*34*	78	61	672
East Midlands	*70.0*	391.5	*35*	*29*	*36*	73	55	569
West Midlands	*67.4*	264.1	*44*	*28*	*28*	68	53	1,064
East Anglia	*68.0*	518.7	*29*	*30*	*41*	73	53	238
South East (SSR)	*51.0*	315.7	*46*	*26*	*28*	74	55	559
South West	*70.1*	248.3	*47*	*25*	*28*	72	54	1,310
Wales	*68.8*	159.0	*48*	*33*	*19*	71	49	947
Scotland	*70.6*	255.5	*44*	*27*	*29*	74	52	373
Northern Ireland	*75.8*	127.5	*47*	*40*	*13*	71	47	1,444

1 1988 for Italy; 1990 for Spain; 1991 for Ireland.
2 The economic value of farms is measured in Standard Gross Margins (SGMs). See Technical notes.
3 European Size Units (ESUs) are an estimate of the financial potential of the holding in terms of the SGMs which might be expected from crops and stock. The threshhold of 8 ESU
   is judged to be the minimum for full-time holdings.
4 1991 for Spain and 1993 for Belgium.
5 1993 for Greece.

Source: Eurostat

2.5 Gross domestic product per head[1], 1994

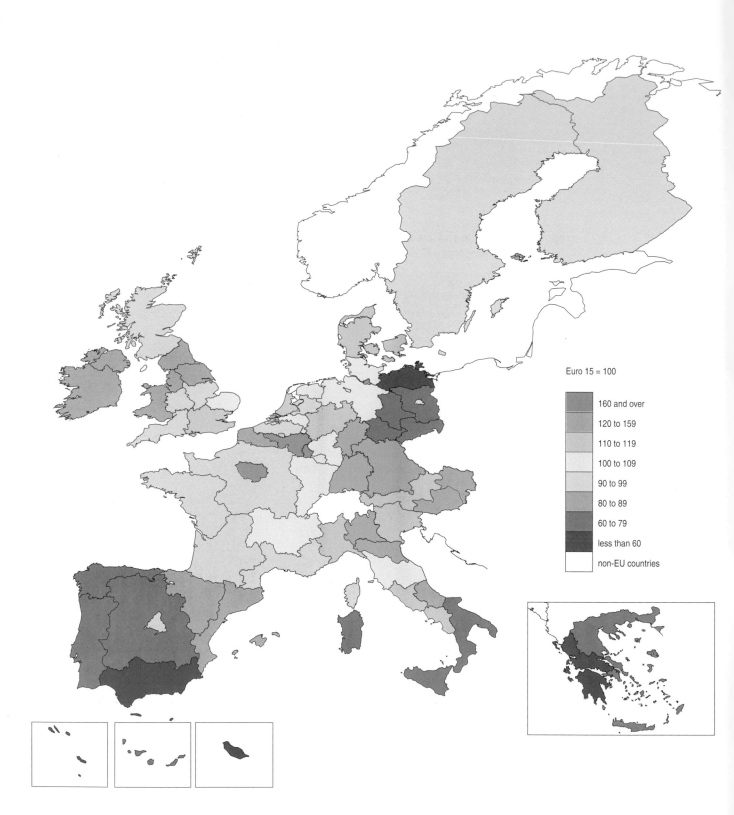

Euro 15 = 100

- 160 and over
- 120 to 159
- 110 to 119
- 100 to 109
- 90 to 99
- 80 to 89
- 60 to 79
- less than 60
- non-EU countries

1 Purchasing Power Standard; see Technical notes.

Source: Eurostat

3 Population and Households

Population change

The South West, the Eastern region and the South East (GOR) have had the fastest growing populations since 1981, while the populations in the North East, Merseyside and Scotland have all fallen.

(Table 3.1)

The largest movement of people between regions is from London to the South East (GOR) with the second largest movement in the opposite direction.

(Table 3.10)

Age

Northern Ireland has the youngest population, with the highest proportion of children and the lowest proportion of pensioners of any region, while the South West has the oldest population.

(Table 3.3)

Births

Scotland has the lowest birth rate and Northern Ireland the highest among all women of child-bearing age, but London has the highest rate among women aged 35 or over.

(Table 3.8)

Deaths

Allowing for the age structure of the population, Scotland has the highest death rates and the South West the lowest.

(Table 3.9)

Social class

London and the South East (GOR) have the highest proportions of economically active people in professional occupations, while the North East followed by Northern Ireland has the highest proportion in unskilled occupations.

(Table 3.14)

Ethnic minorities

One in 100 people in the North East, Wales and Scotland belongs to an ethnic minority group, compared with nearly one in four in London.

(Table 3.15)

Conceptions

Under age conceptions are twice as likely in the North East as in the Eastern region, London or the South East (GOR).

(Table 3.16)

Cohabitation

The proportion of non-married people aged between 18 and 49 who are cohabiting is lowest in Northern Ireland and highest in East Anglia, the South West and the Rest of South East.

(Chart 3.18)

Households

The number of households in the Eastern region and in the South West is projected to grow by around 22 per cent by 2016, double the projected growth in Merseyside.

(Table 3.19)

A third of households in London consist of one person compared with a quarter in the East Midlands, the Eastern region and Northern Ireland.

(Table 3.20)

Introduction

A full population census is conducted every ten years. Preparation for the next census in 2001 began as early as 1993-94 with a development programme which is being taken forward by the Office for National Statistics, the General Register Office for Scotland and the Northern Ireland Statistics and Research Agency. A major census test is being carried out in the United Kingdom in 1997 and this will be followed in 1999 by a full 'dress rehearsal'. This extensive development programme is needed to identify, test, evaluate and develop all the procedures needed for 2001 as the decennial census is the most valuable source of information about the characteristics of people in Britain, particularly for small areas.

A key use of the census is as a benchmark for the population estimates: between censuses the population figures are rolled forward using annual estimates of the components of population change (births, deaths, net migration and other changes). As the decade proceeds, problems with estimating migration in particular progressively affects these rolled forward figures. Thus the census is used as a base for both revising previous years' data and preparing estimates for the following decade.

In general, natural change (that is the difference between births and deaths) and net migration can vary from region to region and from year to year. At a local level, inter-regional migration has more effect than international migration, which tends to be concentrated in a few areas (see Tables 3.10 and 3.11). The UK population has grown by just under 5 per cent since 1971, but this masks quite different growth rates among the regions: growth has been fastest in the Eastern region (18 per cent up to 1995), the South West (17 per cent) and the South East (GOR) (15 per cent). On the other hand, the populations of the North East, Merseyside, London and Scotland were all lower in 1995 than in 1971 (Table 3.1), although by 1995 only Merseyside's was still declining.

One of the biggest changes in social behaviour over the past 15 years has been the tendency of women to delay having their children. This can be seen clearly in Table 3.8 which shows age-specific birth rates for 1981, 1991 and 1995. In every region except Northern Ireland, birth rates among women aged 35 or over were higher in 1995 than they had been in either 1991 or 1981, while there were significant reductions in all regions in the rates among women in their 20s. This pattern is most pronounced in London and the South East (GOR). The delaying of child-bearing is linked to the greater participation of females in both higher education and the labour force. In addition, many women start a second family with their new husband/partner following the breakdown of their first marriage. As a result, the average age of women at childbirth was 28.5 in 1995 compared with 26.8 in 1981.

Another striking change in social behaviour has been the increase in one-person households. In 1981, 23 per cent of households in the United Kingdom consisted of one person, but by 1995 this proportion had risen to more than 28 per cent (Table 3.20). In London a third of all households now consist of one person living alone. There are three main factors associated with this rise in one-person households: the growing number of never married men and to a lesser extent never married women living by themselves, the increase in separations and divorces, and the increased number of elderly widowed women. The growth in the number of one-person households has been a major factor in the reduction in the average household size from 2.72 in 1981 to 2.41 in 1995 and the growth is projected to increase. The total number of households in Great Britain is projected to rise from 23.3 million in 1995 to 25.5 million in 2006 (Table 3.19) and one-person households will account for about three-quarters of this increase.

3.1 Resident population[1]: by gender

Thousands and percentages

	Population (thousands)				Annual growth rate (percentages)	
	1971	1981	1991	1995	1971-1981	1981-1995
Males						
United Kingdom	27,167.3	27,409.2	28,245.6	28,727.5	0.1	0.3
North East	1,304.0	1,283.1	1,267.5	1,272.4	-0.2	-0.1
North West (GOR) & Merseyside	3,422.4	3,357.6	3,348.7	3,376.2	-0.2	-
North West (GOR)	2,626.9	2,627.4	2,652.2	2,686.5	-	0.2
Merseyside	795.5	730.2	696.5	689.7	-0.9	-0.4
Yorkshire and the Humber	2,384.9	2,395.0	2,441.7	2,473.8	-	0.2
East Midlands	1,797.8	1,894.8	1,989.6	2,037.6	0.5	0.5
West Midlands	2,542.4	2,555.6	2,596.3	2,620.8	0.1	0.2
Eastern	2,194.6	2,385.5	2,536.9	2,590.5	0.8	0.6
London	3,611.4	3,277.6	3,352.0	3,431.8	-1.0	0.3
South East (GOR)	3,321.1	3,528.6	3,759.8	3,847.2	0.6	0.6
South West	1,989.9	2,117.2	2,295.6	2,357.2	0.6	0.8
England	22,568.5	22,795.0	23,588.1	24,007.6	0.1	0.4
Wales	1,328.5	1,365.1	1,407.0	1,425.5	0.3	0.3
Scotland	2,515.7	2,494.9	2,469.5	2,489.2	-0.1	-
Northern Ireland	754.6	754.2	780.9	805.2	-	0.5
Females						
United Kingdom	28,760.7	28,943.0	29,562.3	29,878.3	0.1	0.2
North East	1,374.5	1,353.1	1,335.0	1,332.8	-0.2	-0.1
North West (GOR) & Merseyside	3,685.4	3,582.7	3,536.7	3,523.7	-0.3	-0.1
North West (GOR)	2,819.1	2,790.7	2,783.5	2,786.2	-0.1	-
Merseyside	866.3	792.0	753.1	737.5	-0.9	-0.5
Yorkshire and the Humber	2,517.4	2,523.5	2,541.1	2,555.6	-	0.1
East Midlands	1,854.1	1,958.0	2,045.8	2,086.3	0.5	0.5
West Midlands	2,603.6	2,631.1	2,669.1	2,685.6	0.1	0.1
Eastern	2,259.7	2,468.5	2,613.0	2,666.9	0.9	0.6
London	3,918.0	3,528.0	3,538.0	3,575.3	-1.0	0.1
South East (GOR)	3,508.6	3,716.8	3,919.1	4,000.0	0.6	0.5
South West	2,121.9	2,264.1	2,422.1	2,469.7	0.7	0.6
England	23,843.2	24,025.8	24,619.9	24,895.8	0.1	0.3
Wales	1,411.8	1,440.4	1,484.5	1,491.3	0.3	0.2
Scotland	2,719.9	2,685.3	2,637.5	2,647.4	-0.3	-0.1
Northern Ireland	785.8	783.5	820.4	843.7	-	0.5
All persons						
United Kingdom	55,928.0	56,352.2	57,807.9	58,605.8	0.1	0.3
North East	2,678.5	2,636.2	2,602.5	2,605.1	-0.2	-0.1
North West (GOR) & Merseyside	7,107.8	6,940.3	6,885.4	6,899.9	-0.2	-
North West (GOR)	5,446.0	5,418.1	5,435.7	5,472.7	-0.1	0.1
Merseyside	1,661.8	1,522.2	1,449.7	1,427.2	-0.9	-0.5
Yorkshire and the Humber	4,902.3	4,918.4	4,982.8	5,029.5	-	0.2
East Midlands	3,651.9	3,852.8	4,035.4	4,123.9	0.5	0.5
West Midlands	5,146.0	5,186.6	5,265.5	5,306.4	0.1	0.2
Eastern	4,454.3	4,854.1	5,149.8	5,257.4	0.9	0.6
London	7,529.4	6,805.6	6,889.9	7,007.1	-1.0	0.2
South East (GOR)	6,829.7	7,245.4	7,678.9	7,847.2	0.6	0.6
South West	4,111.8	4,381.4	4,717.8	4,826.9	0.6	0.7
England	46,411.7	46,820.8	48,208.1	48,903.4	0.1	0.3
Wales	2,740.3	2,813.5	2,891.5	2,916.8	0.3	0.3
Scotland	5,235.6	5,180.2	5,107.0	5,136.6	-0.2	-0.1
Northern Ireland	1,540.4	1,537.7	1,601.4	1,649.0	-	0.5

1 See Technical notes.

Source: Office for National Statistics; General Register Office for Scotland; Northern Ireland Statistics and Research Agency

3.2 Population change, mid 1981-1995[1] and projected growth 1995-2011[2]

Projected change mid 1981-1995

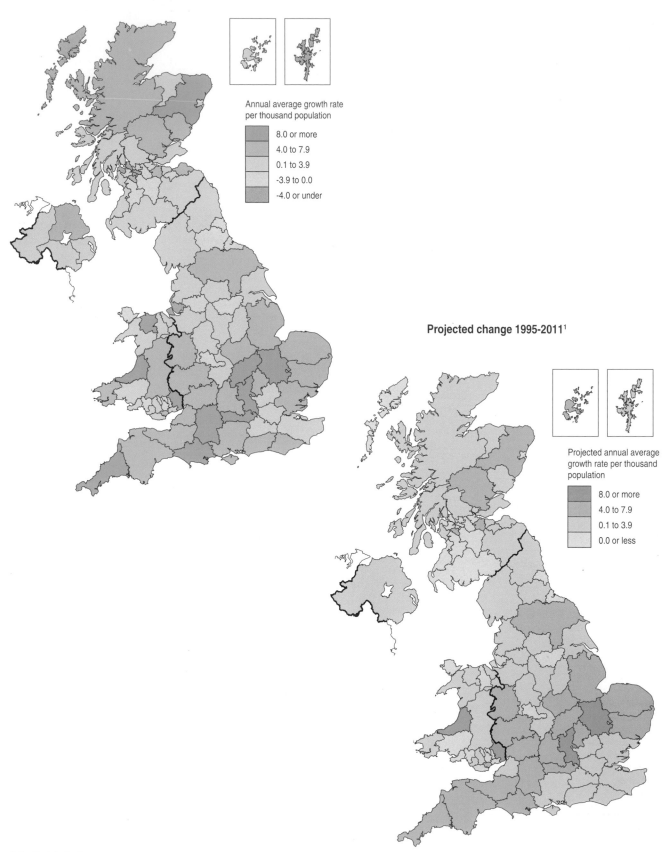

Annual average growth rate
per thousand population

- 8.0 or more
- 4.0 to 7.9
- 0.1 to 3.9
- -3.9 to 0.0
- -4.0 or under

Projected change 1995-2011[1]

Projected annual average
growth rate per thousand
population

- 8.0 or more
- 4.0 to 7.9
- 0.1 to 3.9
- 0.0 or less

1 See Technical notes.
2 Mid-1995 population estimates; 1992-based sub-national projections for England and 1994-based sub-national projections for Wales and Scotland; 1995-based national projections
  for Northern Ireland.

Source: Office for National Statistics; Welsh Office; General Register Office for Scotland; Northern Ireland Statistics and Research Agency

3.3 Resident population[1]: by age and gender, 1995

Thousands and percentages

	0-4	5-15	16-44	Males 45-64 Females 45-59	Males 65-79 Females 60-79	80 and over	All ages
Males (thousands)							
United Kingdom	1,964.6	4,243.4	12,220.7	6,558.6	3,022.6	717.6	28,727.5
North East	84.8	192.8	533.0	294.7	140.0	27.1	1,272.4
North West (GOR) & Merseyside	234.5	518.0	1,411.5	780.4	352.8	79.0	3,376.2
North West (GOR)	186.7	409.5	1,122.9	625.1	279.4	62.9	2,686.5
Merseyside	47.8	108.4	288.6	155.3	73.5	16.1	689.7
Yorkshire and the Humber	169.0	367.0	1,053.0	561.8	262.9	60.1	2,473.8
East Midlands	136.0	298.5	851.5	478.1	222.9	50.6	2,037.6
West Midlands	181.0	394.9	1,091.7	613.7	279.5	60.0	2,620.8
Eastern	174.9	374.2	1,081.4	609.0	281.2	69.7	2,590.5
London	258.6	475.7	1,623.6	695.9	300.2	77.9	3,431.8
South East (GOR)	256.2	557.8	1,618.1	900.6	405.2	109.5	3,847.2
South West	147.1	333.8	953.2	557.7	287.1	78.4	2,357.2
England	1,642.1	3,512.7	10,217.0	5,491.9	2,531.7	612.2	24,007.6
Wales	93.8	216.1	571.9	338.2	168.1	37.5	1,425.5
Scotland	164.1	365.6	1,084.8	567.8	253.0	53.8	2,489.2
Northern Ireland	64.6	149.0	347.0	160.7	69.8	14.1	805.2
Females (thousands)							
United Kingdom	1,870.9	4,026.9	11,825.1	5,244.0	5,272.2	1,639.2	29,878.3
North East	80.6	183.1	522.0	232.7	247.4	67.0	1,332.8
North West (GOR) & Merseyside	221.9	491.5	1,366.8	619.5	629.7	194.3	3,523.7
North West (GOR)	176.8	388.5	1,080.3	494.6	493.0	153.1	2,786.2
Merseyside	45.1	103.0	286.6	124.9	136.7	41.2	737.5
Yorkshire and the Humber	161.1	348.0	1,000.0	447.0	457.4	142.2	2,555.6
East Midlands	128.5	282.4	821.0	375.1	369.7	109.6	2,086.3
West Midlands	172.5	373.7	1,045.1	480.5	477.3	136.6	2,685.0
Eastern	166.9	356.3	1,041.0	484.8	471.6	146.2	2,666.0
London	240.5	454.4	1,594.4	570.8	528.2	180.9	3,575.3
South East (GOR)	243.8	526.6	1,555.7	723.3	706.2	244.3	4,000.0
South West	140.1	315.2	913.0	444.7	487.8	168.8	2,469.7
England	1,562.0	3,331.3	9,859.0	4,378.3	4,375.2	1,390.1	24,895.8
Wales	89.9	205.2	552.5	267.8	289.1	86.8	1,491.3
Scotland	157.3	340.7	1,069.4	465.0	477.7	129.3	2,647.4
Northern Ireland	61.8	141.7	344.2	132.9	130.2	33.0	843.7
All persons (percentages)							
United Kingdom	6.5	14.1	41.0	20.1	14.2	4.0	100.0
North East	6.3	14.4	40.5	20.2	14.9	3.6	100.0
North West (GOR) & Merseyside	6.6	14.6	40.3	20.3	14.2	4.0	100.0
North West (GOR)	6.6	14.6	40.3	20.5	14.1	3.9	100.0
Merseyside	6.5	14.8	40.3	19.6	14.7	4.0	100.0
Yorkshire and the Humber	6.6	14.2	40.8	20.1	14.3	4.0	100.0
East Midlands	6.4	14.1	40.6	20.7	14.4	3.9	100.0
West Midlands	6.7	14.5	40.3	20.6	14.3	3.7	100.0
Eastern	6.5	13.9	40.4	20.8	14.3	4.1	100.0
London	7.2	13.3	45.9	18.1	11.8	3.7	100.0
South East (GOR)	6.4	13.8	40.4	20.7	14.2	4.5	100.0
South West	5.9	13.4	38.7	20.8	16.1	5.1	100.0
England	6.6	14.0	41.1	20.2	14.1	4.1	100.0
Wales	6.3	14.4	38.5	20.8	15.7	4.3	100.0
Scotland	6.3	13.9	41.9	20.1	14.2	3.6	100.0
Northern Ireland	7.7	17.6	41.9	17.8	12.1	2.9	100.0

1 See Technical notes.

Source: Office for National Statistics; General Register Office for Scotland; Northern Ireland Statistics and Research Agency

3.4 Population density, 1995[1]

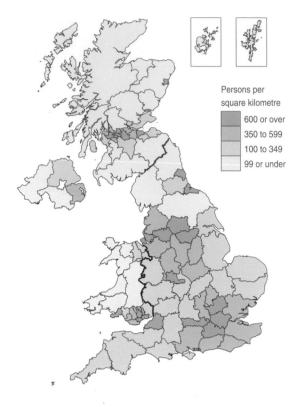

Persons per
square kilometre

- 600 or over
- 350 to 599
- 100 to 349
- 99 or under

1 See Technical notes.

Source: Office for National Statistics; General Register Office for Scotland; Northern Ireland Statistics and Research Agency

3.5 Population under 16[1], 1995

Percentage of
total population

- 21.5 or over
- 20.5 to 21.4
- 19.5 to 20.4
- 19.4 or under

1 See Technical notes.

*Source: Office for National Statistics; General Register Office for
Scotland; Northern Ireland Statistics and Research Agency*

3.6 Population of retirement age[1], 1995

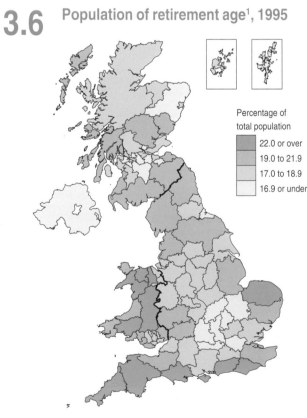

Percentage of
total population

- 22.0 or over
- 19.0 to 21.9
- 17.0 to 18.9
- 16.9 or under

1 Males aged 65 or over, females aged 60 or over. See Technical notes.

*Source: Office for National Statistics; General Register Office for
Scotland; Northern Ireland Statistics and Research Agency*

3.7 Live births, deaths and natural increase in population

Thousands and rates

	Thousands			Rate per 1,000 population		
	1981	1991	1995	1981	1991	1995
Live births[1]						
United Kingdom	730.8	792.5	732.0	13.0	13.7	12.5
North East	34.2	34.9	30.7	13.0	13.4	11.8
North West (GOR) & Merseyside	90.4	97.5	84.3	13.0	14.2	12.2
North West (GOR)	70.4	77.1	67.1	13.0	14.2	12.3
Merseyside	20.0	20.3	17.2	13.2	14.0	12.0
Yorkshire and the Humber	62.6	68.6	62.8	12.7	13.8	12.5
East Midlands	49.2	54.0	49.6	12.8	13.4	12.0
West Midlands	67.5	74.2	67.1	13.0	14.1	12.6
Eastern	62.6	68.4	64.7	12.9	13.3	12.3
London	92.4	105.8	104.1	13.5	15.4	14.9
South East (GOR)	89.0	99.8	95.6	12.3	13.0	12.2
South West	50.4	57.6	54.4	11.5	12.2	11.3
England	598.2	660.8	613.3	12.8	13.7	12.5
Wales	35.8	38.1	34.5	12.7	13.2	11.8
Scotland	69.1	67.0	60.1	13.3	13.1	11.7
Northern Ireland	27.3	26.3	23.9	17.8	16.5	14.5
Deaths[2]						
United Kingdom	658.0	646.2	641.7	11.7	11.2	10.9
North East	32.1	31.8	30.3	12.2	12.2	11.6
North West (GOR) & Merseyside	86.6	82.7	80.1	12.5	12.0	11.6
North West (GOR)	67.6	64.8	62.7	12.5	11.9	11.5
Merseyside	19.0	17.9	17.4	12.4	12.4	12.2
Yorkshire and the Humber	59.1	57.3	55.6	12.0	11.5	11.1
East Midlands	42.8	43.9	43.8	11.1	10.9	10.6
West Midlands	56.4	57.0	57.5	10.9	10.8	10.0
Eastern	50.7	53.3	54.1	10.4	10.3	10.3
London	77.0	68.9	66.8	11.4	10.0	9.5
South East (GOR)	81.3	83.0	84.1	11.2	10.8	10.7
South West	54.4	56.2	56.8	12.4	11.9	11.8
England	541.0	534.0	529.0	11.6	11.1	10.8
Wales	35.0	34.1	35.3	12.4	11.8	12.1
Scotland	63.8	61.0	60.5	12.3	12.0	11.8
Northern Ireland	16.3	15.1	15.3	10.6	9.4	9.3
Natural increase						
United Kingdom	72.8	146.3	90.3	1.3	2.5	1.6
North East	2.1	3.1	0.4	0.8	1.2	0.2
North West (GOR) & Merseyside	3.8	14.8	4.2	0.5	2.2	0.6
North West (GOR)	2.8	12.3	4.4	0.5	2.3	0.8
Merseyside	1.0	2.4	-0.2	0.8	1.6	-0.2
Yorkshire and the Humber	3.5	11.3	7.2	0.7	2.3	1.4
East Midlands	6.4	10.1	5.8	1.7	2.5	1.4
West Midlands	11.1	17.2	9.6	2.1	3.3	1.8
Eastern	11.9	15.1	10.6	2.5	3.0	2.0
London	14.8	36.9	37.3	2.1	5.4	5.4
South East (GOR)	7.7	16.8	11.5	1.1	2.2	1.5
South West	-4.0	1.4	-2.4	-0.9	0.3	-0.5
England	57.2	126.8	84.3	1.2	2.6	1.7
Wales	0.8	4.0	-0.8	0.3	1.4	-0.3
Scotland	5.3	6.0	-0.4	1.0	1.1	-0.1
Northern Ireland	11.0	11.2	8.6	7.2	7.1	5.2

1 Births data for all countries and English regions are based on the mother's usual area of residence. UK figures include births registered in England and Wales to mothers usually resident outside England and Wales. Annual births data are given for year of occurrence in England and Wales, and for year of registration in Scotland and Northern Ireland. See Technical notes.
2 UK death figures include deaths occurring in England and Wales to non-residents of England and Wales. These numbers are excluded from the data for England and Wales and the English regions.

Source: Office for National Statistics; General Register Office for Scotland; Northern Ireland Statistics and Research Agency

3.8 Age specific birth rates

Rates

	Live births per 1,000 women in age groups[1]							
	Under 20	20-24	25-29	30-34	35-39	40 and over	All ages	TPFR[2]
1981								
United Kingdom	28	107	130	70	22	5	62	1.81
North East	34	114	128	60	18	4	62	1.79
North West (GOR) & Merseyside	35	114	130	65	21	5	63	1.85
North West (GOR)	35	115	132	64	20	5	63	1.86
Merseyside	36	109	124	70	23	5	64	1.83
Yorkshire and the Humber	31	117	128	59	18	6	62	1.80
East Midlands	30	113	127	63	19	4	61	1.79
West Midlands	32	108	133	69	20	7	62	1.84
Eastern	22	110	138	70	20	4	61	1.82
London	29	83	114	80	31	6	62	1.71
South East (GOR)	20	97	138	73	23	4	59	1.77
South West	24	103	131	63	18	3	57	1.71
England	28	104	129	69	22	5	61	1.78
Wales	30	121	127	67	21	6	63	1.86
Scotland	31	112	131	66	21	4	63	1.84
Northern Ireland	27	135	173	118	52	13	86	2.59
1991								
United Kingdom	33	89	120	87	32	5	64	1.82
North East	44	102	119	72	23	4	63	1.82
North West (GOR) & Merseyside	42	101	124	84	29	5	67	1.93
North West (GOR)	42	103	125	84	29	5	67	1.94
Merseyside	40	93	121	84	32	5	66	1.87
Yorkshire and the Humber	41	99	122	78	26	4	64	1.85
East Midlands	34	95	126	81	26	4	63	1.83
West Midlands	39	102	126	84	31	5	67	1.93
Eastern	24	86	129	91	31	5	62	1.83
London	29	69	97	96	47	10	64	1.74
South East (GOR)	23	78	122	95	35	5	61	1.80
South West	25	84	125	86	30	5	60	1.77
England	33	89	119	87	32	5	64	1.81
Wales	39	103	127	77	27	5	64	1.88
Scotland	33	82	117	78	27	4	60	1.69
Northern Ireland	29	98	148	107	47	10	76	2.17
1995								
United Kingdom	28	76	108	87	36	7	60	1.71
North East	38	82	107	75	27	4	57	1.67
North West (GOR) & Merseyside	34	83	109	80	32	6	60	1.72
North West (GOR)	34	84	110	80	31	6	60	1.73
Merseyside	34	77	106	79	33	6	58	1.68
Yorkshire and the Humber	36	88	114	78	30	6	61	1.75
East Midlands	29	77	112	84	31	5	59	1.68
West Midlands	33	89	114	83	33	6	62	1.79
Eastern	22	71	112	95	36	6	60	1.71
London	25	69	96	94	51	12	64	1.73
South East (GOR)	21	65	107	98	41	7	60	1.70
South West	23	69	112	89	35	6	58	1.67
England	28	76	108	88	37	7	60	1.71
Wales	35	90	116	79	31	5	60	1.78
Scotland	28	67	101	80	30	5	55	1.55
Northern Ireland	24	72	129	104	46	9	67	1.92

1 The rates for women aged under 20, 40 and over and all ages are based upon the population of women aged 15-19, 40-44 and 15-44 respectively.
2 The Total Period Fertility Rate (TPFR) measures the average number of children which would be born if women were to experience the age-specific fertility rates of the year in question throughout their child-bearing life.

Source: Office for National Statistics; General Register Office for Scotland; Northern Ireland Statistics and Research Agency

3.9 Age-specific death rates: by gender, 1995

Rates and Standardised Mortality Ratios

	Deaths per 1,000 population for specific age groups											SMR[1] (UK = 100)
	Under 1[2]	0-4	5-14	15-24	25-34	35-44	45-54	55-64	65-74	75-84	85 and over	
Males												
United Kingdom	6.8	1.5	0.2	0.8	1.0	1.7	4.2	12.5	36.4	89.3	196.0	100
North East	8.1	1.6	0.2	0.6	0.8	1.7	4.6	14.1	42.9	98.5	202.7	111
North West (GOR) & Merseyside	7.7	1.7	0.2	0.8	1.2	1.8	4.7	14.2	40.6	96.5	196.5	109
North West (GOR)	7.8	1.7	0.2	0.8	1.2	1.8	4.6	13.4	40.0	95.7	194.0	107
Merseyside	7.5	1.6	0.2	0.7	1.1	2.0	5.2	17.2	43.0	99.3	206.6	117
Yorkshire and the Humber	7.7	1.7	0.2	0.7	0.9	1.5	4.2	12.9	37.1	90.9	193.9	101
East Midlands	6.3	1.3	0.1	0.7	0.9	1.5	3.7	11.5	35.4	88.7	193.4	97
West Midlands	7.9	1.8	0.2	0.7	0.8	1.6	4.1	12.9	37.6	94.8	203.2	104
Eastern	5.9	1.3	0.2	0.7	0.8	1.3	3.3	9.9	31.2	84.1	191.7	89
London	6.6	1.6	0.2	0.7	1.2	2.2	4.7	12.8	36.0	86.9	185.8	100
South East (GOR)	5.7	1.3	0.2	0.7	0.8	1.4	3.4	10.3	31.9	83.1	193.8	90
South West	6.0	1.3	0.2	0.7	0.9	1.4	3.5	10.8	31.4	80.2	191.7	89
England	6.8	1.5	0.2	0.7	0.9	1.6	4.0	12.1	35.6	88.3	193.8	98
Wales	6.8	1.5	0.2	1.0	1.1	1.7	4.1	13.2	38.3	93.4	198.9	104
Scotland	6.3	1.4	0.2	1.0	1.4	2.0	5.5	16.4	42.6	95.7	210.6	116
Northern Ireland	7.5	1.7	0.2	1.0	1.1	1.7	4.5	13.7	37.9	95.2	233.2	109
Females												
United Kingdom	5.4	1.2	0.1	0.3	0.5	1.1	2.8	7.4	21.6	57.4	153.6	100
North East	5.3	1.2	0.1	0.3	0.5	1.1	2.8	8.8	25.8	63.4	154.2	110
North West (GOR) & Merseyside	5.4	1.3	0.1	0.3	0.5	1.2	3.1	8.1	24.0	61.3	154.6	106
North West (GOR)	5.4	1.3	0.1	0.3	0.5	1.1	3.1	8.0	23.7	61.3	155.5	106
Merseyside	5.3	1.3	0.1	0.3	0.4	1.4	3.0	8.7	25.2	61.5	151.2	107
Yorkshire and the Humber	6.1	1.4	0.1	0.3	0.5	1.0	2.7	7.5	23.3	57.5	150.4	101
East Midlands	5.2	1.2	0.2	0.2	0.4	1.0	2.7	7.2	21.1	56.6	152.7	99
West Midlands	6.0	1.3	0.1	0.3	0.4	1.0	2.9	7.3	22.0	58.1	157.1	102
Eastern	4.4	1.0	0.1	0.3	0.4	1.0	2.6	6.4	19.0	53.9	154.2	95
London	6.0	1.4	0.1	0.2	0.5	1.1	2.8	7.2	20.9	55.8	144.0	96
South East (GOR)	4.5	1.0	0.1	0.3	0.4	0.9	2.3	6.4	18.7	54.1	152.3	94
South West	4.3	1.0	0.1	0.3	0.4	0.9	2.5	6.3	18.0	51.4	148.3	91
England	5.3	1.2	0.1	0.3	0.4	1.0	2.7	7.2	21.1	56.4	151.6	98
Wales	5.4	1.2	0.1	0.3	0.5	1.2	2.8	8.2	22.1	58.4	153.3	103
Scotland	6.0	1.3	0.1	0.4	0.6	1.2	3.4	9.3	25.6	65.2	171.9	116
Northern Ireland	6.6	1.4	0.2	0.3	0.4	1.2	3.1	8.0	22.5	60.1	173.0	108
All persons												
United Kingdom	6.1	1.4	0.2	0.5	0.7	1.4	3.5	9.9	28.3	69.4	164.3	100
North East	6.7	1.4	0.1	0.5	0.6	1.4	3.7	11.4	33.6	76.2	165.6	110
North West (GOR) & Merseyside	6.6	1.4	0.2	0.5	0.8	1.5	3.9	11.1	31.5	74.1	164.5	107
North West (GOR)	6.6	1.5	0.2	0.5	0.8	1.5	3.9	10.6	31.1	73.9	164.7	106
Merseyside	6.4	1.5	0.1	0.5	0.8	1.7	4.1	12.8	33.1	74.9	163.7	110
Yorkshire and the Humber	6.9	1.5	0.2	0.5	0.7	1.3	3.4	10.1	29.6	69.9	161.0	101
East Midlands	5.8	1.3	0.1	0.5	0.7	1.2	3.2	9.3	27.8	69.1	163.4	98
West Midlands	7.0	1.5	0.2	0.5	0.6	1.3	3.5	10.1	29.2	72.0	168.6	103
Eastern	5.1	1.2	0.2	0.5	0.6	1.1	3.0	8.2	24.6	65.8	164.3	93
London	6.3	1.5	0.1	0.5	0.8	1.7	3.7	10.0	27.8	67.3	154.5	98
South East (GOR)	5.2	1.2	0.1	0.5	0.6	1.2	2.8	8.3	24.7	65.1	163.0	92
South West	5.2	1.2	0.1	0.5	0.7	1.2	3.0	8.5	24.1	62.6	159.8	90
England	6.1	1.4	0.2	0.5	0.7	1.3	3.3	9.6	27.7	68.5	162.3	98
Wales	6.1	1.4	0.1	0.7	0.8	1.5	3.5	10.6	29.5	71.5	164.6	103
Scotland	6.2	1.4	0.2	0.7	1.0	1.6	4.5	12.7	33.1	76.1	181.3	115
Northern Ireland	7.1	1.6	0.2	0.7	0.8	1.4	3.8	10.7	29.2	73.1	187.6	108

1 Standardised Mortality Ratio is the ratio of observed deaths to those expected by applying a standard death ratio to the regional population. See Technical notes.
2 Deaths of infants under 1 year of age per 1,000 live births.

Source: Office for National Statistics; General Register Office for Scotland; Northern Ireland Statistics and Research Agency

3.10 Inter-regional movements[1], 1995

Thousands

					Region of origin									
	United Kingdom	North East	North West (GOR)	Merseyside	Yorkshire & the Humber	East Midlands	West Midlands	Eastern	London	South East (GOR)	South West	Wales	Scotland	Northern Ireland
Region of destination														
United Kingdom	.	46	104	31	98	92	98	119	208	196	108	53	52	12
North East	38	.	5	1	8	3	2	3	4	4	2	1	4	-
North West (GOR)	99	6	.	11	15	8	10	6	9	10	7	7	7	1
Merseyside	25	1	8	.	2	1	2	1	2	2	1	2	1	-
Yorkshire and the Humber	91	10	15	3	.	15	7	8	9	10	6	3	5	1
East Midlands	101	4	10	2	18	.	14	15	10	15	7	3	4	1
West Midlands	90	3	11	2	8	12	.	7	10	14	12	8	3	1
Eastern	135	4	7	2	8	13	8	.	50	25	10	4	5	1
London	171	5	11	3	11	10	12	31	.	56	17	6	7	2
South East (GOR)	219	5	12	3	11	14	15	28	79	.	34	8	8	2
South West	132	3	9	2	7	8	16	12	20	40	.	10	5	1
Wales	55	1	8	2	3	3	9	4	5	8	8	.	2	-
Scotland	49	4	7	1	5	3	3	4	6	7	4	2	.	3
Northern Ireland	14	-	1	-	1	1	1	1	3	2	1	-	2	.

1 Based on patients re-registering with NHS doctors in other parts of the United Kingdom. See Technical notes.

Source: Office for National Statistics; General Register Office for Scotland; Northern Ireland Statistics and Research Agency

3.11 Migration[1]

Thousands

	Inflow					Outflow				
	1981	1986	1991	1993	1995	1981	1986	1991	1993	1995
Internal migration										
North East	31	36	40	38	38	39	46	41	42	46
North West (GOR)	79	90	90	91	99	88	101	94	95	104
Merseyside	23	22	24	24	25	34	37	29	29	31
Yorkshire and the Humber	68	79	85	88	91	73	91	85	88	98
East Midlands	77	102	90	93	101	72	85	81	83	92
West Midlands	67	87	83	83	90	79	95	88	92	98
Eastern	121	145	122	123	135	104	128	113	113	119
London	155	183	149	151	171	187	232	202	203	208
South East (GOR)	202	243	198	206	219	166	204	185	183	196
South West	108	149	121	121	132	88	103	99	101	108
England	94	116	96	99	108	93	101	112	108	108
Wales	45	55	52	52	55	42	50	47	48	53
Scotland	47	44	56	54	49	48	58	47	47	52
Northern Ireland	7	9	13	11	14	10	15	9	12	12
International migration										
United Kingdom	153	250	267	213	245	233	213	239	216	192
North East	4	9	7	4	2	14	7	4	4	3
North West (GOR) & Merseyside	15	26	14	11	17	24	17	19	14	19
North West (GOR)	12	23	13	10	14	18	14	14	10	17
Merseyside	3	3	1	2	3	6	3	5	4	3
Yorkshire and the Humber	9	13	20	16	13	14	14	14	11	12
East Midlands	5	9	12	10	10	10	5	7	9	10
West Midlands	11	11	14	14	16	13	8	18	13	9
Eastern	9	21	26	19	19	18	20	22	26	14
London	49	78	79	61	83	55	51	67	62	50
South East (GOR)	26	38	45	38	50	35	43	37	41	35
South West	10	18	18	16	15	13	16	19	12	19
England	138	223	233	192	224	196	182	207	192	172
Wales	3	8	8	6	8	11	6	6	7	5
Scotland	10	16	22	16	12	21	21	23	15	13
Northern Ireland	2	2	3	-	1	4	4	2	1	2

1 See Technical notes.

Source: National Health Service Central Register and International Passenger Survey, Office for National Statistics; General Register Office for Scotland; Northern Ireland Statistics and Research Agency

3.12 Components of population change, mid-1994 to mid-1995[1,2]

Thousands

	Resident population mid-1994	Births	Deaths	Net natural change	Net civilian migration and other changes	Total change	Resident population mid-1995
United Kingdom	58,394.6	737.8	631.6	106.2	105.0	211.2	58,605.8
North East	2,609.6	31.2	30.4	0.9	-5.4	-4.5	2,605.1
North West (GOR) & Merseyside	6,902.2	86.0	79.7	6.3	-8.6	-2.3	6,899.9
North West (GOR)	5,467.8	68.5	62.4	6.1	-1.2	4.9	5,472.7
Merseyside	1,434.4	17.5	17.3	0.2	-7.4	-7.2	1,427.2
Yorkshire and the Humber	5,025.0	62.8	55.0	7.8	-3.4	4.5	5,029.5
East Midlands	4,102.2	50.2	43.4	6.9	14.9	21.7	4,123.9
West Midlands	5,294.9	67.3	56.6	10.7	0.8	11.5	5,306.4
Eastern	5,223.2	65.4	53.1	12.2	22.0	34.2	5,257.4
London	6,967.5	104.2	66.3	38.0	1.6	39.6	7,007.1
South East (GOR)	7,784.3	96.2	82.6	13.5	49.4	62.9	7,847.2
South West	4,798.4	54.8	55.3	-0.5	28.9	28.4	4,826.9
England	48,707.5	618.2	522.3	95.9	100.1	196.0	48,903.4
Wales	2,913.0	34.8	34.3	0.5	3.2	3.7	2,916.8
Scotland	5,132.4	60.6	59.6	0.9	3.3	4.2	5,136.6
Northern Ireland	1,641.7	24.2	15.3	8.9	-1.6	7.2	1,649.0

1 See Technical notes.
2 The corresponding table in *Regional Trends* 31 mistakenly included 1994 calender year data for births and deaths instead of mid-1993 to mid-1994 data. For the correct data, please contact the Regional Reporting Branch on the telephone number on page 9.

Source: Office for National Statistics; General Register Office for Scotland; Northern Ireland Statistics and Research Agency

3.13 Resident population: by type of area[1], 1995

Percentages and thousands

	Percentage of population in each type of area						Total population (= 100%) (thousands)
	Rural areas	Prospering areas	Maturer areas	Urban centres	Mining and industrial areas	Inner London	
Great Britain	18	22	12	20	21	6	56,957
North East	7	.	.	13	80	.	2,605
North West (GOR) & Merseyside	12	20	6	24	38	.	6,900
North West (GOR)	16	25	7	31	21	.	5,473
Merseyside	.	.	.	.	100	.	1,427
Yorkshire and the Humber	15	5	2	38	41	.	5,029
East Midlands	34	27	.	21	17	.	4,124
West Midlands	27	22	.	46	5	.	5,306
Eastern	15	53	10	23	.	.	5,257
London	.	10	36	.	2	52	7,007
South East (GOR)	11	53	20	17	.	.	7,847
South West	47	17	16	21	.	.	4,827
England	17	25	12	22	16	7	48,903
Wales	33	.	2	.	65	.	2,917
Scotland	20	5	13	17	46	.	5,137

1 Area classifications based on the 1991 Census. See Technical notes.

Source. Office for National Statistics; General Register Office for Scotland

3.14 Social class[1] of economically active population, Spring 1996

Percentages and thousands

	Professional occupations (I)	Managerial and technical (II)	Skilled occupations non-manual (IIIN)	Skilled occupations manual (IIIM)	Partly skilled occupations (IV)	Unskilled occupations (V)	Other[2]	Total economically active population (= 100%) (thousands)
United Kingdom	5.8	28.7	21.7	20.0	15.2	5.5	3.1	28,552
North East	4.7	23.6	20.9	23.4	17.0	6.7	3.7	1,186
North West (GOR) & Merseyside	5.0	27.0	22.8	21.3	15.2	5.5	3.2	3,224
North West (GOR)	5.2	27.7	22.7	21.1	15.1	5.6	2.6	2,610
Merseyside	4.2	23.8	23.2	22.1	15.9	5.1	5.7	614
Yorkshire and the Humber	5.0	25.0	21.5	22.5	17.6	5.5	2.8	2,419
East Midlands	4.9	26.5	20.7	22.3	17.4	5.7	2.4	2,081
West Midlands	4.8	26.7	19.8	22.2	17.6	5.9	2.9	2,587
Eastern	5.9	30.6	22.1	18.9	15.2	4.8	2.5	2,692
London	7.8	34.7	23.3	15.2	11.0	4.2	3.8	3,505
South East (GOR)	7.5	31.5	22.3	17.1	14.1	5.2	2.2	4,013
South West	5.8	30.5	20.6	18.8	14.7	5.7	3.8	2,366
England	6.0	29.2	21.8	19.6	15.1	5.3	3.0	24,073
Wales	4.5	26.9	20.2	22.4	16.5	6.1	3.4	1,303
Scotland	5.4	26.1	22.1	21.8	15.4	6.0	3.1	2,467
Northern Ireland	4.4	25.6	22.5	22.0	12.6	6.3	6.6	710

1 Based on occupation. See Technical notes.
2 Includes members of the armed forces, those who did not state their social class, and for the unemployed those whose previous occupation was more than eight years ago, or those who had never had a job.

Source: Labour Force Survey, Office for National Statistics; Department of Economic Development, Northern Ireland

3.15 Resident population[1]: by ethnic group[2],1995/96[3]

Percentages and thousands

	Black	Indian	Pakistani/ Bangladeshi	Mixed/ other	Total (=100%) (thousands)	White population (thousands)	Total population (thousands)	Ethnic minority population as a percentage of total population
Great Britain	27	27	23	24	3,300	52,927	56,242	6
North East	..	..	33	43	19	2,560	2,580	1
North West (GOR) & Merseyside	12	26	40	22	279	6,547	6,827	4
North West (GOR)	11	28	43	18	255	5,157	5,414	5
Merseyside	..	..	..	65	24	1,389	1,413	2
Yorkshire and the Humber	13	18	53	16	250	4,730	4,980	5
East Midlands	16	58	8	19	200	3,892	4,092	5
West Midlands	17	39	33	12	416	4,836	5,253	8
Eastern	27	21	24	28	158	5,051	5,209	3
London	38	22	15	24	1,558	5,340	6,908	23
South East (GOR)	19	29	17	35	235	7,454	7,690	3
South West	27	18	13	41	77	4,670	4,747	2
England	27	27	23	23	3,192	45,079	48,286	7
Wales	14	15	26	45	42	2,846	2,888	1
Scotland	..	14	40	39	66	5,002	5,068	1

1 Population in private households, students in halls of residence and those in NHS accommodation. See Technical notes to the Labour market chapter.
2 For some ethnic origins in some regions, sample sizes are too small to provide a reliable estimate.
3 Four quarter average Autumn 1995 to Summer 1996.

Source: Labour Force Survey, Office for National Statistics

3.16 Conceptions[1]: by outcome,1994

Percentages and thousands

	Conceptions leading to maternities			Conceptions terminated by abortion		All conceptions			
	Percentages which were			Percentage which were		Percentage which			Of which were at ages under 16 (percentages)
		Outside marriage							
	Within marriage	Joint registration	Sole registration	Within marriage	Outside marriage	Led to maternities	Were terminated by abortion	Total (=100%) (thousands)	
Usual residence of women[2]									
North East	49.2	26.7	8.1	3.1	12.9	84.0	16.0	36.6	1.5
North West (GOR) & Merseyside	49.6	23.9	8.2	3.6	14.7	81.7	18.3	103.6	1.1
North West (GOR)	51.6	23.5	7.2	3.7	14.0	82.3	17.7	82.0	1.1
Merseyside	42.2	25.3	12.2	3.3	17.0	79.7	20.3	21.6	1.1
Yorkshire and the Humber	52.7	23.5	6.5	3.7	13.5	82.8	17.2	75.5	1.3
East Midlands	54.9	22.6	5.8	3.9	12.8	83.3	16.7	59.5	1.1
West Midlands	52.9	21.5	6.3	4.3	15.1	80.7	19.3	82.2	1.3
Eastern	60.0	19.8	4.2	4.2	11.8	84.0	16.0	77.0	0.7
London	47.4	17.5	5.9	6.1	23.1	70.8	29.2	145.9	0.7
South East (GOR)	59.0	19.2	4.2	4.3	13.2	82.5	17.5	115.3	0.7
South West	58.0	20.8	4.9	3.5	12.7	83.8	16.2	64.7	0.9
England	53.4	21.0	5.9	4.3	15.3	80.4	19.6	760.4	1.0
Wales	52.1	24.3	7.2	3.7	12.7	83.6	16.4	41.2	1.2

1 Conception statistics are derived from numbers of registered births and registered abortions. They do not include spontaneous miscarriages and illegal abortions.
2 There are doubts concerning the quality of information collected about usual residence of some women who undergo abortions. The large number in London is probably (in part) a reflection of the fact that many terminations of pregnancy take place there and it is sometimes difficult to collect 'true' usual residence information.

Source: Office for National Statistics

3.17 Marriages[1]

Thousands

	1971	1981	1994
United Kingdom	459.4	397.9	331.3
North East	23.3	19.6	13.2
North West (GOR) & Merseyside	60.0	49.3	36.0
North West (GOR)	48.4	38.7	29.5
Merseyside	11.6	10.6	6.5
Yorkshire and the Humber	39.9	35.7	28.0
East Midlands	27.8	26.7	22.9
West Midlands	42.4	36.0	29.0
Eastern	34.4	33.2	29.3
London	69.3	50.5	44.2
South East (GOR)	55.5	50.3	45.2
South West	29.7	30.9	27.8
England	382.3	332.2	275.5
Wales	22.4	19.8	15.5
Scotland	42.5	36.2	31.5
Northern Ireland	12.2	9.6	8.7

1 Marriages registered outside the United Kingdom are not included.
Source: Office for National Statistics; General Register Office for Scotland; Northern Ireland Statistics and Research Agency

3.18 Cohabitation amongst non-married people aged 18-49, 1993-1995[1]

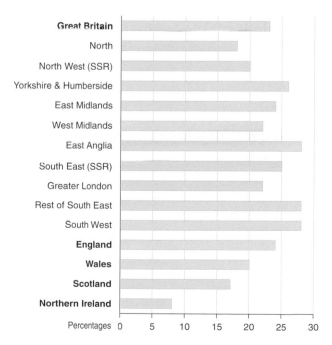

Source: General Household Survey, Office for National Statistics; Continuous Household Survey, Northern Ireland Statistics and Research Agency

3.19 Household numbers and projections

Thousands

	1981	1991	1993	1995	1996[1]	2001[1]	2006[1]	2011[1]	2016[1]
Great Britain	20,177	22,395	22,852	23,315	23,506	24,493	25,454	..	..
North East	977	1,047	1,065	1,076	1,085	1,119	1,153	1,185	1,213
North West (GOR) & Merseyside	2,550	2,721	2,764	2,803	2,820	2,911	3,005	3,105	3,203
North West (GOR)	2,003	2,156	2,194	2,230	2,241	2,319	2,399	2,484	2,568
Merseyside	547	564	570	573	579	592	606	620	635
Yorkshire and the Humber	1,827	1,993	2,033	2,064	2,081	2,156	2,231	2,307	2,380
East Midlands	1,409	1,596	1,637	1,675	1,691	1,775	1,855	1,935	2,014
West Midlands	1,861	2,043	2,081	2,116	2,128	2,199	2,267	2,338	2,410
Eastern	1,764	2,035	2,083	2,142	2,160	2,278	2,390	2,503	2,617
London	2,635	2,842	2,906	2,963	2,986	3,109	3,237	3,368	3,471
South East (GOR)	2,644	3,036	3,105	3,192	3,208	3,369	3,525	3,684	3,843
South West	1,638	1,903	1,947	1,996	2,018	2,129	2,235	2,342	2,448
England	17,306	19,215	19,620	20,027	20,177	21,046	21,897	22,769	23,598
Wales	1,017	1,128	1,148	1,166	1,174	1,211	1,248	1,287	1,318
Scotland	1,854	2,052	2,084	2,121	2,152	2,226	2,293	..	..

1 1992-based projections for England and Scotland; 1994-based projections for Wales. See Technical notes.

Source: Department of the Environment; Welsh Office; The Scottish Office Development Department

3.20 Average household size and one-person households[1]

Numbers and percentages

	Average household size (numbers)					One-person households as a percentage of all households				
	1981	1991	1995	2001	2006	1981	1991	1995	2001	2006
United Kingdom	2.72	2.45	2.41	..	..	22	27	28	..	..
North East	2.67	2.45	2.39	2.31	2.23	23	27	29	32	35
North West (GOR) & Merseyside	2.69	2.49	2.43	2.36	2.30	23	27	29	31	33
North West (GOR)	2.67	2.49	2.42	2.36	2.30	23	27	29	31	33
Merseyside	2.75	2.53	2.45	2.37	2.30	23	28	29	32	34
Yorkshire and the Humber	2.66	2.47	2.40	2.34	2.28	23	27	28	31	33
East Midlands	2.70	2.50	2.43	2.38	2.33	21	25	26	29	30
West Midlands	2.76	2.55	2.48	2.41	2.36	21	25	27	29	31
Eastern	2.71	2.50	2.42	2.36	2.30	20	25	26	29	31
London	2.54	2.39	2.33	2.27	2.23	27	31	33	35	37
South East (GOR)	2.68	2.48	2.41	2.34	2.28	22	25	27	30	32
South West	2.62	2.43	2.37	2.30	2.25	23	26	28	30	32
England	2.67	2.47	2.41	2.34	2.28	23	27	28	31	33
Wales	2.73	2.53	2.47	2.39	2.33	21	25	27	29	31
Scotland	2.77	2.44	2.38	2.28	2.20	22	29	30	33	35
Northern Ireland	3.20	2.91	2.78	..	..	19	23	26	..	..

1 1992-based projections for England and Scotland, 1994-based projections for Wales and 1995-based projections for Northern Ireland. See Technical notes.

Source: Department of the Environment; Welsh Office; The Scottish Office Development Department; Continuous Houshold Survey, Northern Ireland Statistics and Research Agency

4 Education and Training

Grant-maintained schools

Over 37 per cent of secondary pupils in the Eastern region in 1995/96 were in grant-maintained schools compared with less than 1 per cent in the North East and Scotland.

(Table 4.1)

Class sizes

The largest average class sizes in primary schools in Great Britain are in the North West (GOR), while the largest in secondary schools are in the North East; the smallest class sizes in both primary and secondary schools are in Scotland.

(Table 4.2)

Under fives

Eighty-four per cent of the three and four year olds in the North East were in education in 1995/96, the highest proportion in the United Kingdom.

(Table 4.4)

Education and training after age 16

Sixteen year olds in Scotland were the most likely to remain in full or part-time education in 1994/95, while those in the North East were the most likely to be on a government-supported training programme.

(Table 4.5)

Examination results

Pupils in Northern Ireland and the South West were more likely than those in any other region to achieve at least one graded examination result in their last year of compulsory schooling in 1994/95, while those in Merseyside were the least likely.

(Table 4.6)

Among the English regions in 1994/95, the North East had the lowest proportion of 16 year olds achieving GCSE grades A*-C in the three core subjects of the National Curriculum plus a modern language and the South East (GOR) and the South West had the highest.

(Table 4.7)

Further education

In 1994/95, Northern Ireland and the North East had the highest proportions of further education students taking a course leading to an NVQ or equivalent qualification.

(Table 4.8)

Higher education

Higher education students whose home is in the Eastern region are the least likely to study within their own region, while those in Scotland are the most likely.

(Table 4.10)

Expenditure

Capital expenditure accounted for just over 6 per cent of total local education authority expenditure on education in Northern Ireland in 1994-95, nearly four times the proportion in Merseyside.

(Table 4.13)

Training

Among non-manual employees, those in the Yorkshire and Humber region and the North East were the most likely to receive job-related training in Spring 1996 and those in Northern Ireland the least likely.

(Table 4.15)

More than two thirds of those leaving Youth Training in the South East (GOR) during 1995-96 were in employment six months later, compared with half in Merseyside.

(Table 4.17)

Introduction

There are five stages of education: nursery, primary, secondary, further and higher. Primary and secondary education are compulsory for a total of 11 years in Great Britain and 12 years in Northern Ireland. There are differences in the ages at which children enter primary education: in England and Wales, the legal requirement is to start at the age of five, but in practice the majority of rising 5s are in education; in Scotland children generally commence primary school in the August prior to their fifth birthday while in Northern Ireland children who reach their fourth birthday on or before 1 July are required to start school in the following September. The transition between primary and secondary education is normally at age 11 in England, Wales and Northern Ireland and 12 in Scotland. However, some local education authorities in England operate a system of middle schools which cater for pupils on either side of the transition age, and these are deemed either primary or secondary according to the age range of the pupils.

Upon completion of their compulsory education, students have a variety of options. They can seek employment, go into training or continue in post-compulsory education at school or in a further education institution. After (usually) two years of post-compulsory education, and depending on what examination results have been achieved, some students continue their education by going on to university or a college of higher education.

The *Education Reform Act 1988* introduced the National Curriculum to be taught during compulsory schooling in England and Wales. It includes the core subjects of English, mathematics and science, as well as Welsh in Welsh-speaking schools in Wales and eight or nine other foundation subjects including at least one modern language. Unlike England and Wales, there is no National Curriculum in Scotland. Pupils aged between 5 and 14 study a broad curriculum based on national guidelines which set out the aims of study, the ground to be covered, the way pupils should be assessed and the reports parents should receive. At the age of 14, pupils start courses leading to the Scottish Certificate of Education at Standard Grade, the equivalent of the GCSE in England, Wales and Northern Ireland. Table 4.7 shows the percentage of pupils achieving grades A*-C (or equivalent) in the three core subjects of the National Curriculum as it applies in England together with a modern language.

The 1988 Act also gave schools the right to apply for grant-maintained status and receive funding directly from central government. Grant-maintained schools become self governing with responsibility for all aspects of the school's management. By January 1996, there were 448 grant-maintained primary and 642 grant-maintained secondary schools in England, and five and 11 respectively in Wales. At September 1996, three schools in Scotland (two primaries and one secondary) had opted out of education authority control. No fees are payable at any school which is grant-maintained or maintained by the LEA, but it is open to parents, if they choose, to pay for their children to attend private schools.

There has been a strong trend in recent years towards closer integration between academic education and vocational training. It is recognised that education and training are important not only for young people, but throughout a person's working life. Table 4.14 shows the proportions of people meeting the required qualification level for four of the National Targets for Education and Training. The targets have been set using the competence-based National Vocational Qualifications (NVQs) and the Scottish Vocational Qualifications (SVQs) and their vocational and academic equivalents. It should be noted that the data in Table 4.14 relate to the region in which the person is resident, and not where they obtained the qualifications. This can lead to some distortion of the regional picture of educational standards; this is particularly relevant in Northern Ireland, as many qualified young people leave home to enter higher education or seek employment in Great Britain.

4.1 Pupils and teachers: by type of school, 1995/96[1]

| | | Public sector schools | | | | | | |
| | | Primary schools[2] | | Secondary schools | | | | |
	Nursery schools	Total	Of which grant-maintained (percentages)	Total	Of which grant-maintained (percentages)	Non-maintained schools	All special schools	All schools
Pupils[3] (thousands)								
United Kingdom	61.8	5,145.1	2.4	3,677.5	16.0	589.1	113.3	9,586.7
North East	3.0	235.5	0.0	177.4	0.5	15.4	6.4	437.7
North West (GOR) & Merseyside	6.3	663.6	1.3	433.7	9.7	57.1	15.7	1,176.4
North West (GOR)	5.5	521.8	1.6	338.6	10.2	46.2	11.5	923.7
Merseyside	0.8	141.8	0.3	95.0	7.9	10.9	4.2	252.8
Yorkshire and the Humber	2.5	452.5	1.2	333.6	6.1	32.0	8.6	829.3
East Midlands	1.8	357.7	4.2	270.2	19.7	33.4	5.8	668.9
West Midlands	4.4	495.8	1.0	343.9	14.8	44.4	12.6	900.9
Eastern	2.5	426.4	7.2	345.1	37.3	57.4	9.0	840.4
London	5.5	590.0	3.3	370.1	30.4	113.5	11.8	1,091.0
South East (GOR)	2.8	627.6	3.8	448.9	25.3	134.8	17.4	1,231.5
South West	1.6	383.5	3.3	287.5	20.1	58.8	8.5	739.9
England	30.5	4,232.5	2.8	3,010.4	19.3	546.9	95.7	7,916.0
Wales	2.2	281.6	0.4	198.5	4.9	10.0	3.6	495.9
Scotland	24.9	440.8	-	317.0	-	31.2	9.4	823.1
Northern Ireland	4.2	190.2	.	151.6	.	1.0	4.6	351.7
Teachers[3] (thousands)								
United Kingdom	2.9	227.0	2.3	228.2	15.8	57.3	18.4	533.8
North East	0.1	10.0	0.0	10.4	0.5	1.3	0.9	22.7
North West (GOR) & Merseyside	0.3	28.0	1.3	26.1	9.7	4.9	2.7	62.1
North West (GOR)	0.3	21.9	1.6	20.2	10.3	4.0	2.0	48.5
Merseyside	-	6.1	0.3	5.9	7.9	0.9	0.7	13.6
Yorkshire and the Humber	0.1	19.0	1.2	19.0	6.1	2.8	1.4	43.0
East Midlands	0.1	14.9	4.2	16.1	20.4	3.3	0.9	35.3
West Midlands	0.2	21.1	1.0	20.6	15.0	4.3	1.8	47.9
Eastern	0.1	18.8	7.0	20.9	37.6	5.7	1.4	46.9
London	0.3	27.3	3.3	23.4	30.1	10.5	2.1	63.7
South East (GOR)	0.2	27.2	3.8	26.9	26.0	14.3	2.6	71.3
South West	0.1	16.3	3.3	16.8	20.2	6.3	1.2	40.7
England	1.6	182.6	2.9	180.9	19.6	53.4	15.1	433.6
Wales	0.1	12.5	0.4	12.4	4.9	1.0	0.5	26.6
Scotland	1.0	22.6	-	24.6	-	2.8	2.0	53.0
Northern Ireland	0.2	9.3	.	10.3	.	0.1	0.7	20.6
Pupils per teacher[3] (numbers)								
United Kingdom	21.3	22.7	23.1	16.1	16.3	10.3	6.2	18.0
North East	21.3	23.7	.	17.1	17.1	11.9	7.0	19.3
North West (GOR) & Merseyside	20.0	23.7	23.7	16.6	16.5	11.7	5.7	18.9
North West (GOR)	20.3	23.8	23.6	16.7	16.6	11.6	5.7	19.1
Merseyside	17.8	23.3	26.3	16.2	16.3	11.9	5.9	18.5
Yorkshire and the Humber	18.7	23.8	22.6	17.0	16.9	11.3	6.3	19.3
East Midlands	19.2	24.1	23.7	16.8	16.2	10.1	6.1	18.9
West Midlands	23.3	23.5	22.9	16.7	16.4	10.4	7.0	18.8
Eastern	19.3	22.7	23.3	16.5	16.4	10.1	6.5	17.9
London	16.4	21.6	21.9	15.8	16.0	10.8	5.5	17.1
South East (GOR)	17.0	23.0	23.0	16.7	16.2	9.4	6.7	17.3
South West	20.4	23.6	23.9	17.1	17.0	9.4	6.8	18.2
England	19.2	23.2	23.1	16.6	16.3	10.2	6.3	18.3
Wales	19.5	22.5	22.8	16.0	15.8	10.0	6.7	18.7
Scotland	24.3	19.5	13.3	12.9	5.4	10.9	4.7	15.5
Northern Ireland	24.0	20.4	.	14.7	.	10.9	6.7	17.1

1 See Technical notes.
2 For Northern Ireland, figures include pupils and teachers in the preparatory departments attached to grammar schools.
3 Full-time equivalents.

Source: Department for Education and Employment; Welsh Office; The Scottish Office Education and Industry Department; Department of Education, Northern Ireland

4.2 Average class sizes[1]

Numbers

	One teacher classes				All classes[2]			
	Primary		Secondary		Primary		Secondary	
	1990/91	1995/96	1990/91	1995/96	1990/91	1995/96	1990/91	1995/96
Great Britain	..	..	..	..	26.4	27.1	20.8	21.6
North East	26.0	27.1	20.2	22.0	26.5	27.2	21.2	22.5
North West (GOR) & Merseyside	27.1	27.7	20.0	21.8	27.5	28.0	20.7	22.0
North West (GOR)	27.4	27.9	20.1	22.0	27.8	28.1	20.7	22.2
Merseyside	26.0	27.0	19.8	20.9	26.4	27.3	20.8	21.3
Yorkshire and the Humber	25.9	27.6	20.3	21.9	26.4	27.9	20.9	22.1
East Midlands	26.1	27.6	20.0	21.6	26.5	27.8	20.7	21.9
West Midlands	26.3	27.3	20.3	21.8	26.9	27.6	20.8	22.0
Eastern	26.0	26.6	20.7	21.3	26.4	26.8	21.5	21.6
London	25.8	27.0	20.6	21.7	26.2	27.3	21.2	22.0
South East (GOR)	26.7	27.3	20.3	21.4	27.1	27.4	20.9	21.6
South West	26.4	27.3	20.8	21.8	26.7	27.4	21.3	22.0
England	26.3	27.3	20.3	21.7	26.8	27.5	21.0	21.9
Wales	..	..	19.5	..	24.8	25.9	21.0	20.2
Scotland	..	..	..	..	24.7	24.8	18.5	19.5

1 Maintained schools only.
2 Includes classes where more than one teacher may be present.

Source: Department for Education and Employment; Welsh Office; The Scottish Office Education and Industry Department

4.3 Distribution of pupils[1] in the public sector: by size of school, 1995/96

Percentages and thousands

	Maintained primary schools[2]					Maintained secondary schools				
	Number of pupils on the register				Total number of pupils (=100%) (thousands)	Number of pupils on the register				Total number of pupils (=100%) (thousands)
	50 or fewer	51-100	101-200	Over 200		400 or fewer	401-800	801-1,000	Over 1,000	
United Kingdom	1.0	4.0	16.5	78.4	5,313.0	3.6	28.9	23.0	44.5	3,677.5
North East	0.5	2.1	17.1	80.3	249.4	7.4	27.9	19.0	45.7	177.4
North West (GOR) & Merseyside	0.6	2.1	15.6	81.8	685.3	1.2	27.5	25.8	45.5	433.7
North West (GOR)	0.7	2.6	17.3	79.4	536.6	1.4	28.3	27.9	42.4	338.6
Merseyside	0.0	0.3	9.5	90.3	148.6	0.3	24.7	18.4	56.6	95.0
Yorkshire and the Humber	0.8	3.2	14.2	81.8	477.8	6.2	24.2	20.1	49.5	333.6
East Midlands	1.2	5.7	17.9	75.2	373.2	4.9	34.2	18.8	42.2	270.2
West Midlands	0.6	3.1	12.4	84.0	513.1	3.6	32.1	24.3	40.1	343.9
Eastern	1.0	5.3	21.5	72.2	438.9	5.3	32.1	23.7	38.9	345.1
London	-	0.1	5.4	94.4	616.7	0.4	26.4	22.2	51.0	370.1
South East (GOR)	0.5	3.8	18.4	77.4	643.8	2.2	27.3	25.3	45.2	448.9
South West	1.4	8.3	21.9	68.4	391.2	3.0	27.7	20.6	48.7	287.5
England	0.7	3.5	15.5	80.4	4,389.4	3.4	28.7	22.7	45.2	3,010.4
Wales	3.0	6.8	27.7	62.5	292.2	1.9	29.0	20.8	48.3	198.5
Scotland	2.9	5.2	18.3	73.6	440.6	3.6	25.3	26.4	44.7	317.0
Northern Ireland	2.4	8.8	19.3	69.6	190.8	9.8	41.9	23.7	24.6	151.6

1 Full-time and part-time (ie headcounts).
2 Includes 25 preparatory departments attached to grammar schools in Northern Ireland.

Source: Department for Education and Employment; Welsh Office; The Scottish Office Education and Industry Department; Department of Education, Northern Ireland

4.4 Children under five in education, 1995/96

Thousands and percentages

	Under fives in education (thousands)			Participation rates[1] (percentages)		
	Maintained nursery & primary schools	Independent and special schools	All schools	Maintained nursery & primary schools	Independent and special schools	All schools
United Kingdom	836.3	61.4	897.7	53	4	57
North East	56.4	1.2	57.6	82	2	84
North West (GOR) & Merseyside	123.5	5.9	129.3	65	3	68
North West (GOR)	94.6	4.7	99.3	63	3	66
Merseyside	28.8	1.2	30.0	75	3	78
Yorkshire and the Humber	91.4	3.2	94.6	67	2	69
East Midlands	58.1	3.8	61.9	53	3	57
West Midlands	88.5	5.1	93.6	61	4	64
Eastern	57.3	5.7	63.0	41	4	45
London	115.5	11.8	127.3	58	6	64
South East (GOR)	73.2	15.3	88.5	36	8	44
South West	44.5	5.9	50.4	38	5	43
England	708.5	57.8	766.3	54	4	59
Wales	55.9	1.3	57.1	73	2	74
Scotland[2]	48.2	2.1	50.3	36	2	38
Northern Ireland	23.7	0.3	24.0	46	1	46

1 Pupils under five in education as a percentage of the three and four year old population.
2 Excludes pupils aged four in primary schools.

Source: Department for Education and Employment; Welsh Office; The Scottish Office Education and Industry
Department; Department of Education, Northern Ireland

4.5 16 year olds participating in education and government-supported training, 1994/95

Percentages[1]

	Full-time education								
			In further education institutions[2]						
	Maintained schools	Independent schools	Sixth form colleges	Others	Total	Part-time education	Total in full and part-time education	Government-supported training (GST)	All in full-time education and GST[3]
Region of study[3]									
United Kingdom	32.6	6.3	..	25.2	71.9	7.8	79.7	..	..
North East	21.7	3.0	9.5	26.4	60.6	10.2	70.8	21.8	81.3
North West (GOR) & Merseyside	20.2	5.2	14.5	25.6	65.5	8.6	74.0	17.7	82.2
North West (GOR)	15.9	5.0	16.2	27.5	64.6	8.9	73.6	16.7	80.4
Merseyside	34.0	5.7	8.8	19.5	68.1	7.4	75.5	20.9	88.2
Yorkshire and the Humber	26.9	4.0	8.7	25.1	64.7	10.6	75.3	17.0	80.9
East Midlands	31.5	4.5	5.6	25.2	66.7	8.1	74.8	14.8	80.7
West Midlands	26.0	5.6	10.1	27.5	69.2	9.3	78.5	13.9	82.6
Eastern	33.6	6.8	8.5	26.2	75.1	6.2	81.3	9.0	83.6
London	30.9	9.1	8.5	27.4	75.9	5.0	80.8	6.4	81.9
South East (GOR)	29.2	10.7	13.0	24.8	77.8	5.7	83.6	8.3	85.9
South West	30.1	9.5	1.9	33.5	75.0	7.0	82.0	11.1	85.7
England	27.8	6.9	9.5	26.7	71.0	7.6	78.6	12.6	83.0
Wales	37.3	2.1	.	32.2	71.6	7.2	78.8	12.6	83.0
Scotland	63.2	5.1	.	8.5	76.8	11.6	88.3	15.3	92.1
Northern Ireland	53.6	0.1	.	25.1	78.8	4.5	83.3	..	..

1 As a percentage of the estimated 16 year old population at 1 January 1995.
2 Region of domicile for further education students.
3 Excludes overlap between full-time education and government-supported training.

Source: Department for Education and Employment; Welsh Office; The Scottish Office Education and Industry
Department; Department of Education, Northern Ireland

4.6 Examination achievements: by gender, 1994/95[1]

	Pupils in their last year of compulsory education					Pupils/students in education[3] achieving 2 or more A levels/	Average A/AS level points score
	Percentage achieving GCSE or SCE Standard Grade				Total (=100%) (thousands)	3 or more SCE Highers (percentages)	
	5 or more grades A*-C	1-4 grades A*-C	Grades D-G only[2]	No graded results			
Males							
Great Britain[4]	39.6	25.0	26.2	9.2	348.2	26.6	16.1
North East	32.5	22.7	33.1	11.7	17.0	20.0	15.1
North West (GOR) & Merseyside	37.8	22.9	28.8	10.5	43.4	24.8	17.2
North West (GOR)	38.9	23.0	28.5	9.5	34.1	25.0	17.3
Merseyside	33.6	22.5	29.9	14.0	9.3	24.0	16.9
Yorkshire and the Humber	33.9	22.5	32.3	11.3	31.3	22.4	17.1
East Midlands	37.5	24.3	29.5	8.8	25.5	26.0	16.0
West Midlands	36.0	24.0	30.0	9.9	33.3	24.5	16.6
Eastern	42.4	25.8	24.9	7.0	32.8	29.9	15.7
London	36.4	28.1	24.6	10.9	36.2	25.9	15.3
South East (GOR)	45.3	24.6	22.3	7.9	47.9	33.3	16.2
South West	44.4	24.7	24.5	6.5	29.0	29.2	15.8
England	39.0	24.5	27.2	9.3	296.2	26.9	16.2
Wales	35.9	23.2	27.9	13.0	18.6	22.4	14.6
Scotland	46.4	30.4	16.2	7.0	33.4	26.5	.
Females							
Great Britain[4]	48.8	26.8	17.5	6.8	331.4	32.2	15.7
North East	41.0	25.9	23.8	9.3	16.3	25.7	14.6
North West (GOR) & Merseyside	46.4	26.0	20.0	7.6	41.0	29.8	16.5
North West (GOR)	48.0	25.9	19.2	6.9	32.3	30.9	16.8
Merseyside	40.6	26.3	22.6	10.6	8.7	25.9	15.1
Yorkshire and the Humber	43.1	25.9	22.6	8.4	29.5	26.6	16.5
East Midlands	46.4	27.2	19.9	6.5	24.1	30.0	15.5
West Midlands	44.8	27.4	20.6	7.2	31.9	30.7	15.7
Eastern	52.0	28.0	14.8	5.3	31.0	34.7	15.6
London	45.4	30.5	16.1	7.9	35.7	31.2	15.0
South East (GOR)	54.5	26.0	14.0	5.5	45.2	38.5	16.1
South West	54.5	25.7	15.3	4.4	27.4	36.4	15.9
England	48.1	27.0	18.1	6.8	282.0	32.2	15.8
Wales	46.3	24.3	21.1	8.3	17.3	29.4	14.7
Scotland	56.4	27.0	10.8	5.8	32.0	34.5	.
All pupils/students							
United Kingdom[4]	44.4	25.9	21.9	7.9	704.8	29.5	15.9
North East	36.7	24.3	28.6	10.5	33.3	22.8	14.8
North West (GOR) & Merseyside	42.0	24.4	24.5	9.1	84.3	27.2	16.8
North West (GOR)	43.3	24.4	24.0	8.2	66.4	27.8	17.0
Merseyside	37.0	24.3	26.4	12.3	18.0	24.9	16.0
Yorkshire and the Humber	38.4	24.1	27.6	9.9	60.7	24.4	16.8
East Midlands	41.8	25.7	24.8	7.7	49.5	27.9	15.8
West Midlands	40.3	25.7	25.4	8.6	65.2	27.5	16.1
Eastern	47.0	26.9	20.0	6.1	63.7	32.3	15.7
London	40.9	29.3	20.4	9.4	71.9	28.4	15.2
South East (GOR)	49.8	25.3	18.3	6.7	93.1	35.8	16.2
South West	49.3	25.2	20.0	5.5	56.4	32.7	15.9
England	43.5	25.7	22.7	8.1	578.2	29.4	16.0
Wales	40.9	23.8	24.6	10.7	36.0	25.8	14.6
Scotland	51.3	28.7	13.6	6.4	65.4	30.4	.
Northern Ireland	51.3	25.0	19.3	4.4	25.3	34.7	..

1 See Technical notes.
2 No grades above D and at least one in the D-G range.
3 Pupils in schools and students in further education institutions aged 17-19 at the end of the academic year in England, Wales and Northern Ireland as a percentage of the 18 year old population. Pupils in Scotland mostly sit Highers one year earlier and the figures relate to the results of pupils in Year S5 as a percentage of the 17 year old population.
4 England and Wales only for 'Average A/AS level points score'.

Source: Department for Education and Employment; Welsh Office; The Scottish Office Education and Industry Department; Department of Education, Northern Ireland

4.7 Pupils[1] achieving GCSE grades A*-C[2]: by selected subjects and gender, 1994/95[3]

Percentages

	English	Mathematics	Science — Any science[4]	Science — Single award	Science — Double award	Any modern language[5]	French	Geography	History	Craft Design Technology	All core subjects[6]
Males											
Great Britain	43.2	40.6	44.0	2.0	..	27.3	20.6	23.7	17.7	22.0	..
North East	35.1	34.0	36.3	0.9	28.1	19.4	14.1	20.0	15.8	16.6	15.7
North West (GOR) & Merseyside	40.9	38.3	40.8	1.1	32.1	26.1	19.5	22.8	18.2	20.1	20.2
North West (GOR)	41.7	39.7	42.2	1.2	34.1	26.8	19.5	23.6	18.5	20.6	20.8
Merseyside	38.3	33.3	35.5	0.8	24.6	23.5	19.7	19.8	17.1	18.0	18.0
Yorkshire and the Humber	36.6	35.4	38.2	0.7	32.0	23.9	17.2	21.8	15.8	19.4	17.9
East Midlands	39.2	39.0	42.6	1.4	37.1	23.3	18.4	22.7	15.5	22.1	18.7
West Midlands	38.9	36.5	40.0	0.8	32.7	24.8	18.4	23.2	16.6	20.8	18.4
Eastern	45.2	43.8	45.8	1.5	39.3	27.2	21.2	26.3	20.7	23.1	21.9
London	40.0	37.6	38.0	2.1	27.6	27.2	19.1	19.3	19.1	16.3	19.2
South East (GOR)	47.4	45.7	47.8	2.0	36.0	33.5	27.0	26.7	21.4	21.9	26.5
South West	46.1	45.3	48.9	1.4	39.2	31.6	25.3	27.0	19.4	25.8	25.3
England	41.7	40.0	42.5	1.4	33.9	27.1	20.7	23.6	18.4	20.8	21.0
Wales[7]	38.5	37.9	41.2	1.5	32.1	18.4	15.3	24.9	15.3	23.3	..
Scotland	59.6	47.3	59.1	7.3	.	33.8	23.5	23.7	13.2	32.5	28.2
Females											
Great Britain	60.9	41.2	44.8	2.8	..	42.1	32.5	21.2	22.8	28.9	..
North East	52.3	35.3	36.5	2.0	28.4	33.0	25.2	17.9	20.6	23.8	23.8
North West (GOR) & Merseyside	50.2	38.7	41.5	1.6	34.2	40.9	31.2	19.2	22.6	26.5	28.2
North West (GOR)	59.5	40.4	42.8	1.7	36.0	42.2	31.5	20.1	23.3	27.9	29.3
Merseyside	53.4	32.3	36.4	1.2	27.6	36.1	30.1	15.9	20.0	21.3	24.1
Yorkshire and the Humber	55.2	36.8	39.2	1.7	33.3	38.9	28.4	19.4	20.6	28.9	26.6
East Midlands	58.1	38.7	42.3	2.7	37.1	36.8	29.4	20.1	20.0	31.5	26.6
West Midlands	57.4	36.5	40.3	1.3	36.1	37.9	28.5	21.6	21.6	31.4	25.6
Eastern	64.2	44.3	46.1	2.6	39.6	42.1	32.9	24.2	26.1	32.5	31.1
London	55.8	38.1	39.0	3.8	32.4	40.3	28.6	19.1	22.8	21.2	20.3
South East (GOR)	65.1	46.0	48.6	3.0	40.1	48.6	38.5	24.6	25.7	26.6	34.0
South West	65.1	45.3	48.9	3.0	39.9	47.8	38.8	24.7	24.4	35.9	34.4
England	59.6	40.4	43.0	2.5	36.1	41.5	31.9	21.4	23.0	28.5	29.1
Wales[7]	56.8	40.2	42.1	3.0	33.3	34.0	29.3	20.0	21.9	35.6	..
Scotland	74.7	48.5	61.8	5.6	.	52.2	39.5	19.8	20.9	28.7	39.1
All pupils											
Great Britain	51.8	40.9	44.4	2.4	..	34.5	26.4	22.5	20.2	25.4	..
North East	43.5	34.6	36.4	1.5	28.3	26.0	19.5	19.0	18.1	20.1	19.7
North West (GOR) & Merseyside	49.3	38.5	41.1	1.3	33.1	33.3	25.2	21.1	20.4	23.2	24.1
North West (GOR)	50.4	40.0	42.5	1.4	35.0	34.3	25.3	21.9	20.9	24.2	24.9
Merseyside	45.6	32.8	35.9	1.0	26.1	29.6	24.7	17.9	18.5	19.6	21.0
Yorkshire and the Humber	45.6	36.1	38.7	1.2	32.6	31.2	22.6	20.6	18.1	24.1	22.1
East Midlands	48.4	38.9	42.5	2.0	37.1	29.9	23.7	21.4	17.7	26.7	22.6
West Midlands	47.9	36.5	40.2	1.1	34.4	31.2	23.3	22.4	19.1	26.0	21.9
Eastern	54.4	44.0	45.9	2.0	39.4	34.4	26.9	25.3	23.3	27.7	26.4
London	47.8	37.8	38.9	3.0	30.0	33.7	23.8	19.2	21.0	18.7	22.7
South East (GOR)	56.0	45.9	48.2	2.5	38.0	40.8	32.6	25.7	23.5	24.1	30.6
South West	55.3	45.3	48.9	2.2	39.5	39.5	31.9	25.9	21.8	30.7	29.7
England	50.4	40.2	42.7	1.9	35.0	34.1	26.1	22.5	20.7	24.5	24.9
Wales[7]	47.3	39.0	41.6	2.2	32.7	25.9	22.0	22.5	18.5	29.2	..
Scotland	67.0	47.9	60.4	6.5	.	42.8	31.3	21.8	17.0	30.6	33.5

1 Pupils in their last year of compulsory schooling.
2 SCE Standard Grade awards at grades 1-3 in Scotland.
3 See Technical notes.
4 Includes double award, single award and individual science subjects.
5 Including French.
6 The core subjects of the National Curriculum applicable in England are English, mathematics and a science. Figures in this column also include a modern language. The National Curriculum does not apply in Scotland.
7 Welsh is included as a core subject in Welsh-speaking schools. In 1994/95, 6.1 per cent of pupils achieved GCSE grade A* to C in Welsh as a first language and a further 13.2 per cent in Welsh as a second language.

Source: Department for Education and Employment; Welsh Office; The Scottish Office Education and Industry Department

4.8 Home students in further education[1]: by level of course of study[2], 1994/95

Percentages and thousands

	Courses leading to NVQ[3] or equivalent qualifications (percentages)						All courses not leading to a specified qualification (percentages)	Total all FE students[1] (=100%) (thousands)
	Level 1	Level 2	Level 3	Level unknown	Other specified courses[4]	All courses		
Region of domicile								
North East	3.8	18.0	30.8	27.1	3.3	83.1	16.9	99.4
North West (GOR) & Merseyside	3.3	17.1	27.4	19.9	5.1	72.8	27.2	308.2
North West (GOR)	3.3	16.8	28.1	18.2	4.7	71.1	28.9	250.0
Merseyside	3.5	18.3	24.6	26.9	6.7	79.9	20.1	58.0
Yorkshire and the Humber	2.3	13.4	22.1	22.4	4.0	64.2	35.8	233.9
East Midlands	3.7	15.1	25.6	23.3	3.9	71.7	28.3	161.1
West Midlands	3.3	12.3	24.0	23.7	3.8	67.1	32.9	245.6
Eastern	2.7	16.2	27.7	19.6	3.9	70.1	29.9	187.8
London	5.8	15.0	24.6	16.5	7.5	69.4	30.6	291.1
South East (GOR)	2.6	16.1	31.2	16.9	3.5	70.2	29.8	276.1
South West	3.1	14.7	28.6	19.5	2.8	68.6	31.4	183.5
England	3.4	15.2	26.6	20.3	4.4	70.0	30.0	1,986.8
Wales	3.8	11.1	15.4	27.8	20.5	78.6	21.4	100.9
Scotland	1.2	6.8	3.2	70.4	-	81.6	18.4	162.3
Northern Ireland	0.1	2.1	11.5	71.4	-	85.2	14.8	72.0
Other[5]	0.8	0.9	1.0	43.5	0.1	46.4	53.6	31.4

1 Further education institutions only. For institutions in Scotland and Northern Ireland figures relate to number of enrolments not the number of students. See Technical notes.
2 Highest level of qualification aimed for by students.
3 SVQ in Scotland.
4 Includes Access to FE, Access to HE and Basic education courses. Additionally, in Wales includes GCSE and GCE courses.
5 Includes Channel Islands, Isle of Man and home students whose region of domicile was unknown or unclassified.

Source: Department for Education and Employment; Welsh Office; The Scottish Office Education and Industry Department; Department of Education, Northern Ireland

4.9 Home students in further education: by age and region of domicile, 1994/95[1]

Percentages and thousands

	Full-time/sandwich students aged		Part-time day students aged		Evening only students aged		All students aged		Total FE students (=100%) (thousands)
	18 or under	19 or over	18 or under	19 or over	18 or under	19 or over	18 or under	19 or over	
Region of domicile									
United Kingdom[2]	22.1	10.2	6.5	28.4	1.8	31.0	30.4	69.6	2,353.5
North East	24.4	8.5	7.9	27.1	2.1	30.0	34.4	65.6	99.4
North West (GOR) & Merseyside	23.1	11.1	5.9	28.6	1.5	29.7	30.5	69.5	308.2
North West (GOR)	24.1	10.4	5.8	27.4	1.5	30.8	31.5	68.5	250.2
Merseyside	18.6	14.2	6.2	34.1	1.7	25.2	26.4	73.6	58.0
Yorkshire and the Humber	18.5	9.0	6.4	30.4	2.2	33.5	27.1	72.9	233.9
East Midlands	21.6	10.3	6.2	28.0	1.6	32.4	29.4	70.6	161.1
West Midlands	21.1	11.5	6.2	29.4	1.5	30.2	28.9	71.1	245.6
Eastern	25.1	7.4	5.6	27.3	1.5	33.2	32.2	67.8	187.8
London	22.1	13.5	3.4	29.2	1.3	30.4	26.8	73.2	291.1
South East (GOR)	28.3	7.9	4.9	23.7	1.4	33.8	34.6	65.4	276.1
South West	23.6	8.4	5.7	26.1	1.2	34.9	30.6	69.4	183.5
England	23.1	10.0	5.6	27.9	1.6	31.9	30.2	69.8	1,986.8
Wales	26.0	10.8	5.2	22.3	2.7	33.0	33.9	66.1	100.9
Scotland	10.9	12.1	17.5	36.1	2.0	21.4	30.4	69.6	162.3
Northern Ireland	25.1	3.4	12.0	21.6	7.7	30.2	44.8	55.2	72.0
Other[2]	0.1	22.5	0.2	61.4	-	15.8	0.3	99.7	31.4

1 See Technical notes. Excludes further education students in higher education institutions, adult education centres and private institutions. Ages as at beginning of the academic year.
2 Includes Channel Islands, Isle of Man, and home students whose region of domicile was unknown or unclassified.

Source: Department For Education and Employment; Welsh Office; The Scottish Office Education and Industry Department; Department of Education, Northern Ireland

4.10 Undergraduate and postgraduate students[1]: by region of study and domicile, 1995/96[2]

Percentages and thousands

	Region of study												All students (=100%) (thousands)
	North East	North West (GOR) & Merseyside	Yorkshire and the Humber	East Midlands	West Midlands	Eastern	London	South East (GOR)	South West	Wales	Scotland	Northern Ireland	
Region of domicile													
United Kingdom[3]	4.8	11.2	9.1	7.0	8.7	6.2	15.2	11.8	6.5	5.0	12.0	2.5	1,537.3
North East	68.8	6.0	9.5	3.5	2.3	1.4	2.0	1.7	0.8	0.6	3.4	-	58.3
North West (GOR) & Merseyside	4.2	61.7	11.3	3.9	6.3	1.4	2.5	2.3	1.6	2.5	2.2	-	160.4
Yorkshire and the Humber	7.0	8.5	61.4	6.5	4.4	2.1	2.8	2.5	1.3	1.1	2.4	-	98.9
East Midlands	3.2	7.2	14.9	46.6	9.0	4.0	4.5	4.8	2.8	1.7	1.4	-	92.6
West Midlands	1.7	6.6	6.2	7.9	56.9	2.2	4.0	4.9	4.5	3.9	1.1	-	118.3
Eastern	2.0	3.8	5.9	8.1	5.0	42.9	14.4	10.5	4.3	1.6	1.5	-	118.1
London	0.9	2.7	2.5	2.4	2.8	5.2	66.2	12.3	2.7	1.0	1.2	-	200.2
South East (GOR)	1.7	3.6	4.2	5.0	5.0	4.5	16.1	48.4	7.3	2.7	1.7	-	190.3
South West	1.3	3.5	3.6	3.9	5.9	3.0	7.0	13.9	50.6	5.9	1.4	-	104.7
England	5.9	12.8	11.3	8.3	10.4	7.4	17.9	14.1	7.8	2.4	1.7	-	1,141.7
Wales	0.8	6.6	2.9	3.1	4.5	1.7	3.5	4.8	5.3	65.7	0.9	-	70.7
Scotland	0.8	0.8	0.7	0.4	0.4	0.4	0.8	0.7	0.3	0.2	94.5	-	167.3
Northern Ireland	1.6	3.7	1.8	1.3	1.3	1.4	2.2	1.5	0.7	1.2	10.1	73.2	50.6

1 See Technical notes. Open University students are excluded.
2 1994/95 for higher education students studying in further education institutions in England.
3 Includes higher education students whose region of domicile in the United Kingdom was unknown.

Source: Department for Education and Employment; Welsh Office; The Scottish Office Education and Industry Department; Department of Education, Northern Ireland

4.11 Higher education students[1]: by region of domicile and subject, 1995/96

Percentages and thousands

	Medicine & dentistry & subjects allied to medicine	Biological sciences	Mathematical & physical sciences	Engineering & technology	Social sciences	Business & financial studies	Languages & related studies	Creative arts	Education	Multidisciplinary studies	Other Courses	All HE students (=100%) (thousands)
Region of domicile												
United Kingdom[2]	9.3	4.2	9.5	7.5	10.2	13.3	5.0	5.1	8.6	19.1	8.2	1,553.3
North East	10.8	4.0	12.2	7.7	10.9	12.2	5.2	5.0	9.2	14.2	8.5	55.4
North West (GOR) & Merseyside	10.8	4.4	10.2	7.5	10.2	11.9	4.8	4.6	9.8	18.0	7.8	153.0
North West (GOR)	10.2	4.5	10.6	7.7	10.1	12.3	4.7	4.9	9.8	17.2	7.8	120.1
Merseyside	13.0	4.1	8.8	6.5	10.3	10.6	4.9	3.7	9.7	20.9	7.7	32.8
Yorkshire and the Humber	7.9	3.9	10.1	7.4	11.2	12.7	4.8	5.0	10.2	17.9	8.7	94.7
East Midlands	9.0	3.8	9.6	7.7	10.2	12.1	3.6	5.5	9.1	22.3	7.1	95.4
West Midlands	9.7	4.0	10.0	7.6	10.8	13.0	4.3	5.3	8.9	19.0	7.5	113.7
Eastern	9.2	4.4	8.8	6.3	9.6	10.7	4.9	5.7	8.6	24.0	7.8	118.2
London	10.4	4.0	9.3	6.5	12.5	13.5	5.9	5.7	6.7	17.8	7.7	203.2
South East (GOR)	8.2	4.2	8.7	6.2	8.6	11.2	5.6	5.9	9.5	23.3	8.5	195.0
South West	7.8	4.5	9.5	6.9	9.0	10.4	4.7	6.2	10.2	22.7	8.2	107.4
England[3]	9.5	4.2	9.7	7.0	10.4	11.7	5.3	5.4	8.8	19.8	8.1	1,233.4
Wales	9.0	3.9	9.6	8.2	8.5	12.4	4.8	4.9	10.1	19.2	9.4	75.5
Scotland	6.8	4.1	8.7	10.9	8.9	22.5	2.5	4.1	7.0	16.2	8.3	180.4
Northern Ireland	9.4	4.7	9.4	7.2	11.3	18.7	5.4	3.2	7.7	13.0	10.0	53.5

1 See Technical notes. Open University students are included. For England, higher education students studying in further education institutions are excluded.
2 Includes higher education students whose region of domicile in the United Kingdom was unknown.
3 Includes higher education students who lived in England but whose specific region of domicile was unknown.

Source: Department for Education and Employment; Welsh Office; The Scottish Office Education and Industry Department; Department of Education, Northern Ireland

4.12 New student awards made by local education authorities: by region of domicile, 1994/95[1]

Thousands and rates

	Mandatory awards					Discretionary awards[1]			
	First degrees	Teacher training	Other higher education	Total	Rates[2]	Higher education	Further education	Total	Rates[2]
United Kingdom	244.4	36.0	62.0	342.4	5,008	..	..	..	..
North East	9.7	1.6	2.4	13.6	4,240	0.2	6.6	6.8	2,124
North West (GOR) & Merseyside	29.2	4.8	5.6	39.6	4,770	1.5	23.1	24.5	2,956
North West (GOR)	23.6	3.7	4.5	31.9	4,885	1.0	19.5	20.5	3,140
Merseyside	5.5	1.0	1.1	7.7	4,341	0.4	3.6	4.0	2,274
Yorkshire and the Humber	17.9	3.2	3.7	24.8	4,016	0.5	11.5	12.0	1,950
East Midlands	15.9	2.5	2.9	21.3	4,390	0.3	7.2	7.5	1,537
West Midlands	19.3	2.7	3.6	25.6	4,030	0.2	7.4	7.6	1,200
Eastern	21.5	3.1	3.1	27.8	4,700	0.3	10.5	10.8	1,827
London	35.3	4.1	5.1	44.6	6,160	1.1	11.8	12.9	1,775
South East (GOR)	35.2	4.7	5.2	45.1	5,093	3.2	24.3	27.5	3,106
South West	19.3	3.4	3.3	26.0	4,874	1.0	10.0	11.0	2,068
England	203.2	30.2	35.0	268.4	4,773	8.3	112.4	120.6	2,146
Wales	12.1	2.8	2.4	17.3	5,098	0.1	13.2	13.3	3,918
Scotland	19.4	2.3	22.0	43.7	6,896	..	..	..	..
Northern Ireland	9.6	0.7	2.7	13.0	5,415	0.7	2.3	3.0	1,250

1 See Technical notes.
2 Rate per 10,000 population aged 18 in the summer of 1994.

Source: Department for Education and Employment; The Scottish Office Education and Industry
Department; Department of Education, Northern Ireland

4.13 Local education authority expenditure, 1994-95

	Percentage of total LEA expenditure[1]								Current expenditure per pupil[5] (£ per pupil)	
	Pre-primary & primary schools	Secondary schools	Special schools	Continuing education	Administration & inspection[2,3]	Other educational services[4]	Capital expenditure	Total (= 100%) (£ million)	Nursery/ primary pupils	Secondary pupils
United Kingdom	37.5	36.0	5.8	14.1	1.5	1.6	3.6	25,034.1	1,670	2,340
North East	38.7	37.7	5.2	15.1	0.5	..	2.7	1,099.8	1,620	2,130
North West (GOR) & Merseyside	38.8	35.7	6.4	15.6	0.6	..	2.9	3,007.0	1,570	2,260
North West (GOR)	38.9	35.3	6.0	15.9	0.5	..	3.3	2,349.1	1,570	2,230
Merseyside	38.2	36.8	7.9	14.5	0.9	..	1.7	657.9	1,570	2,370
Yorkshire and the Humber	39.4	37.7	4.6	15.1	0.3	..	2.9	2,104.2	1,620	2,170
East Midlands	37.5	39.9	5.0	14.5	0.4	..	2.6	1,682.6	1,630	2,320
West Midlands	39.1	36.2	6.0	15.3	0.7	..	2.7	2,263.9	1,650	2,240
Eastern	36.4	39.5	5.4	15.0	0.8	..	2.9	2,108.1	1,670	2,250
London	39.0	31.4	6.8	17.6	1.2	..	3.9	3,329.7	1,940	2,630
South East (GOR)	36.3	35.4	6.6	16.6	0.6	..	4.6	3,052.7	1,640	2,240
South West	36.1	37.1	5.6	16.7	0.4	..	4.1	1,823.1	1,550	2,180
England	38.0	36.2	5.9	15.9	0.7	..	3.4	20,471.1	1,660	2,270
Wales	35.5	34.1	3.8	13.0	5.0	5.5	3.1	1,315.3	1,640	2,260
Scotland	34.9	37.1	6.1	0.8	5.5	10.5	5.1	2,454.1	1,850	2,890
Northern Ireland	35.8	30.5	4.3	9.8	4.4	9.0	6.2	793.6	1,550	2,330

1 See Technical notes.
2 Includes LEA expenditure on grant-maintained schools.
3 Administration costs in Scotland are treated differently from administration costs in England and Wales.
4 Includes school catering services in Wales, Scotland and Northern Ireland. Expenditure on central services under this heading in England has been recharged to columns 1-4.
5 These figures must be interpreted carefully in the light of different educational structures between regions.

Source: Department for Education and Employment; Welsh Office; The Scottish Office Education and Industry
Department; Department of Education, Northern Ireland

4.14 Progress towards achieving the National Targets for Education and Training[1,2]: by gender, Spring 1996

Percentages

	Foundation learning: percentage of the population				Lifetime learning: percentages of those in employment of working age[3]			
	Aged 19-21 qualified to at least NVQ level 2 or equivalent		Aged 21-23 qualified to at least NVQ level 3 or equivalent		Qualified to at least NVQ level 3 or equivalent		Qualified to at least NVQ level 4 or equivalent	
	Males	Females	Males	Females[4]	Males	Females	Males	Females
United Kingdom	67	70	47	41	46	35	24	24
North East	70	73	51	42	46	31	20	21
North West (GOR) & Merseyside	65	67	47	39	46	33	23	23
North West (GOR)	65	68	50	40	47	33	24	23
Merseyside	65	63	38	..	41	35	20	22
Yorkshire and the Humber	68	69	45	38	45	31	21	21
East Midlands	54	69	48	42	44	31	23	21
West Midlands	64	66	46	36	42	31	21	21
Eastern	67	64	40	34	43	32	22	21
London	74	70	53	45	51	44	32	32
South East (GOR)	65	68	50	41	48	35	27	23
South West	76	78	45	40	45	35	24	24
England	67	69	47	40	46	34	24	23
Wales	58	63	45	37	44	32	22	22
Scotland	73	81	51	49	53	42	26	27
Northern Ireland	71	69	41	47	42	35	19	26

1 See Technical notes for details of the targets.
2 The questions on qualifications in the Labour Force Survey were changed substantially in Spring 1996. Figures are therefore not directly comparable with those for earlier years.
3 Males aged 16-64 and females aged 16-59.
4 For Merseyside the sample size is too small to provide a reliable estimate.

Source: Department for Education and Employment from the Labour Force Survey

4.15 Employees of working age[1] receiving job-related training[2], Spring 1996

Percentages[3] and hours

	Manual					Non manual				
	On-the-job training only	Off-the-job training only	Both on and off-the-job training	Any job-related training	Average number of hours training in the last week[4]	On-the-job training only	Off-the-job training only	Both on and off-the-job training	Any job-related training	Average number of hours training in the last week[4]
United Kingdom	2.9	4.7	1.6	9.2	17.1	4.4	10.9	3.0	18.3	13.3
North East	2.2	5.1	..	9.0	17.6	5.7	11.4	3.7	20.8	11.1
North West (GOR) & Merseyside	2.7	4.5	1.5	8.7	16.3	4.5	11.3	3.4	19.2	12.1
North West (GOR)	2.6	4.6	1.5	8.6	17.6	4.4	11.4	3.4	19.3	12.3
Merseyside	..	..	..	8.8	10.9	4.6	11.0	..	19.1	11.4
Yorkshire and the Humber	3.1	4.8	1.8	9.8	15.5	5.4	12.6	3.5	21.4	13.6
East Midlands	2.5	4.1	..	7.9	15.6	4.4	9.4	2.4	16.2	11.4
West Midlands	2.8	4.2	1.3	8.3	16.3	4.7	10.4	3.5	18.6	11.8
Eastern	3.2	5.5	2.1	10.8	16.3	4.5	10.8	2.8	18.1	12.8
London	3.0	5.2	1.7	9.9	15.6	4.5	11.5	2.8	18.8	14.2
South East (GOR)	3.1	5.5	1.7	10.3	15.4	4.2	11.0	2.6	17.8	13.4
South West	3.5	4.6	1.5	9.6	17.1	4.2	11.1	3.2	18.5	14.2
England	2.9	4.8	1.6	9.4	16.1	4.6	11.1	3.0	18.7	13.0
Wales	2.9	4.8	..	9.5	18.3	5.3	11.1	3.1	19.5	14.2
Scotland	2.8	4.7	1.4	8.8	25.0	3.7	9.7	2.6	16.1	16.1
Northern Ireland	..	..	..	4.9	..	..	8.9	..	12.4	13.8

1 Males aged 16-64 and females aged 16-59.
2 Job-related education or training received in the four weeks before interview. In some cases sample sizes are too small to provide reliable estimates.
3 As a percentage of all employees of working age.
4 Question was only asked of those who had received training in the week before interview.

Source: Department for Education and Employment from the Labour Force Survey

4.16 Government-supported training[1]: trainees on programmes by gender, March 1996

Percentages and thousands

	Training for work			Youth Training			Modern apprenticeships		
	Males	Females	Total (=100%) (thousands)	Males	Females	Total (=100%) (thousands)	Males	Females	Total (=100%) (thousands)
Great Britain	70	30	85.3	59	41	258.2	71	29	27.9
North East	74	26	7.3	61	39	15.0	59	41	2.3
North West (GOR) & Merseyside	70	30	13.1	58	42	40.0	67	33	6.5
North West (GOR)	69	31	7.7	59	41	29.9	66	34	5.5
Merseyside	71	29	5.4	53	47	10.1	73	27	1.0
Yorkshire and the Humber	72	28	8.5	59	41	22.4	69	31	3.9
East Midlands	72	28	5.6	58	42	21.0	68	32	2.5
West Midlands	70	30	6.9	56	44	24.0	75	25	2.3
Eastern	68	32	4.8	59	41	22.5	71	29	1.6
London	61	39	10.1	57	43	16.4	64	36	1.9
South East (GOR)	68	32	5.7	56	44	30.1	61	39	1.7
South West	71	29	6.3	61	39	19.7	75	25	1.8
England	69	31	68.2	58	42	211.0	69	31	24.7
Wales	72	28	4.7	61	39	13.2	82	18	3.0
Scotland	76	24	12.4	66	34	34.0	95	5	0.2
Northern Ireland[1]	65	35	6.1	68	32	12.1	.	.	.

1 Northern Ireland schemes differ from those in Great Britain: see Technical notes. Adults and young people on schemes in Northern Ireland are comprised mainly of those on the Jobskills Scheme but also include 4,233 persons remaining on the Youth Training Programme and 101 remaining on the Job Training Programme. Modern apprenticeships did not come into operation in Northern Ireland until July 1996.

Source: Department for Education and Employment; The Scottish Office Education and Industry Department; Training and Employment Agency, Northern Ireland

4.17 Training for Work and Youth Training leavers[1], 1995-96

Percentages and thousands

	Training for Work						Youth Training					
	Status six months after leaving[2] (percentages)				Gained qualifi-cation[4] (percent-ages)	All leavers[5] (thou-sands)	Status six months after leaving[2] (percentages)				Gained qualifi-cation[4] (percent-ages)	All leavers[5] (thou-sands)
	In employ-ment	In further educ-ation or training	Unemp-loyed	Other[3]			In employ-ment	In further educ-ation or training	Unemp-loyed	Other[3]		
Great Britain	39	6	47	9	..	283.6	62	13	19	7	..	297.5
North East	39	5	48	8	51	22.5	53	17	25	6	52	20.2
North West (GOR) & Merseyside	40	5	47	8	45	46.1	60	16	19	5	49	49.7
North West (GOR)	41	4	47	8	42	28.0	64	14	17	5	50	35.2
Merseyside	38	6	48	8	50	18.1	50	20	24	6	47	14.5
Yorkshire and the Humber	39	6	47	8	44	30.3	61	15	18	6	51	30.2
East Midlands	44	4	43	9	44	19.0	64	13	17	6	49	24.3
West Midlands	40	6	46	9	50	28.1	67	12	16	6	56	28.0
Eastern	40	4	46	10	50	17.7	66	13	15	7	53	20.9
London	35	5	50	10	46	35.3	59	14	21	7	53	23.2
South East (GOR)	40	4	47	10	51	20.4	69	10	15	6	51	30.1
South West	38	5	46	10	51	19.9	65	15	14	6	51	21.2
England	39	5	47	9	48	239.4	63	13	18	6	51	248.0
Wales	40	5	47	8	45	13.7	59	14	21	6	43	15.9
Scotland	36	14	43	7	..	30.5	52	15	22	11	..	33.6
Northern Ireland[1]	37	13	45	5	48	3.0	71	2	17	9	79	3.0

1 Schemes in Northern Ireland differ from those in Great Britain: see Technical notes.
2 Status on completion of courses in Northern Ireland.
3 Scotland figure includes non-respondents to the Highlands and Islands Enterprise follow-up questionnaire.
4 In Northern Ireland, full qualifications gained by all leavers including early leavers. These are expressed as a percentage of persons who completed the course.
5 All those who left the programme during 1995-96 except in Northern Ireland where the figure covers completers of courses only and does not include early leavers.

Source: Department for Education and Employment; The Scottish Office Education and Industry Department; Training and Employment Agency, Northern Ireland

5 Labour market

Economic activity

Nearly 66 per cent of people aged 16 or over in the South East (GOR) were economically active in Spring 1996 compared with less than 56 per cent in Merseyside, the highest and lowest proportions.

(Tables 5.1 and 5.3)

Employees

Half of all female employees in the South West worked part-time in Spring 1996 compared with a third in London.

(Table 5.6)

The North East and Scotland were the only two regions in Great Britain in Spring 1996 where there were more men than women on casual or fixed-term contracts.

(Table 5.7)

In 1995, 38 per cent of male employees in the West Midlands worked in manufacturing, three and a half times the proportion in London.

(Table 5.8)

The self-employed

Over 70 per cent of the self-employed in the North East and in London in Spring 1996 were in service industries compared with 43 per cent in Northern Ireland.

(Table 5.9)

Qualifications

London and Scotland have the most highly qualified workforce with more than two fifths qualified to at least A level standard or equivalent.

(Table 5.10)

Labour disputes

Both the North East and London lost 88 days per 1,000 employees due to labour disputes in 1996, two and a half times the rate in Northern Ireland.

(Chart 5.11)

Hours of work

Weekend working is most common in Wales and least common in London.

(Table 5.14)

Full-time employees in the Eastern region and in the South East (GOR) worked the longest hours in Spring 1996, at almost 45 hours a week on average.

(Table 5.15)

Earnings

Average gross weekly earnings in April 1996 ranged from £514 in London to £337 in Northern Ireland for men and from £365 in London to £249 in the East Midlands for women.

(Tables 5.16 and 5.17)

Unemployment

The ILO unemployment rate in Merseyside in Spring 1996 was 13.3 per cent, more than double the proportions in the Eastern region, the South East (GOR) and the South West.

(Table 5.21)

One in five of the ILO unemployed in the Eastern region in 1995/96 was aged 50 or over compared with one in nine in Wales.

(Table 5.25)

Introduction

There are four main sources used in this chapter: the Labour Force Survey (LFS), the Short-term Turnover and Employment Survey (STTES), the New Earnings Survey (NES) and the claimant unemployment count. Problems can arise in drawing together data on the same subject from different sources. For example, the question in the LFS as to whether the respondent is employed produces a measure of employment based on the number of persons, whereas a question addressed to employers asking the number of people they employ, as in the STTES, produces a measure of the number of jobs. Thus if someone has a second job they will be included twice.

Similarly the number of people who are classified by the LFS as unemployed (which corresponds to the International Labour Organisation (ILO) definition of unemployment) differs from the number of people claiming unemployment benefits and satisfying the conditions for the receipt of benefit (claimant unemployment). Both measures have their advantages and disadvantages. The ILO measure, as well as being the international standard, allows unemployment to be viewed as one part of an integrated classification of the whole population aged 16 or over by economic status. Although changes to the benefit system may affect the labour market behaviour of respondents to the LFS, the ILO definition itself is entirely independent of the benefit system. However, as it is sample based, it is not reliable for areas smaller than counties or the larger local authority districts. The claimant count on the other hand is available quickly, monthly and at relatively little expense. Because it is a 100 per cent count it also provides precise information for very small areas. However, it can be affected by changes to the benefit system, such as the introduction of the Jobseeker's Allowance (JSA) which replaced Unemployment Benefit and Income Support for unemployed people from 7 October 1996.

The ILO unemployment rate is based on the resident economically active populations of local areas whilst the claimant count rate is based, very largely, on the number of jobs in each area and, consequently, on the population whose place of work is in each area. The two can therefore occasionally vary quite markedly. One example is London, where inward commuting is an important feature of the local labour market and where, as a consequence, the ILO unemployment rate tends to be significantly higher than the equivalent claimant unemployment rate. Time series of these two measures of unemployment appear as Tables 5.20 and 5.21.

Table 5.3 drawn from the LFS looks at the labour force and economic activity. One of the most significant changes in the British labour market this century has been the increased participation of women. In 1971 women made up 38 per cent of the labour force compared with 44 per cent in 1996. Whether a woman is economically active or not depends to some extent on whether she has a family and, if so, on the number and ages of her children. Although men are still more likely than women to be economically active at all ages, the gap has closed in the last 25 years.

On average full-time employees are working longer hours than they used to. The average number of hours that full-time male employees worked in a week, including both paid and unpaid overtime but excluding meal breaks, increased from 44.5 hours in 1985 to 45.8 hours in Spring 1996; for women the increase was from 39.6 to 40.6 hours. Table 5.15 shows that the longest hours were worked in the Eastern and South East (GOR) regions. Hours worked also vary by occupation: for example those working in banking, finance and insurance in Northern Ireland worked an average of just over 40 hours per week in Spring 1996, while employees in the agriculture and fishing industry in Scotland worked an average of almost 51 hours. The figures on hours worked in Table 5.17, drawn from the NES, are lower than those in Table 5.15 because they exclude unpaid overtime.

Glossary of terms

Employees (Labour Force Survey) — A household-based measure of persons aged 16 or over who regard themselves as paid employees. People with two or more jobs are counted only once.

Employees in employment (employer survey-based measure) — A measure, obtained from surveys of employers, of jobs held by civilians who are paid by an employer who runs a PAYE tax scheme. People with two or more jobs are counted in each job.

The self-employed — A household-based measure of persons aged 16 or over who regard themselves as self-employed in their main job, that is who work on their own account, whether or not they have employees, and are responsible for payment of their own income tax and National Insurance contributions.

Government-supported employment and training programmes — A household-based measure of persons aged 16 or over participating in Youth Training, Training for Work or Community Action programmes, or a programme administered by a Training and Enterprise Council (England and Wales), Local Enterprise Company (Scotland) or the Training and Employment Agency (Northern Ireland).

Work-related government-supported training participants — A count, obtained from administrative returns, of all participants who receive some form of work experience in the course of their placement, but who do not have a contract of employment and are not self-employed.

The labour force in employment — A household-based measure of employees, self-employed persons, participants in government-supported employment and training programmes, and persons doing unpaid family work.

The workforce in employment — A measure of employees in employment (obtained from employer-based surveys), self employed persons, all HM Forces, and participants on work-related government-supported training programmes.

The claimant unemployed — A measure, known as the claimant count, and derived from administrative sources, which counts as unemployed those people who are claiming unemployment-related benefits (Jobseeker's Allowance from October 1996) at Employment Service local offices (formerly Unemployment Benefit Offices).

The ILO unemployed — An International Labour Organisation (ILO) recommended measure, used in household surveys such as the Labour Force Survey, which counts as unemployed those aged 16 or over who are without a job, are available to start work in the next two weeks and who have been seeking a job in the last four weeks, or are waiting to start a job already obtained.

The workforce — The **workforce in employment** *plus* the **claimant unemployed**.

The economically active/ the labour force — The **labour force in employment** *plus* the **ILO unemployed**.

Claimant unemployment rate — The percentage of the **workforce** who are **claimant unemployed**.

ILO unemployment rate — The percentage of the **economically active** who are **ILO unemployed**.

The economically inactive — Persons who are neither part of the labour force in employment nor ILO unemployed. For example, all people under 16, those retired or looking after a home, or those permanently unable to work.

The population of working age — Males aged 16 to 64 years and females aged 16 to 59 years.

Economic activity rate — The percentage of the population in a given age group which is in the **labour force**.

5.1 Economic activity[1], Spring 1996

Percentages and thousands

| | In employment | | | | | | | All aged 16 or over[3] (=100%) (thousands) | Economic activity rates (percentages) | |
| | Employees | | Self-employed | Total[2] | ILO unem-ployed | Total econom-ically active | Econom-ically inactive | | | |
	Full-time	Part-time							Males	Females
United Kingdom	36.9	12.5	7.2	57.3	5.1	62.4	37.6	45,725	71.9	53.5
North East	34.8	11.9	4.3	51.9	6.3	58.2	41.8	2,037	67.6	49.4
North West (GOR) & Merseyside	35.7	12.3	6.3	55.2	5.1	60.3	39.7	5,349	69.4	51.7
North West (GOR)	36.9	12.4	6.8	57.0	4.5	61.5	38.5	4,246	70.8	52.7
Merseyside	30.9	11.8	4.5	48.2	7.4	55.6	44.4	1,104	64.2	47.8
Yorkshire and the Humber	35.7	13.4	6.6	56.5	5.0	61.5	38.5	3,932	70.5	52.9
East Midlands	38.8	13.3	6.7	59.4	4.8	64.2	35.8	3,241	73.4	55.3
West Midlands	37.5	12.3	6.2	56.9	5.8	62.7	37.3	4,127	72.8	53.0
Eastern	38.8	13.3	8.3	61.1	4.0	65.1	34.9	4,133	74.8	55.7
London	38.1	10.0	7.9	56.9	7.2	64.1	35.9	5,466	73.5	55.3
South East (GOR)	38.8	13.6	8.8	61.7	3.9	65.6	34.4	6,114	75.3	56.6
South West	34.0	13.9	9.2	58.1	3.9	62.0	38.0	3,816	71.0	53.5
England	37.1	12.6	7.4	57.9	5.1	63.0	37.0	38,214	72.4	54.0
Wales	32.3	12.0	7.0	52.3	4.7	57.1	42.9	2,283	66.4	48.3
Scotland	37.7	11.8	5.6	56.0	5.3	61.3	38.7	4,025	70.9	52.4
Northern Ireland	34.2	10.0	6.7	53.3	5.7	59.0	41.0	1,202	70.3	48.6

1 See Technical notes.
2 Includes those on government-supported employment and training schemes and unpaid family workers.
3 Population in private households, student halls of residence and NHS accommodation.

Source: Labour Force Survey, Office for National Statistics; Department of Economic Development, Northern Ireland

5.2 Labour force[1]: by age, Spring 1996

Percentages and thousands

| | Percentages aged | | | | All ages (= 100%) (thousands) |
	16-24	25-44	Females 45-59 Males 45-64	Females 60+ Males 65+	
United Kingdom	16.1	50.5	30.6	2.8	28,552
North East	17.6	51.3	29.2	2.0	1,186
North West (GOR) & Merseyside	16.7	50.9	30.2	2.2	3,224
North West (GOR)	16.5	50.8	30.5	2.2	2,610
Merseyside	17.6	51.0	29.0	2.5	614
Yorkshire and the Humber	15.9	51.3	30.6	2.1	2,419
East Midlands	15.6	49.7	32.1	2.6	2,081
West Midlands	16.5	49.3	31.5	2.7	2,587
Eastern	15.9	48.6	32.3	3.2	2,692
London	14.9	55.7	26.6	2.8	3,505
South East (GOR)	15.3	48.4	32.9	3.4	4,013
South West	15.3	48.5	32.5	3.7	2,366
England	15.8	50.5	30.9	2.8	24,073
Wales	17.2	49.6	30.8	2.5	1,303
Scotland	17.0	51.5	29.2	2.2	2,467
Northern Ireland	19.7	51.5	26.1	2.8	710

1 See Technical notes.

Source: Labour Force Survey, Office for National Statistics; Department of Economic Development, Northern Ireland

5.3 Labour force and economic activity rates[1]

Thousands and percentages

	Labour force (thousands)					Economic activity rates (percentages)				
	1992	1993	1994	1995	1996	1992	1993	1994	1995	1996
Males										
United Kingdom	16,187	16,021	15,996	15,981	15,992	73.8	72.9	72.5	72.2	71.9
North East	676	671	665	653	668	68.8	68.2	67.4	66.9	67.6
North West (GOR) &										
Merseyside	1,857	1,825	1,818	1,795	1,800	72.1	70.7	70.4	69.2	69.4
North West (GOR)	1,506	1,477	1,480	1,462	1,462	73.3	72.2	72.3	70.4	70.8
Merseyside	351	348	338	333	337	67.2	65.3	63.4	64.2	64.2
Yorkshire and the Humber	1,383	1,374	1,359	1,379	1,355	72.7	72.1	71.2	72.1	70.5
East Midlands	1,154	1,152	1,145	1,153	1,167	74.1	73.6	72.8	72.9	73.4
West Midlands	1,490	1,474	1,486	1,469	1,472	74.0	73.2	73.7	72.8	72.8
Eastern	1,515	1,514	1,514	1,543	1,526	76.9	76.3	75.3	76.2	74.8
London	1,967	1,978	1,950	1,950	1,948	74.8	75.1	73.9	73.8	73.5
South East (GOR)	2,250	2,217	2,212	2,216	2,232	76.8	75.6	75.6	75.3	75.3
South West	1,325	1,301	1,318	1,329	1,315	73.5	71.9	72.3	72.3	71.0
England	13,617	13,506	13,466	13,486	13,483	74.2	73.4	73.0	72.8	72.4
Wales	744	719	732	722	734	68.2	65.7	66.8	65.6	66.4
Scotland	1,425	1,390	1,100	1,071	1,369	74.3	72.4	72.8	71.1	70.9
Northern Ireland	401	406	399	403	406	72.2	71.8	69.9	70.2	70.3
Females										
United Kingdom	12,395	12,426	12,436	12,445	12,561	53.0	53.1	53.1	53.1	53.5
North East	532	530	519	511	518	50.1	50.0	49.1	48.9	49.4
North West (GOR) &										
Merseyside	1,418	1,430	1,426	1,395	1,425	51.3	51.8	51.8	50.5	51.7
North West (GOR)	1,139	1,147	1,160	1,131	1,148	52.2	52.8	53.4	52.2	52.7
Merseyside	279	283	266	263	276	47.6	48.2	45.6	44.6	47.8
Yorkshire and the Humber	1,059	1,072	1,060	1,055	1,064	52.6	53.3	52.7	52.5	52.9
East Midlands	888	899	882	896	913	54.6	55.1	53.9	54.6	55.3
West Midlands	1,096	1,104	1,118	1,110	1,115	52.1	52.5	53.2	52.8	53.0
Eastern	1,149	1,149	1,161	1,163	1,167	55.3	55.6	55.7	55.5	55.7
London	1,511	1,540	1,518	1,526	1,557	53.5	54.6	53.9	54.2	55.3
South East (GOR)	1,755	1,725	1,746	1,742	1,782	56.4	55.1	55.9	55.7	56.6
South West	1,014	1,040	1,040	1,045	1,050	52.3	53.5	53.4	53.5	53.5
England	10,421	10,489	10,468	10,444	10,590	53.4	53.7	53.6	53.4	54.0
Wales	564	559	566	583	569	48.1	47.7	48.2	49.6	48.3
Scotland	1,119	1,092	1,118	1,121	1,098	53.4	52.1	53.4	53.5	52.4
Northern Ireland	290	285	285	297	303	48.7	46.1	46.1	48.0	48.6
All persons										
United Kingdom	28,581	28,448	28,433	28,426	28,552	63.1	62.7	62.5	62.4	62.4
North East	1,208	1,200	1,184	1,165	1,186	59.1	58.7	57.9	57.6	58.2
North West (GOR) &										
Merseyside	3,275	3,255	3,243	3,190	3,224	61.3	60.9	60.8	59.6	60.3
North West (GOR)	2,645	2,624	2,639	2,503	2,610	62.5	62.2	62.6	61.1	61.5
Merseyside	630	631	604	597	614	56.9	56.3	54.1	53.8	55.6
Yorkshire and the Humber	2,442	2,446	2,419	2,434	2,419	62.4	62.5	61.7	62.1	61.5
East Midlands	2,042	2,051	2,026	2,048	2,081	64.2	64.2	63.2	63.6	64.2
West Midlands	2,586	2,578	2,604	2,579	2,587	62.8	62.6	63.2	62.6	62.7
Eastern	2,664	2,664	2,675	2,706	2,692	65.9	65.8	65.3	65.7	65.1
London	3,478	3,518	3,468	3,476	3,505	63.8	64.5	63.6	63.7	64.1
South East (GOR)	4,005	3,942	3,958	3,958	4,013	66.3	65.0	65.4	65.2	65.6
South West	2,339	2,341	2,358	2,374	2,366	62.5	62.4	62.6	62.6	62.0
England	24,039	23,996	23,934	23,930	24,073	63.5	63.3	63.0	62.8	63.0
Wales	1,308	1,279	1,298	1,304	1,303	57.8	56.4	57.2	57.3	57.1
Scotland	2,543	2,482	2,517	2,492	2,467	63.4	61.8	62.6	62.0	61.3
Northern Ireland	691	691	683	700	710	60.1	58.4	57.5	58.7	59.0

1 At Spring of each year. Based on population aged 16 or over in private households, student halls of residence and NHS accommodation. See Technical notes.

Source: Labour Force Survey, Office for National Statistics; Department of Economic Development, Northern Ireland

5.4 Labour force and economic activity projections[1,2]

Thousands and percentages

	Labour force (thousands)				Economic activity rates (percentages)					
	Males		Females		Males		Females		All persons	
	2001	2006	2001	2006	2001	2006	2001	2006	2001	2006
Standard Statistical Regions										
United Kingdom	16,277	16,376	13,192	13,715	*71.5*	*70.0*	*55.5*	*56.7*	*63.3*	*63.3*
North	798	791	654	669	*66.8*	*65.1*	*52.0*	*52.9*	*59.2*	*58.9*
North West (SSR)	1,685	1,685	1,387	1,433	*68.9*	*67.5*	*54.1*	*55.3*	*61.3*	*61.3*
Yorkshire and Humberside	1,377	1,383	1,114	1,152	*70.1*	*68.6*	*55.0*	*56.1*	*62.4*	*62.3*
East Midlands	1,185	1,203	955	1,004	*72.1*	*70.8*	*56.4*	*57.7*	*64.2*	*64.2*
West Midlands	1,487	1,481	1,183	1,224	*72.5*	*70.9*	*55.7*	*57.0*	*64.0*	*63.9*
East Anglia	645	664	516	548	*74.2*	*72.8*	*57.8*	*59.1*	*65.9*	*65.9*
South East (SSR)	5,191	5,255	4,201	4,400	*74.1*	*72.8*	*57.5*	*59.0*	*65.6*	*65.8*
Greater London	1,991	2,022	1,600	1,686	*73.7*	*72.9*	*56.3*	*58.2*	*64.8*	*65.4*
Rest of South East	3,200	3,233	2,601	2,715	*74.4*	*72.8*	*58.3*	*59.5*	*66.2*	*66.0*
South West	1,381	1,412	1,124	1,181	*71.6*	*70.2*	*55.9*	*57.2*	*63.6*	*63.6*
England	13,751	13,874	11,134	11,610	*72.0*	*70.6*	*56.0*	*57.3*	*63.9*	*63.9*
Wales	737	737	599	620	*65.1*	*63.5*	*50.2*	*51.1*	*57.4*	*57.2*
Scotland	1,376	1,347	1,152	1,167	*71.0*	*69.2*	*55.3*	*56.3*	*62.9*	*62.5*
Northern Ireland	414	418	306	318	*68.9*	*67.5*	*47.9*	*48.7*	*58.0*	*57.8*

1 See Technical notes.
2 Projected from 1994 estimates.

Source: Labour Force Survey, Office for National Statistics; Department of Economic Development, Northern Ireland

5.5 Employment structure of the civilian workforce[1], September 1996

Thousands

	Employees in employment	Self-employed[2]	Claimant unemployed	WRGT[3]	Civilian workforce		
					Males	Females	Total
Standard Statistical Regions							
United Kingdom	22,330	3,373	2,104	206	15,543	12,470	28,012
North	1,076	130	131	20	748	609	1,356
North West (SSR)	2,347	309	234	24	1,613	1,300	2,913
Yorkshire and Humberside	1,896	267	189	20	1,331	1,040	2,372
East Midlands	1,565	228	131	13	1,070	867	1,937
West Midlands	2,063	271	189	17	1,436	1,103	2,539
East Anglia	811	143	59	7	578	443	1,021
South East (SSR)	7,237	1,190	645	34	5,066	4,040	9,106
Greater London	3,232	445	363	16	2,277	1,779	4,056
Rest of South East	4,005	745	282	18	2,789	2,261	5,050
South West	1,802	365	143	13	1,271	1,053	2,324
England	18,797	2,903	1,720	148	13,114	10,455	23,569
Wales	970	164	103	10	689	558	1,247
Scotland	1,988	228	191	27	1,308	1,126	2,434
Northern Ireland	574	78	90	21	432	330	762

1 See Technical notes.
2 With or without employees.
3 Work-Related Government-supported Training.

Source: Short-term Turnover and Employment Survey, Office for National Statistics;
Department of Economic Development, Northern Ireland

5.6 Part-time employees[1]: by gender, Spring 1996

Percentages[2]

	Males			Females		
	Manual	Non-manual	All males	Manual	Non-manual	All females
United Kingdom	8.4	7.1	7.7	58.7	38.4	44.5
North East	7.1	7.2	7.2	61.6	38.5	46.2
North West (GOR) & Merseyside	7.9	6.9	7.4	59.1	39.0	45.4
North West (GOR)	8.0	6.5	7.2	58.4	38.9	45.0
Merseyside	7.7	8.4	8.0	61.7	39.7	46.8
Yorkshire and the Humber	7.3	8.1	7.7	62.1	41.2	48.6
East Midlands	6.6	7.7	7.1	54.9	41.2	46.1
West Midlands	6.2	5.8	6.1	58.2	39.7	46.1
Eastern	9.3	6.4	7.6	61.0	40.2	46.2
London	11.6	7.9	9.2	52.7	28.0	33.0
South East (GOR)	10.0	7.0	8.1	61.8	38.9	45.2
South West	11.7	7.8	9.3	61.8	45.5	50.2
England	8.6	7.2	7.8	59.3	38.4	44.7
Wales	7.9	7.2	7.7	59.9	42.2	48.7
Scotland	7.2	7.0	7.1	54.2	36.9	42.2
Northern Ireland	6.5	4.1	5.3	52.7	36.0	40.5

1 Based on employees' own definition of part-time. See Technical notes.
2 Part-time employees as a percentage of all employees.

Source: Labour Force Survey, Office for National Statistics; Department of Economic Development, Northern Ireland

5.7 Temporary employees: by type of work and gender, Spring 1996[1]

Percentages and thousands

	Seasonal work, agency temping & casual work and other temporary work		Contract for fixed period/ fixed task		All temporary employees[2] (=100%) (thousands)	All temporary employees as a percentage of all employees
	Males	Females	Males	Females		
United Kingdom	20.3	28.2	24.3	27.1	1,586	7.1
North East	17.4	21.6	40.6	20.4	80	8.4
North West (GOR) & Merseyside	15.9	27.9	25.4	30.8	156	6.1
North West (GOR)	16.2	27.2	26.3	30.3	130	6.3
Merseyside	..	..	..	..	26	5.6
Yorkshire and the Humber	19.4	25.2	26.4	29.1	130	6.8
East Midlands	22.2	28.3	19.7	29.8	102	6.1
West Midlands	21.4	24.1	25.9	28.6	126	6.2
Eastern	24.0	27.1	20.7	28.1	144	6.8
London	21.0	30.3	20.9	27.8	228	8.8
South East (GOR)	21.0	30.3	23.0	25.6	217	6.9
South West	23.4	32.3	17.1	27.2	133	7.4
England	20.7	28.1	23.5	27.7	1,317	7.0
Wales	17.1	34.6	24.9	23.4	84	8.4
Scotland	18.9	25.3	31.3	24.5	156	7.9
Northern Ireland	..	..	..	..	29	5.7

1 For some regions, sample sizes are too small to provide a reliable estimate. See Technical notes.
2 Includes those who did not state type of temporary work but percentages are based on totals excluding them.

Source: Labour Force Survey, Office for National Statistics; Department of Economic Development, Northern Ireland

5.8 Employees in employment: by industry and gender, 1995[1]

Percentages and thousands

	Agriculture, hunting, forestry & fishing	Mining, quarrying (inc oil & gas extraction)	Manufacturing	Electricity, gas, water	Construction	Distribution, hotels & catering, repairs
Males						
United Kingdom	2.1	0.5	25.7	1.2	6.3	20.0
North East	1.1	0.7	30.8	1.4	9.3	16.1
North West (GOR) & Merseyside	1.3	0.2	30.5	1.1	6.7	19.4
North West (GOR)	1.5	0.2	31.4	1.2	6.7	19.5
Merseyside	0.4	0.1	25.5	0.7	6.4	18.6
Yorkshire and the Humber	1.8	0.6	30.6	1.1	7.1	20.5
East Midlands	2.5	0.7	35.1	1.3	5.5	20.0
West Midlands	1.1	0.3	38.1	1.1	5.7	18.9
Eastern	3.8	0.4	25.7	1.2	5.6	21.0
London	0.1	0.3	10.7	0.5	4.4	21.1
South East (GOR)	2.5	0.2	20.9	1.2	4.8	22.5
South West	3.3	0.6	25.3	1.6	5.6	21.6
England	1.8	0.4	25.8	1.1	5.7	20.5
Wales	3.0	0.9	31.6	1.6	6.6	17.5
Scotland	3.2	1.7	22.3	1.6	10.9	17.4
Northern Ireland	6.0	0.6	24.2	1.5	7.4	17.9
Females						
United Kingdom	0.6	0.1	10.9	0.4	1.2	25.0
North East	0.3	-	12.8	0.4	1.4	23.1
North West (GOR) & Merseyside	0.5	-	12.3	0.3	1.1	25.3
North West (GOR)	0.5	-	13.1	0.4	1.1	25.7
Merseyside	0.1	-	8.9	0.1	0.8	23.3
Yorkshire and the Humber	0.4	0.1	12.1	0.3	1.4	26.2
East Midlands	0.7	0.1	17.2	0.4	1.5	24.0
West Midlands	0.3	-	14.7	0.5	1.3	25.0
Eastern	1.0	0.1	10.9	0.3	1.2	26.1
London	0.1	0.1	6.1	0.2	1.1	22.7
South East (GOR)	0.7	-	8.4	0.4	1.1	25.1
South West	1.0	0.1	9.3	0.5	1.2	27.0
England	0.5	0.1	10.9	0.4	1.2	24.9
Wales	1.0	0.1	12.4	0.4	1.1	24.1
Scotland	0.8	0.2	9.7	0.4	1.4	26.6
Northern Ireland	0.8	0.1	11.9	0.2	0.9	21.8

5.8 *(continued)*

Percentages and thousands

	Transport, storage & communication	Financial & business services	Public administration & defence	Education, social work & health services	Other	Whole economy (=100%) (thousands)
Males						
United Kingdom	8.7	15.9	6.6	8.9	4.0	11,158
North East	7.7	10.5	7.6	10.7	4.1	432
North West (GOR) & Merseyside	8.8	13.5	5.8	9.0	3.8	1,254
North West (GOR)	8.6	13.5	5.6	8.2	3.5	1,049
Merseyside	9.9	13.5	7.1	12.7	5.1	206
Yorkshire and the Humber	8.4	12.1	5.7	8.6	3.5	958
East Midlands	7.5	11.0	4.9	8.5	3.1	785
West Midlands	7.0	11.9	5.2	7.6	3.1	1,059
Eastern	9.6	16.1	5.2	8.1	3.3	972
London	11.8	29.8	7.6	7.7	6.0	1,646
South East (GOR)	9.4	19.3	6.3	9.5	3.4	1,437
South West	7.3	14.6	7.5	9.1	3.4	865
England	9.0	16.9	6.2	8.6	3.9	9,407
Wales	7.1	9.2	8.3	10.2	4.0	476
Scotland	8.4	12.4	7.0	10.5	4.6	987
Northern Ireland	5.9	7.0	12.7	12.0	4.8	288
Females						
United Kingdom	3.0	17.7	6.2	30.3	4.7	10,856
North East	2.3	12.1	8.4	33.8	5.5	439
North West (GOR) & Merseyside	2.8	15.7	6.4	31.0	4.7	1,242
North West (GOR)	2.9	15.8	6.3	29.9	4.3	1,009
Merseyside	2.2	15.2	7.2	36.0	6.2	233
Yorkshire and the Humber	2.7	15.0	6.2	31.1	4.3	917
East Midlands	2.5	12.0	5.4	31.8	4.0	762
West Midlands	2.5	15.7	5.5	30.1	4.3	949
Eastern	3.2	17.6	5.4	29.9	4.4	927
London	4.7	29.3	6.6	22.8	6.4	1,546
South East (GOR)	3.5	19.6	5.2	31.6	4.4	1,426
South West	2.4	16.5	5.9	31.8	4.3	877
England	3.1	18.4	6.0	29.8	4.7	9,086
Wales	1.8	11.9	7.5	34.9	4.9	470
Scotland	2.6	16.9	6.6	30.2	4.6	1,012
Northern Ireland	1.8	8.9	8.2	41.2	4.4	288

1 At September. Figures are based on SIC 1992. See Technical notes.

Source: Office for National Statistics; Department of Economic Development, Northern Ireland

5.9 Self-employed: by broad industry group[1], Spring 1996

Percentages and thousands

	Agriculture & fishing	Manufacturing	Construction	Services[2]	Total self-employed[3] (=100%) thousands
United Kingdom	7.7	7.6	24.2	60.5	3,286
North East	..	..	15.6	70.9	87
North West (GOR) & Merseyside	7.8	7.0	24.5	60.7	339
North West (GOR)	8.9	7.1	24.6	59.4	289
Merseyside	..	..	24.1	68.1	50
Yorkshire and the Humber	6.4	6.5	25.9	61.3	258
East Midlands	7.6	8.8	28.9	54.8	216
West Midlands	9.3	8.0	25.9	56.8	258
Eastern	5.7	9.8	25.7	58.8	343
London	..	6.1	21.0	72.2	431
South East (GOR)	3.0	8.9	27.4	60.8	537
South West	13.8	8.4	20.7	57.0	353
England	6.3	7.9	24.5	61.3	2,820
Wales	16.7	7.1	24.8	51.3	160
Scotland	12.0	5.9	19.8	62.3	225
Northern Ireland	27.4	..	25.5	42.7	81

1 Based on SIC 1992. In some cases, sample sizes are too small to provide a reliable estimate. See Technical notes.
2 Includes SIC 1992 groups C and E, Energy and Water.
3 Total includes those who did not state their industry and those whose workplace is outside the United Kingdom, but percentages are based on figures which exclude them.
Source: Labour Force Survey, Office for National Statistics; Department of Economic Development, Northern Ireland

5.10 Economically active of working age[1]: by highest qualification[2], Spring 1996

Percentages and thousands

	Degree or equivalent[3]	Higher education below degree	GCE A level or equivalent	Apprenticeship	GCE O level or equivalent	CSE below grade 1	Other qualifications[4]	No qualifications	Total[5] (= 100%) (thousands)
United Kingdom	14.0	9.0	12.5	11.5	22.0	4.0	9.6	17.4	27,764
North East	10.0	9.0	11.8	14.8	21.7	5.3	9.2	18.3	1,163
North West (GOR) & Merseyside	12.6	9.2	11.8	13.0	23.2	4.5	8.0	17.7	3,152
North West (GOR)	13.1	9.4	11.7	13.3	23.1	4.5	7.9	17.1	2,554
Merseyside	10.6	8.6	12.4	11.5	23.6	4.9	8.3	20.2	599
Yorkshire and the Humber	12.0	8.0	12.2	12.3	22.3	4.3	9.7	19.1	2,368
East Midlands	12.3	8.9	11.0	12.2	21.9	4.7	8.8	20.1	2,026
West Midlands	11.3	8.4	11.6	10.5	21.8	4.5	10.0	21.9	2,518
Eastern	13.0	7.9	12.3	11.0	24.6	4.8	10.1	16.2	2,606
London	23.1	7.5	12.1	7.8	19.5	3.0	12.5	14.7	3,406
South East (GOR)	14.9	9.6	13.3	10.3	23.4	4.9	8.8	14.7	3,875
South West	13.6	9.5	12.6	10.9	24.3	4.7	8.6	15.7	2,278
England	14.3	8.7	12.2	11.1	22.5	4.5	9.6	17.2	23,392
Wales	11.3	9.7	11.8	10.9	23.5	3.8	9.9	19.1	1,271
Scotland	12.9	12.2	16.9	14.7	17.1	0.5	9.7	16.1	2,412
Northern Ireland	12.2	8.4	9.8	16.4	19.8	2.3	6.7	24.3	690

1 Men aged 16-64 and women aged 16-59.
2 See Technical notes. Data are not directly comparable with earlier years due to a change in the LFS questionnaire.
3 Includes NVQ level 4 qualifications.
4 Includes YTS certificate.
5 Includes those who did not state their qualifications, but percentages are based on figures excluding them.
Source: Labour Force Survey, Office for National Statistics; Department of Economic Development, Northern Ireland

5.11 Working days lost due to labour disputes[1], 1996

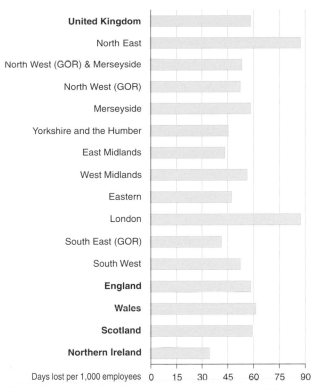

Days lost per 1,000 employees	0 15 30 45 60 75 90
United Kingdom	
North East	
North West (GOR) & Merseyside	
North West (GOR)	
Merseyside	
Yorkshire and the Humber	
East Midlands	
West Midlands	
Eastern	
London	
South East (GOR)	
South West	
England	
Wales	
Scotland	
Northern Ireland	

1 Regional rates are based on data for stoppages that exclude widespread disputes that cannot be allocated to a specific region. These are included in the United Kingdom strike rate only.

Source: Office for National Statistics

5.12 Employees absent due to sickness, Spring 1996[1]

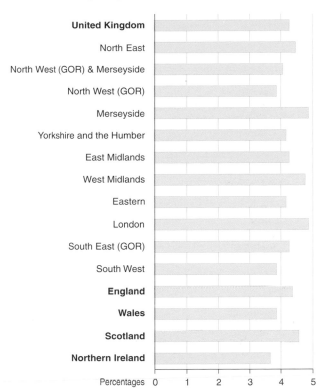

Percentages	0 1 2 3 4 5
United Kingdom	
North East	
North West (GOR) & Merseyside	
North West (GOR)	
Merseyside	
Yorkshire and the Humber	
East Midlands	
West Midlands	
Eastern	
London	
South East (GOR)	
South West	
England	
Wales	
Scotland	
Northern Ireland	

1 Percentages of employees absent from work due to illness or injury for at least one day in the week before interview. See Technical notes.

Source: Labour Force Survey, Office for National Statistics; Department of Economic Development, Northern Ireland

5.13 Trade union membership, 1995 and 1996[1]

Percentages[2]

| | All employees | | 1996 | | | |
| | | | Manual | | Non-manual | |
	1995	1996	Males	Females	Males	Females
United Kingdom	32.1	31.3	36.7	22.8	30.0	32.4
North East	42.3	42.4	47.2	36.7	40.1	42.8
North West (GOR) & Merseyside	38.9	37.9	42.9	26.8	37.6	39.0
North West (GOR)	37.3	36.0	41.0	24.1	36.3	37.1
Merseyside	46.2	46.0	51.6	39.3	43.6	46.6
Yorkshire and the Humber	34.9	35.4	40.1	27.9	34.5	36.0
East Midlands	31.4	32.2	37.7	27.0	29.8	32.5
West Midlands	32.8	32.0	37.3	26.0	29.6	32.2
Eastern	25.8	24.6	29.5	11.9	25.3	26.2
London	28.9	26.2	31.3	20.5	23.1	28.0
South East (GOR)	23.1	22.6	27.2	13.3	22.9	23.4
South West	26.4	27.4	30.2	12.5	30.2	31.1
England	30.6	30.0	35.6	21.6	28.6	31.1
Wales	43.9	41.0	46.3	29.0	41.5	43.3
Scotland	38.4	36.4	39.1	28.1	35.8	38.4
Northern Ireland	39.5	40.7	43.8	33.1	39.7	41.5

1 Autumn quarter of each year.
2 As a percentage of all employees in each region, excluding those who did not say whether they belonged to a trade union.

Source: Labour Force Survey, Office for National Statistics; Department of Economic Development, Northern Ireland

5.14 Shift work and Saturday/Sunday working[1]: by gender, Spring 1996

Percentages[2]

	Males				Females			
	Permanent night shifts	Other shift working	Saturdays	Sundays	Permanent night shifts	Other shift working	Saturdays	Sundays
United Kingdom	1.4	14.5	28.7	14.0	1.2	11.0	22.1	12.2
North East	1.9	20.4	30.4	17.6	..	11.5	27.1	13.5
North West (GOR) & Merseyside	1.6	15.9	30.9	15.6	1.3	11.3	23.7	14.0
North West (GOR)	1.6	15.3	31.2	15.6	1.3	11.4	24.2	14.1
Merseyside	..	18.7	29.5	15.5	..	10.7	21.4	13.8
Yorkshire and the Humber	1.5	16.8	30.3	14.8	1.1	11.5	23.5	12.3
East Midlands	1.6	13.9	30.6	12.1	1.4	10.9	20.7	11.4
West Midlands	1.8	13.6	27.8	12.1	..	10.7	22.2	12.1
Eastern	1.3	12.6	28.0	11.6	1.3	10.6	21.2	11.9
London	0.9	11.8	24.2	11.6	..	9.2	16.2	9.3
South East (GOR)	1.3	13.0	27.1	13.2	1.2	10.6	21.1	11.3
South West	0.9	12.0	30.8	14.6	1.4	10.8	25.3	13.9
England	1.4	14.0	28.6	13.4	1.1	10.7	21.8	12.0
Wales	..	19.2	33.7	18.8	..	11.6	26.9	16.2
Scotland	1.5	17.6	27.8	17.5	2.2	14.3	23.3	12.7
Northern Ireland	..	12.8	25.8	13.7	..	8.8	17.1	9.6

1 Saturday, Sunday and shift work are not mutually exclusive. Figures cover people who usually work shift patterns/Saturdays/Sundays. For some regions, sample sizes are too small to provide a reliable estimate. See Technical notes.
2 Percentages of all in employment who responded to the question.

Source: Labour Force Survey, Office for National Statistics; Department of Economic Development, Northern Ireland

5.15 Average weekly hours[1] of work of full-time employees: by industry[2], Spring 1996

Hours

	Agriculture & fishing	Energy & water	Manu-facturing	Con-struction	Distribution, hotels & restaurants	Trans-port & communi-cation	Banking, finance & insurance	Public admin-istration, education, health	Other services	All industries[3]
United Kingdom	48.1	46.1	44.2	45.7	44.4	46.5	43.1	42.5	43.9	44.0
North East	..	50.5	44.2	45.0	43.6	45.0	42.5	42.3	41.9	43.7
North West (GOR) & Merseyside	..	43.8	43.6	45.5	44.4	46.5	42.3	41.6	44.5	43.5
North West (GOR)	..	43.8	43.7	45.1	44.5	46.6	42.6	41.4	44.6	43.5
Merseyside	..	..	42.5	47.4	44.0	46.2	41.0	42.4	44.2	43.2
Yorkshire and the Humber	48.6	45.6	44.2	45.3	44.1	48.2	43.0	42.4	42.8	44.0
East Midlands	47.3	48.3	44.2	46.2	44.8	46.8	44.2	42.1	44.9	44.3
West Midlands	49.1	44.5	44.1	45.5	44.7	46.7	42.9	42.2	44.8	44.0
Eastern	46.7	45.6	44.8	45.9	44.9	47.3	43.7	43.5	45.6	44.7
London	..	44.0	44.0	47.2	44.4	44.8	43.8	43.1	43.5	44.0
South East (GOR)	46.0	45.0	45.0	46.8	45.2	46.5	43.5	43.4	44.3	44.6
South West	48.2	44.8	44.3	45.5	44.1	47.6	42.1	43.0	41.9	43.8
England	47.5	45.6	44.3	45.9	44.6	46.5	43.3	42.7	43.9	44.1
Wales	..	47.1	44.5	45.0	43.1	48.3	41.6	42.4	43.5	43.8
Scotland	50.7	47.9	43.9	44.9	43.5	46.6	41.6	41.1	43.9	43.3
Northern Ireland	..	..	42.5	43.3	43.3	45.2	40.3	41.5	41.3	42.4

1 Usual hours including paid and unpaid overtime and excluding meal breaks. See Technical notes.
2 Based on SIC 1992.
3 Includes those whose workplace is outside the United Kingdom, and those who did not specify their industry.

Source: Labour Force Survey, Office for National Statistics; Department of Economic Development, Northern Ireland

5.16 Average weekly earnings[1]: by industry[2] and gender, April 1996

£ per week

	Whole economy			Agriculture, forestry fishing & hunting		Manufacturing	
	Males	Females	All persons	Males	Females	Males	Females
United Kingdom	389.9	282.3	350.3	264.5	214.3	378.1	245.1
North East	347.7	252.4	314.1	..	..	367.5	228.1
North West (GOR) & Merseyside	367.8	264.2	329.6	259.7	..	371.9	235.8
North West (GOR)	369.0	262.4	330.5	..	..	373.5	234.5
Merseyside	361.7	271.3	325.4	..	..	361.5	247.1
Yorkshire and the Humber	350.7	252.5	316.4	263.4	..	351.3	218.5
East Midlands	352.9	248.7	317.9	272.6	..	354.4	212.2
West Midlands	360.1	256.9	324.3	..	..	348.3	225.1
Eastern	382.3	279.9	345.7	286.0	..	400.2	264.5
London	514.3	364.9	454.3	..	..	505.0	361.8
South East (GOR)	412.7	292.7	367.4	290.6	..	425.1	276.5
South West	364.8	261.1	326.5	235.9	..	365.9	243.8
England	396.2	286.6	356.0	269.0	217.5	381.6	249.7
Wales	345.5	250.5	313.1	..	..	359.6	227.9
Scotland	363.6	262.0	324.9	258.1	..	376.0	229.9
Northern Ireland	337.4	256.9	306.2	180.3	..	300.1	195.2

	Mining, quarrying & Electricity, gas, water		Construction		Distribution, hotels & catering, repairs		Transport, storage & communication	
	Males	Females	Males	Females	Males	Females	Males	Females
United Kingdom	471.0	341.1	356.5	249.2	328.4	225.7	367.0	298.9
North East	..	..	313.1	..	282.5	188.1	314.9	226.3
North West (GOR) & Merseyside	445.4	..	341.1	..	319.2	215.2	346.3	267.5
North West (GOR)	449.5	..	343.9	..	317.5	216.6	352.2	270.1
Merseyside	..	..	..	..	326.9	207.8	322.5	..
Yorkshire and the Humber	442.5	..	333.0	..	304.4	200.9	326.1	..
East Midlands	439.9	..	335.5	..	318.6	211.3	326.4	244.1
West Midlands	458.7	..	332.7	..	320.0	203.1	331.1	268.3
Eastern	435.1	..	384.1	..	330.4	224.3	364.2	276.4
London	..	430.7	449.6	..	388.6	288.2	458.7	381.8
South East (GOR)	508.7	..	416.6	266.6	368.5	246.5	383.3	302.4
South West	..	..	322.8	..	299.1	205.4	334.5	247.4
England	468.2	342.2	363.6	253.7	336.2	230.5	373.7	302.7
Wales	419.8	..	327.9	..	268.2	183.3	311.2	..
Scotland	534.6	..	337.3	227.2	281.1	200.7	329.5	276.6
Northern Ireland	375.2	..	295.5	..	276.6	188.0	323.1	281.1

	Financial & business services		Public administration & defence		Education, social work & health services		Other	
	Males	Females	Males	Females	Males	Females	Males	Females
United Kingdom	487.9	307.6	400.4	291.2	410.0	312.0	346.4	274.4
North East	377.8	233.7	362.0	269.0	376.9	294.6	..	..
North West (GOR) & Merseyside	416.9	267.2	389.1	276.6	404.7	300.8	..	238.3
North West (GOR)	418.7	267.3	397.0	278.4	410.6	298.1	296.3	246.9
Merseyside	408.8	266.9	359.2	270.8	389.6	308.6	..	..
Yorkshire and the Humber	386.3	249.4	387.6	277.1	394.7	297.8	296.1	219.1
East Midlands	379.6	250.8	382.7	269.3	391.4	296.7	..	..
West Midlands	427.4	258.7	386.5	280.4	414.6	301.7	334.4	228.7
Eastern	424.8	291.1	384.5	290.3	409.5	317.5	313.1	245.9
London	660.8	406.8	457.9	353.4	455.4	358.5	464.3	381.9
South East (GOR)	470.4	307.7	400.9	295.3	411.1	321.2	330.4	262.3
South West	437.5	269.0	377.1	266.4	393.3	296.8	310.7	..
England	499.2	314.1	403.5	296.9	410.9	313.4	355.1	282.8
Wales	354.7	235.6	373.2	275.3	404.1	286.0	..	..
Scotland	413.8	266.5	371.3	258.6	411.2	310.1	300.8	220.3
Northern Ireland	390.3	251.9	423.0	264.2	389.3	314.9	292.8	221.3

1 Average gross weekly earnings; data relate to full-time employees on adult rates whose pay for the survey pay period was not affected by absence. See Technical notes.
2 Classification is based on SIC 1992.

Source: New Earnings Survey, Office for National Statistics; Department of Economic Development, Northern Ireland

5.17 Average weekly earnings and hours: by gender, April 1996[1]

	Average gross weekly earnings								Percentage of employees who received overtime pay	Average weekly hours	
		of which								Total including overtime (hours)	Overtime (hours)
		Overtime pay	PBR etc pay[2]	Shift etc premium pay	Percentage earning under						
	Total (£)	(£)	(£)	(£)	£170	£220	£300	£400			
All full-time male employees											
United Kingdom	389.9	26.5	15.5	6.3	6.4	18.0	41.0	65.1	34.9	41.7	3.1
North East	347.7	28.6	13.7	8.4	7.8	21.1	47.5	72.5	37.3	41.9	3.3
North West (GOR) & Merseyside	367.8	28.2	14.0	7.6	6.7	19.3	43.5	67.7	37.1	41.9	3.3
North West (GOR)	369.0	28.0	14.9	7.3	6.6	19.2	43.6	67.7	37.3	42.0	3.3
Merseyside	361.7	29.2	9.9	8.9	7.1	19.8	43.3	67.6	35.9	41.4	3.4
Yorkshire and the Humber	350.7	27.9	16.8	6.5	7.7	21.2	46.5	71.9	38.0	42.3	3.5
East Midlands	352.9	29.6	14.2	6.3	7.3	20.0	45.5	71.4	39.5	42.4	3.6
West Midlands	360.1	27.5	16.1	6.9	6.4	18.7	43.9	70.1	37.6	41.9	3.3
Eastern	382.3	28.3	13.9	5.4	5.6	16.4	39.6	64.9	35.7	42.3	3.2
London	514.3	22.4	19.0	5.1	3.4	9.7	26.1	47.1	26.4	40.4	2.3
South East (GOR)	412.7	25.2	18.4	4.7	5.3	16.1	37.0	60.6	32.5	41.6	2.8
South West	364.8	24.4	12.7	5.9	7.8	20.6	44.5	68.9	35.5	41.5	2.9
England	396.2	26.4	15.9	6.1	6.1	17.3	39.9	64.1	34.6	41.7	3.0
Wales	345.5	27.5	13.3	9.7	8.7	22.8	47.6	72.0	37.1	42.1	3.3
Scotland	363.6	25.9	14.4	7.1	7.2	20.5	45.7	69.2	35.7	41.8	3.1
Northern Ireland	337.4	28.1	8.5	5.3	11.4	26.2	50.7	71.0	36.1	41.3	3.1
Full-time manual male employees											
United Kingdom	300.1	42.4	13.7	10.5	9.2	25.9	57.8	83.5	53.1	44.8	5.3
North East	298.4	42.2	16.0	12.0	10.0	26.8	59.8	83.3	51.5	44.4	5.1
North West (GOR) & Merseyside	301.6	43.9	12.7	12.5	8.7	25.3	57.5	82.7	53.9	44.8	5.5
North West (GOR)	300.2	43.6	12.8	11.9	8.6	25.3	58.0	83.1	54.1	44.8	5.5
Merseyside	308.3	45.2	12.1	15.6	9.1	25.2	55.0	80.9	52.8	44.7	5.6
Yorkshire and the Humber	292.8	43.1	18.0	10.2	9.7	27.8	59.5	85.4	55.4	45.1	5.6
East Midlands	294.1	44.6	16.2	9.9	10.1	26.2	59.1	85.7	56.7	45.2	5.7
West Midlands	297.1	41.7	16.6	11.0	8.3	24.8	56.5	85.2	54.1	44.4	5.3
Eastern	308.7	46.5	10.8	9.6	7.2	22.9	54.6	81.8	56.2	45.4	5.6
London	336.8	43.2	12.3	10.3	7.0	18.6	46.2	74.1	47.8	45.0	5.1
South East (GOR)	307.7	44.2	10.7	8.7	8.0	24.4	56.0	81.6	54.2	45.2	5.2
South West	282.7	38.2	9.3	9.9	11.1	30.1	63.4	88.4	53.6	44.4	4.9
England	302.8	43.2	13.6	10.4	8.8	25.0	56.7	83.0	53.8	44.9	5.3
Wales	295.0	38.6	14.0	14.8	10.9	29.5	59.2	83.5	49.8	44.5	4.9
Scotland	290.9	39.1	15.1	9.9	9.7	28.4	62.7	85.1	50.2	44.5	4.9
Northern Ireland	261.4	37.3	10.5	8.2	16.9	38.3	72.4	90.8	49.1	44.0	4.7
Full-time non-manual male employees											
United Kingdom	462.7	13.6	17.0	2.8	4.2	11.6	27.4	50.2	20.0	39.1	1.3
North East	406.0	12.5	11.1	4.0	5.2	14.4	33.0	59.7	20.5	39.0	1.2
North West (GOR) & Merseyside	429.3	13.6	15.3	3.0	4.8	13.7	30.5	53.7	21.4	39.1	1.3
North West (GOR)	433.6	13.4	16.9	3.1	4.7	13.4	30.0	53.3	21.5	39.3	1.3
Merseyside	409.6	14.7	8.0	2.8	5.3	14.9	32.8	55.5	20.7	38.5	1.4
Yorkshire and the Humber	410.0	12.3	15.5	2.7	5.7	14.5	33.1	58.1	20.1	39.3	1.3
East Midlands	413.1	14.3	12.2	2.5	4.4	13.8	31.7	56.8	22.0	39.6	1.4
West Midlands	425.0	12.9	15.5	2.7	4.5	12.5	31.1	54.5	20.7	39.2	1.3
Eastern	442.6	13.4	16.4	1.9	4.3	11.2	27.4	51.0	18.9	39.6	1.2
London	585.7	14.0	21.7	2.9	2.0	6.1	18.0	36.2	17.8	38.6	1.2
South East (GOR)	477.9	13.4	23.2	2.3	3.6	11.0	25.3	47.6	19.0	39.4	1.3
South West	431.4	13.2	15.5	2.6	5.2	12.8	29.1	53.1	20.8	39.0	1.2
England	468.9	13.4	17.8	2.7	4.0	11.2	27.0	49.5	19.7	39.1	1.3
Wales	406.8	14.0	12.4	3.4	6.1	14.7	33.6	58.0	21.8	39.2	1.3
Scotland	434.0	13.1	13.7	4.5	4.8	12.9	29.2	53.7	21.7	39.1	1.3
Northern Ireland	408.2	19.5	6.7	2.7	6.2	14.9	30.6	52.6	23.9	38.9	1.6

5.17 *(continued)*

| | Average gross weekly earnings | | | | | | | | Percentage of employees who received overtime pay | Average weekly hours | |
| | Total (£) | Overtime pay (£) | PBR etc pay[2] (£) | Shift etc premium pay (£) | Percentage earning under | | | | | Total including overtime (hours) | Overtime (hours) |
					£170	£220	£300	£400			
All full-time female employees											
United Kingdom	282.3	6.8	6.9	2.9	*18.6*	*39.4*	*65.2*	*83.8*	18.6	37.6	0.9
North East	252.4	6.2	5.1	3.5	*24.9*	*48.6*	*73.3*	*89.1*	18.1	37.6	0.8
North West (GOR) & Merseyside	264.2	6.6	7.2	3.0	*20.4*	*44.5*	*69.9*	*87.0*	18.4	37.6	0.9
North West (GOR)	262.4	6.4	7.6	2.9	*21.1*	*45.4*	*70.5*	*87.6*	18.6	37.6	0.9
Merseyside	271.3	7.2	5.5	3.5	*17.9*	*41.2*	*67.4*	*84.6*	17.6	37.2	0.9
Yorkshire and the Humber	252.5	7.5	6.1	2.8	*25.1*	*49.5*	*73.3*	*88.9*	20.9	37.8	1.0
East Midlands	248.7	7.0	7.1	2.8	*25.0*	*50.4*	*74.6*	*89.5*	20.3	38.0	1.0
West Midlands	256.9	5.9	8.1	2.9	*22.5*	*46.8*	*72.9*	*87.9*	17.3	37.7	0.8
Eastern	279.9	6.8	5.8	2.4	*17.1*	*38.1*	*66.0*	*84.6*	19.9	37.7	0.9
London	364.9	7.9	9.5	2.6	*6.0*	*16.5*	*41.3*	*69.1*	16.7	37.3	0.8
South East (GOR)	292.7	6.7	7.7	2.4	*14.5*	*34.5*	*63.0*	*82.6*	18.5	37.8	0.8
South West	261.1	5.9	5.5	3.4	*22.1*	*45.2*	*71.6*	*87.8*	19.5	37.5	0.8
England	286.6	6.8	7.3	2.8	*17.6*	*38.1*	*64.0*	*83.1*	18.6	37.6	0.9
Wales	250.5	5.6	4.5	3.9	*25.6*	*47.9*	*75.0*	*89.9*	17.1	37.9	0.8
Scotland	262.0	7.5	4.7	3.9	*22.2*	*46.1*	*70.8*	*87.6*	20.6	37.6	0.9
Northern Ireland	256.9	6.1	3.5	3.4	*27.6*	*47.3*	*70.4*	*85.5*	14.9	37.4	0.7
Full-time manual female employees											
United Kingdom	194.4	12.1	7.7	5.4	*44.8*	*71.6*	*91.2*	*97.9*	29.3	40.2	1.9
North East	184.8	9.1	10.2	8.0	*51.9*	*73.4*	*93.7*	*98.8*	22.1	39.7	1.4
North West (GOR) & Merseyside	190.7	11.7	9.7	4.4	*45.5*	*73.3*	*91.3*	*98.6*	28.0	40.1	1.9
North West (GOR)	191.7	11.8	9.5	4.4	*45.0*	*73.1*	*90.9*	*98.4*	28.0	40.1	1.9
Merseyside	184.4	11.3	10.9	4.1	*48.4*	*74.2*	*93.5*	*100.0*	27.4	39.9	2.1
Yorkshire and the Humber	182.6	13.9	7.6	5.6	*52.4*	*77.3*	*93.6*	*98.2*	31.3	40.3	2.2
East Midlands	181.8	12.0	11.8	3.7	*50.1*	*79.2*	*95.0*	*99.0*	29.4	40.2	2.0
West Midlands	191.5	12.1	12.3	6.1	*45.6*	*72.6*	*92.3*	*99.0*	28.5	40.3	2.0
Eastern	197.0	14.0	6.1	4.5	*44.2*	*71.0*	*90.0*	*97.8*	32.6	40.6	2.2
London	239.5	14.9	4.8	5.1	*25.1*	*51.1*	*79.1*	*91.7*	31.5	40.8	2.1
South East (GOR)	204.0	12.0	5.1	5.7	*38.3*	*67.0*	*89.8*	*97.6*	30.7	40.4	1.8
South West	185.5	10.6	5.7	6.2	*50.3*	*76.0*	*92.9*	*98.8*	29.6	39.8	1.6
England	196.5	12.5	8.1	5.3	*44.0*	*70.8*	*90.6*	*97.6*	29.7	40.3	1.9
Wales	184.8	11.0	7.3	5.1	*47.2*	*74.3*	*94.4*	*98.6*	26.5	40.3	1.7
Scotland	189.7	11.7	4.8	6.7	*45.8*	*72.4*	*93.1*	*98.6*	29.6	40.0	1.8
Northern Ireland	171.0	7.2	8.8	4.7	*57.7*	*84.6*	*96.2*	*99.6*	22.2	39.2	1.2
Full-time non-manual female employees											
United Kingdom	301.7	5.7	6.7	2.4	*12.8*	*32.3*	*59.4*	*80.7*	16.2	37.0	0.6
North East	270.2	5.5	3.7	2.4	*17.8*	*42.1*	*68.0*	*86.5*	17.1	37.0	0.6
North West (GOR) & Merseyside	280.6	5.4	6.6	2.7	*14.8*	*38.1*	*65.1*	*84.4*	16.2	37.0	0.6
North West (GOR)	279.7	5.1	7.2	2.5	*15.2*	*38.6*	*65.6*	*85.0*	16.2	37.1	0.6
Merseyside	284.0	6.6	4.7	3.4	*13.4*	*36.3*	*63.5*	*82.3*	16.2	36.8	0.7
Yorkshire and the Humber	270.4	5.8	5.8	2.1	*18.1*	*42.4*	*68.1*	*86.6*	18.3	37.1	0.7
East Midlands	271.1	5.3	5.5	2.5	*16.6*	*40.8*	*67.7*	*86.3*	17.3	37.2	0.7
West Midlands	276.4	4.1	6.9	2.0	*15.6*	*39.1*	*67.1*	*84.6*	14.0	36.9	0.5
Eastern	296.7	5.3	5.7	2.0	*11.6*	*31.5*	*61.2*	*81.9*	17.3	37.1	0.6
London	379.5	7.1	10.0	2.3	*3.8*	*12.4*	*36.9*	*66.5*	15.0	36.9	0.7
South East (GOR)	309.5	5.7	8.2	1.8	*9.9*	*28.3*	*58.0*	*79.8*	16.1	37.3	0.6
South West	277.0	4.9	5.4	2.8	*16.2*	*38.7*	*67.2*	*85.5*	17.4	37.0	0.6
England	305.6	5.7	7.2	2.3	*12.1*	*31.2*	*58.4*	*80.1*	16.2	37.1	0.6
Wales	270.4	3.9	3.7	3.6	*19.0*	*39.9*	*69.2*	*87.3*	14.2	37.2	0.5
Scotland	282.8	6.3	4.6	3.1	*15.4*	*38.5*	*64.4*	*84.5*	18.0	37.0	0.7
Northern Ireland	278.8	5.9	2.2	3.1	*20.0*	*37.8*	*63.8*	*82.0*	13.0	37.0	0.6

1 Data relate to full-time employees on adult rates whose pay for the survey pay-period was not affected by absence. See Technical notes.
2 PBR etc pay is payments-by-results, bonuses, commission and other incentive payments.

Source: New Earnings Survey, Office for National Statistics; Department of Economic Development, Northern Ireland

5.18 Vacancies¹ at jobcentres

Thousands

	1992	1993	1994	1995	1996
United Kingdom	117.1	127.8	157.9	182.9	226.0
North East	4.8	4.9	5.6	6.4	8.1
North West (GOR) &					
Merseyside	16.1	16.9	20.4	22.7	26.8
North West (GOR)	12.9	13.7	16.8	18.7	21.9
Merseyside	3.2	3.2	3.6	4.0	4.9
Yorkshire and the Humber	7.9	9.9	11.8	13.3	16.7
East Midlands	7.3	8.7	10.9	12.8	14.8
West Midlands	7.6	8.9	12.3	15.3	18.8
Eastern	10.0	10.2	13.0	14.8	17.8
London	8.3	10.0	13.2	16.5	28.8
South East (GOR)	14.4	15.3	20.7	22.8	28.2
South West	9.0	9.6	12.5	14.4	19.1
England	85.4	94.5	120.3	138.9	179.0
Wales	8.6	9.6	11.2	13.3	14.5
Scotland	18.9	18.5	19.9	23.2	25.5
Northern Ireland	4.3	5.2	6.5	7.4	7.0

1 Vacancies remaining unfilled, seasonally adjusted annual averages.

Source: Office for National Statistics

5.19 Redundancies¹, Spring 1996

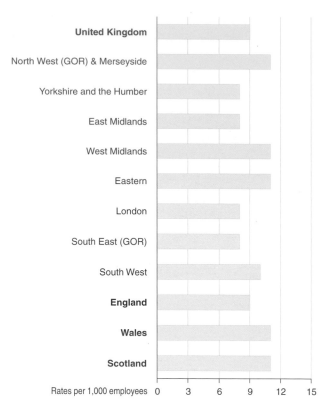

Rates per 1,000 employees

1 Relates to those made redundant in the three months prior to each interview. See Technical notes. For the North East and Northern Ireland, sample sizes are too small to provide reliable estimates.

Source: Labour Force Survey, Office for National Statistics

5.20 Claimant unemployment rates¹

Percentages

	Seasonally adjusted annual averages				
	1992	1993	1994	1995	1996
United Kingdom	9.7	10.3	9.3	8.2	7.5
North East	12.1	12.9	12.4	11.6	10.6
North West (GOR) &					
Merseyside	10.5	10.6	9.9	8.7	8.0
North West (GOR)	9.4	9.5	8.7	7.6	6.9
Merseyside	15.0	15.1	14.9	13.7	13.1
Yorkshire and the Humber	9.9	10.2	9.6	8.7	8.0
East Midlands	9.0	9.5	8.7	7.6	6.8
West Midlands	10.3	10.8	9.9	8.3	7.4
Eastern	8.7	9.4	8.1	6.9	6.1
London	10.5	11.6	10.7	9.7	8.9
South East (GOR)	8.0	8.6	7.3	6.2	5.4
South West	9.2	9.5	8.1	7.0	6.2
England	9.6	10.2	9.2	8.1	7.3
Wales	10.0	10.3	9.3	8.7	8.2
Scotland	9.4	9.7	9.3	8.1	7.9
Northern Ireland	13.8	13.7	12.6	11.4	10.9

1 See Technical notes.

Source: Office for National Statistics

5.21 ILO unemployment rates¹

Percentages

	Spring quarter of each year				
	1992	1993	1994	1995	1996
United Kingdom	9.7	10.3	9.6	8.6	8.2
North East	11.8	12.0	12.5	11.4	10.8
North West (GOR) &					
Merseyside	10.1	10.8	10.3	9.0	8.4
North West (GOR)	9.1	9.8	9.5	8.3	7.3
Merseyside	14.0	15.4	13.6	11.7	13.3
Yorkshire and the Humber	10.1	10.0	9.9	8.7	8.1
East Midlands	8.8	9.1	8.3	7.5	7.4
West Midlands	10.7	11.8	10.0	9.0	9.2
Eastern	7.7	9.2	8.2	7.5	6.2
London	12.0	13.2	13.1	11.5	11.3
South East (GOR)	7.8	8.0	7.1	6.4	6.0
South West	9.1	9.2	7.5	7.8	6.3
England	9.7	10.3	9.5	8.6	8.1
Wales	8.9	9.6	9.3	8.8	8.3
Scotland	9.5	10.2	10.0	8.3	8.7
Northern Ireland	12.3	12.5	11.7	11.0	9.7

1 See Technical notes.

Source: Labour Force Survey, Office for National Statistics; Department of Economic Development, Northern Ireland

5.22 Claimant unemployment: by sub-region[1], January 1997

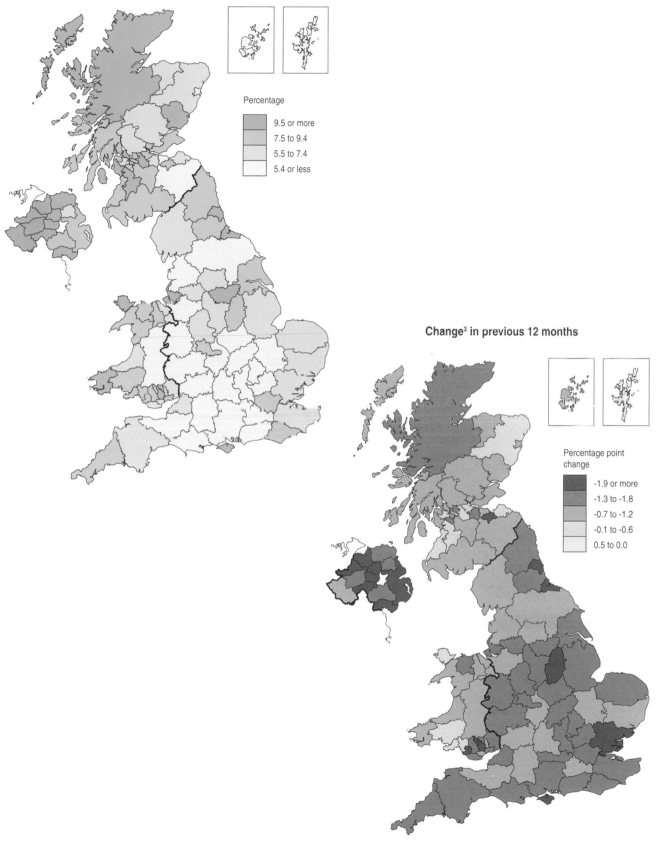

Unemployment rate[2], January 1997

Percentage

- 9.5 or more
- 7.5 to 9.4
- 5.5 to 7.4
- 5.4 or less

Change[3] in previous 12 months

Percentage point
change

- -1.9 or more
- -1.3 to -1.8
- -0.7 to -1.2
- -0.1 to -0.6
- 0.5 to 0.0

1 See Technical notes. Data are workforce-based. Travel-to-work areas for Northern Ireland.
2 Not seasonally adjusted.
3 Percentage point change in unemployment rate between January 1996 and January 1997.

Source: Office for National Statistics; Department of Economic Development, Northern Ireland

5.23 Unemployed claimants[1] by duration and gender, January 1997

Percentages and thousands

	2 weeks or less	Over 2 and up to 8 weeks	Over 8 and up to 13 weeks	Over 13 and up to 26 weeks	Over 26 weeks up to 1 year	Over 1 and up to 2 years	Over 2 and up to 3 years	Over 3 and up to 5 years	Over 5 years	Total (= 100%) (thou-sands)
Males										
United Kingdom	6.0	14.1	9.0	15.0	17.0	16.0	6.9	7.2	8.8	1,463.5
North East	5.1	13.9	8.9	14.4	16.5	16.1	7.2	7.6	10.3	85.9
North West (GOR) &										
Merseyside	6.5	15.4	9.5	15.3	17.5	15.2	5.9	6.0	8.5	180.4
North West (GOR)	7.4	17.1	10.5	15.9	17.5	14.4	5.4	5.2	6.7	125.7
Merseyside	4.5	11.6	7.4	14.1	17.4	17.1	7.2	7.9	12.8	54.7
Yorkshire and the Humber	6.2	15.3	9.9	15.5	16.9	15.6	6.3	5.9	8.4	137.5
East Midlands	6.9	15.8	9.5	14.8	16.3	15.3	6.4	6.5	8.6	91.2
West Midlands	5.9	13.5	8.4	14.3	17.3	15.8	6.6	7.5	10.7	126.6
Eastern	7.4	15.5	9.6	15.6	16.5	15.9	6.5	6.8	6.2	98.6
London	4.2	9.6	7.0	14.3	17.6	18.6	9.5	10.2	9.0	233.8
South East (GOR)	7.4	15.1	9.6	15.2	16.6	16.5	6.8	6.7	6.3	132.3
South West	7.2	15.8	10.2	16.1	16.6	15.4	6.2	6.0	6.5	101.4
England	6.1	14.0	9.0	15.0	17.0	16.3	7.0	7.3	8.4	1,187.6
Wales	5.8	15.0	10.1	16.3	17.4	16.7	5.8	5.7	7.2	75.3
Scotland	6.3	16.8	10.2	16.2	18.0	14.1	5.4	5.6	7.4	144.5
Northern Ireland	3.4	8.1	5.3	10.4	14.1	14.9	8.3	11.0	24.4	56.0
Females										
United Kingdom	8.7	15.6	10.7	18.7	18.8	13.9	5.0	4.4	4.1	444.3
North East	8.8	15.8	10.2	17.8	19.4	13.9	4.9	4.5	4.7	21.4
North West (GOR) &										
Merseyside	10.0	17.5	10.9	18.8	18.6	12.7	4.2	3.6	3.8	50.2
North West (GOR)	11.1	19.1	11.8	19.2	18.1	11.2	3.6	2.8	2.9	35.2
Merseyside	7.5	13.7	8.7	17.7	19.6	16.2	5.5	5.3	5.7	15.0
Yorkshire and the Humber	9.1	16.8	11.2	18.6	18.9	13.0	4.5	3.5	4.3	39.1
East Midlands	9.8	16.0	11.2	19.2	18.5	13.2	4.1	3.9	4.2	27.7
West Midlands	8.3	14.6	9.6	18.3	19.6	14.1	5.2	5.0	5.4	39.4
Eastern	9.5	16.1	11.2	19.0	18.7	13.5	4.5	4.4	3.1	32.3
London	5.8	11.8	9.2	18.8	20.0	17.2	7.3	6.0	3.9	82.0
South East (GOR)	9.7	16.2	11.0	19.0	17.7	14.1	5.0	4.3	3.1	40.9
South West	10.2	17.0	12.2	19.2	17.0	13.0	4.5	3.6	3.3	34.4
England	8.6	15.3	10.5	18.8	18.9	14.3	5.2	4.5	3.9	367.3
Wales	9.5	17.4	11.8	19.2	18.7	12.4	4.0	3.6	3.4	21.1
Scotland	9.8	18.5	12.3	18.6	19.0	11.4	3.6	3.2	3.7	41.1
Northern Ireland	6.6	12.3	7.7	17.4	18.4	13.9	6.3	7.0	10.5	14.8

1 Not seasonally adjusted. See Technical notes.

Source: Office for National Statistics

5.24 Unemployed claimants[1]: by age and gender, January 1997

Percentages and thousands

	Percentage aged						Total (= 100%) (thousands)
	Under 20	20-29	30-39	40-49	50-59	60 or over	
Males							
United Kingdom	6.7	34.1	25.9	17.3	14.8	1.2	1,463.5
North East	8.1	33.6	25.2	17.1	15.1	0.9	85.9
North West (GOR) & Merseyside	7.6	36.8	25.0	16.3	13.3	1.0	180.4
North West (GOR)	7.6	36.9	24.5	16.3	13.6	1.1	125.7
Merseyside	7.7	36.5	26.1	16.1	12.7	0.9	54.7
Yorkshire and the Humber	7.3	35.4	24.6	16.6	14.9	1.1	137.5
East Midlands	6.8	34.8	24.1	17.1	15.7	1.4	91.2
West Midlands	6.7	34.6	25.1	17.0	15.3	1.3	126.6
Eastern	6.4	32.3	24.6	18.2	16.8	1.8	98.6
London	4.7	33.2	30.8	17.3	12.9	1.1	233.8
South East (GOR)	6.0	31.8	25.3	18.6	16.7	1.6	132.3
South West	6.5	33.0	24.4	18.2	16.6	1.3	101.4
England	6.5	34.0	26.0	17.3	14.9	1.3	1,187.6
Wales	7.7	36.0	24.5	16.6	14.3	0.9	75.3
Scotland	7.8	34.7	24.6	16.9	14.7	1.3	144.5
Northern Ireland	5.6	31.9	27.6	19.3	14.7	0.8	56.0
Females							
United Kingdom	12.5	35.6	17.7	17.4	16.7	-	444.3
North East	15.9	33.2	16.5	18.1	16.4	-	21.4
North West (GOR) & Merseyside	14.9	36.9	16.9	16.2	15.0	-	50.2
North West (GOR)	14.7	36.5	17.0	16.4	15.4	-	35.2
Merseyside	15.4	37.9	16.5	15.9	14.2	-	15.0
Yorkshire and the Humber	14.6	35.8	16.1	17.3	16.3	-	39.1
East Midlands	13.1	35.7	16.7	17.5	16.9	-	27.7
West Midlands	13.6	35.6	16.5	16.9	17.4		09.4
Eastern	11.8	33.2	16.6	19.4	18.9	0.1	32.3
London	8.9	39.4	21.2	16.0	14.4	0.1	82.0
South East (GOR)	10.8	33.3	17.8	18.8	19.2	0.1	40.9
South West	11.3	34.4	16.9	18.9	18.5	-	34.4
England	12.3	35.9	17.8	17.4	16.6	0.1	367.3
Wales	14.5	35.2	16.4	17.3	16.6	-	21.1
Scotland	14.0	33.1	17.7	17.8	17.5	-	41.1
Northern Ireland	12.1	36.5	17.7	16.5	17.2	-	14.8

1 Not seasonally adjusted. See Technical notes.

Source: Office for National Statistics

5.25 ILO unemployed: by age, 1995/96[1]

Percentages and thousands

	Percentage aged				All ILO unemployed of working age (= 100%) (thousands)
	16-24	25-34	35-49	Males 50-64/ females 50-59	
United Kingdom	30.5	27.9	26.4	15.2	2,366
North East	30.5	26.9	27.0	15.5	131
North West (GOR) & Merseyside	34.7	26.8	25.3	13.1	272
North West (GOR)	34.8	25.8	25.7	13.6	195
Merseyside	34.5	29.3	24.2	12.0	78
Yorkshire and the Humber	31.8	30.5	24.2	13.5	197
East Midlands	29.9	29.7	26.2	14.2	149
West Midlands	30.3	25.4	28.2	16.1	229
Eastern	30.6	23.4	26.2	19.8	182
London	25.4	34.0	26.4	14.2	395
South East (GOR)	31.1	23.7	27.5	17.6	248
South West	30.4	26.0	25.4	18.2	162
England	30.2	27.9	26.3	15.6	1,965
Wales	34.8	26.1	27.8	11.3	110
Scotland	31.6	28.0	25.6	14.8	218
Northern Ireland	29.2	28.9	28.9	13.1	72

1 Average of four quarters ending Summer 1996. See Technical notes.

Source: Labour Force Survey, Office for National Statistics; Department of Economic Development, Northern Ireland

6 Housing

Stock of dwellings
The stock of dwellings in Northern Ireland rose by nearly 20 per cent between 1981 and 1995, almost five times the rate of growth in Merseyside.
(Table 6.1)

Tenure
The rate of owner-occupation in Scotland rose by just over 10 per cent between 1991 and 1995, the highest increase.
(Table 6.2)

New homes
In 1995, private developers built two and a half times as many homes per head of population in Northern Ireland as in London.
(Table 6.4)

Type of dwelling
Scotland and London have the highest proportions of households living in purpose-built flats at 36 and 30 per cent respectively, compared with 7 per cent in the East Midlands and Northern Ireland.
(Table 6.5)

Overcrowding
One in 20 households in London and Northern Ireland in 1995-96 lived in overcrowded accommodation, roughly double the proportion in all other regions.
(Table 6.6)

Council Tax bandings
Three in every four properties in the North East is in Band A or B (the lowest bands) for Council Tax compared with one in four in the South East (GOR) and one in six in London.
(Table 6.7)

Rents
Within Great Britain, the average private sector rent in 1995-96 ranged from £52 per week in Wales to £116 per week in London.
(Table 6.8)

House prices
House prices were higher in 1996 than in 1993 in all regions, but the difference ranged from 2 per cent in the North East and the North West (GOR) to 25 per cent in Northern Ireland.
(Table 6.10)

Council house sales
Local authorities in the South East (GOR) have sold or transferred more than half their housing stock since 1979, while those in the North East, the North West (GOR) and the Yorkshire and Humber region have reduced their stocks by about a quarter.
(Table 6.11)

Homelessness
Mortgage arrears was the principal reason cited by 15 per cent of households accepted as homeless in the Eastern region in 1995, compared with only 1 per cent in Northern Ireland.
(Table 6.13)

Introduction

Changes in the stock of dwellings are affected by a number of factors other than the building of new homes: some existing properties are converted, some are demolished either to make way for new development or because they are defective, some are closed as unfit for habitation and others that were previously closed are made fit again.

There has been a fall in the stock of local authority housing since the early 1980s for two major reasons. The first is the sale of dwellings to sitting tenants and others - for example to people who work in the borough/district (Table 6.11). The second reason is the introduction in Great Britain of Large Scale Voluntary Transfers (LSVTs). Under this scheme, a local authority can transfer all or part of its housing stock to a new landlord, usually a non-profit-making housing association registered with the Housing Corporation or Scottish Homes. Some local authorities in England now have no housing stock following LSVTs. At the same time, the main responsibility for building new social housing in England and Wales has been transferred from local authorities to housing associations (Table 6.4)

The introduction to the Population Chapter highlights the projected growth in the number of households, particularly one-person households: this may have implications for the number, types and sizes of dwellings required in the future. Table 6.5 looks at the types of dwelling in which households live. The most striking differences among the regions are the high proportions of households in London and Scotland living in flats and the very low proportion of London households living in detached houses.

One way of addressing the need for more housing in future, apart from reducing the number of vacant properties, may be to make better use of under-occupied dwellings. The extent to which a dwelling is overcrowded or under-occupied may be calculated from a number of indicators. One commonly used measure is the bedroom standard which compares the number of bedrooms available to a household with a calculation of the number required according to the bedroom standard, details of which are given in the Technical notes. Table 6.6 shows the proportions of households whose accommodation is below, at or above the bedroom standard. Around a third of households in all regions except the North East, London and Scotland are in accommodation with at least two bedrooms above the standard. The lower proportions in London (22 per cent) and Scotland (20 per cent) reflect the high proportion of flats in those regions. In London, it may also partly reflect the higher prices of property.

The Survey of English Housing 1995-96 asked households renting from a local authority or housing association whether they would be interested in moving to a smaller property. For this purpose, under-occupancy was defined as more than one bedroom per person or households which said they had too many bedrooms. Although under this definition there was a high level of under-occupancy among tenants in the North East (40 per cent), this was not accompanied by a particularly high level of interest in moving to a smaller property (8 per cent). The lowest levels of interest were in the Eastern region and the South West (4 and 5 per cent respectively).

Local authorities have the primary responsibility for dealing with homelessness. Their main duty is to secure accommodation for those whom they accept as homeless (see Technical notes). The Survey of English Housing 1995-96 provides information on the experience of homelessness. This was most common among people living in London where 10 per cent of respondents to the survey (either the head of household or their partner) said they had had some experience of homelessness in the previous ten years compared with between 4 and 6 per cent in the other English regions (Table 6.14)

6.1 Stock of dwellings[1]

	Thousands						Percentage increase 1981-1995	Rates per 1,000 population 1995
	1981	1991	1992	1993	1994	1995		
United Kingdom	21,586	23,711	23,881	24,062	24,247	24,430	*13.2*	417
North East	1,020	1,077	1,082	1,088	1,094	1,100	*7.8*	422
North West (GOR) & Merseyside	2,660	2,803	2,818	2,834	2,852	2,870	*7.9*	416
North West (GOR)	2,094	2,228	2,240	2,253	2,267	2,281	*8.9*	417
Merseyside	566	575	578	581	585	589	*4.1*	413
Yorkshire and the Humber	1,901	2,031	2,044	2,058	2,072	2,087	*9.8*	415
East Midlands	1,484	1,646	1,661	1,676	1,693	1,709	*15.2*	414
West Midlands	1,941	2,089	2,102	2,117	2,132	2,146	*10.6*	404
Eastern	1,859	2,110	2,130	2,151	2,174	2,196	*18.1*	418
London	2,682	2,928	2,945	2,960	2,975	2,993	*11.6*	427
South East (GOR)	2,750	3,120	3,145	3,171	3,197	3,223	*17.2*	411
South West	1,728	1,983	2,000	2,015	2,031	2,048	*18.5*	424
England	18,025	19,788	19,927	20,071	20,219	20,371	*13.0*	417
Wales	1,089	1,190	1,199	1,208	1,218	1,227	*12.7*	421
Scotland	1,970	2,160	2,175	2,193	2,210	2,232	*13.3*	434
Northern Ireland	502	573	580	590	600	600	*19.5*	364

1 At 31 December each year. See Technical notes.

Source: Department of the Environment; Welsh Office; The Scottish Office Development Department;
Department of the Environment, Northern Ireland

6.2 Tenure of dwellings[1]

Percentages

	Owner -occupied			Rented from local authority or New Town[2,3]			Rented from private owners with job or business			Rented from housing association		
	1991	1993	1995	1991	1993	1995	1991	1993	1995	1991	1993	1995
Great Britain	*66*	*67*	*67*	*21*	*20*	*19*	*10*	*10*	*10*	*3*	*4*	*4*
North East	*58*	*59*	*59*	*31*	*30*	*29*	*7*	*7*	*8*	*4*	*4*	*4*
North West (GOR) & Merseyside	*67*	*67*	*68*	*21*	*21*	*20*	*8*	*8*	*8*	*4*	*4*	*4*
North West (GOR)	*69*	*69*	*70*	*21*	*21*	*20*	*8*	*8*	*8*	*3*	*3*	*3*
Merseyside	*62*	*63*	*63*	*24*	*23*	*22*	*9*	*9*	*9*	*5*	*5*	*5*
Yorkshire and the Humber	*65*	*65*	*65*	*24*	*22*	*22*	*8*	*9*	*10*	*2*	*3*	*3*
East Midlands	*71*	*70*	*71*	*19*	*18*	*18*	*9*	*9*	*9*	*2*	*2*	*3*
West Midlands	*67*	*67*	*68*	*23*	*22*	*21*	*7*	*8*	*8*	*3*	*3*	*4*
Eastern	*71*	*71*	*71*	*17*	*16*	*15*	*10*	*10*	*10*	*3*	*4*	*5*
London	*57*	*57*	*57*	*24*	*22*	*22*	*13*	*14*	*15*	*5*	*6*	*7*
South East (GOR)	*74*	*74*	*74*	*12*	*11*	*10*	*11*	*11*	*11*	*3*	*4*	*5*
South West	*72*	*72*	*72*	*14*	*13*	*12*	*12*	*12*	*12*	*2*	*3*	*4*
England	*67*	*67*	*68*	*20*	*19*	*18*	*10*	*10*	*10*	*3*	*4*	*4*
Wales	*71*	*71*	*71*	*18*	*18*	*17*	*8*	*8*	*8*	*3*	*3*	*4*
Scotland	*52*	*56*	*58*	*38*	*34*	*31*	*7*	*7*	*7*	*3*	*3*	*4*
Northern Ireland[4]	*65*	*67*	*69*	*29*	*27*	*25*	*4*	*3*	*4*	*2*	*2*	*2*

1 As at 31 December each year. See Technical notes.
2 Including Scottish Homes, formerly the Scottish Special Housing Association.
3 Northern Ireland Housing Executive in Northern Ireland.
4 Changes in the method of data collection mean that the 1995 figures for Northern Ireland are not strictly comparable with either the 1995 data for Great Britain or the Northern Ireland figures for earlier years. The figures are based on total occupied stock.

Source: Department of the Environment; Welsh Office; The Scottish Office Development Department;
Department of the Environment, Northern Ireland

6.3 Renovations by sector[1]

Thousands of dwellings[2]

| | Grants paid to private owners and tenants[3,4] | | | | Work completed for housing associations[3] | | Work completed for local authorities and new towns[3,5,6] | |
| | All | | Of which grants for disabled facilities[3] | | | | | |
	1991	1995	1991	1995	1991	1995	1991	1995
United Kingdom	136.3	139.5	..	28.4	8.5	..	267.7	413.2
North East	4.9	4.8	0.5	1.3	0.1	..	22.4	17.8
North West (GOR) & Merseyside	15.1	13.7	1.5	3.5	0.8	..	24.5	30.0
North West (GOR)	11.7	11.4	1.3	2.9	..	..	22.1	25.6
Merseyside	3.5	2.3	0.2	0.5	..	..	2.4	4.1
Yorkshire and the Humber	10.3	9.3	2.7	2.8	0.5	..	9.4	21.7
East Midlands	8.5	9.6	1.0	2.2	0.3	..	14.0	13.9
West Midlands	12.3	9.5	1.0	2.3	0.4	..	19.9	50.2
Eastern	6.3	8.5	1.0	2.5	0.5	..	9.3	29.7
London	7.5	11.2	0.6	2.0	2.6	..	29.4	77.1
South East (GOR)	11.7	15.5	1.4	3.8	1.0	..	21.8	26.6
South West	8.6	10.9	1.3	2.8	0.3	..	25.4	41.1
England	85.4	92.5	11.0	22.5	6.4	..	177.3	308.1
Wales	21.2	17.3	1.2	3.1	0.3	0.2	10.5	16.7
Scotland	23.5	19.0	1.7	2.0	1.7	1.3	70.4	82.2
Northern Ireland	6.2	10.7	..	0.8	0.1	0.1	9.5	6.2

1 See Technical notes.
2 Figures for Wales and Northern Ireland are for thousands of grants.
3 Figures for Scotland and, except for housing associations, for Northern Ireland are for work approved.
4 In England grants paid under the *Housing Act 1985* and earlier legislation refer to the number of dwellings whereas grants paid under the *Local Government and Housing Act 1989* refer to the number of grants.
5 Including Scottish Homes.
6 Northern Ireland Housing Executive in Northern Ireland.

Source: Department of the Environment; Welsh Office; The Scottish Office Development Department; Department of the Environment, Northern Ireland

6.4 New dwellings[1] completed: by sector

Thousands and rates per 1,000 population

| | Private enterprise[2] | | | | Housing associations | | | | Local authorities, new towns and government departments[3] | | | |
| | Thousands | | Rates | | Thousands | | Rates | | Thousands | | Rates | |
	1991	1995	1991	1995	1991	1995	1991	1995	1991	1995	1991	1995
United Kingdom	159.1	156.3	2.8	2.7	20.8	39.2	0.4	0.7	11.2	3.5	0.2	0.1
North East	5.4	6.0	2.1	2.3	1.0	1.3	0.4	0.5	0.1	-	0.1	-
North West (GOR) & Merseyside	15.4	16.0	2.2	2.3	3.0	4.6	0.4	0.7	0.5	-	0.1	-
North West (GOR)	12.9	13.0	2.4	2.4	2.1	3.4	0.4	0.6	0.2	-	-	-
Merseyside	2.4	3.0	1.7	2.1	0.8	1.2	0.6	0.8	0.3	-	0.2	-
Yorkshire and the Humber	11.1	11.7	2.2	2.3	2.0	3.5	0.4	0.7	0.2	-	-	-
East Midlands	14.0	13.9	3.5	3.4	1.0	2.4	0.3	0.6	0.7	0.2	0.2	0.1
West Midlands	13.6	12.7	2.6	2.4	1.5	2.7	0.3	0.5	1.0	0.1	0.2	-
Eastern	18.9	18.1	3.8	3.4	0.6	3.4	0.1	0.6	1.5	0.1	0.3	-
London	12.8	11.0	1.9	1.6	2.7	5.2	0.4	0.7	0.7	0.1	0.1	-
South East (GOR)	23.0	21.3	3.0	2.7	2.3	5.0	0.3	0.6	2.3	0.1	0.3	-
South West	17.0	14.0	3.6	2.9	1.1	3.0	0.2	0.6	1.1	0.2	0.2	-
England	131.2	124.6	2.7	2.5	15.3	31.1	0.3	0.6	8.1	0.8	0.2	-
Wales	7.3	6.5	2.6	2.2	2.5	2.3	0.9	0.8	0.4	0.2	0.1	0.1
Scotland	15.5	18.2	3.0	3.5	2.3	5.0	0.4	1.0	1.7	1.2	0.3	0.2
Northern Ireland	5.2	6.8	3.2	4.1	0.8	0.7	0.5	0.4	1.0	1.3	0.6	0.8

1 Permanent dwellings only ie those with a life expectancy of 60 years or more. See Technical notes.
2 Includes private landlords (persons or companies) and owner-occupiers.
3 Northern Housing Executive in Northern Ireland.

Source: Department of the Environment; Welsh Office; The Scottish Office Development Department; Department of the Environment, Northern Ireland

6.5 Households: by type of dwelling, 1995-96

Percentages

	Det-ached house	Semi-det-ached house	Terraced house	Purpose-built flat or mais-onette	Other[1]
North East	10	41	34	13	2
North West (GOR) &					
Merseyside	16	39	34	9	3
North West (GOR)	18	38	33	9	2
Merseyside	10	42	36	8	5
Yorkshire and the					
Humber	19	41	29	9	2
East Midlands	29	37	25	7	2
West Midlands	20	38	28	11	2
Eastern	28	33	25	12	4
London	5	18	30	30	17
South East (GOR)	29	29	23	13	6
South West	29	27	25	11	7
England	20	33	28	13	5
Wales	24	32	32	8	3
Scotland	18	21	22	36	3
Northern Ireland	32	24	35	7	2

1 Includes converted flats which are particularly common in London.
Source: Survey of English Housing, Department of the Environment;
General Household Survey, Office for National Statistics;
Continuous Household Survey, Northern Ireland Statistics and
Research Agency

6.6 Difference from bedroom standard[1], 1995-96

Percentages

	One or more below	At stan-dard	One above	Two or more above
North East	2	28	44	25
North West (GOR) &				
Merseyside	3	27	39	31
North West (GOR)	3	27	40	30
Merseyside	3	28	37	32
Yorkshire and the Humber	2	27	40	31
East Midlands	2	24	40	33
West Midlands	3	27	37	33
Eastern	2	26	38	34
London	5	41	31	22
South East (GOR)	2	27	37	34
South West	2	27	37	34
England	3	29	38	31
Wales	2	26	38	35
Scotland	3	38	40	20
Northern Ireland	5	24	38	33

1 This concept is used as an indicator of occupation density. See Technical notes.
Source: Survey of English Housing, Department of the Environment;
General Household Survey, Office for National Statistics;
Continuous Household Survey, Northern Ireland Statistics and
Research Agency

6.7 Residential properties: by Council Tax bandings, 1995-96[1]

Percentages and thousands

	Percentage of residential properties classified to								Total number of properties (=100%) (thousands)
	Band A	Band B	Band C	Band D	Band E	Band F	Band G	Band H	
North East	60.9	13.8	13.5	6.3	3.1	1.4	0.8	0.1	1,101
North West (GOR) & Merseyside	45.2	18.7	17.2	9.2	5.1	2.6	1.8	0.2	2,885
North West (GOR)	43.6	19.0	17.5	9.6	5.5	2.8	1.9	0.2	2,291
Merseyside	51.5	17.9	16.4	7.3	3.7	1.8	1.3	0.1	594
Yorkshire and the Humber	47.6	19.5	16.2	7.9	4.9	2.4	1.5	0.1	2,092
East Midlands	39.9	22.8	18.0	9.6	5.3	2.6	1.6	0.2	1,711
West Midlands	33.7	25.2	19.1	10.2	6.2	3.3	2.1	0.2	2,155
Eastern	14.6	21.8	27.1	17.1	10.0	5.3	3.7	0.4	2,202
London	3.3	13.6	27.0	25.4	15.5	7.5	6.1	1.6	3,006
South East (GOR)	8.7	16.6	26.3	20.0	13.3	7.8	6.3	0.9	3,246
South West	17.2	25.0	23.6	15.5	10.1	5.1	3.1	0.3	2,063
England	26.6	19.4	21.8	14.6	9.0	4.7	3.4	0.5	20,460
Wales	20.2	25.9	20.0	15.0	11.8	4.2	2.7	0.3	1,194
Scotland	27.5	25.7	15.3	11.1	11.0	5.3	3.6	0.4	2,213

1 Figures for England and Wales relate to dwellings on valuation lists at 16 October 1995, and for Scotland at 10 October 1995. See Technical notes.
Source: Department of the Environment; Welsh Office; The Scottish Office Development Department

6.8 Average weekly rents: by tenure, 1996[1]

£ per week

	Private sector average rent[2]	Local authorities[3]	Housing associations[4]
North East	63.0	33.3	37.4
North West (GOR) &			
Merseyside	68.0	37.3	35.7
North West (GOR)	69.0	36.2	37.4
Merseyside	64.0	41.0	32.9
Yorkshire and the Humber	56.0	31.4	39.6
East Midlands	56.0	34.1	43.3
West Midlands	58.0	36.8	41.3
Eastern	66.0	41.3	43.7
London	116.0	52.7	50.3
South East (GOR)	77.0	46.1	48.5
South West	67.0	40.8	45.5
England	76.0	40.0	44.0
Wales	52.0	37.2	40.9
Scotland	53.0	31.3	30.2
Northern Ireland	..	32.6	..

1 See Technical notes.
2 1995-96 average across the whole sector (excluding rent free). Figures for England are combined averages from the Family Resources Survey and the Survey of English Housing.
3 Unrebated rents at April 1996. Northern Ireland Housing Executive average unrebated rent for Northern Ireland.
4 Rents covering whole stock at 31 March 1996, from Housing Corporation returns.

Source: Department of Social Security; Department of the Environment; Welsh Office; The Scottish Office Development Department; Scottish Homes; Department of the Environment, Northern Ireland

6.9 Housing costs of owner occupiers, 1995-96[1]

£ per week

	Mortgage payments	Endowment policies	Structural insurance	Service payments	Total
Great Britain	29.2	6.7	4.4	0.6	40.9
North East	22.5	6.2	3.9	0.3	32.9
North West (GOR) &					
Merseyside	23.9	5.7	4.1	0.3	34.0
North West (GOR)	23.7	5.5	4.1	0.3	33.6
Merseyside	24.8	6.5	4.5	0.4	36.2
Yorkshire and the Humber	23.9	6.0	3.9	0.3	34.1
East Midlands	24.7	6.4	4.0	0.2	35.3
West Midlands	24.9	6.1	3.8	0.4	35.2
Eastern	33.6	7.4	4.6	0.5	46.1
London	43.2	7.8	5.5	2.0	58.5
South East (GOR)	37.5	8.0	5.1	0.8	51.4
South West	27.7	5.9	4.4	0.5	38.5
England	30.0	6.7	4.4	0.6	41.8
Wales	19.5	4.8	3.6	0.1	28.0
Scotland	27.6	7.7	4.1	0.3	39.7
Northern Ireland	19.6	5.3	2.2	0.4	27.6

1 See Technical notes.

Source: Family Resources Survey, Department of Social Security; Family Expenditure Survey, Northern Ireland Statistics and Research Agency

6.10 Dwelling prices, mortgages and income of borrowers[1]

	Index of dwelling prices[2] (1993=100)				Average dwelling price, 1996 (£ thousands)			Mortgages, 1996		Average recorded income, 1996[4] (£ thousands per annum)
	1993	1994	1995	1996	All dwellings	Excluding LA sitting tenants	First-time buyers[3]	Total number of loans (thousands)	Of which first-time buyers (percentages)	
United Kingdom	100.0	102.5	103.2	107.0	70.6	72.4	48.7	969.7	47.0	24.7
North East	100.0	102.7	98.7	101.9	51.3	53.6	36.4	36.0	52.8	19.4
North West (GOR) & Merseyside	..	..	..	..	58.3	59.3	41.8	92.7	52.7	21.6
North West (GOR)	100.0	102.8	102.1	102.1	58.1	59.1	41.6	76.8	52.8	21.5
Merseyside	100.0	100.9	95.0	104.3	59.4	60.5	42.4	15.9	52.2	21.9
Yorkshire and the Humber	100.0	98.4	98.6	103.2	57.4	58.7	40.4	70.2	50.8	21.5
East Midlands	100.0	102.2	102.4	108.4	59.8	61.1	41.4	69.5	46.8	22.1
West Midlands	100.0	100.5	103.2	106.4	64.6	66.1	44.5	80.5	47.2	23.0
Eastern	100.0	101.4	102.8	106.6	74.3	75.6	51.1	105.3	45.0	26.2
London	100.0	105.2	106.2	108.9	94.7	96.4	67.3	121.3	49.8	31.6
South East (GOR)	100.0	104.2	104.6	109.9	88.3	89.4	58.5	168.1	40.2	28.8
South West	100.0	103.1	104.1	108.1	68.4	69.3	49.4	93.3	41.7	23.2
England	100.0	102.7	103.3	106.9	73.1	74.5	50.4	836.9	46.4	25.3
Wales	100.0	101.3	99.4	103.8	55.4	56.5	41.9	43.1	52.4	20.9
Scotland	100.0	101.1	102.2	105.8	57.5	62.3	38.4	65.1	49.3	21.9
Northern Ireland	100.0	103.9	116.0	125.1	47.9	52.0	34.6	24.6	53.3	19.1

1 See Technical notes.
2 Figures are based on all lenders. Data are therefore not comparable with those in earlier editions of *Regional Trends*, which were based on building societies' lending only. The index adjusts for the mix of dwellings (by size, type and whether new or second hand) and excludes those bought at non-market prices.
3 Includes LA sitting tenants.
4 The income of borrowers is the total recorded income taken into account when the mortgage is granted.

Source: Department of the Environment

6.11 Sales and transfers of local authority dwellings[1]

Thousands and percentages

	April 1979 to March 1996				Sales 1995-96				Stock at 1 April 1996[4]	Total sales and transfers April 1979 to March 1996 as a percentage of notional stock at 1 April 1979[5]
	Right-to-buy sales[2]	Other sales	Large scale voluntary transfers[3]	Total sales and transfers	Right-to-buy sales[2]	Other sales	Large scale voluntary transfers	Total sales and transfers		
United Kingdom	1,591	346	250	2,187	47	7	45	99	4,456	33
North East	107	5	-	112	3	-	-	3	302	27
North West (GOR) & Merseyside	145	38	8	191	3	1	4	8	532	27
North West (GOR)	109	23	8	140	3	1	4	8	413	25
Merseyside	36	15	-	51	-	-	-	-	119	30
Yorkshire and the Humber	131	14	8	153	3	-	-	3	447	26
East Midlands	116	15	-	131	3	-	-	3	297	31
West Midlands	148	24	16	188	4	-	2	6	433	30
Eastern	138	42	39	219	4	-	-	4	306	42
London	193	67	12	272	5	1	-	6	628	30
South East (GOR)	163	50	114	327	4	-	28	32	293	53
South West	111	18	26	155	3	-	11	14	232	40
England	1,252	273	223	1,748	32	2	45	79	3,470	34
Wales	95	6	1	102	2	-	-	2	206	33
Scotland	244	-	26	270	13	-	-	13	632	29
Northern Ireland[6]	.	67	.	67	.	5	.	5	148	31

1 Includes shared ownership deals and dwellings transferred to housing associations and private developers. Excludes New Towns. Figures for Scotland exclude sales by Scottish Homes.
2 Right-to-buy sales were introduced in Great Britain in October 1980. Figure for United Kingdom therefore relates to Great Britain.
3 Figure for United Kingdom relates to Great Britain. For Scotland includes large scale voluntary transfers and trickle transfers to housing associations.
4 For Scotland includes 12,617 houses transferred from the new towns of Glenrothes and East Kilbride to local authority stock in 1995-96.
5 Calculated as sales in the period April 1979 to March 1996 expressed as a percentage of stock at 1 April 1996 plus sales in the period April 1979 to March 1996.
6 The NI Housing Executive is responsible for public sector housing in Northern Ireland. Under the *Housing (NI) Order 1992* NIHE operates a voluntary house sales scheme which is comparable to the Right-to-buy scheme in Great Britain.

Source: Department of the Environment; Welsh Office; The Scottish Office Development Department;
Department of the Environment, Northern Ireland

6.12 County Court actions for mortgage possessions[1]

Thousands

	1991			1994			1995			1996		
	Actions entered	Suspended orders	Orders made	Actions entered	Suspended orders	Orders made	Actions entered	Suspended orders	Orders made	Actions entered	Suspended orders	Orders made
North East	6.0	2.9	1.9	3.2	2.4	1.2	3.3	2.1	1.0	3.5	2.0	1.1
North West (GOR) & Merseyside	22.3	8.6	7.5	12.2	6.2	3.7	12.8	6.7	4.0	12.7	7.7	4.0
North West (GOR)	17.9	6.9	6.1	9.7	5.4	3.1	10.2	5.5	3.4	9.9	6.3	3.5
Merseyside	4.4	1.7	1.4	2.5	0.8	0.6	2.6	1.2	0.6	2.8	1.4	0.5
Yorkshire and the Humber	14.1	5.1	5.7	7.6	3.2	2.3	7.4	3.6	2.2	7.6	3.9	2.6
East Midlands	13.5	4.5	5.2	6.0	3.2	2.4	6.5	3.3	2.1	5.9	3.0	2.0
West Midlands	17.7	6.5	6.9	8.6	4.4	2.6	8.2	4.2	2.4	7.6	3.9	2.1
Eastern	18.6	6.0	8.4	9.3	4.2	3.6	8.5	4.3	3.4	8.3	4.0	3.4
London	35.3	13.1	14.4	15.5	8.4	6.8	12.1	6.7	6.0	11.4	6.4	4.8
South East (GOR)	32.2	13.2	13.2	13.6	7.9	5.6	13.0	7.6	5.3	11.6	6.6	4.0
South West	16.7	5.8	6.5	7.4	3.5	2.5	7.1	3.4	2.4	6.3	3.3	2.4
England	176.4	65.6	69.9	83.5	43.3	30.7	78.9	41.9	28.8	74.9	40.7	26.4
Wales	10.2	3.5	4.0	4.4	2.3	1.5	5.3	2.7	1.6	4.9	2.7	1.4
Northern Ireland [2]	3.1	..	..	1.4	..	..	1.2	..	..	1.2	..	..

1 Local authority and private. See Technical notes.
2 Mortgage possession actions are heard in Chancery Division of Northern Ireland High Court.

Source: The Court Service; Northern Ireland Court Service

6.13 Households accepted as homeless: by reason[1]; and households in temporary accommodation: by type, 1995

Percentages and numbers

	Reasons for homelessness						Total house-holds accepted as homeless (=100%) (numbers)	Households in temporary accommodation on 31 December 1995			
	No longer willing or able to remain with		Break-down of relation-ship with partner	Mort-gage arrears	Rent arrears or other reason for loss of rented or tied accomm-odation	Other reasons[2]		Hostels	Bed & Breakfast	Other[3]	Total (=100%) (numbers)
	Parents	Relatives or friend									
England & Wales	18	12	23	8	22	17	130,281	22	10	68	44,688
North East	21	12	30	7	16	13	6,270	51	19	30	430
North West (GOR) &											
Merseyside	16	11	27	7	17	21	17,400	60	12	28	2,140
North West	15	11	28	7	16	22	14,440	56	14	30	1,840
Merseyside	22	10	22	7	21	18	2,960	83	3	13	300
Yorkshire and the Humber	18	11	30	6	18	17	10,290	49	7	44	1,160
East Midlands	17	9	29	9	20	17	9,170	39	3	58	1,420
West Midlands	16	13	29	6	17	19	18,130	33	7	61	1,220
Eastern	17	7	20	15	29	11	8,810	30	4	66	2,740
London	19	20	15	5	20	21	26,930	14	11	75	26,060
South East (GOR)	17	11	16	13	32	12	14,250	25	10	65	6,430
South West	13	7	19	12	35	13	10,030	24	9	67	2,540
England	17	12	23	8	22	17	121,280	22	10	68	44,140
Wales	21	8	20	7	26	18	9,001	34	11	55	548
Northern Ireland	32		20	1	11	36	4,319	16	..	84	2,151

1 See Technical notes.
2 A large proportion of the Northern Ireland total is classified as 'Other reasons' due to differences in the definitions used.
3 For Northern Ireland the figure relates to private and Northern Ireland Housing Executive accommodation.

Source: Department of the Environment; Welsh Office; Department of the Environment, Northern Ireland

6.14 Experience of homelessness[1] in the previous ten years, 1995-96

Percentages and thousands

	Experience of homelessness[1] (percentages)					All households (=100%) (thousands)
	Approached council and accepted as homeless	Approached council and not accepted as homeless	Did not approach council but has been homeless	Total reporting homelessness	Was not homeless	
North East	3	1	-	5	95	1,095
North West (GOR) & Merseyside	3	1	1	5	95	2,656
Yorkshire and the Humber	4	1	1	6	95	2,066
East Midlands	3	1	1	5	95	1,614
West Midlands	3	1	1	5	95	2,066
Eastern	3	1	1	5	94	2,094
London	7	2	2	10	90	2,729
South East (GOR)	3	1	1	5	95	3,116
South West	3	1	1	5	96	2,038
England	4	1	1	6	94	19,473

1 By heads of household or their partner.

Source: Survey of English Housing, Department of the Environment

7 Health

Infant deaths

The infant mortality rate in 1995 ranged from 5.1 in the Eastern region to 7.1 in Northern Ireland.

(Table 7.2)

Limiting long-standing illness

About half of elderly people in Northern Ireland and Wales have a limiting long-standing illness compared with around a third in the South East (GOR).

(Table 7.4)

Hearing difficulties

Nearly a quarter of men in the North East and Wales and about a sixth of women in the Yorkshire and Humber region reported in 1995-96 that they had a hearing difficulty, the highest proportions.

(Table 7.6)

Private medical insurance

Nearly one in five people in the South East (GOR) had private medical insurance in 1995-96 compared with one in 20 in Scotland and one in 25 in Wales.

(Table 7.7)

Smoking

On average, the heaviest smokers are in Scotland and Northern Ireland.

(Table 7.8)

Eating habits

In 1994, nearly two thirds of people in the South West ate fruit on at least five days a week compared with just under half in the North West.

(Table 7.10)

Cancer registration

Lung cancer registration rates are highest in Scotland, closely followed by the Northern and the Mersey Regional Health Authorities areas, and lowest in the East Anglian and the South Western RHA areas.

(Table 7.15)

Death rates

Allowing for the age structure of the population, Scotland had the highest death rates in 1995 for all causes of death while the South and West and the Anglia and Oxford Regional Health Authority areas had the lowest.

(Table 7.16)

Waiting lists

At the end of September 1996, the West Midlands NHS region had the lowest proportion of patients waiting more than 12 months for admission to an NHS hospital.

(Table 7.17)

Hospital beds

The West Midlands Regional Health Authority area had the highest rate of throughput per hospital bed in 1995-96 of all the RHAs in England, and North Thames the lowest.

(Table 7.18)

GP list sizes

Within England, the average GP list size in 1995 ranged from just over 2,000 in the North West Thames Regional Health Authority area to just over 1,700 in the South and West RHA area.

(Table 7.21)

Introduction

T he regional breakdown within England for many of the tables in this chapter is the Regional Health Authority (RHA) areas. On 1 April 1994 there was a reorganisation of the then 14 RHAs to form eight. From 1 April 1996 the eight RHAs were replaced by NHS Regional Office areas involving some minor boundary changes. Some of the statistics in this edition relate to the original 14 RHAs, but most relate to the April 1994 structure. Maps of the both these structures appear on page 214 of the Technical notes. Due to differences in the collection of health statistics across the United Kingdom, it is not always possible to show national totals.

There are a wide range of data on health-related behaviour, morbidity and mortality available. Some of these are from administrative sources, for example registrations of deaths, notifications of certain diseases and hospital records, whilst others are from household surveys. Surveys are important because they can also cover individuals who are not in contact with health care services and can cover other inter-related factors such has lifestyle, housing conditions and local environment which can effect a person's health.

Tables 7.14 and 7.16 show death rates by cause. The rates have been adjusted to take account of the differences in age structures across the regions, a process known as age-standardisation. The method used for the tables in this edition of *Regional Trends* is standardisation to the mid-1991 population estimates for the United Kingdom. Standardisation is carried out separately for males and females, using the actual age structure of the UK population for each. Thus in Table 7.16 it is possible to compare standardised rates for different conditions for each gender separately, but not possible to compare male and female rates. To be able to do this there is a second methodology: standardisation to the European Standard Population. This is the same for both males and females and so standardised rates can be compared for each gender and between males and females. The European Standard, although artificial, is particularly useful for international comparisons and looking at trends. The effect of standardising to the European Standard Population compared with the UK population is to reduce the death rates, significantly in the case of females. This is because the European Standard Population does not accurately reflect the number of elderly in the UK population, particularly elderly women. As most deaths are associated with old age, this under-representation reduces rates for men by around 10 per cent and for women by around 45 per cent compared with those standardised to the UK population. Tables 7.14 and 7.16 standardised to the European Standard Population are available from the Regional Reporting Branch of the Office for National Statistics.

Most people required to wait for admission to hospital are admitted within a few months, but about half of patients (excluding live births) treated in hospitals are emergency cases and do not come from the waiting lists. The waiting list figures in Table 7.17 represent a snapshot of those waiting at September 1996 and how long they had been waiting at that time.

It is open to District Health Authorities and GP fundholders to purchase healthcare from any Trust hospital if, for example, the treatment is thought to be better or the cost is lower or the waiting time shorter. Tables 7.18 and 7.23 look at hospital activity from two perspectives: patients (including private patients) treated in NHS hospitals in the region and NHS healthcare purchased for patients living in the region. The tables thus illustrate the difference between the region providing the treatment and the region of residence of the patient (although there are definitional differences between the two tables to bear in mind also). Another example of this is Table 7.12 which shows the number of AIDs cases. While the United Kingdom totals for region of treatment and region of residence are the same, the regional distributions are different.

7.1 Population and vital statistics: Regional Health Authority areas, 1995

Thousands and rates

	Population aged (mid-year estimates) (thousands)					Vital statistics (rates)				
	0-15	16-64	65-84	85 or over	All ages	Live births[1]	Still births[2]	Deaths[3]	Perinatal mortality[4]	Infant mortality[5]
United Kingdom	12,105.8	37,275.0	8,180.9	1,044.1	58,605.8	60.1	5.6	10.9	8.9	6.2
Northern and Yorkshire	1,384.0	4,208.5	942.5	114.2	6,649.2	59.1	5.8	11.2	9.3	6.6
North West	1,410.3	4,167.4	920.2	115.6	6,613.5	60.0	5.4	11.6	8.6	6.6
Trent	973.0	3,052.1	689.1	82.1	4,796.3	59.1	5.9	11.0	9.6	6.6
West Midlands	1,122.2	3,360.8	739.1	84.5	5,306.5	62.2	5.9	10.8	10.1	7.0
Anglia and Oxford	1,110.3	3,420.9	694.1	90.0	5,315.3	59.7	4.8	9.5	7.3	5.2
North Thames	1,414.1	4,488.3	854.2	115.7	6,872.3	63.1	6.0	9.7	9.0	5.6
South Thames	1,345.4	4,322.0	968.6	145.4	6,781.5	61.1	5.5	11.1	8.6	5.7
South and West	1,288.7	4,104.1	1,030.3	145.7	6,568.8	58.2	4.7	11.4	7.6	5.5
England	10,048.0	31,124.1	6,838.0	893.3	48,903.4	60.4	5.5	10.8	8.8	6.1
Wales	605.0	1,806.4	450.6	54.9	2,916.8	60.4	5.1	12.1	7.8	6.1
Scotland	1,035.8	3,323.3	700.1	77.4	5,136.6	54.5	6.6	11.8	9.6	6.2
Northern Ireland	417.0	1,021.2	192.1	18.6	1,649.0	66.8	6.1	9.3	10.4	7.1

1 Per 1,000 women aged 15-44.
2 Per 1,000 live and still births. A still birth relates to a baby born dead after 24 completed weeks gestation or more.
3 Per 1,000 population.
4 Still births and deaths of infants under 1 week of age per 1,000 live and still births.
5 Deaths of infants under 1 year of age per 1,000 live births.

Source: Office for National Statistics; General Register Office for Scotland;
Northern Ireland Statistics and Research Agency

7.2 Still births, perinatal mortality and infant mortality

Rates

	Still births[1]				Perinatal mortality[2]				Infant mortality[3]		
	1981	1993[4]	1993[4]	1995	1981	1993[4]	1993[4]	1995	1981	1993	1995
United Kingdom	6.6	4.4	5.7	5.6	12.0	7.6	9.0	8.9	11.2	6.3	6.2
North East	7.5	4.6	5.9	6.8	12.6	7.9	9.2	10.4	10.4	6.7	6.7
North West (GOR) & Merseyside	7.0	4.5	5.8	5.5	12.7	7.7	9.0	8.6	11.3	6.5	6.6
North West (GOR)	7.0	4.5	5.9	5.7	12.6	7.9	9.3	8.9	11.1	6.8	6.6
Merseyside	6.9	4.7	5.6	4.6	12.8	7.0	8.0	7.2	12.0	5.4	6.4
Yorkshire and the Humber	7.8	4.6	5.9	5.4	13.5	8.0	9.4	9.2	12.1	7.3	6.9
East Midlands	6.2	3.9	5.4	5.5	11.4	7.2	8.7	8.6	11.0	6.6	5.8
West Midlands	7.0	4.4	6.0	5.9	12.9	8.4	9.9	10.1	11.7	7.1	7.0
Eastern	5.5	3.9	5.2	5.2	10.0	6.8	8.1	7.7	9.7	5.4	5.1
London	6.3	4.9	6.1	6.3	10.3	8.2	9.5	9.7	10.7	6.4	6.3
South East (GOR)	5.8	4.0	5.4	4.9	10.5	7.0	8.3	7.7	10.3	5.3	5.2
South West	6.3	4.0	5.0	4.6	10.8	6.9	7.9	7.4	10.4	5.8	5.2
England	6.5	4.3	5.7	5.5	11.7	7.6	8.9	8.8	10.9	6.3	6.1
Wales	7.3	4.5	5.8	5.1	14.1	7.0	8.3	7.8	12.6	5.5	6.1
Scotland	6.3	4.8	6.4	6.6	11.6	8.0	9.6	9.6	11.3	6.5	6.2
Northern Ireland	8.7	4.1	5.2	6.1	15.3	7.7	8.8	10.4	13.2	7.1	7.1

1 Rate per 1,000 live and still births.
2 Still births and deaths of infants under 1 week of age per 1,000 live and still births.
3 Deaths of infants under 1 year of age per 1,000 live births.
4 On 1 October 1992 the legal definition of a still birth was altered from a baby born dead after 28 completed weeks gestation or more to one born dead after 24 weeks gestation or more. Figures are given on both the old and new definitions for continuity/comparison.

Source: Office for National Statistics; General Register Office for Scotland;
Northern Ireland Statistics and Research Agency

7.3 Life expectation at birth: by gender, 1992[1]

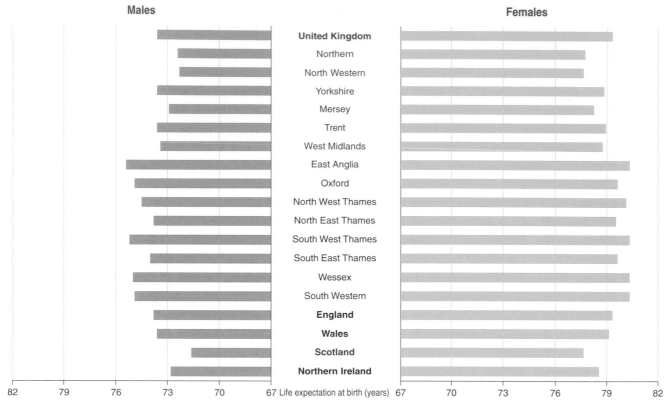

Males | **Females**

United Kingdom
Northern
North Western
Yorkshire
Mersey
Trent
West Midlands
East Anglia
Oxford
North West Thames
North East Thames
South West Thames
South East Thames
Wessex
South Western
England
Wales
Scotland
Northern Ireland

82   79   76   73   70   67   Life expectation at birth (years)   67   70   73   76   79   82

1 Expectation of life is the average total number of years which a person could be expected to live from birth if they experienced the mortality rates of 1992 throughout their lifetime. See Technical notes.

Source: Government Actuary's Department

7.4 Consultations with an NHS general medical practitioner[1] and reports of limiting long-standing illness[2]: by age, 1995-96[3]

Percentages

	Persons who consulted an NHS general medical practitioner						Persons who reported limiting long-standing illness					
	0-4	5-15	16-44	45-64	65 or over	All ages	0-4	5-15	16-44	45-64	65 or over	All ages
United Kingdom	21	11	14	16	21	16	4	8	12	27	42	19
North East	17	16	12	15	19	15	2	12	10	35	44	21
North West (GOR) & Merseyside	22	8	15	19	27	17	3	7	14	33	43	21
Yorkshire and the Humber	20	7	13	18	23	15	5	10	11	27	44	20
East Midlands	17	9	14	17	24	16	3	7	13	25	39	18
West Midlands	24	9	15	16	15	15	7	10	13	28	42	21
Eastern	17	11	14	13	21	15	5	8	12	22	41	17
London	23	12	13	16	17	15	2	10	12	28	41	19
South East (GOR)	22	14	14	15	18	15	2	6	10	20	35	15
South West	20	12	12	12	21	14	7	8	13	23	42	19
England	20	11	14	16	21	15	4	8	12	26	41	19
Wales	23	8	17	16	26	17	7	6	12	33	51	22
Scotland	29	13	14	17	25	17	4	7	12	29	42	20
Northern Ireland	22	10	14	19	23	16	6	6	12	30	52	19

1 In the 14 days before interview.
2 See Technical notes.
3 Care must be taken in interpreting the data in this table as some cells are based on sample sizes of less than 100.

Source: General Household Survey, Office for National Statistics;
Continuous Household Survey, Northern Ireland Statistics and Research Agency

7.5 Dental attendance, 1995-96

Percentages

| | Adults who have regular check-ups[1] | | Children who had visited a dentist[2] | |
	Males	Females	Within the previous 6 months	12 months ago or longer
United Kingdom	47	61	79	5
North East	41	60	85	7
North West (GOR) & Merseyside	45	61	80	3
Yorkshire and the Humber	44	59	83	4
East Midlands	51	61	81	6
West Midlands	48	62	76	5
Eastern	50	64	81	3
London	35	46	68	11
South East (GOR)	49	64	81	4
South West	53	68	82	5
England	46	60	79	5
Wales	55	62	78	6
Scotland	47	64	78	3
Northern Ireland	42	56	72	7

1 Adults with some natural teeth.
2 For a check-up or to get used to the dentist. Base excludes children who had never visited a dentist.

Source: General Household Survey, Office for National Statistics; Continuous Household Survey, Northern Ireland Statistics and Research Agency

7.6 Hearing difficulties: by gender[1], 1995-96

Percentages

| | Males | | Females | |
	Difficulty with hearing, no aid	Use hearing aids	Difficulty with hearing, no aid	Use hearing aids
United Kingdom	15	3	10	3
North East	19	5	11	3
North West (GOR) & Merseyside	15	4	9	4
Yorkshire and the Humber	18	3	13	4
East Midlands	15	3	10	2
West Midlands	16	3	9	3
Eastern	15	2	9	2
London	14	2	10	2
South East (GOR)	14	3	10	3
South West	14	4	9	4
England	15	3	10	3
Wales	18	6	12	3
Scotland	17	4	10	4
Northern Ireland	13	2	10	2

1 People aged 16 or over.

Source: General Household Survey, Office for National Statistics; Continuous Household Survey, Northern Ireland Statistics and Research Agency

7.7 Private medical insurance: by age, 1995-96

Percentages

| | Percentages of people with private medical insurance cover aged | | | | |
	0-15	16-44	45-64	65 or over	All ages
Great Britain	8	10	12	5	9
North East	6	7	9	2	7
North West (GOR) & Merseyside	5	8	11	3	7
Yorkshire and the Humber	5	7	12	3	7
East Midlands	9	10	10	7	9
West Midlands	6	8	11	8	8
Eastern	8	10	12	6	10
London	10	13	11	6	11
South East (GOR)	17	18	22	11	18
South West	6	9	10	5	8
England	8	11	13	6	10
Wales	2	2	8	1	4
Scotland	4	5	6	2	5

Source: General Household Survey, Office for National Statistics

7.8 Cigarette smoking amongst people aged 16 or over: by gender, 1994-95

Percentages and numbers

	Percentage of people who smoke cigarettes		Smokers' average weekly consumption (numbers)		Percentage of smokers with daily consumption of		
	Males	Females	Males	Females	1 - 9 cigarettes	10 - 19 cigarettes	20 or more cigarettes
Standard Statistical Regions							
United Kingdom	28	26	113	96	25	40	36
North	29	27	120	100	24	39	37
North West (SSR)	26	28	114	103	22	40	38
Yorkshire and Humberside	29	28	115	99	23	41	36
East Midlands	28	24	111	101	23	39	38
West Midlands	25	23	119	97	22	41	36
East Anglia	27	21	104	92	25	41	34
South East (SSR)	29	25	109	89	29	40	31
Greater London	32	26	110	88	29	40	31
Rest of South East	27	25	108	90	29	40	31
South West	27	22	104	90	30	37	33
England	28	25	111	95	26	40	34
Wales	28	27	105	90	30	37	33
Scotland	31	29	131	111	16	38	46
Northern Ireland	29	27	128	106	18	39	43

Source: General Household Survey, Office for National Statistics;
Continuous Household Survey, Northern Ireland Statistics and Research Agency

7.9 Alcohol consumption[1] amongst people aged 16 or over: by gender, 1994-95

Percentages

	Consumption levels of males (units per week)				Consumption levels of females (units per week)			
	Non-drinker	Under 1 - 10	11 - 21	22 or more	Non-drinker	Under 1 - 7	8 -14	15 or more
Standard Statistical Regions								
United Kingdom	8	44	22	26	14	58	15	13
North	7	37	25	31	18	53	15	13
North West (SSR)	6	41	23	30	13	58	16	13
Yorkshire and Humberside	9	41	20	29	12	55	17	15
East Midlands	6	45	21	28	11	60	15	13
West Midlands	7	42	22	28	16	59	14	12
East Anglia	7	50	22	22	10	63	13	14
South East (SSR)	8	46	21	25	14	58	14	14
Greater London	12	43	20	24	20	54	14	13
Rest of South East	5	48	22	25	11	60	15	14
South West	5	49	23	23	11	62	15	12
England	7	44	22	27	14	58	15	13
Wales	10	40	23	27	15	58	16	11
Scotland	7	44	24	24	13	61	17	9
Northern Ireland	22	37	20	21	33	48	12	7

1 Comparative consumption levels are different for males and females. See Technical notes.

Source: General Household Survey, Office for National Statistics;
Continuous Household Survey, Northern Ireland Statistics and Research Agency

7.10 Eating habits amongst people aged 16 or over, 1994[1]

Percentages

	Ate vegetables or salad[2]	Usually drank skimmed milk	Ate fruit[2]	Ate high fibre cereal	Usually ate whole-meal bread	Used solid cooking fat	Ate confec-tionery[2]	Took sugar in tea/coffee	Added salt in cooking
Northern and Yorkshire	71	12	52	39	27	19	20	34	65
North West	69	17	49	42	26	14	19	37	69
Trent	77	15	53	43	23	20	23	37	68
Anglia and Oxford	83	16	59	45	26	14	24	36	66
West Midlands	77	17	55	41	21	18	22	40	73
North Thames	82	14	59	40	26	9	19	38	69
South Thames	83	16	59	42	27	8	21	33	69
South and West	82	15	63	41	29	11	22	32	69
England	78	15	56	42	26	14	21	36	68

1 See Technical notes.
2 On at least five days a week.

Source: Health Survey for England, Department of Health

7.11 Drug addicts notified[1]

Numbers and percentages

	All addicts notified[2]					Of which new addicts (percentages)				
	1991	1992	1993	1994	1995	1991	1992	1993	1994	1995
United Kingdom	20,820	24,703	27,976	33,952	37,164	38	39	41	40	40
North East	125	168	418	399	621	50	52	53	49	56
North West (GOR) & Merseyside	6,085	6,837	7,461	8,593	8,830	37	36	37	33	33
North West (GOR)	3,106	3,713	4,608	5,636	6,463	44	44	42	39	37
Merseyside	2,979	3,124	2,853	2,957	2,367	30	27	28	23	22
Yorkshire and the Humber	953	1,557	2,205	3,228	4,245	49	59	55	52	52
East Midlands	404	663	699	781	971	37	34	40	43	43
West Midlands	966	1,160	1,218	1,511	1,812	37	37	49	43	49
Eastern	1,159	1,324	1,416	1,656	1,944	30	34	32	33	40
London	6,423	7,011	7,682	8,321	8,307	37	35	37	34	35
South East (GOR)	1,499	1,953	2,044	2,476	2,814	39	40	43	42	39
South West	1,147	1,567	1,904	2,524	3,153	42	44	49	47	43
England	18,761	22,240	25,047	29,489	32,697	38	38	41	38	39
Wales	528	579	659	735	886	42	41	47	39	41
Scotland	1,499	1,849	2,220	3,691	3,542	48	47	47	49	41
Northern Ireland	32	35	50	37	39	28	54	52	62	56

1 Number of addicts notified throughout the year. Under the *Misuse of Drugs (Notification of and Supply to addicts) Regulations 1973*, doctors were required to notify the Chief Medical Officer at the Home Office with particulars of persons whom they considered, or suspected, to be addicted to any of the 14 controlled drugs.
2 Cumulative register.

Source: Home Office

7.12 Exposure category of HIV-1 infected persons and of AIDS cases: cumulative totals to end-1996

Numbers

	Sexual intercourse			Injecting drug use		Blood[2]	Other[3]/ undetermined		Total cases reported to 31 December 1996[4]
	Between men[1]	Between men and women							
		Males	Females	Males	Females		Males	Females	
HIV-1 infected persons: region of report									
United Kingdom	17,292	2,484	2,938	2,049	938	1,434	908	340	28,447
Northern and Yorkshire	599	115	110	78	39	166	21	6	1,136
North West	1,044	129	104	77	42	173	58	9	1,634
Trent	401	96	73	49	17	77	14	12	739
West Midlands	492	81	79	43	16	162	22	7	902
Anglia and Oxford	515	124	134	104	38	151	20	8	1,096
North Thames	9,644	1075	1,382	569	307	255	522	175	13,981
South Thames	2,714	484	670	269	113	182	150	78	4,664
South and West	774	119	106	82	23	83	30	15	1,235
England	16,183	2,223	2,658	1,271	595	1,246	837	310	25,387
Wales	252	61	37	16	4	59	26	4	459
Scotland	769	188	223	759	336	109	44	26	2,454
Northern Ireland	88	12	20	3	3	20	1	0	147
AIDS cases: region of report									
United Kingdom[5]	9,786	1,066	942	589	250	737	228	128	13,726
Northern and Yorkshire	303	48	31	18	9	101	7	4	521
North West	538	58	32	32	10	88	14	5	777
Trent	209	39	25	17	5	33	5	5	338
West Midlands	211	32	23	5	5	48	6	1	331
Anglia and Oxford	319	49	40	44	11	86	10	2	561
North Thames	5,793	491	457	172	82	123	107	64	7,289
South Thames	1,460	208	223	75	28	106	49	27	2,176
South and West	452	56	36	16	10	63	11	7	651
England	9,285	981	867	379	160	648	209	115	12,644
Wales	108	13	10	2	2	29	6	2	172
Scotland	341	67	58	207	86	50	11	11	831
Northern Ireland	48	5	7	1	2	9	1	0	73
AIDS cases: region of residence									
United Kingdom[6]	9,786	1,066	942	589	250	737	228	128	13,726
Northern and Yorkshire	319	45	30	16	8	105	6	4	533
North West	537	52	27	32	10	82	14	5	759
Trent	223	42	28	16	6	32	5	5	357
West Midlands	214	30	21	4	5	57	8	1	340
Anglia and Oxford	377	52	42	49	13	62	10	3	608
North Thames	4,031	409	389	142	70	92	72	34	5,239
South Thames	2,651	214	249	89	35	102	50	37	3,427
South and West	513	55	40	16	9	69	13	8	723
England	8,919	900	829	367	156	609	178	97	12,055
Wales	128	15	12	2	2	34	5	2	200
Scotland	340	64	55	205	85	49	11	9	818
Northern Ireland	43	3	7	1	1	9	1	0	65

1 Includes men who had also injected drugs.
2 Blood/blood factor and tissue recipients.
3 Includes mother to infant transmission.
4 Components may not add to totals as in some cases gender was not recorded.
5 Includes 6 cases reported in the Channel Islands.
6 Includes people whose region of residence was either the Channel Islands, the Isle of Man, abroad or unknown.

Source: Public Health Laboratory Service, Communicable Disease Surveillance Centre;
Scottish Centre for Infection and Environmental Health

7.13 Notifications of measles[1]

Rates per 100,000 population

	1985	1986	1987	1988	1989	1990	1991	1992	1993	1994	1995
United Kingdom	185	159	81	159	54	27	20	21	21	40	15
North East	230	174	125	99	73	55	18	24	21	38	18
North West (GOR) & Merseyside	196	219	94	187	65	31	22	23	21	42	15
North West (GOR)	173	247	77	185	72	31	21	23	21	47	15
Merseyside	277	117	158	193	39	29	24	22	20	23	14
Yorkshire and the Humber	199	214	97	240	87	37	30	26	27	42	20
East Midlands	140	269	54	151	46	24	17	18	20	25	12
West Midlands	200	169	105	327	59	32	25	20	21	25	15
Eastern	208	184	60	149	40	22	17	19	17	39	15
London	192	77	62	132	32	20	15	15	16	26	14
South East (GOR)	163	93	94	108	41	18	15	16	14	22	11
South West	167	140	76	112	31	19	12	28	12	19	11
England	187	163	84	168	51	27	19	20	19	30	14
Wales	334	173	82	205	65	21	19	16	22	56	18
Scotland	89	138	53	44	66	39	33	34	37	121	25
Northern Ireland	178	69	77	151	92	21	21	19	30	58	16

1 See Technical notes.

Source: Office for National Statistics; Information and Statistics Division, Scottish Health Service;
Department of Health and Social Services, Northern Ireland

7.14 Cervical and breast cancer: screening and age-adjusted death rates

Percentages and rates

	Cervical screening programme percentage of target population screened at 31 March each year[1]			Age-adjusted death rates from cervical cancer[2]		Breast screening programmes percentage of women invited for screening who attended[3]			Age-adjusted death rates from breast cancer[2]	
	1992	1995	1996	1991	1995	1991-92	1994-95	1995-96	1991	1995
United Kingdom	..	..	..	8.4	6.5	72	77	76	68.7	61.3
Northern and Yorkshire	84	87	87	9.6	7.3	74	80	77	63.7	55.6
North West	83	85	84	10.9	8.0	71	78	77	65.5	59.6
Trent	88	89	89	9.6	6.2	78	80	81	69.7	64.9
West Midlands	84	87	86	7.7	7.5	72	79	78	72.9	63.5
Anglia and Oxford	85	88	87	8.0	5.6	79	83	82	71.8	66.1
North Thames	65	77	78	7.0	5.8	59	68	66	71.8	62.9
South Thames	74	84	84	6.8	5.8	69	72	74	70.7	58.6
South and West	87	87	86	6.5	6.1	77	81	79	70.7	61.5
England	80	85	85	8.2	6.5	72	77	76	69.4	61.2
Wales	79	84	84	11.4	6.8	72	80	77	64.9	60.6
Scotland	80	81	83	8.8	7.3	72	69	72	65.3	62.7
Northern Ireland	..	..	..	6.9	3.3	63	74	72	65.9	59.9

1 For England figures relate to women aged 20-64 years for 1992, 25-64 years for 1995 and 1996. For Wales figures relate to women aged 20-64. The calculation of data for England and Wales involves subtracting the 'number of women with recall ceased' (women who as a result of surgery etc do not require screening) from the target population. For Scotland, figures relate to women aged 20-59 years. In 1992 information was not collected centrally and is an estimate based on local board data. For 1995 and 1996 the figures relate to the percentage of women aged 20-59 screened in the previous 5.5 years, as at 31 December for 1994 and 1995 respectively. Medically ineligible women are excluded from the calculated figure. See Technical notes.
2 Deaths per 100,000 women aged 20 or over. Standardised to the1991 United Kingdom mid-year estimate population. See Technical notes.
3 Women aged 50-64 years. Figures for Scotland exclude early recalls.

Source: Office for National Statistics; Department of Health; Welsh Office; General Register Office for Scotland;
Information and Statistics Division, Scottish Health Service; Northern Ireland Statistics and Research Agency;
Department of Health and Social Services, Northern Ireland

7.15 Incidence of lung cancer [1,2]: by gender

Rates and thousands

	Registrations of lung cancer (rates per 100,000 population)											Total registrations (thousands)
	1981	1982	1983	1984	1985	1986	1987	1988	1989	1990	1991	1991[3]
Males												
Northern	132.0	131.8	125.0	125.7	125.6	124.0	116.7	119.9	118.5	116.6	114.0	1.9
North Western	127.2	129.7	123.7	125.1	123.4	119.2	114.5	110.1	113.9	105.9	102.8	2.1
Yorkshire	109.8	115.0	110.6	106.5	112.1	100.5	102.6	106.2	101.7	93.8	94.9	1.9
Mersey	125.2	133.7	130.3	122.8	126.8	123.6	115.3	114.9	115.4	120.1	113.2	1.4
Trent	108.6	104.8	110.0	106.8	104.3	101.1	98.5	96.5	91.2	84.2	84.5	2.2
West Midlands	113.5	114.3	118.5	111.2	110.5	105.4	99.0	98.8	96.0	91.9	94.8	2.7
East Anglian	93.0	95.1	90.8	87.0	91.9	80.4	83.9	81.3	77.6	74.7	69.1	0.9
Oxford	102.3	100.1	95.9	94.5	97.8	91.1	87.4	89.6	80.7	84.6	84.4	1.0
North East Thames	112.4	127.0	115.0	115.9	120.5	113.1	111.6	109.4	97.8	93.4	92.9	1.8
North West Thames	97.8	76.5	87.0	69.9	106.2	93.8	91.8	95.4	89.1	84.9	81.8	1.4
South West Thames	109.5	98.0	99.8	96.9	99.4	90.9	89.4	83.4	76.0	85.2	78.3	1.3
South East Thames	111.3	106.6	109.2	103.5	106.7	98.6	100.0	100.7	88.2	92.5	86.5	1.8
Wessex	101.6	94.4	97.9	91.9	94.3	83.8	83.5	88.0	82.4	84.0	77.6	1.4
South Western	93.4	92.2	87.1	81.1	83.8	74.1	77.5	73.1	71.6	70.8	72.5	1.5
England	110.5	109.2	108.3	103.9	108.0	100.7	98.6	98.2	93.3	91.5	89.4	23.1
Wales[4]	104.0	105.0	86.2	100.6	106.4	96.7	98.3	101.6	113.0	94.8	..	1.5
Scotland	135.8	132.4	136.1	137.8	133.1	126.7	128.6	122.5	120.0	117.2	118.4	3.1
Northern Ireland[5]	87.2	91.5	94.3	93.3	96.6	97.7	94.1	95.0	101.0	92.2	88.5	0.6
Females												
Northern	33.6	36.9	35.4	41.2	38.3	40.2	42.7	46.2	46.1	47.4	48.5	1.0
North Western	32.2	34.4	34.0	39.2	37.3	36.9	36.7	41.0	39.3	39.7	38.0	1.0
Yorkshire	28.4	30.9	30.4	32.7	30.8	33.2	35.4	35.2	36.1	36.3	35.0	0.9
Mersey	37.2	40.9	36.1	36.0	39.8	44.0	39.6	45.1	45.6	47.9	44.4	0.7
Trent	28.8	27.2	28.7	29.3	29.3	29.6	29.0	30.0	27.6	28.3	28.6	0.9
West Midlands	24.5	24.4	26.3	26.1	27.5	27.7	27.8	29.3	29.3	27.0	32.1	1.1
East Anglian	25.9	22.8	25.2	21.0	24.9	26.4	25.9	26.7	26.5	25.3	23.9	0.4
Oxford	28.8	28.9	26.4	30.7	30.9	30.4	31.9	29.0	26.9	28.6	30.1	0.5
North East Thames	28.3	31.4	32.8	32.5	37.9	31.6	33.7	36.9	33.8	33.9	32.2	0.8
North West Thames	27.6	22.1	28.0	21.2	35.7	31.3	32.0	35.2	32.5	32.1	33.6	0.8
South West Thames	29.4	29.3	29.1	29.8	31.3	29.7	31.0	29.0	26.9	29.4	30.2	0.7
South East Thames	28.6	30.2	30.1	30.6	33.3	32.9	32.0	33.2	33.4	34.4	31.6	0.9
Wessex	26.4	25.6	28.2	24.9	30.1	26.8	29.1	30.4	28.2	26.5	25.4	0.6
South Western	24.7	23.1	23.3	23.9	23.6	22.4	26.2	22.8	25.0	25.1	24.5	0.7
England	28.8	29.1	29.7	30.1	32.2	31.5	32.3	33.5	32.6	32.8	32.7	11.0
Wales[4]	27.2	28.5	23.9	29.8	30.7	27.6	46.6	33.3	36.9	33.0	..	0.7
Scotland	38.5	41.0	40.1	44.1	45.1	44.1	46.0	46.1	46.2	50.0	49.1	1.7
Northern Ireland[5]	25.0	24.4	25.7	28.4	23.0	30.8	27.1	31.4	28.5	33.0	28.7	0.3

1 Figures relate to malignant neoplasms of the trachea, bronchus and lung registered by 31 December 1995 for England, Wales and Northern Ireland. Registered by 12 September 1996 for Scotland.
2 Cancer registration rates are standardised to the European Standard Population for the purpose of comparison with other European countries.
3 1990 for Wales.
4 The Welsh Cancer and Intelligence Surveillance Unit are in the process of validating these data and they may be subject to amendment in the future.
5 All rates for Northern Ireland are likely to be underestimates due to incompleteness of the registry.

Source: Office for National Statistics; Information and Statistics Division, Scottish Health Service; Northern Ireland Cancer Registry

7.16 Age-adjusted mortality rates[1]: by cause[2] and gender, 1995

Rates per 100,000 population

	All circulatory diseases			All respiratory diseases			All injuries and poisonings				
	Total	Ischaemic heart disease	Cerebro-vascular disease	Total	Bronchitis and allied conditions	Cancer[3]	Total	Road traffic accidents	Suicides and open verdicts	All other causes	All causes
Males											
United Kingdom	442	279	84	150	60	279	42	9	17	123	1,037
Northern and Yorkshire	469	304	89	153	62	294	44	9	19	121	1,080
North West	485	313	90	177	75	303	45	9	19	123	1,133
Trent	443	284	84	154	60	277	38	10	15	123	1,034
West Midlands	470	292	93	156	67	282	38	9	15	130	1,076
Anglia and Oxford	385	235	73	134	49	252	40	11	16	113	923
North Thames	403	257	69	157	60	259	37	6	15	128	985
South Thames	401	242	74	150	58	270	35	7	15	118	974
South and West	399	248	76	120	45	255	38	9	16	116	927
England	431	271	81	150	59	274	39	9	16	121	1,015
Wales	466	297	88	161	71	285	49	11	21	122	1,083
Scotland	520	329	116	146	63	322	59	12	25	147	1,195
Northern Ireland	508	331	97	178	57	277	61	12	14	105	1,129
Females											
United Kingdom	465	225	140	174	42	250	23	4	6	167	1,078
Northern and Yorkshire	480	246	143	181	51	261	23	4	6	174	1,120
North West	502	254	146	199	57	260	21	4	6	162	1,144
Trent	464	233	136	172	43	250	22	4	5	172	1,079
West Midlands	487	231	146	167	40	248	23	3	5	173	1,097
Anglia and Oxford	417	193	129	164	33	234	23	4	5	167	1,005
North Thames	413	202	115	188	41	250	20	3	5	170	1,041
South Thames	426	193	124	170	36	235	18	3	6	152	1,001
South and West	417	194	131	143	29	232	21	3	6	170	982
England	450	218	133	173	41	246	21	4	5	167	1,057
Wales	494	237	144	176	47	247	26	4	5	158	1,101
Scotland	576	278	197	166	51	288	36	5	8	180	1,245
Northern Ireland	545	287	163	235	45	235	27	4	5	123	1,166
All persons											
United Kingdom	455	253	112	163	51	265	32	6	11	146	1,062
Northern and Yorkshire	475	275	117	168	56	270	33	7	12	148	1,102
North West	494	283	119	188	65	281	33	6	12	143	1,138
Trent	457	260	111	165	52	266	30	7	10	148	1,065
West Midlands	481	263	120	163	54	266	30	6	10	152	1,092
Anglia and Oxford	405	217	102	151	42	246	31	8	10	141	975
North Thames	410	231	93	174	51	256	28	4	10	149	1,019
South Thames	415	218	100	161	47	253	27	5	10	135	990
South and West	411	222	104	133	38	245	29	6	11	144	962
England	443	246	108	162	50	261	30	6	11	145	1,041
Wales	482	268	117	169	59	267	37	8	13	141	1,096
Scotland	547	302	157	156	57	304	47	8	16	164	1,217
Northern Ireland	526	308	131	207	51	255	44	8	9	114	1,147

1 Rates standardised to the mid-1991 United Kingdom population. See Technical notes.
2 Deaths at ages under 28 days occurring in England and Wales are not assigned an underlying cause.
3 Malignant neoplasms only.

Source: Office for National Statistics; General Register Office for Scotland;
Northern Ireland Statistics and Research Agency

7.17 NHS hospital waiting lists[1]: by patients' region of residence[2], at 30 September 1996[3]

Thousands and percentages

	Ordinary admissions					Day case admissions				
		Months waited (percentages)			Patients admitted from the waiting list per month[4] (thousands)		Months waited (percentages)			Patients admitted from the waiting list per month[4] (thousands)
	Total waiting (thousands)	Less than 6	6 but less than 12	12 or over		Total waiting (thousands)	Less than 6	6 but less than 12	12 or over	
Patients' region of residence[2]										
Northern and Yorkshire	65.5	70.7	26.6	2.7	17.6	69.3	79.4	19.5	1.1	22.4
North West	78.6	71.3	27.8	0.9	17.0	91.1	80.2	19.6	0.2	27.3
Trent	56.4	72.4	23.8	3.8	9.2	50.1	78.2	19.4	2.4	11.6
West Midlands	38.0	86.8	13.0	0.2	10.3	46.1	90.0	9.9	0.1	14.6
Anglia and Oxford	58.3	73.0	25.6	1.4	12.5	50.4	80.6	18.7	0.7	15.2
North Thames	77.6	70.8	26.8	2.4	15.9	74.6	80.7	18.2	1.1	25.8
South Thames	73.6	71.3	27.0	1.7	16.3	77.8	80.0	19.4	0.6	22.8
South and West	68.7	77.6	20.5	1.9	15.3	61.9	84.6	14.8	0.6	19.9
England	516.9	73.4	24.6	1.9	114.1	521.2	81.4	17.8	0.8	159.6
Wales[3]	41.1	..	..	11.6	11.9	26.1	..	..	5.8	16.8
Scotland	46.1	81.9	16.7	1.4	21.5	33.79	89.4	9.9	0.7	20.6
Northern Ireland	22.9	61.5	25.9	12.6	5.9	18.4	71.2	20.2	8.6	7.2

1 Comprises NHS patients on waiting lists but excludes private patients. Figures exclude patients undergoing a series of repeat admissions and those who are temporarily suspended from the waiting list for medical or social reasons.
2 Region of treatment for Wales, Scotland and Northern Ireland.
3 Figures for Wales relate to 31 March 1997.
4 Average for the three months ending 30 September 1996 for England, for the 12 months ending 30 September 1996 for Scotland and Northern Ireland, and for the six months ending 31 March 1997 for Wales. The figures relate to admissions from waiting lists plus booked admissions.

Source: Department of Health; Welsh Office; Information and Statistics Division, Scottish Health Service; Department of Health and Social Services, Northern Ireland

7.18 Hospital activity[1], year ending 31 March 1996

	In-patients (all specialties)				Average length of stay in hospital[2] (mean) (days)				Total accident and emergency attend-ances (thousands)
	Average daily available beds per 1,000 population	Cases[1] treated per available bed	Cases[1] treated per 1,000 population	Finished consultant episodes[1] (thousands)	Non-psychiatric specialties	Psychiatric specialties	Day cases (thousands)	Total out-patient attend-ances[3] (thousands)	
United Kingdom	4.6	..	..	..	..	..	3,557	48,893	17,449
Northern and Yorkshire	4.6	40	184	1,224	6	125	415	5,749	2,010
North West	4.6	43	194	1,281	6	94	520	5,943	2,309
Trent	4.0	43	172	825	6	66	238	3,890	1,241
West Midlands	3.9	45	175	928	6	94	283	4,142	1,632
Anglia and Oxford	3.8	41	155	823	6	60	260	3,781	1,078
North Thames	4.4	37	165	1,132	7	202	410	6,519	2,088
South Thames	4.0	39	156	1,058	6	84	343	5,410	2,111
South and West	4.1	41	168	1,102	6	41	372	4,565	1,766
England[4]	4.2	41	171	8,379	6	94	2,845	40,118	14,234
Wales	5.5	32	177	516	7	60	262	2,570	996
Scotland	7.9	24	190	973	9	95	354	4,791	1,546
Northern Ireland	6.0	30	184	304	8	64	96	1,414	673

1 Finished consultant episodes in England. Data for Wales and Northern Ireland relate to discharges and deaths. Data for Scotland relate to discharges and deaths and transfers to other specialties within hospital. See Technical notes.
2 For England figures relate to 1994-95. The mean length of stay for psychiatric patients may be affected for some regions due to the closure and transfer of patients in long-stay hospitals to more appropriate accommodation.
3 Consultant out-patient attendances in Scotland.
4 Special Health Authorities are not shown separately but are included in England totals.

Source: Department of Health; Welsh Office; Information and Statistics Division, Scottish Health Service; Department of Health and Social Services, Northern Ireland

7.19 Pharmaceutical services[1],1991 and 1995[2]

	Prescription items dispensed (millions)[1]		Percentage of prescription items exempt from charge[3,4]		Number of prescription items per person		Average net ingredient cost[5] (£ per person)		Average net ingredient cost[5] (£ per prescription item)	
	1991	1995	1991	1995	1991	1995	1991	1995	1991	1995
United Kingdom	499.9	582.5	..	84.8	8.6	9.9	59.9	77.9	6.9	7.8
Northern	28.7	33.2	81.5	85.0	9.3	10.7	64.1	81.1	6.9	7.6
North Western	39.9	45.5	81.8	85.0	10.0	11.3	65.2	82.9	6.5	7.3
Yorkshire	33.6	38.6	81.0	84.4	9.1	10.3	59.6	75.9	6.5	7.3
Mersey	23.7	27.1	83.2	86.2	9.8	11.2	65.9	84.8	6.7	7.6
Trent	41.6	49.1	80.3	86.5	8.8	10.2	58.4	76.7	6.7	7.5
West Midlands	45.8	53.0	81.1	84.9	8.7	10.0	58.1	74.3	6.7	7.4
East Anglian	16.6	20.1	77.8	81.2	8.0	9.4	56.6	76.1	7.1	7.1
Oxford	17.7	20.9	74.3	78.6	6.9	7.9	52.6	66.1	7.6	8.3
North East Thames	30.1	35.3	80.5	85.1	7.9	9.2	56.2	70.6	7.1	7.7
North West Thames	25.6	29.8	76.9	82.0	7.3	8.4	53.7	72.0	7.3	8.6
South West Thames	21.6	25.0	76.7	81.2	7.2	8.3	54.6	71.6	7.5	8.7
South East Thames	29.8	34.9	79.9	84.4	8.0	9.3	55.8	74.1	6.9	7.9
Wessex	23.4	27.3	78.2	82.0	8.0	9.1	57.6	73.1	7.2	8.1
South Western	28.4	33.6	79.8	83.6	8.2	9.5	58.2	75.2	7.1	8.0
England	406.5	473.3	80.0	83.8	8.4	9.7	58.4	75.3	6.9	7.8
Wales	31.2	36.3	..	86.3	10.4	12.4	70.0	92.8	6.5	7.5
Scotland	46.0	53.0	85.6	89.0	9.0	10.3	65.7	86.9	7.3	8.4
Northern Ireland	16.2	19.9	90.7	94.0	9.9	12.1	81.3	100.7	8.2	8.3

1 Figures relate to NHS prescription items dispensed by community pharmacists, and appliance contractors, dispensing doctors and prescriptions submitted by prescribing doctors for items personally administered.
2 For Wales figures relate to 1991 and 1995-96. For Scotland figures relate to 1991-92 and 1995.
3 For England figures relate to items dispensed by community pharmacists and appliance contractors only. Items dispensed by dispensing doctors and personal administration are not analysed into exempt, non exempt or other categories and are therefore excluded. Personally administered items are free of charge.
4 Figures for the English regions, England and Wales exclude prescriptions for which prepayment certificates have been purchased. For Scotland and Northern Ireland they are included.
5 Net ingredient cost is the cost of medicines before any discounts and does not include any dispensing costs or fees. Figures for 1991 have been revalued to 1995 prices as estimated by the general index of retail prices.

Source: Department of Health; Welsh Office; Pharmacy Practice Division, Scottish Health Service; Central Services Agency, Northern Ireland

7.20 NHS Hospital and Community Health Service staff: by type of staff[1], 30 September 1995

Percentages and thousands

	Direct care staff (percentages)				Management and support staff (percentages)			Total staff[1] (=100%) (thousands)
	Medical and Dental[2]	Nursing, midwifery and health visiting[3]	Scientific, therapeutic and technical	All direct care staff	Adminis- tration[4] and estates	Other	All management and support staff	
Northern and Yorkshire	7.1	44.6	11.7	63.3	21.3	15.4	36.7	104.4
North West	7.1	47.0	12.4	66.4	20.2	13.3	33.6	106.2
Trent	6.6	43.9	12.2	62.7	21.2	16.1	37.3	75.0
West Midlands	6.6	43.5	12.1	62.2	22.0	15.8	37.9	79.0
Anglia and Oxford	7.0	45.7	12.3	65.0	21.7	13.3	35.0	70.9
North Thames	8.6	44.2	13.0	65.7	22.4	11.9	34.3	104.2
South Thames	7.7	43.0	12.2	63.0	23.0	14.1	37.0	97.0
South and West	6.2	44.4	12.1	62.7	20.5	16.8	37.3	95.7
England[5]	7.0	43.7	12.4	63.1	22.4	14.5	36.9	755.6
Wales	6.2	43.1	11.8	61.1	21.1	17.8	38.9	54.1
Scotland	6.7	48.3	11.6	66.6	18.6	14.7	33.4	108.5
Northern Ireland	6.3	44.0	10.8	61.1	25.1	13.8	38.9	33.7

1 Whole-time equivalents. See Technical notes.
2 Locums are excluded.
3 Excludes nurse teachers, Project 2000 students, other nurse and midwife learners (except in Northern Ireland), agency nurses, and Bank nurses (except in England and Northern Ireland).
4 For Northern Ireland figure includes staff supporting Personal Social Services in Healthcare Facilities and Health and Social Services Boards but excludes home helps.
5 The England totals include staff in special health authorities and other statutory authorities which are not assigned to a specific region.

Source: Department of Health; Welsh Office; Information and Statistics Division, Scottish Health Service; Department of Health and Social Services, Northern Ireland

7.21 General practitioners: numbers and list sizes, 1 October 1995

Numbers and percentages

| | General Medical Practitioners | | | | | | | General Dental Practitioners | | | |
| | Number of unrestricted principals[1] | Average list size | GP fundholders[2] | | | Percentage of population covered by GP fundholders | Number of opticians[3] | Number of dentists[4] | Persons registered with a dentist as a percentage of the population[5] | Average list size |
			Number of funds	Number of practices	Number of GPs					
United Kingdom	32,977	1,833	..	3,163	12,581	..	..	19,317	55	1,678
Northern and Yorkshire	3,749	1,835	266	320	1,495	40	1,035	2,052	58	1,936
North West	3,391	1,934	252	345	1,247	37	952	2,083	61	1,875
Trent	2,555	1,902	238	316	1,156	46	770	1,339	58	2,084
West Midlands	2,799	1,938	284	400	1,392	50	767	1,474	56	2,008
Anglia and Oxford	2,932	1,830	207	235	1,177	41	984	1,616	52	1,710
North Thames	3,776	2,008	272	376	1,300	35	1,494	2,569	53	1,412
South Thames	3,640	1,946	287	391	1,509	41	1,406	2,591	52	1,349
South and West	3,860	1,716	202	230	1,180	32	1,082	2,227	57	1,693
England	26,702	1,887	2,008	2,613	10,456	40	6,778	15,951	56	1,711
Wales	1,719	1,730	123	146	541	39	553	876	55	1,852
Scotland	3,553	1,506	250	286	1,134	33	1,081	1,909	50	1,336
Northern Ireland	1,003	1,731	..	118	450	..	269	581	58	1,637

1 An unrestricted principal is a medical practitioner who provides the full range of general medical services and whose list is not limited to any particular group or persons. Doctors may also practise in the general medical services as restricted principals, assistants, associates or trainees.
2 Figures for the English Regional Health Authorities and for England relate to 1 April 1995, for Wales they relate to 31 March 1996 and for Northern Ireland they relate to 31 March 1997. For Scotland comprises practices in all phases of fundholding (including preparatory/pilot).
3 Optometrists and Opthalmic Medical Practitioners contracted to perform NHS sight tests at 31 December 1995 (31 March 1996 for Optometrists in Scotland). As some practitioners have contracts in more than one region or country, the sum of the English regions does not equal the England total nor is it possible to calculate a United Kingdom figure.
4 At 30 September 1995. Includes assistants and vocational trainees. Dentists are assigned to the region where they carry out their main work.
5 Registrations with dentists practising in each region.

Source: Department of Health; Welsh Office; Information and Statistics Division, Scottish Health Service; Central Services Agency, Northern Ireland

7.22 General medical practice staff[1], 1991 and 1995

Percentages and numbers

| | 1991 | | | | | | 1995 | | | | | |
	Practice managers	Computer operators	Secretaries/ clerical staff/ receptionists	Nurses	Other	All whole-time equivalents (=100%) (numbers)	Practice/ Fund managers[2]	Computer operators	Secretaries/ clerical staff/ receptionists	Nurses	Other	All whole-time equivalents (=100%) (numbers)
Great Britain	11.4	1.8	65.2	17.5	4.1	56,836	13.7	3.5	60.1	16.2	6.4	69,132
Northern and Yorkshire	12.5	1.7	65.7	16.8	3.2	6,604	12.3	3.8	61.0	16.0	6.8	8,014
North West	10.4	1.2	69.3	15.2	3.9	6,470	13.1	3.3	63.4	14.2	5.9	7,508
Trent	10.8	2.4	60.9	18.3	7.5	4,648	14.2	3.3	58.2	16.4	8.0	5,469
West Midlands	11.4	1.1	64.9	17.4	5.2	4,745	13.1	3.4	59.6	17.7	6.2	6,099
Anglia and Oxford	10.6	3.1	60.9	19.3	6.2	5,848	11.9	4.1	56.3	18.1	9.6	6,477
North Thames	11.2	1.6	67.1	17.8	2.3	7,375	13.3	3.2	60.8	16.9	5.8	8,507
South Thames	12.5	2.9	64.6	17.7	2.4	6,640	14.6	4.2	59.7	14.8	6.8	9,088
South and West	13.6	2.0	59.0	21.6	3.8	6,402	12.3	3.5	59.4	18.1	6.8	8,092
England	11.7	2.0	64.3	18.0	4.1	48,731	13.1	3.6	59.9	16.4	6.9	59,254
Wales	10.8	1.8	68.2	17.6	1.5	2,976	12.0	4.3	59.9	16.9	6.9	3,668
Scotland	9.8	..	72.2	12.6	5.4	5,130	20.4	2.5	61.6	13.8	1.7	6,209

1 Whole-time equivalents. GPs themselves are not included in this table.
2 The figure for Scotland includes other administrative staff.

Source: Department of Health; Welsh Office; Information and Statistics Division, Scottish Health Service

7.23 Health services and treatment for patients purchased by health authorities and GP fundholders[1], 1995-96

Thousands and percentages

	Finished consultant episodes		Accident & emergency attendances	Outpatient first attendances	Community & paramedical contacts	Ambulance journeys (emergency & urgent)	Learning disabilities		Mental illness	
	Total	Of which General & acute (percentages)					Hospital bed days	Community bed days[2]	Hospital bed days	Community bed days[2]
Region of purchaser										
Northern and Yorkshire	1,552	88.2	2,014	1,408	16,761	586	630	691	1,798	339
North West	1,648	88.7	2,220	1,391	20,337	655	128	959	1,638	566
Trent	1,052	87.3	1,267	1,039	12,766	393	281	552	1,159	349
West Midlands	1,078	86.9	1,679	1,045	11,936	441	354	463	989	207
Anglia and Oxford	976	87.1	1,079	1,058	12,456	298	444	331	1,156	281
North Thames	1,332	86.2	2,000	1,459	14,636	550	593	675	2,243	624
South Thames	1,313	86.4	2,092	1,498	16,275	515	727	1,291	1,630	761
South and West	1,403	87.1	1,770	1,332	16,487	403	430	858	1,440	266
England	10,354	87.3	14,121	10,229	121,655	3,842	3,588	5,820	12,054	3,392
Scotland	976	90.5	1,546	1,327	..	435	1,105	..	3,325	..

1 Figures are on a 'purchaser basis' and relate to activity purchased, using NHS funds, by health authorities and GP fundholders for their patients. This includes activity purchased from private hospitals and NHS hospitals but excludes private patients.
2 In nursing homes, residential care homes and group homes.

Source: Department of Health; Information and Statistics Division, Scottish Health Service

7.24 People in residential care homes for older people[1] and adults with physical disabilities[2]: by sector and by age, at 31 March 1996[3]

	Percentage of residents in			Percentage of residents aged[4]			Number of residents[5] (all ages) (= 100%)	Number of residents (all ages) per 1,000 population
	Local authority homes	Voluntary homes	Private homes	Under 65	65 to 84	85 or over		
Standard Statistical Regions								
North	29	11	60	4	48	49	15,220	4.9
North West (SSR)	17	22	61	4	46	50	33,922	5.3
Yorkshire and Humberside	25	9	65	3	44	53	25,384	5.0
East Midlands	27	10	63	3	44	53	18,941	4.6
West Midlands	30	13	58	5	44	51	21,841	4.1
East Anglia	28	13	59	4	39	58	10,401	4.9
South East (SSR)	22	24	54	5	39	56	75,705	4.2
Greater London	34	31	34	3	41	55	19,537	2.8
Rest of South East	18	21	61	5	39	56	56,168	5.1
South West	13	17	71	4	39	57	32,335	6.7
England	22	18	60	4	42	54	233,749	4.8
Wales	39	9	52	4	46	50	12,863	4.4
Scotland	48	28	25	5	44	51	15,976	3.1

1 For England figures include some residents needing nursing care in dual-registered homes ie registered as residential care homes and nursing homes, but exclude residents in homes for older mentally ill people.
2 Includes people with sensory disabilities.
3 For Wales and Scotland figures relate to 31 March 1995.
4 For Scotland the age breakdown is based on long-stay residents only.
5 Figures include holiday/respite residents.

Source: Department of Health; Welsh Office; The Scottish Office Home Department

7.25 Children looked after by local authorities, year ending 31 March 1995[1]

	Total children looked after per thousand resident population[2]			Manner of accommodation (percentages)			Number of children looked after[4] (=100%)
	Children admitted	Ceased to be looked after[3]	Looked after[4]	Foster homes	Community homes	Other	
Standard Statistical Regions							
North	3.3	3.3	4.9	61	16	23	3,500
North West (SSR)	2.9	2.8	4.9	59	17	24	7,500
Yorkshire and Humberside	3.1	3.1	5.2	62	13	25	6,000
East Midlands	2.5	2.8	4.0	64	11	25	3,700
West Midlands	2.7	2.8	4.6	65	12	23	5,700
East Anglia	2.5	2.5	3.5	77	8	16	1,600
South East (SSR)	2.7	2.7	4.1	63	10	27	16,600
Greater London	3.0	3.0	5.3	62	10	29	8,200
Rest of South East	2.5	2.4	3.4	64	11	25	8,300
South West	3.2	3.2	4.1	72	8	20	4,200
England	2.8	2.8	4.4	64	14	23	48,800
Wales[5]	4.2	4.3	4.4	68	10	23	2,793
Northern Ireland	1.9	2.6	5.6	63	12	25	2,624

1 English regional figures are estimates which take account of missing or incomplete data. Estimated figures are rounded to the nearest hundred. Comparable data are not available for Scotland due to differences in legislation.
2 Rates are based on mid-1994 estimates of population aged under 18.
3 For Northern Ireland data refer to all discharges from care, not individual children discharged from care; some children may be admitted and discharged on more than one occasion.
4 At 31 March. For Northern Ireland data refer to children in care; they are therefore not strictly comparable with those for England and Wales.
5 Figures exclude the former county of Gwynedd.

Source: Department of Health; Welsh Office; Department of Health and Social Services, Northern Ireland

7.26 Children and young people on child protection registers: by age and category[1], at 31 March 1995

	Percentage aged					Number of children on registers[2] (= 100%)	Rate per 10,000 children aged under 18	Percentage of children in each category of abuse[3]				
	Under 1	1-4	5-9	10-15	16 or over			Neglect	Physical injury	Sexual abuse	Emotional abuse	Other[4]
Standard Statistical Regions												
North	8	30	30	29	3	3,287	46	33	33	24	18	1
North West (SSR)	9	33	30	25	3	4,345	29	32	43	25	8	1
Yorkshire and Humberside	8	32	31	26	2	4,965	43	28	41	30	9	2
East Midlands	12	31	29	26	2	3,245	35	25	42	35	8	1
West Midlands	8	32	30	27	3	3,074	25	33	42	27	11	1
East Anglia	10	24	28	33	5	1,048	9	27	35	33	13	-
South East (SSR)	8	30	30	29	3	11,963	36	36	33	22	17	1
Greater London	7	29	32	29	3	6,002	39	42	33	17	15	1
Rest of South East	9	30	29	28	2	5,961	34	31	32	26	19	-
South West	7	32	31	28	2	3,027	29	27	35	29	17	1
England	8	31	30	28	3	34,954	32	32	37	26	13	1
Wales	10	34	29	25	2	1,668	25	25	38	16	15	7
Northern Ireland	6	29	32	29	4	1,523	33	25	10	12	10	45

1 Data for Scotland are not available in the same form; however, the total number of children on protection registers at 31 March 1995 was 2,601.
2 Includes a number of unborn children.
3 The total of the percentages exceed 100 as children in mixed categories are counted more than once. For Wales, the figure for 'other' relates to mixed categories.
4 For England data relate to children or young people on the child protection registers who have not been allocated a specific category. For Northern Ireland the category includes 'Grave concern', which is no longer used in English and Welsh statistics.

Source: Department of Health; Welsh Office; Department of Health and Social Services, Northern Ireland

8 Lifestyles

Household income Average weekly household income in 1995-96 was highest in London, at £446, and lowest in Northern Ireland, at £323.

(Tables 8.1 and 8.2)

People in the Eastern region, London and the South East (GOR) are more than twice as likely to live in households in the top fifth of the income distribution as people in the North East.

(Table 8.3)

Savings In 1995-96, 11 per cent of households in the South East (GOR) and the South West had at least one member with a Personal Equity Plan, more than double the proportion in the North East, Wales and Scotland.

(Table 8.4)

Income tax The average income tax payable by men in 1994-95 ranged from £2,630 in Wales to £4,890 in London.

(Chart 8.6)

Benefits In 1995-96, 27 per cent of households in the North East received Family Credit or Income Support compared with 14 per cent in South East (GOR).

(Table 8.7)

Household expenditure Average weekly household expenditure in 1995-96 ranged from £261 in the North East to £327 in London.

(Table 8.9)

Households in London spent the most on housing in 1995-96, those in Northern Ireland the most on food, on fuel, light and power and on clothing and footwear, and those in the East Midlands the most on motoring and fares.

(Table 8.9)

In 1994-1995, people in London spent an average of £5.50 per head per week on eating out, nearly double the average amount spent by people in the North (SSR).

(Table 8.10)

Consumption In 1994-1995, people in the North (SSR) ate the most meat and meat products, those in Wales ate the most vegetables and vegetable products, while those in London ate the most fruit.

(Table 8.11)

Consumer goods The proportion of households in the South East (GOR) owning a dishwasher, 28 per cent, is almost three times that in the North East (10 per cent).

(Table 8.12)

Leisure Old age pensioners in the North West watched an average of 38 hours of television each week in 1996, seven hours more than those in the East region who watched the least.

(Table 8.13)

National lottery Three in every four households in the North East, Merseyside and the West Midlands participated in the National Lottery Saturday draw in 1995-96, compared with three in five in London, the South East (GOR) and Northern Ireland.

(Table 8.15)

Introduction

This chapter looks at the way we live. The first three tables show the source and distribution of household income. The chapter goes on to look at income tax payable, benefits, household expenditure, ownership of consumer durables, and some aspects of how we spend our leisure time.

Tables 8.3, 8.4, 8.7 and 8.12 are from the Department of Social Security's Family Resources Survey (FRS). The survey is mainly about household incomes, but it also includes detailed questions covering a variety of subjects which have a bearing on household income. In previous editions of *Regional Trends*, Table 8.12 was from the Family Expenditure Survey (FES), the Office for National Statistics' long-running source of information on household income and expenditure. The FRS provides more precise information because of its larger size. Tables 8.1 and 8.2 on household income in 1995-96 continue to be drawn from the FES, however, for direct comparability with the expenditure information in Table 8.9

Table 8.3 is a new table to *Regional Trends*. It shows how the distribution of income in each region in 1994-95 compared with that of Great Britain as a whole. Individuals were ranked according to their household equivalised disposable income, that is, after adjustment for the size and composition of the household (see Technical notes). As, for example, 25 per cent of individuals in Wales were in the bottom quintile group compared with 20 per cent of the population of Great Britain, Wales was over-represented in the bottom group. Similarly, the South West was over-represented in the middle quintile and the South East (GOR) was over-represented in the top quintile group. No adjustment has been made for regional differences in the cost of living and hence this table cannot be used to compare the relative standards of living of the regions.

Table 8.9 shows household expenditure by main commodity and service. The area of expenditure where there is most regional variation, both in cash terms and as a percentage of total expenditure, is housing: in London nearly 19 per cent of total household expenditure in 1995-96 was on housing, almost double the proportion in Northern Ireland, at 10 per cent. This is also reflected in the figures shown in Tables 6.8 - 6.10 in the Housing chapter.

Since its introduction in November 1994, the National Lottery has become something of an institution. The FES indicates that around two thirds of households participated in the Saturday Draw during the period October 1995 to March 1996 (Table 8.14). Households in London, the South East (GOR) and Northern Ireland were less likely than average to participate, while those in the North East, Merseyside and the West Midlands were more likely. Expenditure per participating household as measured by the FES averaged £3.20 per week.

Some 27 per cent of the National Lottery's proceeds are allocated to good causes divided between five separate funds administered by the Arts Councils, a Charities Board, the Millennium Commission, the National Heritage Fund and the Sports Councils. By the end of 1996, more than 19,300 grants had been awarded to the value of £3,153 million (Table 8.15). London appears to have received a disproportionately high value of grants, but many of the largest grants were to institutions which have a national significance.

The ONS sometimes receives requests for the Retail Prices Index (RPI) on a regional basis. This information is not available. The RPI is designed to measure price changes over time rather than the differences in price levels between different groups within the reference population, which is what is generally required. It would be possible (with some enlargement of the sample of price collections and perhaps some enlargement of the FES to produce more precise regional data on expenditure) to compile indices which showed regional changes in prices, but there is no reason to doubt that in practice these indices would move in much the same way as the UK index.

8.1 Household income: by source, 1995-96[1]

Percentages and £

	Percentage of average gross weekly household income						Average gross weekly household income[3] (= 100%) (£)
	Wages and salaries	Self employ- ment	Invest- ments	Annuities and pensions[2]	Social security benefits[3]	Other income	
United Kingdom	64.3	8.6	4.8	6.8	13.7	1.7	380.9
North East	61.1	5.4	4.5	8.9	19.3	0.9	337.9
North West (GOR) & Merseyside	62.2	8.8	4.4	6.3	16.4	1.9	354.2
North West (GOR)	63.4	8.3	4.2	6.1	16.0	2.1	352.6
Merseyside	57.1	11.2	5.4	7.3	18.2	0.9	361.3
Yorkshire and the Humber	64.2	8.0	3.8	6.2	16.1	1.7	344.2
East Midlands	68.5	8.6	3.8	5.9	11.5	1.7	394.3
West Midlands	65.5	7.6	3.2	6.0	15.7	1.9	348.3
Eastern	63.2	8.1	6.3	8.5	12.5	1.5	394.5
London	68.6	8.8	4.5	5.7	10.5	2.0	445.8
South East (GOR)	63.6	10.9	6.3	7.5	10.4	1.2	438.1
South West	63.2	9.8	5.9	7.2	12.0	2.0	393.2
England	64.6	8.8	4.9	6.8	13.2	1.7	388.7
Wales	59.0	8.7	5.4	7.7	16.5	2.7	361.0
Scotland	65.1	7.0	3.2	6.5	16.5	1.8	336.4
Northern Ireland[4]	62.1	7.0	2.6	5.2	21.6	1.5	322.8

1 See Technical notes.
2 Other than social security benefits.
3 Excluding Housing Benefit and Council Tax Benefit (rates rebate in Northern Ireland).
4 Northern Ireland data are obtained from an enhanced sample, but the United Kingdom figures are obtained from the main Family Expenditure Survey sample.

Source: Family Expenditure Survey, Office for National Statistics; Northern Ireland Statistics and Research Agency

8.2 Distribution of household income, 1995-96[1]

Percentages and £

	Percentage of households in each weekly income group								Average gross weekly income[2] (£)	
	Under £80	£80 but under £125	£125 but under £175	£175 but under £275	£275 but under £375	£375 but under £475	£475 but under £650	£650 or over	Per house- hold	Per person
United Kingdom	9.6	11.2	10.0	14.9	13.8	12.3	12.9	15.4	380.9	156.1
North East	13.9	13.9	10.6	15.3	11.2	11.5	10.6	13.0	337.9	135.6
North West (GOR) & Merseyside	10.3	11.8	11.9	14.7	12.7	13.6	10.7	14.3	354.2	140.5
North West (GOR)	9.8	12.1	11.2	14.8	13.6	13.2	11.1	14.2	352.6	138.3
Merseyside	12.3	10.3	15.1	14.4	8.9	15.1	8.9	15.1	361.3	151.2
Yorkshire and the Humber	9.8	11.4	13.1	16.8	12.8	13.8	9.9	12.3	344.2	141.9
East Midlands	8.4	10.4	10.0	14.3	14.7	13.2	13.6	15.5	394.3	159.5
West Midlands	9.5	11.0	9.8	15.1	16.4	12.2	14.2	11.8	348.3	138.4
Eastern	7.7	10.6	8.7	16.4	13.9	13.8	13.8	15.1	394.5	161.0
London	10.8	12.4	7.2	11.8	11.0	10.1	14.7	22.0	445.8	189.1
South East (GOR)	7.8	9.2	8.2	13.8	14.5	10.7	15.6	20.2	438.1	185.1
South West	8.0	11.0	8.6	14.4	14.8	14.9	13.5	14.8	393.2	160.2
England	9.3	11.1	9.7	14.6	13.6	12.6	13.2	15.9	388.7	159.0
Wales	9.4	10.9	10.9	16.2	17.1	10.3	11.2	13.9	361.0	144.3
Scotland	11.8	12.1	10.8	15.6	14.9	10.8	11.1	13.1	336.4	143.3
Northern Ireland[3]	12.3	11.5	12.0	17.8	11.5	12.4	11.8	10.6	322.8	118.2

1 See Technical notes.
2 Excluding Housing Benefit and Council Tax Benefit (rates rebate in Northern Ireland).
3 Northern Ireland data are obtained from an enhanced sample, but the United Kingdom figures are obtained from the main Family Expenditure Survey sample.

Source: Family Expenditure Survey, Office for National Statistics; Northern Ireland Statistics and Research Agency

8.3 Income distribution of individuals, 1994-95[1]

Percentages

	Quintile groups of individuals ranked by net equivalised household income				
	1	2	3	4	5
Great Britain	20	20	20	20	20
North East	25	26	20	18	12
North West (GOR) & Merseyside	23	22	20	19	16
Yorkshire and the Humber	26	23	19	18	14
East Midlands	20	21	22	20	17
West Midlands	20	22	20	21	17
Eastern	17	17	19	21	26
London	19	17	18	18	28
South East (GOR)	14	17	19	22	28
South West	18	20	23	22	17
England	20	20	20	20	21
Wales	25	22	20	19	14
Scotland	22	20	21	20	18

1 See Introduction to chapter and Technical notes.

Source: Department of Social Security from Households Below Average Income

8.4 Households[1] with different types of saving, 1995-96

Percentages[2]

	Accounts						Other savings					
	Current[3]	Post Office	TESSA	Other building society[4]	Other bank	Other account[5]	Gilts or unit trusts	Stocks & shares	National Savings	Save As You Earn	Premium Bonds	PEPs
Great Britain	80	13	12	56	21	2	7	21	8	2	28	8
North East	76	10	7	45	17	1	4	12	5	1	16	5
North West (GOR) & Merseyside	77	11	11	53	18	2	6	17	7	3	24	7
North West (GOR)	79	11	11	55	19	2	6	18	7	3	25	7
Merseyside	69	10	9	42	14	1	5	14	8	2	21	6
Yorkshire and the Humber	76	11	12	54	23	2	6	18	7	2	27	6
East Midlands	82	14	13	57	22	2	7	21	9	2	29	7
West Midlands	78	13	12	59	21	2	7	20	8	2	27	9
Eastern	85	16	15	66	22	2	9	26	11	3	37	10
London	78	11	11	58	15	2	6	21	8	2	27	6
South East (GOR)	89	16	15	66	22	4	10	28	11	3	38	11
South West	86	17	12	64	22	4	10	25	10	2	35	11
England	81	13	12	59	20	3	7	22	9	2	30	8
Wales	77	12	7	46	17	1	5	15	7	1	22	5
Scotland	68	8	9	38	30	2	5	16	5	1	17	5

1 Households in which at least one member has an account. See Technical notes.
2 As a percentage of all households.
3 A current account may be either a bank or building society account.
4 All building society accounts excluding current accounts and TESSAs.
5 All accounts yielding interest but excluding high street bank and building society accounts.

Source: Family Resources Survey, Department of Social Security

8.5 Distribution of income liable to assessment for tax, 1994-95[1]

Percentages and thousands

	£3,445-£4,999	£5,000-£7,499	£7,500-£9,999	£10,000-£14,999	£15,000-£19,999	£20,000-£29,999	£30,000-£49,999	£50,000 and over	Individuals with incomes of £3,445 or more (= 100%) (thousands)
	Percentage of individuals in each income range								
United Kingdom[2]	11.9	16.7	14.5	22.7	14.6	13.1	4.6	1.9	26,900
North East	13.4	17.6	16.2	22.7	14.1	11.9	3.1	1.0	1,060
North West (GOR) & Merseyside	13.3	16.6	16.3	21.9	15.0	11.7	4.0	1.2	2,960
North West (GOR)	13.1	16.4	16.7	22.2	14.5	11.9	4.0	1.2	2,450
Merseyside	14.3	17.6	14.1	20.5	17.5	10.9	4.1	1.0	510
Yorkshire and the Humber	14.6	19.2	13.6	23.5	13.3	11.4	3.2	1.2	2,320
East Midlands	13.6	19.1	13.7	23.2	13.8	12.0	3.1	1.5	1,990
West Midlands	10.3	17.7	15.8	24.8	14.1	12.4	3.6	1.3	2,320
Eastern	10.7	14.8	13.8	22.5	14.6	15.3	5.8	2.5	2,380
London	9.9	12.2	13.3	21.4	17.3	15.9	6.5	3.5	3,110
South East (GOR)	10.2	15.8	12.5	22.1	14.5	15.1	6.7	3.1	3,890
South West	13.0	17.7	17.5	21.7	13.2	11.9	3.8	1.2	2,340
England[2]	11.9	16.4	14.5	22.5	14.6	13.4	4.7	2.0	22,400
Wales	11.4	19.4	16.2	22.5	15.1	12.1	2.5	0.8	1,190
Scotland	12.7	17.6	13.3	24.4	14.7	12.0	4.0	1.3	2,450
Northern Ireland	12.2	18.7	15.2	24.6	13.6	11.4	3.1	1.2	624

1 See Technical notes.
2 Figures for United Kingdom include members of HM Forces and others who are liable to some UK tax but reside overseas on a long-term basis. In addition the United Kingdom and England totals include a very small number of individuals who could not be allocated to a region.

Source: Survey of Personal Incomes, Board of Inland Revenue

8.6 Average income tax payable, 1994-1995[1]

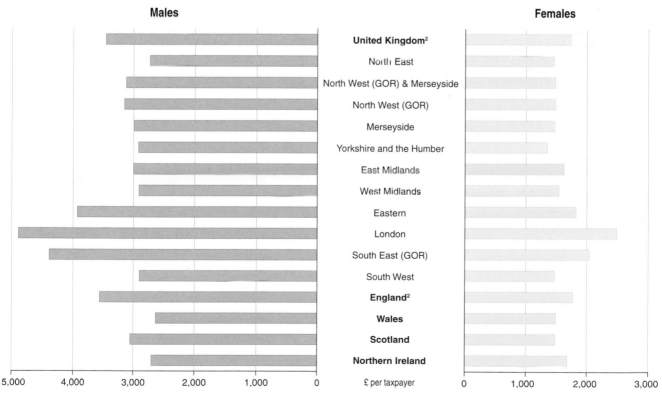

Males   **Females**

United Kingdom[2]
North East
North West (GOR) & Merseyside
North West (GOR)
Merseyside
Yorkshire and the Humber
East Midlands
West Midlands
Eastern
London
South East (GOR)
South West
England[2]
Wales
Scotland
Northern Ireland

5,000 4,000 3,000 2,000 1,000 0 £ per taxpayer 0 1,000 2,000 3,000

1 See Technical notes.
2 Figures for United Kingdom include members of HM Forces and others who are liable to some UK tax but reside overseas on a long-term basis. In addition the United Kingdom and England averages include a very small number of individuals who could not be allocated to a region.

Source: Survey of Personal Incomes, Board of Inland Revenue

8.7 Households in receipt of benefit[1], by type of benefit, 1995-96

Percentages[2]

	Family Credit or Income Support	Housing Benefit	Council Tax Benefit	Unemploy- ment Benefit	Retirement Pension	Incapacity or Disablement Benefits[3]	Child Benefit or One Parent Benefit	Any benefit
Great Britain	21	20	25	1	30	15	32	75
North East	27	26	35	2	28	20	29	78
North West (GOR) & Merseyside	25	23	31	1	30	20	34	79
Yorkshire and the Humber	22	20	27	1	32	16	31	77
East Midlands	21	18	24	2	28	15	33	74
West Midlands	22	20	27	1	32	16	34	77
Eastern	16	15	20	2	32	12	32	73
London	25	26	29	2	26	12	31	72
South East (GOR)	14	13	17	1	30	10	31	70
South West	18	17	22	1	34	13	31	76
England	21	19	25	1	30	14	32	75
Wales	25	20	27	2	33	24	32	82
Scotland	24	28	28	1	30	18	32	77

1 Households in which at least one member is currently in receipt of benefit. See Technical notes.
2 As a percentage of all households.
3 Incapacity Benefit, Disability Living Allowance (Care and Mobility components), Severe Disablement Allowance, Industrial Injuries Disability Benefit, War Disablement Benefit and Attendance Allowance.

Source: Family Resources Survey, Department of Social Security

8.8 Eligibility for free school meals[1], 1995/96

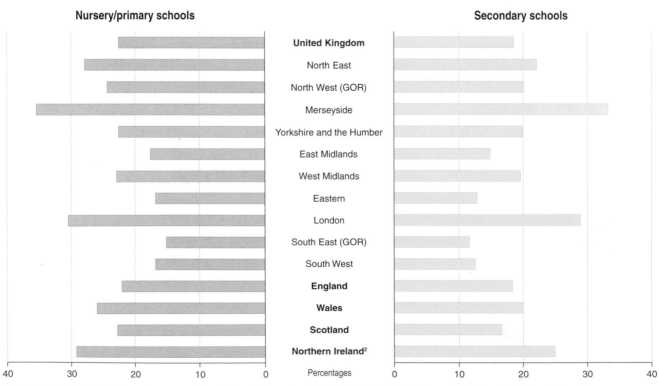

1 Pupils known to be eligible for free meals as a percentage of all pupils (day pupils only in England). In Scotland excludes pupils attending schools not providing meals.
2 Figures relate to pupils entitled to free school meals (ie entitlement is granted when an application for free school meals is made).

Source: Department for Education and Employment; Welsh Office; The Scottish Office Education and Industry Department; Department of Education, Northern Ireland

8.9 Household expenditure: by commodity and service, 1995-96[1]

£ per week and percentages

	Housing	Fuel, light & power	Food	Alcohol and tobacco	Clothing and footwear	House-hold goods and services	Motoring and fares	Leisure goods and services	Miscellan-eous and personal goods and services	Average house-hold expend-iture	Average expend-iture per person
£ per week											
United Kingdom	48.2	12.9	52.9	17.2	17.2	38.6	43.2	45.8	13.9	289.9	118.8
North East	39.2	12.7	47.8	19.0	17.0	34.3	37.0	42.5	11.6	261.1	104.7
North West (GOR) & Merseyside	44.6	13.2	51.4	20.7	17.1	38.5	43.4	41.3	12.3	282.5	112.1
North West (GOR)	44.5	13.2	51.7	20.6	16.5	38.8	46.1	40.3	12.9	284.7	111.7
Merseyside	44.8	13.3	50.2	21.2	19.4	37.3	31.2	45.6	9.7	272.8	114.1
Yorkshire and the Humber	42.2	12.9	49.4	18.6	15.8	35.9	34.5	44.1	17.3	270.7	111.6
East Midlands	47.4	13.2	52.6	18.0	18.7	39.8	51.0	51.1	14.5	306.2	123.8
West Midlands	45.1	12.8	51.2	18.4	14.9	35.3	41.3	44.3	12.3	275.7	109.5
Eastern	53.7	12.5	54.6	14.7	17.6	41.0	48.3	48.3	14.2	304.9	124.5
London	61.4	12.0	58.2	16.5	18.8	45.1	44.7	54.0	16.4	327.0	138.7
South East (GOR)	57.8	12.8	55.4	15.2	17.2	42.5	48.4	50.1	14.8	314.1	132.7
South West	49.0	12.6	51.9	14.9	17.3	36.3	40.8	44.4	13.8	281.0	114.5
England	50.0	12.7	52.9	17.2	17.2	39.2	43.7	46.9	14.3	294.2	120.4
Wales	40.6	14.7	51.5	15.6	16.0	35.8	37.7	41.9	11.7	265.5	106.1
Scotland	40.5	13.1	52.2	18.5	17.0	33.5	40.3	40.6	12.3	267.9	114.1
Northern Ireland[2]	28.7	15.7	60.2	17.8	21.3	43.7	46.2	39.0	14.1	286.7	105.0
As a percentage of average weekly household expenditure											
United Kingdom	16.6	4.5	18.2	5.9	5.9	13.3	14.9	15.8	4.8	100.0	
North East	15.0	4.9	18.3	7.3	6.5	13.1	14.2	16.3	4.4	100.0	
North West (GOR) & Merseyside	15.8	4.7	18.2	7.3	6.0	13.6	15.3	14.6	4.4	100.0	
North West (GOR)	15.6	4.6	18.2	7.2	5.8	13.6	16.2	14.1	4.5	100.0	
Merseyside	16.4	4.0	18.4	7.8	7.1	13.7	11.5	16.7	3.6	100.0	
Yorkshire and the Humber	15.6	4.8	18.3	6.9	5.8	13.3	12.7	16.3	6.4	100.0	
East Midlands	15.5	4.3	17.2	5.9	6.1	13.0	16.7	16.7	4.7	100.0	
West Midlands	16.4	4.6	18.6	6.7	5.4	12.8	15.0	16.1	4.5	100.0	
Eastern	17.6	4.1	17.9	4.8	5.8	13.4	15.8	15.9	4.7	100.0	
London	18.8	3.7	17.8	5.0	5.7	13.8	13.7	16.5	5.0	100.0	
South East (GOR)	18.4	4.1	17.6	4.8	5.5	13.5	15.4	15.9	4.7	100.0	
South West	17.4	4.5	18.5	5.3	6.1	12.9	14.5	15.8	4.9	100.0	
England	17.0	4.3	18.0	5.9	5.8	13.3	14.9	15.9	4.8	100.0	
Wales	15.3	5.5	19.4	5.9	6.0	13.5	14.2	15.8	4.4	100.0	
Scotland	15.1	4.9	19.5	6.9	6.3	12.5	15.0	15.1	4.6	100.0	
Northern Ireland[2]	10.0	5.5	21.0	6.2	7.4	15.2	16.1	13.6	4.9	100.0	

1 See Technical notes.
2 Northern Ireland data are obtained from an enhanced sample, but the United Kingdom figures are obtained from the main Family Expenditure Survey sample

Source: Family Expenditure Survey, Office for National Statistics; Northern Ireland Statistics and Research Agency

8.10 Expenditure on selected foods bought for household consumption and expenditure on eating out, 1994-1995[1]

£ per person per week

	Liquid and processed milk and cream	Cheese	Eggs	Uncooked carcass meat and poultry	Other meat and meat products	Fish	Vegetables and vegetable products[2]	Fresh and other fruit	Bread	Total household food[3]	Eating out[3,4]
Standard Statistical Regions											
Great Britain	1.42	0.48	0.17	1.62	1.96	0.72	2.04	1.07	0.69	13.51	3.85
North	1.32	0.34	0.18	1.54	2.09	0.75	1.90	0.78	0.72	12.88	2.80
North West (SSR)	1.39	0.40	0.16	1.57	1.97	0.69	1.90	0.92	0.71	12.91	3.85
Yorkshire & Humberside	1.42	0.45	0.16	1.54	1.90	0.74	1.94	0.96	0.70	13.06	3.52
East Midlands	1.51	0.50	0.16	1.56	1.96	0.69	2.08	1.02	0.69	13.61	3.59
West Midlands	1.38	0.51	0.17	1.72	1.83	0.70	2.05	1.03	0.68	13.41	3.50
East Anglia/South East(SSR)[5]	1.45	0.53	0.18	1.65	1.98	0.78	2.21	1.25	0.65	14.16	4.55
Greater London	1.37	0.53	0.20	1.78	1.90	0.84	2.31	1.44	0.64	14.40	5.52
South West	1.47	0.55	0.18	1.56	1.72	0.71	2.06	1.21	0.65	13.52	3.50
England	1.43	0.48	0.17	1.61	1.94	0.74	2.07	1.09	0.68	13.58	3.92
Wales	1.41	0.43	0.17	1.71	1.98	0.66	2.07	0.99	0.72	13.26	3.41
Scotland	1.29	0.45	0.17	1.59	2.21	0.63	1.70	0.92	0.75	12.98	3.47

1 See Technical notes.
2 Including tomatoes, fresh potatoes and potato products.
3 Excluding soft and alcoholic drinks and confectionery.
4 Individual expenditure on all food consumed outside the home and not obtained from household stocks, whether consumed by the purchaser or others or both. Expenditure which is to be reclaimed as business expenses is not included.
5 Data shown are averages for East Anglia and the South East (SSR) combined.

Source: National Food Survey, Ministry of Agriculture, Fisheries and Food

8.11 Household consumption of selected foods, 1990-1991 and 1994-1995[1]

Kilograms per person per week[2]

	Liquid and processed milk and cream		Meat and meat products		Fish		Vegetables & vegetable products[3]		Fresh and other fruit		Bread	
	1990-1991	1994-1995	1990-1991	1994-1995	1990-1991	1994-1995	1990-1991	1994-1995	1990-1991	1994-1995	1990-1991	1994-1995
Standard Statistical Regions												
Great Britain	2.15	2.18	0.97	0.94	0.14	0.14	2.24	2.07	0.92	0.98	0.78	0.76
North	2.08	2.11	1.03	1.08	0.15	0.16	2.44	2.20	0.83	0.75	0.86	0.83
North West (SSR)	2.11	2.19	0.98	0.94	0.14	0.14	2.23	2.01	0.81	0.87	0.77	0.78
Yorkshire & Humberside	2.13	2.25	0.97	0.98	0.16	0.16	2.21	2.15	0.85	0.94	0.76	0.78
East Midlands	2.35	2.37	0.91	0.94	0.14	0.14	2.26	2.21	0.95	0.99	0.75	0.80
West Midlands	2.02	2.16	0.99	0.97	0.13	0.14	2.33	2.22	0.70	0.98	0.89	0.80
East Anglia/South East (SSR)[4]	2.12	2.14	0.95	0.91	0.15	0.15	2.17	2.01	1.11	1.09	0.71	0.69
Greater London	2.02	2.01	1.00	0.89	0.16	0.16	2.15	2.00	1.15	1.21	0.68	0.64
South West	2.25	2.20	0.96	0.89	0.13	0.14	2.45	2.14	0.98	1.14	0.74	0.71
England	2.13	2.19	0.97	0.94	0.14	0.15	2.26	2.09	0.95	1.00	0.76	0.75
Wales	2.29	2.23	1.02	1.05	0.14	0.14	2.41	2.29	0.74	0.93	0.89	0.83
Scotland	2.20	2.10	0.92	0.92	0.13	0.12	2.02	1.71	0.82	0.83	0.83	0.79

1 See Technical notes.
2 Except equivalent litres of milk and cream.
3 Including tomatoes, fresh potatoes and potato products.
4 Data shown are averages for East Anglia and the South East (SSR) combined.

Source: National Food Survey, Ministry of Agriculture, Fisheries and Food

8.12 Households with selected durable goods,1995-96[1]

Percentages

	Micro-wave oven	Wash-ing machine	Tumble drier	Dish-washer	Refrig-erator[2]	Deep freezer[2]	Tele-phone	Tele-vision	Video	Home com-puter	Central heating
Great Britain	69	89	50	19	99	88	92	98	77	23	85
North East	70	88	44	10	98	84	87	98	76	17	92
North West (GOR) & Merseyside	71	89	50	15	99	88	90	98	78	21	80
Yorkshire and the Humber	71	92	50	15	98	86	91	98	76	21	79
East Midlands	72	93	54	19	99	89	91	99	80	21	89
West Midlands	71	89	52	18	99	87	91	98	76	22	81
Eastern	72	90	54	25	99	91	94	99	79	27	90
London	60	82	41	17	99	87	93	97	74	24	85
South East (GOR)	70	90	54	28	99	91	96	98	80	28	89
South West	69	89	50	21	99	88	94	98	75	23	83
England	69	89	50	19	99	88	92	98	78	23	85
Wales	75	90	47	15	99	89	89	99	77	19	86
Scotland	67	91	49	15	99	84	88	99	76	18	84
Northern Ireland	68	90	37	18	99	79	89	97	73	16	92

1 See Technical notes.
2 Fridge-freezers are attributed to both Refrigerator and Deep freezer.

Source: Family Resources Survey, Department of Social Security, Continuous Household Survey, Northern Ireland Statistics and Research Agency

8.13 Average weekly television viewing[1]: by age, 1992 and 1996

Hours[2]

	1992 Persons aged				All persons aged 4 or over	1996 Persons aged				All persons aged 4 or over
	4-15	16-34	35-64	65 or over		4-15	16-34	35-64	65 or over	
United Kingdom[3]	19.6	23.4	27.5	37.7	26.7	17.7	21.5	26.2	36.2	25.1
North East	20.0	24.8	30.5	34.0	27.4	16.0	22.7	27.2	32.4	24.9
North West	19.4	23.3	28.3	39.7	27.1	17.6	22.0	26.3	38.3	25.5
Yorkshire	19.7	23.1	28.7	34.8	26.6	18.2	22.1	27.5	34.2	25.6
Midlands	18.6	22.8	25.3	38.7	25.5	16.4	20.1	24.2	36.1	23.6
East	17.5	20.1	23.2	32.0	22.8	17.6	18.9	22.4	31.1	22.1
London	19.0	21.5	24.8	36.4	24.6	16.1	19.2	23.2	35.6	22.7
South, South East and Channel Islands	17.5	21.4	24.3	32.8	24.0	16.3	19.0	24.1	34.0	23.4
South West	17.7	22.2	24.2	31.4	24.1	16.8	21.0	24.4	34.2	24.3
Wales and West	18.8	23.0	26.6	30.5	25.0	16.6	21.4	25.0	33.2	24.1
Border	20.0	26.8	27.4	37.0	27.5	18.2	19.7	29.0	34.6	26.1
Central Scotland	19.9	25.2	32.6	41.8	29.8	18.4	20.7	29.2	36.8	26.5
Northern Scotland	19.3	20.2	26.5	41.5	26.1	18.6	20.9	26.4	34.1	25.2
Ulster	22.9	25.7	29.7	36.3	27.8	18.3	23.1	27.9	36.4	25.5

1 Including timeshift, ie viewing of broadcast material recorded at home and played back within seven days of recording.
2 Per person in UK private households containing a television set in working order.
3 Figures for the regions exclude viewing of other regions' broadcasts, whereas figures for the United Kingdom include all viewing, and are therefore higher.

Source: Broadcasters' Audience Research Board Ltd

8.14 Adults taking a holiday[1]: by region of domicile, 1996

Percentages

	A holiday abroad	A holiday in Great Britain	Any holiday
Standard Statistical Regions			
Great Britain	34	35	58
North	34	25	51
North West (SSR)	40	36	61
Yorkshire and Humberside	30	33	55
East Midlands	23	37	52
West Midlands	30	36	57
East Anglia	24	46	63
South East (SSR)	39	32	61
Greater London	41	25	58
Rest of South East	37	37	63
South West	22	37	50
England	33	34	57
Wales	36	43	65
Scotland	35	36	63

1 Defined as four or more nights away.

Source: British Tourist Authority

8.15 Participation in the National Lottery, 1995-96[1]

Percentages and £

	Percentage of house-holds participating	Average household expenditure[2] (£)
United Kingdom	67	3.2
North East	74	3.5
North West (GOR) & Merseyside	68	3.2
North West (GOR)	67	3.2
Merseyside	76	2.9
Yorkshire and the Humber	70	2.8
East Midlands	71	3.3
West Midlands	74	3.4
Eastern	66	3.0
London	60	3.7
South East (GOR)	58	3.0
South West	66	3.2
England	67	3.2
Wales	65	3.2
Scotland	72	3.0
Northern Ireland[3]	59	2.6

1 Participation in the Saturday Draw only over the period October 1995 to March 1996.
2 Average weekly expenditure of participating households.
3 Northern Ireland data are obtained from an enhanced sample, but the United Kingdom figures are obtained from the main Family Expenditure Survey sample.

Source: Family Expenditure Survey, Office for National Statistics; Northern Ireland Statistics and Research Agency

8.16 The National Lottery grants: totals to end-1996

Numbers and £ million

	Number of grants awarded	Total value of grants (£ million)
United Kingdom[1]	19,321	3,153.0
North East	494	125.1
North West (GOR) & Merseyside	1,317	371.1
North West (GOR)	1,007	300.1
Merseyside	310	71.0
Yorkshire and the Humber	924	200.0
East Midlands	724	114.9
West Midlands	1,185	252.9
Eastern	963	140.4
London	1,797	785.2
South East (GOR)	1,269	243.9
South West	1,175	250.4
England	9,848	2,483.8
Wales	1,551	180.1
Scotland	1,710	371.8
Northern Ireland	1,033	80.0

1 Includes 5,179 grants worth £37.4 million made UK-wide.

Source: Department of National Heritage

9 Crime and Justice

Crime rates
The North East had the highest recorded crime rate in England and Wales in 1995, one and three quarters times the rate in the Eastern region, which was the lowest.

(Table 9.1)

The robbery rate in London was nearly 15 times higher than in Wales in 1995, and twice that in Merseyside, the region with the second highest rate.

(Table 9.1)

Victims
Nearly two in every five households in the Yorkshire and Humber region suffered at least one crime against their property in 1995 compared with less than one in five in Scotland and Northern Ireland.

(Table 9.2)

Clear-ups
Within England and Wales, the police forces in Wales were the most successful in clearing up crimes in 1995 with about a third of recorded offences cleared up.

(Table 9.3)

Firearms
The number of offences recorded in which firearms were reported to have been used more than doubled in Merseyside and the South West between 1991 and 1995, but nearly halved in London.

(Table 9.4)

Drug seizures
Nearly a third of seizures of Class A drugs in the United Kingdom in 1995 were in London.

(Table 9.5)

Offenders
Police in the Eastern region were more likely than those in the other regions of England and Wales to caution the under 18s for an indictable offence in 1995 and the police in Merseyside were the least likely.

(Table 9.6)

Within England and Wales, the North East has proportionately the most known offenders among their youngsters aged under 18 and the South West the fewest.

(Table 9.7)

Sentences
Around 8 per cent of people found guilty of drink-driving in the East Midlands and in Merseyside in 1995 were given a custodial sentence, double the UK average.

(Table 9.9)

Courts in Scotland which impose a custodial sentence on adult offenders are more likely to impose a short sentence than those elsewhere in the United Kingdom.

(Table 9.10)

Police manpower
There is one police officer or full-time reserve for every 144 people in Northern Ireland compared with one officer for every 530 people the Eastern region.

(Table 9.11)

Introduction

C rime is something which affects all of us as individuals to varying degrees. Variation exists not only in the effect of criminal activity on our everyday lives but also in the legal frameworks and crime recording systems in existence to deal with such activity in the United Kingdom. The differences are significant and result in the lack of comparability of the figures in the three jurisdictions (England and Wales, Scotland and Northern Ireland); it has not always been possible therefore to include figures for the United Kingdom in this chapter. The lack of comparability means careful interpretation of the information in the chapter is required.

There are two main measures of crime: one is the statistics of crimes recorded by the police (Table 9.1) and the other is crime surveys. The main surveys are the British Crime Survey (BCS) (which relates to England and Wales), the Scottish Crime Survey (SCS) and the Northern Ireland Crime Survey. The surveys show a higher level of crime than the police statistics. This is because not all crimes are reported to the police and not all of those reported are subsequently recorded by them. During 1995 less than half the offences counted in the BCS were reported to the police. There are various reasons for this but most frequent were that victims felt the incident was not serious enough, that the police would not be able to do very much or that they would not be interested. The surveys count only those incidents that are technically criminal by applying a legal definition of crime, and do not simply accept respondents' definitions of what happened. Nevertheless, as with the statistics of crime recorded by the police, the information in surveys is limited; they cover only a selection of crime types and a selection of the population and results are subject to sampling error. Hence neither system - recorded crime nor crime surveys - fully records the scale of crime.

The surveys also provide information on people's perceptions of the likelihood of becoming a victim of crime. Nearly a third of adults participating in the BCS thought it was certain, very likely or fairly likely they would be burgled in the coming year. One in six thought the same about mugging. People were more pessimistic in areas with higher crime rates, as one would expect; for example, nearly twice as many people in inner city areas as elsewhere rated the chance of mugging as at least fairly likely. However the reality is that in 1995 just over 6 per cent of households in England and Wales overall were burgled (including attempts), which puts the annual risk for the average household at one in 16. In the Yorkshire and Humber region the risk rose to one in 11, while in Scotland and Northern Ireland it fell to around one in 35. The risk of mugging was considerably lower at less than one in 100.

Table 9.12 presents the results from the BCS and SCS on fear of crime. A detailed analysis of the 1994 BCS showed that worry about mugging and 'feeling unsafe' was *not* related to having been a victim of street crime, although those who knew other victims were more anxious. But for other crimes, such as burglary, having been a victim oneself did increase worry.

Table 9.5 shows the number of seizures of controlled drugs in 1995. The police made nearly 112 thousand seizures during the year, some 16 times more than Customs Officers. However, comparing the quantity seized as opposed to the number of seizures, the reverse is the case: Customs Officers seized almost 54,532 kg of controlled drugs, nearly eight times the 6,913 kg seized by the police. This clearly shows that although the police make a far greater number of seizures, they are on average very much smaller in quantity than those made by Customs Officers, reflecting the different roles of the two organisations in the fight against drugs.

Regional Trends 32, © Crown copyright 1997

9.1 Notifiable offences recorded by the police[1]: by offence group, 1995 and percentage change, 1994-1995

Rates per 100,000 population and percentages

	Violence against the person	Sexual offences	Burglary	Robbery	Theft and handling stolen goods	Fraud and forgery	Criminal damage[2]	Other	Total
1995									
England & Wales	412	59	2,401	132	4,750	258	1,771	98	9,880
North East	411	46	3,520	86	5,397	220	2,929	101	12,709
North West (GOR) & Merseyside	384	52	2,575	140	4,884	248	2,037	121	10,442
North West (GOR)	336	49	2,620	126	4,798	236	2,098	113	10,376
Merseyside	565	65	2,405	193	5,214	297	1,802	152	10,693
Yorkshire and the Humber	422	61	3,808	107	5,772	226	2,040	104	12,538
East Midlands	546	67	2,670	88	4,837	248	1,984	88	10,528
West Midlands	370	47	2,628	167	4,787	230	1,684	69	9,981
Eastern	304	47	1,533	40	3,846	189	1,224	72	7,255
London	521	88	2,309	396	5,176	447	1,968	124	11,029
South East (GOR)	350	52	1,726	45	4,344	219	1,459	91	8,287
South West	387	59	1,977	56	4,400	233	1,175	86	8,373
England	409	59	2,429	138	4,796	261	1,774	97	9,963
Wales	454	51	1,934	27	3,989	207	1,712	118	8,491
Percentage change 1994-1995									
England & Wales	-3	-5	-2	13	-5	-9	-2	5	-3
North East	-4	-19	4	23	-11	-16	-5	23	-5
North West (GOR) & Merseyside	4	8	-2	17	-1	-9	3	16	-
North West (GOR)	2	7	-3	10	-5	-18	2	12	-3
Merseyside	6	16	5	37	15	42	12	35	13
Yorkshire and the Humber	-2	-3	-4	12	-3	-10	2	2	-2
East Midlands	4	-10	-1	13	-6	13	-	9	0
West Midlands	-8	-7	-4	12	1	-7	-2	6	-2
Eastern	-4	-4	-10	11	-2	-9	5	4	-3
London	-15	-7	7	14	-6	2	-13	4	-5
South East (GOR)	7	-9	-	7	-6	-12	4	1	-3
South West	3	-13	-7	-2	-9	-23	-3	5	-7
England	-3	-6	-2	13	-5	-9	-2	6	-3
Wales	-2	5	-3	23	0	-8	-2	4	-6
Scotland[3]									
1995	308	63	1,445	104	4,323	431	1,685	903	9,261
Percentage change 1994-1995	9	-10	-16	1	-6	-7	-2	13	-5
Northern Ireland[3]									
1995	312	102	997	93	2,029	296	229	112	4,170
Percentage change 1994-1995	7	26	-3	-2	1	-4	23	-1	1

1 See Technical notes.
2 The Northern Ireland figures exclude criminal damage valued at under £200 in 1994 and 1995.
3 Figures for Scotland and Northern Ireland are not comparable with those for England and Wales, nor with each other, because of the differences in the legal systems, recording practices and classification.

Source: Home Office; The Scottish Office Home Department; Royal Ulster Constabulary

9.2 Offences committed against households, 1995[1]

Rates and percentages

	Offences per 10,000 households[2]				Percentage of households[2] victimised at least once			
	Vandalism	Burglary[3]	Vehicle thefts[4]	All household offences[5]	Vandalism	Burglary[3]	Vehicle thefts[4]	All household offences[5]
Standard Statistical Regions								
North	1,293	1,015	3,325	6,280	8.5	7.7	23.1	34.5
North West (SSR)	2,068	1,016	3,166	6,862	12.3	7.8	22.2	37.0
Yorkshire and Humberside	1,591	1,237	3,722	7,368	10.1	8.9	24.9	38.1
East Midlands	1,530	698	2,794	5,602	9.1	5.6	20.1	31.6
West Midlands	1,349	821	2,574	5,336	9.5	6.4	19.2	31.3
East Anglia	1,454	604	1,264	4,639	10.1	3.6	9.1	26.0
South East (SSR)	1,675	735	2,606	5,546	10.7	5.5	18.5	31.2
Greater London	1,477	918	3,018	5,656	9.9	7.2	20.2	31.9
Rest of South East	1,795	623	2,399	5,479	11.3	4.5	17.6	30.7
South West	1,570	638	2,380	5,611	9.1	5.1	17.0	30.2
England	1,622	830	2,745	5,893	10.3	6.3	19.4	32.5
Wales	1,485	805	2,778	5,381	9.2	6.3	21.1	30.7
Scotland	1,105	386	1,337	3,211	6.4	3.0	9.6	18.6
Northern Ireland	814	330	930	2,775	4.7	2.6	7.0	16.4

1 See Technical notes.
2 The vehicle theft risks are based on vehicle-owning households only.
3 The term used in Scotland is housebreaking. The figures include attempts at burglary/housebreaking.
4 Comprises theft of vehicles, thefts from vehicles and associated attempts.
5 Comprises the three individual categories plus thefts of bicycles and other household thefts.

Source: British Crime Survey, Home Office; Scottish Crime Survey, The Scottish Office Home Department; Northern Ireland Crime Survey, Northern Ireland Office

9.3 Notifiable offences cleared up by the police[1,2]: by offence group, 1995

Percentages

	Violence against the person	Sexual offences	Burglary	Robbery	Theft and handling stolen goods	Fraud and forgery	Criminal damage[3]	Trafficking in controlled drugs	Other[4]	Total[3,4]
England & Wales	77	76	21	23	23	50	19	98	94	26
North East	75	79	15	29	25	51	20	100	97	25
North West (GOR) & Merseyside	74	83	22	24	26	64	19	99	99	28
North West (GOR)	77	84	23	26	26	64	20	99	98	28
Merseyside	67	82	19	20	26	64	15	99	99	27
Yorkshire and the Humber	79	79	16	25	20	50	14	101	101	21
East Midlands	82	82	22	33	23	46	18	98	97	26
West Midlands	77	75	29	20	23	35	15	94	94	26
Eastern	79	74	22	27	26	48	18	101	93	28
London	65	58	22	18	18	46	31	95	82	25
South East (GOR)	81	80	19	32	24	51	18	98	93	26
South West	84	84	19	29	22	54	22	100	96	26
England	76	75	21	22	23	50	19	98	94	26
Wales	84	90	28	48	33	51	23	97	96	34
Scotland[5]	77	77	17	29	26	80	21	100	98	35
Northern Ireland[5]	67	82	19	19	31	63	33	86	94	36

1 See Technical notes.
2 Some offences cleared up in 1995 may have been initially recorded in an earlier year; hence figures can be higher than 100 per cent.
3 Figures for England and Wales exclude criminal damage valued at £20 or under. The Northern Ireland figure excludes criminal damage valued at under £200.
4 The Northern Ireland figure incudes Offences against the State.
5 Figures for Scotland and Northern Ireland are not comparable with those for England and Wales, nor with each other, because of the differences in the legal systems, recording practices and classification.

Source: Home Office; The Scottish Office Home Department; Royal Ulster Constabulary

9.4 Firearms

Numbers and rates

	Offences recorded[1] by the police in which firearms were reported[2] to have been used					Number of firearm and shot gun certificates on issue per 1,000 population[3]					Firearms surrendered during last amnesty 1996[4]
	1991	1992	1993	1994	1995	1991	1992	1993	1994	1995	
United Kingdom	15,267	16,676	16,978	15,795	15,394	18	18	17	17	17	22,939
North East	693	742	687	767	723	11	10	10	10	10	931
North West (GOR) & Merseyside	1,473	1,671	2,118	2,044	2,308	11	10	10	10	10	1,910
North West (GOR)	1,075	1,210	1,488	1,397	1,465	12	12	11	11	11	1,665
Merseyside	398	461	630	647	843	5	5	5	5	5	245
Yorkshire and the Humber	1,494	1,948	2,146	2,264	2,270	14	13	13	13	13	1,271
East Midlands	904	1,078	1,044	970	1,014	20	19	19	19	18	1,941
West Midlands	1,063	1,328	1,372	1,394	1,510	17	17	17	16	15	1,758
Eastern	865	954	898	808	771	25	24	23	23	23	2,690
London	3,706	3,584	3,513	2,186	1,918	7	6	6	6	6	1,062
South East (GOR)	1,193	1,371	1,371	1,526	1,367	20	19	19	19	18	3,409
South West	285	263	416	569	588	29	26	26	25	25	3,264
England	11,676	12,939	13,565	12,528	12,469	16	16	16	15	15	18,236
Wales	453	366	386	449	635	24	23	23	23	22	1,275
Scotland	1,921	1,959	1,776	1,788	1,715	21	20	20	20	20	3,428
Northern Ireland	1,217	1,412	1,251	1,030	575	54	54	54	54	53	.

1 See Technical notes.
2 'Alleged' in Scotland.
3 Certificates on issue as at 31 December.
4 From 3 June to 30 June 1996. The amnesty did not apply in Northern Ireland.

Source. Home Office; The Scottish Office Home Department; Royal Ulster Constabulary

9.5 Seizures of controlled drugs[1]: by type of drug, 1995

Number of seizures

	Class A drugs					Class B drugs			
	Heroin	Cocaine	LSD	Ecstasy	All class A drugs[2]	Cannabis excluding plants	Cannabis plants	Ampheta-mines	All class B drugs[2]
United Kingdom[3]	6,468	2,191	1,155	5,513	17,344	91,325	6,125	15,443	101,445
North East	87	40	41	348	520	3,070	262	898	3,732
North West (GOR) & Merseyside	1,376	150	112	549	2,266	8,603	460	1,631	9,774
North West (GOR)	1,111	58	83	406	1,738	6,477	400	1,343	7,449
Merseyside	265	92	29	143	528	2,126	60	288	2,325
Yorkshire and the Humber	952	43	86	302	1,527	5,752	716	1,468	6,723
East Midlands	138	20	82	320	610	4,469	548	1,439	5,382
West Midlands	235	37	74	275	708	4,806	459	786	5,369
Eastern	216	73	47	349	729	5,713	622	1,054	6,305
London	1,628	1,071	216	1,519	5,449	21,366	715	2,544	23,244
South East (GOR)	303	135	107	450	1,069	8,326	820	1,533	9,179
South West	456	79	103	406	1,345	6,910	834	1,329	7,695
England	5,391	1,648	868	4,518	14,223	69,015	5,436	12,682	77,403
Wales	152	23	90	174	545	4,671	383	986	5,255
Scotland	738	69	107	523	1,496	10,381	273	1,525	11,346
Northern Ireland	0	3	55	220	255	649	19	72	691
British Transport Police[3]	49	9	6	24	118	560	11	34	581
Customs and Excise[3]	138	439	29	54	707	6,049	3	144	6,169

1 See Technical notes.
2 Since a seizure may involve drugs other than those listed, figures for individual drugs cannot be added together to produce totals.
3 Figures for the British Transport Police and the Customs and Excise cannot be split by region or country, but are included in the UK totals.

Source: Home Office

9.6 Offenders given a police caution[1]: by age and gender

Percentages[2]

	Persons aged 10 - 17					Persons aged 18 or over				
	1991	1992	1993	1994	1995	1991	1992	1993	1994	1995
Males										
England & Wales	66	70	69	66	64	20	25	27	27	28
North East	63	63	62	61	59	13	18	22	26	30
North West (GOR) & Merseyside	62	65	65	62	59	17	22	23	23	21
North West (GOR)	63	66	65	64	61	17	23	25	24	22
Merseyside	58	63	63	55	48	17	19	18	20	19
Yorkshire and the Humer	65	67	63	64	61	17	20	19	20	19
East Midlands	67	67	67	64	65	20	23	24	24	26
West Midlands	67	68	68	66	62	17	24	28	28	29
Eastern	72	79	76	75	74	19	27	30	29	31
London	64	69	67	65	63	27	32	34	36	40
South East (GOR)	74	79	79	73	69	22	29	33	29	27
South West	65	72	76	73	68	22	29	33	32	30
England	66	70	69	66	64	20	25	28	28	29
Wales	63	64	64	57	59	12	17	19	20	22
Females										
England & Wales	84	88	87	85	84	40	47	48	46	46
North East	84	85	85	83	83	39	44	45	50	54
North West (GOR) & Merseyside	81	86	85	84	82	35	43	42	40	37
North West (GOR)	81	86	85	84	83	37	45	47	41	39
Merseyside	81	86	85	84	72	30	36	30	34	30
Yorkshire and the Humber	83	87	86	85	84	41	45	43	43	42
East Midlands	86	86	87	84	85	47	51	51	48	51
West Midlands	86	89	88	86	85	44	52	54	51	51
Eastern	88	91	90	90	90	41	50	53	51	52
London	81	87	86	84	83	40	46	45	44	47
South East (GOR)	89	92	91	89	85	46	53	54	50	47
South West	78	86	89	87	83	42	51	53	50	48
England	84	88	88	86	84	41	48	48	46	46
Wales	79	83	83	78	78	23	36	39	34	39
All persons										
England & Wales	70	74	73	71	68	23	29	31	31	31
North East	68	68	67	66	65	18	23	26	31	34
North West (GOR) & Merseyside	66	70	69	67	64	20	26	27	26	24
North West (GOR)	66	70	69	68	66	20	27	29	27	25
Merseyside	63	68	68	61	52	19	22	20	22	21
Yorkshire and the Humber	69	72	68	69	67	21	25	23	24	23
East Midlands	72	71	72	69	71	24	27	28	28	30
West Midlands	71	73	72	71	68	22	29	32	32	33
Eastern	76	82	80	79	78	23	31	34	33	34
London	67	73	71	69	67	29	34	36	37	41
South East (GOR)	77	83	82	77	73	26	33	37	32	30
South West	68	75	79	76	72	25	33	37	35	33
England	70	74	73	71	69	24	29	31	31	32
Wales	66	68	68	62	63	14	20	22	22	24

1 Offenders committing an indictable offence who on admission of guilt were given a formal oral caution by the police. See Technical notes.
2 Those cautioned as a percentage of persons found guilty or cautioned.

Source: Home Office

9.7 Offenders found guilty or cautioned[1]: by type of offence and age, 1991 and 1995

Rates per 100,000 population in the relevant age group

	1991						1995					
	Violence against the person plus common assault[2]	Sexual off-ences	Burglary, robbery and theft[3]	Drugs off-ences	Other indict-able off-ences[4]	All indictable offences *plus* common assult[2]	Violence against the person plus common assault[2]	Sexual off-ences	Burglary, robbery and theft[3]	Drugs off-ences	Other indict-able off-ences[4]	All indictable offences *plus* common assult[2]
Age 10-17												
England & Wales												
North East	388	39	2,890	66	182	3,565	632	32	3,617	249	338	4,868
North West (GOR) &												
Merseyside	364	39	2,479	205	292	3,379	425	26	1,923	252	256	2,882
North West (GOR)	355	44	2,530	182	272	3,383	445	29	2,105	250	267	3,096
Merseyside	398	17	2,290	287	369	3,361	348	17	1,236	258	214	2,073
Yorkshire and the Humber	392	50	2,794	101	209	3,546	435	25	2,213	148	207	3,028
East Midlands	437	64	2,391	48	195	3,135	462	37	2,036	138	166	2,839
West Midlands	376	49	2,368	65	369	3,227	409	35	2,026	162	246	2,877
Eastern	252	29	1,896	95	182	2,454	345	26	1,826	185	201	2,583
London	271	20	1,540	291	224	2,346	287	14	1,463	358	228	2,350
South East (GOR)	211	23	1,658	107	170	2,169	292	16	1,533	140	190	2,171
South West	213	27	1,375	67	154	1,836	266	18	1,432	111	167	1,994
England	313	36	2,090	129	209	2,777	375	24	1,886	198	218	2,701
Wales	342	43	2,351	65	362	3,163	405	21	1,950	193	299	2,868
Age 18 or over												
England & Wales												
North East	151	18	548	38	139	894	181	18	610	153	202	1,164
North West (GOR) &												
Merseyside	156	19	638	130	221	1,164	154	16	581	195	244	1,190
North West (GOR)	159	18	620	109	183	1,009	160	16	585	191	233	1,185
Merseyside	143	21	705	207	363	1,439	128	17	562	209	284	1,200
Yorkshire and the Humber	175	19	555	61	173	983	155	16	474	127	195	966
East Midlands	202	21	517	45	152	938	163	17	387	111	143	821
West Midlands	167	21	523	63	198	972	142	15	415	129	194	895
Eastern	110	13	428	73	131	755	113	11	348	136	132	740
London	155	22	546	223	193	1,140	137	13	490	355	243	1,238
South East (GOR)	100	14	428	86	132	760	107	12	346	130	122	717
South West	121	15	436	58	138	768	119	13	366	130	126	754
England	146	18	516	99	171	949	137	14	441	173	182	948
Wales	149	16	503	79	211	958	165	16	460	194	213	1,049

1 See Technical notes.
2 Following the introduction of a charging standard on 31 August 1994, some people who would have been charged with an indictable offence are now charged with common assult,
  a summary offence. Common assults have therefore been included for comparability between the years.
3 Includes handling stolen goods.
4 Includes fraud and forgery.

Source: Home Office

9.8 Persons found guilty of offences[1,2]; by gender and type of sentence, 1995

	Result as a percentage of number of persons sentenced						Persons convicted	
	Absolute or condit- ional discharge	Fine	All community penalties	Fully sus- pended sentence[3]	Immed- iate custodial sentence[4]	Otherwise dealt with	Rates[5]	Numbers (= 100%)
Males								
England & Wales	9	72	10	-	7	2	45.8	1,125,244
North East	14	62	13	-	8	2	44.8	55,315
North West (GOR) & Merseyside	10	71	10	-	7	2	56.8	184,968
North West (GOR)	10	70	10	-	7	2	57.3	148,447
Merseyside	9	74	9	-	7	1	54.8	36,521
Yorkshire and the Humber	11	66	14	-	8	2	41.5	99,188
East Midlands	9	70	11	-	7	2	40.9	80,694
West Midlands	8	74	11	-	7	1	45.9	116,152
Eastern	7	76	9	-	6	2	40.2	96,258
London	7	76	8	-	7	1	53.2	186,273
South East (GOR)	9	73	10	-	6	2	37.4	134,626
South West	8	76	9	-	5	2	43.3	99,202
England	9	72	10	-	7	2	45.4	1,052,676
Wales	10	73	9	-	6	1	52.5	72,568
Scotland[6]	9	72	7	.	11	1	60.6	130,778
Northern Ireland	7	69	2	8	7	7	44.0	29,572
Females								
England & Wales	12	79	7	-	2	1	8.5	217,983
North East	14	78	7	-	1	1	10.4	13,493
North West (GOR) & Merseyside	13	76	8	-	2	1	9.8	33,530
North West (GOR)	14	74	8	-	2	1	9.4	25,272
Merseyside	10	81	6	-	2	1	11.5	8,258
Yorkshire and the Humber	16	70	11	-	2	1	6.9	17,107
East Midlands	11	81	6	-	1	1	9.4	19,120
West Midlands	12	79	7	-	1	1	8.2	21,290
Eastern	10	80	7	-	2	1	7.5	18,570
London	9	81	6	-	3	1	9.1	33,400
South East (GOR)	11	80	6	-	2	1	7.0	26,381
South West	10	82	6	-	1	1	8.8	21,075
England	11	79	7	-	2	1	8.5	203,966
Wales	13	78	6	-	1	1	9.7	14,017
Scotland[6]	19	70	6	.	3	2	9.5	22,178
Northern Ireland	15	66	1	5	2	11	4.7	3,400

1 See Technical notes.
2 The coverage of the table is all offences, including motoring offences. A defendant is recorded only once for each set of court proceedings, against the principal offence.
3 Fully suspended sentences are not available to courts in Scotland.
4 Includes Young Offenders Institutions and unsuspended imprisonment. In Scotland includes custodial sentences imposed following a sentence deferred for good behaviour.
5 Rates per 1,000 population aged 10 or over.
6 To improve comparability excludes breaches of probation and community service orders normally included in Scottish figures. Most children aged under 16 are dealt with under the Children's Hearing system.

Source: Home Office; The Scottish Office Home Department; Royal Ulster Constabulary

9.9 Persons[1] found guilty of driving etc after consuming alcohol or drugs[2]: custodial sentences and average fines, 1991 and 1995

	1991					1995				
	Total pro-ceedings (numbers)	Total found guilty (numbers)	Percentage attracting custodial sentence	Average length of sentence (months)	Average fine(£)[3]	Total pro-ceedings (numbers)	Total found guilty (numbers)	Percentage attracting custodial sentence	Average length of sentence (months)	Average fine(£)[3]
United Kingdom	110,053	103,419	2.5	3.1	280	100,070	92,714	4.0	3.1	298
North East	4,881	4,616	2.4	3.6	199	3,844	3,544	3.5	3.5	227
North West (GOR) & Merseyside	14,347	13,641	2.8	3.3	266	12,747	12,004	4.7	3.0	292
North West (GOR)	10,945	10,563	2.7	3.2	269	10,211	9,728	4.0	3.2	296
Merseyside	3,402	3,078	2.9	3.5	256	2,536	2,276	7.8	2.7	271
Yorkshire and the Humber	9,413	8,833	3.4	2.9	287	7,869	7,307	4.1	2.9	306
East Midlands	6,669	6,184	3.6	2.9	277	5,362	4,889	8.0	2.8	299
West Midlands	10,891	10,219	2.0	3.5	288	9,432	8,844	4.3	3.4	324
Eastern	8,043	7,495	2.2	2.9	306	7,466	6,965	4.4	2.9	323
London	16,084	14,919	2.9	2.8	294	16,187	14,505	4.7	2.8	310
South East (GOR)	13,368	12,530	2.1	2.9	288	12,471	11,651	2.9	3.2	326
South West	8,210	7,762	2.4	3.3	293	7,440	6,960	2.8	3.5	295
England	91,906	86,199	2.6	3.1	282	82,818	76,669	4.3	3.0	306
Wales	5,868	5,531	2.6	3.6	243	5,157	4,795	3.4	3.5	270
Scotland	8,675	8,444	1.8	3.6	297	7,786	7,583	2.3	4.0	318
Northern Ireland	3,604	3,245	1.7	7.2	94	4,309	3,667	1.4	4.4	129

1 In Scotland, a person is included only if driving etc after consumption of alcohol or drugs was the main offence of which they were found guilty.
2 See Technical notes.
3 Where a fine was the principal penalty. Figures for 1991 relate to the average fine revalued to 1995 prices as estimated by the general index of retail prices.

Source: Home Office; The Scottish Office Home Department; Royal Ulster Constabulary

9.10 Persons aged 21 or over sentenced to immediate imprisonment: by gender and by length of sentence imposed for principal[1] offence, 1995

Percentages and numbers

	Males				Females			
	Length of sentence			Number of males sentenced to immediate imprisonment (= 100%)	Length of sentence			Number of females sentenced to immediate imprisonment (= 100%)
	One year or less	Over one year but less than four years	Four years or over		One year or less	Over one year but less than four years	Four years or over	
United Kingdom	76	17	7	68,942	83	12	5	3,851
North East	72	21	7	3,085	81	15	4	107
North West (GOR) & Merseyside	75	18	6	10,314	85	12	4	680
North West (GOR)	75	18	7	8,207	84	12	4	503
Merseyside	77	17	6	2,107	86	10	3	177
Yorkshire and the Humber	71	22	7	5,620	78	13	8	218
East Midlands	74	20	6	4,130	80	15	5	149
West Midlands	74	20	6	5,617	81	16	3	218
Eastern	75	19	6	4,312	89	9	2	247
London	73	18	9	11,254	81	14	5	894
South East (GOR)	71	21	8	5,986	72	17	11	343
South West	76	18	7	3,778	78	16	6	159
England	74	19	7	54,096	81	14	5	3,015
Wales	73	20	6	3,090	78	19	3	134
Scotland[2]	88	7	5	10,278	95	4	1	658
Northern Ireland	73	15	12	1,478	86	7	7	44

1 Figures for Scotland are for the length of sentence in total given for all offences and not just for the principal offence. Figures on sentence lengths for principal offences only are not available for Scotland.
2 Excludes breaches of probation and community service orders.

Source: Home Office; The Scottish Office Home Department; Northern Ireland Office

9.11 Police manpower: by type, 1995-96[1]

| | Police officers on ordinary duty[2] | | | | | Special constables and civilian staff (rates per 1,000 officers on ordinary duty) | | Traffic wardens (numbers) |
| | | Percentage of which | | Population per officer[3] | Officers per 100 sq km | Special con-stables[4] | Civilian staff | |
	Number	Ethnic minorities	Women officers					
United Kingdom[5]	150,631	1.5	14.0	389	62	154	398	5,032
North East	6,490	0.8	13.5	401	76	131	370	161
North West (GOR) & Merseyside	17,633	1.5	15.3	391	124	119	383	501
North West (GOR)	13,222	1.5	15.2	414	98	134	393	366
Merseyside	4,411	1.7	15.5	324	673	75	354	136
Yorkshire and the Humber	11,581	1.8	14.0	434	75	159	402	285
East Midlands	8,286	2.4	13.6	498	53	229	393	242
West Midlands	12,350	2.8	17.1	430	95	207	395	319
Eastern	9,501	1.2	14.5	530	50	222	410	355
London	28,213	2.9	14.5	266	1,788	68	521	1,539
South East (GOR)	14,859	1.1	14.7	510	79	177	410	458
South West	9,494	0.7	12.9	508	40	275	403	349
England	118,405	1.9	14.6	413	91	157	426	4,207
Wales	6,439	0.6	11.9	453	31	193	386	178
Scotland[6]	14,430	0.3	13.0	356	18	130	304	495
Northern Ireland[7]	11,357	..	9.2	144	84	129	228	152

1 Full-time equivalents as at 31 March 1996 for England and Wales and for Scotland. Actual numbers (whether full or part-time) as at 31 March 1996 for Northern Ireland.
2 Includes full-time Reserves in Northern Ireland.
3 Based on mid-1995 population estimates.
4 These are part-time Reserves in Northern Ireland.
5 Great Britain for ethnic minorities.
6 For civilian staff and traffic wardens, part-time staff are counted as half full-time.
7 The figure for civilian staff relates to those who work to the Chief Constable and not to those who work to the Police Authority for Northern Ireland.

Source: Home Office; The Scottish Office Home Department; Royal Ulster Constabulary

9.12 Fear of crime and feelings of insecurity: by gender, 1996[1]

Percentages

| | Worry about falling victim of specific crimes: percentage feeling 'very' worried | | | | | | | Feelings of insecurity, walking alone at night: percentage feeling 'very' or 'fairly' unsafe | | | |
| | Theft of a car[2] | | Burglary | | Mugging | | Rape | Men | | Women | |
	Men	Women	Men	Women	Men	Women	Women	16-59	60 or over	16-59	60 or over
Standard Statistical Regions											
North	27	43	19	33	9	29	30	13	18	46	57
North West (SSR)	24	28	26	31	18	33	38	12	32	47	65
Yorkshire and Humberside	30	30	19	29	9	26	28	9	25	44	65
East Midlands	30	34	19	33	12	29	38	12	19	39	58
West Midlands	24	30	20	29	15	31	38	14	30	42	66
East Anglia	12	23	8	23	8	28	33	9	15	40	55
South East (SSR)	19	21	16	22	12	22	29	13	26	41	60
Greater London	23	22	22	27	16	26	30	18	39	44	63
Rest of South East	18	20	13	19	9	19	28	9	20	40	59
South West	20	18	13	20	9	21	28	9	22	33	56
England	23	26	18	26	12	26	32	12	25	42	61
Wales	31	31	21	25	12	28	32	9	23	43	52
Scotland	..	..	13	20	10	20	25	17	31	43	61

1 See Technical notes.
2 Based on vehicle owners only; 'don't know' responses are excluded.

Source: British Crime Survey, Home Office; Scottish Crime Survey, The Scottish Office Home Department

10 Transport

Cars

One in six cars licensed to addresses in the West Midlands in 1995 was a company car compared with one in 17 in the North East, Merseyside and Wales.

(Table 10.1)

Around four in every five households in the South East (GOR) and the South West have at least one car compared with three in five in the North East, Merseyside, London and Scotland.

(Table 10.2)

However...

On average, households in the North East and in Scotland have the newest cars while those in London have the oldest.

(Table 10.3)

Traffic

The average daily traffic flow on major roads in London in 1995 was almost five times greater than that on major roads in Scotland.

(Table 10.4)

Road accidents

In 1995, the fatal or serious accident rate per vehicle kilometre on major roads in London was more than twice that for any other region of Great Britain.

(Table 10.6)

About one in five road casualties in London and in Scotland in 1995 was a pedestrian compared with one in ten in the Eastern region.

(Table 10.7)

Journeys

In the Yorkshire and Humber region and in Scotland around 18 per cent of women's journeys were for commuting in 1993-1995 compared with just over 11 per cent in Merseyside.

(Table 10.8)

On average, people living in the Yorkshire and Humber region travel the shortest distance to work, while those in the South East and the Eastern region travel the furthest (but with the fastest average speed).

(Chart 10.9)

On average, people living in London and the East Midlands walk the furthest and those in Wales the shortest distance.

(Table 10.10)

People living in London, Scotland and the North East travel, on average, more than 1,000 miles per year by public transport.

(Table 10.10)

Someone living in the South East travels an average of 8,100 miles per year compared with 4,900 for someone living in Merseyside.

(Table 10.10)

Introduction

T he demand for transport has been increasing steadily for many years. Passenger traffic by all modes has roughly tripled compared with 40 years ago and the volume of freight traffic has more than doubled. Many peoples' lifestyles now require them to travel further and more often.

Road is the dominant form of transport, accounting for 94 per cent of passenger traffic in 1995. Motor vehicle traffic grew by 2 per cent in 1994 and a further 2 per cent in 1995. Department of Transport forecasts predict that motor vehicle traffic will increase by somewhere between 11 and 18 per cent between 1994 (the base year for the forecasts) and the year 2000. This increase will be due to a combination of more vehicles being licensed and people using their vehicles more frequently for shorter distances. Table 10.1 shows the number of cars currently licensed; there were increases between 1994 and 1995 in all regions except London where the number fell by nearly 1 per cent. The average daily traffic flow on major roads across the United Kingdom as a whole in 1995 was 11 thousand vehicles per day (Table 10.4). This varied considerably both by region and by type of road, although not surprisingly the volume was highest in London.

The Government has adopted a target of reducing the total number of road casualties in Great Britain by a third from the 1981-1985 baseline average by the year 2000. The scope of the target in Northern Ireland is narrower: to reduce the total number of people killed or seriously injured by a third, again by the year 2000. There are considerable regional variations in the rates of accidents and casualties (Tables 10.6 and 10.7). However, there are many reasons why accident rates per head vary between regions. For example, they will be affected by the mix of pedestrian and vehicle traffic within each region. In Scotland, for instance, rates of pedestrian casualties are higher generally than elsewhere as lower car ownership means more people on foot, especially in highly populated areas such as Glasgow.

Other factors to bear in mind in interpreting accident and casualties statistics are the length of different types of road and the amount of traffic using those different road types. The evidence of the figures is that motorways are the safest roads on which to travel, despite the fact that the average speed is higher on motorways than on other road types. It is estimated that human error is the main or a contributory factor in 95 per cent of all road accidents.

Tables 10.8 and 10.10 and Chart 10.9 are drawn from the National Travel Survey, the household survey designed to provide information on personal travel in Great Britain. Table 10.8 shows that there are clear differences between males and females for the purposes of journeys, but that people's travel patterns are similar in all regions of the United Kingdom. Over the period 1993-1995, each person in Great Britain travelled an average of 6,510 miles a year, 22 per cent further than in 1985/86. Time spent travelling averaged 358 hours (or 15 days) per person per year. About 59 per cent of this time was spent in a car and a further 21 per cent was spent walking. People on average walked furthest in London and the East Midlands, cycled furthest in the Eastern region, and travelled furthest on public transport in London, the North East and Scotland (Table 10.10).

Regional Trends 32, © Crown copyright 1997

10.1 Motor cars currently licensed and new registrations[1]

Thousands and percentages

	Currently licensed[2]				Percentage company cars 1995[3]	New registrations			Percentage company cars 1996[3]
	1992	1993	1994	1995		1994	1995	1996	
United Kingdom	20,937	21,256	21,708	21,917	10	1,983	2,019	..	..
North East	734	747	756	765	6	66	68	74	40
North West (GOR) & Merseyside	2,303	2,360	2,407	2,426	11	223	227	235	52
North West (GOR)	1,910	1,957	1,999	2,017	12	190	193	199	56
Merseyside	393	403	408	409	6	33	34	36	25
Yorkshire and the Humber	1,607	1,632	1,656	1,674	9	131	131	138	44
East Midlands	1,398	1,423	1,451	1,464	10	138	140	140	62
West Midlands	2,023	2,067	2,116	2,146	16	244	266	275	63
Eastern	2,142	2,170	2,218	2,260	10	194	193	200	50
London	2,287	2,302	2,343	2,326	15	274	278	277	71
South East (GOR)	3,154	3,213	3,263	3,273	10	284	278	292	57
South West	1,916	1,948	1,980	1,997	9	120	121	130	55
England	17,565	17,862	18,191	18,330	11	1,674	1,702	1,762	57
Wales	981	974	982	986	6	67	68	73	40
Scotland	1,537	1,574	1,603	1,618	9	143	145	154	45
Northern Ireland	493	500	509	523	9	77	81	..	..

1 Figures for United Kingdom include motor vehicles where the county of the registered keeper is unknown.
2 At 31 December.
3 Within the Private and light goods tax class only.

Source: Annual Vehicle Census/Vehicle Information Database, Department of Transport; Department of the Environment, Northern Ireland

10.2 Availablility of cars[1], 1995-96

Percentages

	Percentage of households with			
	No car	One car	Two cars	Three or more cars
United Kingdom	30	46	21	3
North East	39	43	16	3
North West (GOR) & Merseyside	30	47	19	3
North West (GOR)	28	49	19	4
Merseyside	39	40	19	1
Yorkshire and the Humber	36	42	20	2
East Midlands	25	46	25	4
West Midlands	29	44	23	4
Eastern	24	44	27	5
London	39	44	15	2
South East (GOR)	19	46	30	6
South West	22	49	24	5
England	29	45	22	4
Wales	30	45	22	2
Scotland	38	42	19	2
Northern Ireland	31	48	17	3

1 Includes cars and light vans normally available to the household.
Source: General Household Survey, Office for National Statistics; Continuous Household Survey, Northern Ireland Statistics and Research Agency

10.3 Age of household cars, 1993-1995

Percentages

	Age of car[1]		
	Under 3 years old	3-6 years old	7 years or more
Great Britain	28	37	34
North East	35	38	27
North West (GOR) & Merseyside	30	36	34
North West (GOR)	31	36	33
Merseyside	27	36	36
Yorkshire and the Humber	28	43	29
East Midlands	30	39	31
West Midlands	29	36	35
Eastern	28	37	36
London	23	35	42
South East (GOR)	30	36	34
South West	25	36	39
England	28	37	35
Wales	23	38	39
Scotland	34	42	24

1 Age of newest car or light van normally available to the household.
Source: National Travel Survey, Department of Transport

10.4 Average daily motor vehicle flows[1]: by major road class, 1995

Thousand vehicles per day

| | Motorway | Built-up major | | | Non built-up major | | | All major roads |
		Trunk	Principal	Total	Trunk	Principal	Total	
United Kingdom	60	19	15	15	15	7	10	11
North East	45	16	13	13	19	9	13	14
North West (GOR) & Merseyside	58	16	16	16	15	9	11	19
North West (GOR)	60	14	16	16	14	8	10	18
Merseyside	46	27	16	16	25	13	19	20
Yorkshire and the Humber	52	17	15	15	19	8	12	16
East Midlands	66	20	13	14	16	8	11	14
West Midlands	69	20	17	17	15	8	10	18
Eastern	77	16	14	14	24	11	16	19
London	88	42	22	25	59	23	50	29
South East (GOR)	73	17	16	16	26	13	16	22
South West	54	16	13	13	16	8	10	13
England	65	23	16	16	20	9	13	18
Wales	50	10	10	10	9	5	7	9
Scotland	34	11	12	12	8	3	5	6
Northern Ireland[2]	25	17	11	14	8	5	6	9

1 Annual average daily flow is the number of vehicles passing a point per year divided by 365. See Technical notes.
2 Northern Ireland Primary Class 1 roads are shown as trunk roads. Non-primary Class 1 roads are shown as principal roads.

Source: Department of Transport; Department of the Environment, Northern Ireland

10.5 Distribution of traffic and accidents on major roads, 1995

| | Distribution of traffic (percentages) | | | Major road traffic (=100%) (100 million vehicle kms) | Distribution of accidents (percentages) | | | Total accidents | |
	Motorways	Built - up 'A'	Non built - up 'A'		Motorways	Built - up 'A'	Non built - up 'A'	On major roads (= 100%) (numbers)	On all roads (numbers)[1]
Great Britain	26.0	29.0	45.0	2,725	6.4	64.5	29.1	114,723	230,376
North East	9.6	26.6	63.8	94	3.0	56.7	40.4	3,509	8,309
North West (GOR) & Merseyside	37.9	34.5	27.6	323	9.1	72.6	18.3	15,318	31,020
North West (GOR)	39.2	31.8	29.0	286	10.0	69.5	20.5	12,440	24,573
Merseyside	27.0	54.1	18.9	37	5.1	86.0	8.9	2,878	6,447
Yorkshire and the Humber	25.9	32.7	41.4	219	6.3	65.5	28.1	8,847	19,954
East Midlands	21.4	22.3	56.3	215	5.1	51.8	43.1	7,757	15,902
West Midlands	36.9	28.6	34.5	255	8.1	63.7	28.1	9,540	20,030
Eastern	22.4	18.4	59.2	298	9.7	44.7	45.6	10,035	21,074
London	10.5	73.7	15.8	190	1.8	94.7	3.4	23,732	37,978
South East (GOR)	35.9	21.8	42.3	485	11.0	51.6	37.4	15,803	32,037
South West	22.7	22.7	54.5	255	6.0	47.4	46.5	7,906	17,272
England	27.7	29.4	42.9	2,334	6.7	66.3	27.1	102,447	203,576
Wales	16.5	27.8	55.7	139	4.6	48.3	47.1	4,547	10,275
Scotland	15.5	26.2	58.3	252	4.3	50.6	45.1	7,729	16,525
Northern Ireland	13.4	35.8	50.8	76	..	..	..	..	6,792

1 Includes B, C and unclassified roads. See Technical notes.

Source: Department of Transport; Welsh Office; The Scottish Office Development Department; Department of the Environment, Northern Ireland; Royal Ulster Constabulary

10.6 Fatal and serious road accidents[1]

Numbers and rates

	Fatal and serious accidents on all roads						Fatal and serious accidents on major roads[2]			
	Numbers			Rates per 100,000 population			Numbers		Rates per 100 million vehicle kms	
	1981-1985 average[3]	1991	1995	1981-1985 average[3]	1991	1995	1991	1995	1991	1995
Great Britain	67,839	47,919	41,777	124	85	73	24,340	21,109	9.4	7.8
North East	2,255	1,769	1,309	86	68	50	734	568	8.3	6.0
North West (GOR) & Merseyside	6,178	4,914	4,879	90	71	71	2,506	2,404	8.4	7.4
North West (GOR)	5,079	3,901	4,146	94	72	76	2,030	2,058	7.7	7.2
Merseyside	1,099	1,013	733	73	70	51	476	346	14.4	9.4
Yorkshire and the Humber	5,714	4,352	3,709	117	87	74	2,084	1,711	10.1	7.8
East Midlands	5,334	3,451	3,466	138	86	84	1,796	1,754	9.3	8.2
West Midlands	6,525	4,447	4,000	126	84	75	2,055	1,895	8.5	7.4
Eastern	6,884	4,802	4,248	140	93	81	2,264	1,999	7.7	6.7
London	7,588	7,267	5,922	112	105	85	4,395	3,666	23.8	19.3
South East (GOR)	10,169	5,843	5,295	139	76	67	2,882	2,686	6.1	5.5
South West	6,697	3,793	2,843	158	80	59	1,833	1,349	7.1	5.3
England	57,344	40,638	35,671	123	84	73	20,549	18,032	9.2	7.7
Wales	3,083	2,112	1,677	107	73	57	1,139	853	8.9	6.1
Scotland	7,412	5,169	4,429	144	101	86	2,652	2,224	12.1	8.8
Northern Ireland	..	1,381	1,271	..	85	77	..	..	..	..

1 See Technical notes.
2 Motorways, A(M) roads and A roads.
3 Used as a basis for the government targets for reducing road casualties in Great Britain, and fatal and serious road casualties in Northern Ireland, by a third by the year 2000.

Source: Department of Transport; Royal Ulster Constabulary

10.7 Road casualties[1]: by age and by type of road user, 1995

Percentages and numbers

	Percentage of all road casualties								All road casualties (=100%) (numbers)	Percentage change over 1981-85 average[4]
	Who were aged[2]			Type of road user						
	0 - 15	16 - 59	60 or over	Pedestrians	Pedal cyclists	Motor cyclists	Car occupants[3]	Other road users		
United Kingdom	14.1	73.9	10.0	15.0	7.9	7.4	62.9	6.9	322,231	..
North East	17.5	71.9	10.6	18.6	6.9	3.1	63.5	7.9	11,514	3.7
North West (GOR) & Merseyside	15.8	74.6	9.5	15.5	7.2	4.7	65.3	7.3	43,620	20.2
North West (GOR)	15.6	75.0	9.3	15.3	7.5	5.0	65.1	7.1	34,447	18.5
Merseyside	16.5	73.0	10.5	16.0	6.4	3.3	66.1	8.2	9,173	26.9
Yorkshire and the Humber	16.0	72.9	11.0	16.8	7.9	6.5	61.1	7.7	27,279	5.3
East Midlands	13.9	74.0	9.5	13.0	7.6	7.7	64.8	6.8	22,331	-3.2
West Midlands	15.1	73.4	9.9	15.0	7.4	6.6	64.6	6.3	27,473	-0.8
Eastern	12.4	75.5	9.7	10.2	8.7	8.1	67.5	5.5	29,253	-3.4
London	11.6	72.1	8.8	20.8	10.0	12.1	49.3	7.7	44,995	-16.9
South East (GOR)	12.2	75.3	10.1	10.9	9.3	9.0	65.5	5.4	43,408	-4.6
South West	12.4	75.7	11.6	11.8	8.2	9.6	64.4	6.0	23,500	-10.8
England	13.8	74.0	9.9	14.8	8.4	7.9	62.3	6.7	273,373	-2.5
Wales	15.1	73.4	11.5	13.7	5.0	5.4	69.5	6.5	14,950	3.8
Scotland	17.7	70.7	11.6	20.9	6.0	4.4	60.5	8.2	22,183	-18.2
Northern Ireland	14.7	77.3	8.0	10.5	3.3	2.1	75.4	8.7	11,725	..

1 See Technical notes.
2 Excludes age not reported.
3 Includes occupants of taxis and minibuses.
4 Used as a basis for the government targets for reducing road casualties in Great Britain, and fatal and serious road casualties in Northern Ireland, by a third by the year 2000.

Source: Department of Transport; Royal Ulster Constabulary

10.8 Journeys per person per year[1]: by journey purpose and gender, 1993-1995[2]

Percentages and numbers

	Commuting	Business	Education	Shopping	Other personal business	Leisure	Average number of journeys (=100%) (numbers)
Males							
Great Britain	21.6	6.8	5.0	16.2	20.2	30.2	795
North East	22.3	3.0	4.5	18.9	19.6	31.6	738
North West (GOR) & Merseyside	20.9	6.0	4.4	17.0	21.8	30.0	793
North West (GOR)	20.9	6.7	3.6	16.4	22.3	30.1	798
Merseyside	20.9	3.9	6.8	18.7	20.0	29.6	776
Yorkshire and the Humber	22.9	6.7	5.4	15.8	19.1	30.1	757
East Midlands	21.4	8.0	4.2	15.6	19.6	31.2	858
West Midlands	21.6	5.6	5.5	17.1	19.5	30.7	824
Eastern	23.8	7.4	5.1	16.3	18.4	29.1	840
London	21.8	7.0	6.8	14.3	20.6	29.6	715
South East (GOR)	20.5	8.4	4.5	16.3	21.2	29.1	861
South West	20.5	7.3	4.6	16.4	19.0	32.2	811
England	21.6	6.9	5.0	16.2	20.1	30.2	802
Wales	22.3	5.4	4.9	18.0	18.8	30.5	714
Scotland	22.2	6.1	4.1	15.3	21.6	30.8	775
Females							
Great Britain	15.7	2.2	5.0	22.8	22.7	31.6	693
North East	14.4	1.2	4.7	26.4	20.8	32.6	661
North West (GOR) & Merseyside	14.2	1.7	4.8	24.4	23.2	31.6	695
North West (GOR)	15.1	2.1	4.5	23.6	23.2	31.5	702
Merseyside	11.4	0.5	6.0	27.0	23.2	32.0	676
Yorkshire and the Humber	18.4	2.0	5.1	21.8	20.6	32.1	653
East Midlands	16.4	3.0	4.8	22.7	19.6	33.4	717
West Midlands	15.9	1.6	5.2	23.0	23.9	30.3	720
Eastern	16.5	2.3	5.7	22.5	22.1	30.8	712
London	16.2	2.8	6.1	21.1	24.1	29.6	642
South East (GOR)	14.4	2.4	4.4	22.3	24.9	31.5	778
South West	14.4	2.4	4.5	23.0	21.8	34.0	692
England	15.6	2.2	5.0	22.8	22.8	31.6	700
Wales	13.7	1.9	5.9	23.2	21.0	34.2	621
Scotland	18.0	1.7	4.1	23.1	22.2	30.9	674

1 Within Great Britain only. Figures relate to region of residence of the traveller and therefore some journeys may have been undertaken outside of this region. Journeys of less than
   1 mile are excluded.
2 See Technical notes.

Source: National Travel Survey, Department of Transport

10.9 Travel to work: distance travelled and average speed, 1993-1995[1]

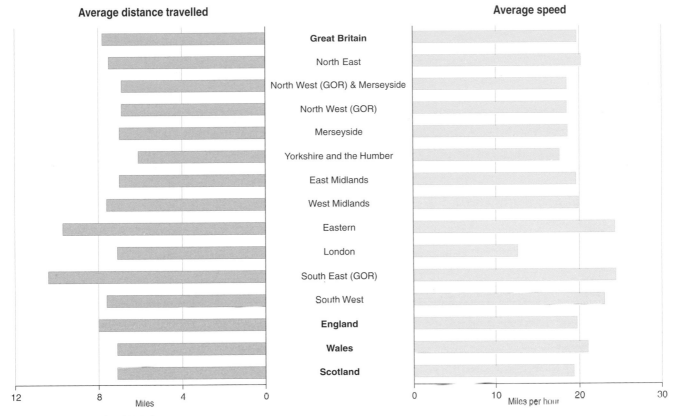

1 By region of residence. See Technical notes.

Source: National Travel Survey, Department of Transport

10.10 Distance travelled per person per year[1]: by mode of transport, 1993-1995[2]

Miles

	Walk	Pedal cycle	Cars and other private road vehicles	Public transport	All modes of transport
Great Britain	200	37	5,473	801	6,511
North East	195	40	4,377	1,016	5,627
North West (GOR) & Merseyside	209	29	5,017	755	6,010
North West (GOR)	210	30	5,448	699	6,387
Merseyside	205	23	3,706	925	4,859
Yorkshire and the Humber	196	32	4,922	704	5,853
East Midlands	232	51	6,278	464	7,024
West Midlands	174	28	5,319	633	6,154
Eastern	177	60	6,415	795	7,447
London	241	32	3,565	1,236	5,073
South East (GOR)	187	43	7,032	846	8,108
South West	185	54	6,568	596	7,402
England	201	40	5,521	801	6,563
Wales	153	20	5,235	349	5,757
Scotland	217	21	5,143	1,085	6,466

1 Within Great Britain only. Figures relate to region of residence of the traveller and therefore some journeys may have been undertaken outside of this region.
2 See Technical notes.

Source: National Travel Survey, Department of Transport

10.11 Road haulage[1] and rail freight traffic[2]

Million tonnes

Loading region[3]	Road haulage						Rail freight			
	1991	1992	1993	1994	1995	1996	1991-92	1992-93	1993-94	1994-95
United Kingdom	1,547	1,505	1,575	1,641	1,658	1,685	135.2	121.7	102.4	95.5
North	97	86	90	102	95	99	12.9	11.9	8.8	7.6
North West (SSR)	165	162	171	186	181	186	7.4	5.5	3.3	1.8
Yorkshire and Humberside	179	176	182	186	187	199	42.9	41.0	34.5	36.8
East Midlands	149	145	155	165	158	166	25.9	24.2	20.4	18.1
West Midlands	143	142	157	152	163	162	6.1	4.5	3.5	2.5
East Anglia	84	80	86	83	88	78	1.6	1.3	1.5	0.5
South East (SSR)	313	309	314	344	339	348	5.8	4.8	5.2	2.6
Greater London	74	67	76	80	83	76	2.7	2.2	1.6	1.3
Rest of the South East	240	242	237	264	256	272	3.1	2.6	3.6	1.3
South West	136	120	122	129	141	133	9.9	9.3	9.0	9.1
England	1,265	1,221	1,278	1,347	1,352	1,369	112.5	102.5	86.2	79.0
Wales	92	87	89	96	100	98	13.7	12.2	11.2	11.1
Scotland	148	157	158	155	157	162	9.0	7.0	5.0	5.4
Northern Ireland	41	41	50	43	49	54	.	.	.	.

1 Traffic carried by UK registered vehicles only. International road haulage is considered to be loaded at the port of entry. Includes weight of containers.
2 Excludes international traffic. Includes weight of containers. Northern Ireland Railways do not operate a local freight service, therefore UK figures related to Great Britain. Figures are not available from 1995-96 onwards following privatisation of the rail industry.
3 Standard Statistical Regions.

Source: Department of Transport; Department of the Environment, Northern Ireland

10.12 Air Terminal passengers[1] at selected airports: by domestic and international flights

Millions

	Domestic flights				International flights			
	1986	1991	1994	1995	1986	1991	1994	1995
Newcastle	0.4	0.5	0.7	0.7	0.8	1.0	1.7	1.8
Manchester	1.5	1.9	2.3	2.4	6.0	8.2	12.1	12.1
Leeds/Bradford	0.2	0.4	0.4	0.4	0.3	0.3	0.4	0.5
East Midlands	0.3	0.3	0.3	0.3	0.9	0.8	1.3	1.5
Birmingham	0.5	0.7	0.8	0.9	1.6	2.5	3.9	4.3
Luton	-	0.2	0.1	0.1	1.9	1.7	1.7	1.7
Stansted	0.1	0.3	0.5	0.8	0.5	1.4	2.8	3.1
Heathrow	5.6	6.7	7.1	7.3	25.7	33.5	44.3	46.8
Gatwick	1.1	1.0	1.6	1.8	15.2	17.7	19.4	20.6
Bristol	-	0.1	0.2	0.3	0.4	0.6	1.1	1.2
Cardiff	-	0.1	0.1	0.1	0.4	0.5	0.9	0.9
Aberdeen	0.9	1.3	1.5	1.5	0.6	0.7	0.7	0.7
Edinburgh	1.4	1.9	2.4	2.6	0.2	0.4	0.6	0.7
Glasgow	1.7	2.3	2.6	2.8	1.4	1.9	2.9	2.6
Belfast City	0.2	0.5	1.2	1.3	-	-	-	-
Belfast International	1.4	1.8	1.4	1.6	0.4	0.4	0.6	0.7

1 Arrivals and departures.

Source: Department of Transport

11 Environment

Rainfall

Northern Ireland was the only region in the United Kingdom to receive at least its average rainfall during 1996.

(Table 11.1)

Water consumption

Non-metered customers of the Southern Water and Sewage Company used on average 27 litres per head per day more than those of the Yorkshire Water and Sewage Company in 1995-96.

(Table 11.3)

Water pollution

On average, Wales and the South Western region have the highest quality rivers and canals, within England and Wales.

(Table 11.4)

In 1995, prosecutions for water pollution incidents were more likely in Northern Ireland than in any other region.

(Table 11.5)

Northern Ireland, Wessex and Yorkshire coastal regions have the best records of bathing waters complying with EU standards, while the North West coastal region has the poorest record.

(Table 11.6)

Acidity

The areas where critical loads for freshwater and soil vegetation acidity are exceeded occur mainly in the upland areas of the north and west of Great Britain.

(Chart 11.7)

Air pollution

Black smoke and sulphur dioxide concentrations have reduced greatly in most parts of the United Kingdom since the 1970s, but there are still significant local variations.

(Table 11.8)

Ozone pollution is at its worst in the South East (GOR), particularly in Kent and East and West Sussex.

(Chart 11.9)

Radiation

The South West is the region of England most affected by high levels of radon.

(Chart 11.10)

Heritage

London has over twice as many entries per 10 square kilometres on the listed buildings register as Merseyside, the region with the second highest density.

(Table 11.11)

The coastline of the South West accounts for over 40 per cent of the total length of Defined Heritage Coasts of England and Wales, the highest proportion of any region.

(Table 11.12)

Land

Almost two thirds of all land changing to urban uses in the East Midlands in 1992 had been land in rural uses.

(Table 11.14)

Regional Trends 32, © Crown copyright 1997

Introduction

W ater resources, water use, water quality and the health of the aquatic environment are all affected by climatic conditions which vary not only from region to region and from year to year, but also from season to season. They are also affected by strongly seasonal losses owing to evaporation. Table 11.1 shows the last 11 years' annual rainfall total in each region expressed as a percentage of the region's 1961-1990 average rainfall and highlights in particular the exceptionally dry conditions experienced across the United Kingdom in 1996.

An interesting feature of recent years is the increased concentration of rainfall in the winter half year (October to March). Table 11.2 shows winter and summer half year rainfall for the last three years. It clearly demonstrates the unusually wet winter of 1994-1995; indeed, December to February in this period was the wettest on record for the United Kingdom. This was followed by the long, hot summer of 1995 where April to August was the driest five-month sequence for over 200 years in England and Wales. Figures for 1995-1996 show a very dry winter was followed by another dry summer. Winter 1995-1996 apart, the accentuation in the half-yearly rainfall contrasts has important implications for water resources: the limited winter evaporation increases the effectiveness of winter rainfall in replenishing resources, but the lower summer rainfall puts increased pressure on water resources at the very time when demand increases.

Table 11.3 shows estimated water consumption per head for those households served by the ten water and sewage companies of England and Wales. There are also 18 smaller companies which only supply water which are not included in the table. The hot, dry summer of 1995 stimulated higher than usual demand for water. The industry as a whole reported a 5 per cent increase in water consumption from 146 litres per head per day in 1994-95 to 154 in 1995-96 for those households without a water meter. However among households with a meter consumtion rose from 131 litres per head per day to 134, an increase of only 2 per cent. Per head consumption in 1995-96 was therefore 13 per cent lower in households with a meter than in those without. This may partly reflect the fact that many customers who choose to have a meter installed are low users, but the figures do suggest that the use of water meters encourages people to conserve water.

Water leakage has become an increasingly important issue as more demand is put on resources. Taken in aggregate again, the industry reported a 1° per cent fall in estimated total water leakage between 1994-95 and 1995-96. The total amount lost in 1995-96 was 4,979 megalitres (or 221 litres per property per day) which represents around 30 per cent of the distribution input.

Variations in rainfall and consequently river flow can have a considerable effect on freshwater quality and the aquatic environment. Lower than average rainfall and low river flows are likely to have an adverse effect on river quality because there is a reduced dilution of pollution; water abstractions during periods of increased demand can also have a detrimental affect. On the other hand, effluent treatment works better in hot, dry weather and river quality benefits from fewer storms. Various aspects of water quality are shown in this chapter, namely the chemical quality of rivers and canals (Table 11.4), water pollution incidents (Table 11.5) and bathing water standards (Table 11.6).

11.1 Rainfall[1]

Percentages and millimetres

	Annual rainfall as a percentage of the 1961-1990 rainfall average											1961-1990 rainfall average (millimetres) (=100%)
	1986	1987	1988	1989	1990	1991	1992	1993	1994	1995	1996[2]	
United Kingdom	112	98	107	97	112	95	113	107	113	98	87	1,079
North West	109	104	110	89	105	93	103	97	113	85	78	1,201
Northumbria	110	112	106	71	101	94	99	113	103	96	84	853
Severn Trent	109	102	102	96	91	86	112	111	114	90	82	754
Yorkshire	114	101	106	81	95	82	102	109	108	84	84	821
Anglian	108	115	103	91	79	79	118	122	108	91	79	596
Thames	110	104	96	94	80	88	116	112	108	100	77	688
Southern	109	106	93	86	90	90	103	117	122	98	83	778
Wessex	112	89	96	97	88	91	101	115	123	111	93	839
South West	114	92	106	96	100	93	96	118	126	100	96	1,173
England	109	102	102	89	91	87	106	111	113	93	83	823
Wales[3]	115	99	107	98	101	94	107	105	121	92	88	1,355
Scotland	114	94	112	104	134	102	121	104	112	104	88	1,436
Northern Ireland	110	91	112	91	117	96	109	109	110	101	102	1,059

1 The regions of England shown in this table correspond to the original nine English regions of the National Rivers Authority; the NRA became part of the Environment Agency upon its creation in April 1996. See Technical notes.
2 Figures are provisional for November and December 1996.
3 The figures in this table relate to the country of Wales; in Tables 11.4 - 11.6 they relate to the Environment Agency Welsh Region.

Source: Meteorological Office; Institute of Hydrology

11.2 Winter and summer half-year rainfall[1,2]

Percentages and millimetres

	Rainfall as a percentage of the 1961-1990 winter and summer rainfall averages						1961-1990 rainfall average for winter (=100%) (millimetres)	1961-1990 rainfall average for summer (=100%) (millimetres)
	1993-1994		1994 - 1995		1995 - 1996			
	Winter	Summer	Winter	Summer	Winter	Summer		
United Kingdom	124	95	132	73	86	76	609	471
North West	113	93	141	58	62	75	669	534
Northumbrian	121	82	127	69	92	73	456	397
Severn Trent	131	101	133	62	85	70	397	357
Yorkshire	117	91	132	60	72	72	441	380
Anglian	140	105	125	69	77	63	298	298
Thames	130	94	138	68	95	63	362	327
Southern	134	118	144	71	83	71	444	335
Wessex	138	105	147	78	110	81	477	361
South West	136	111	135	71	99	86	718	456
England	129	98	136	65	84	70	444	379
Wales[3]	128	99	137	64	83	83	796	560
Scotland	118	90	130	85	84	77	836	601
Northern Ireland	121	94	116	64	111	102	597	462

1 Winter rainfall is the October - March accumulation; Summer rainfall is the April - September accumulation.
2 The regions of England shown in this table correspond to the original nine regions of the National Rivers Authority; the NRA became part of the Environment Agency upon its creation in April 1996. See Technical notes.
3 The figures in this table relate to the country of Wales; in Tables 11.4 - 11.6 they relate to the Environment Agency Welsh Region.

Source: Meteorological Office; Institute of Hydrology

11.3 Estimated household water consumption[1]

Litres per head per day

Water and sewage companies	Unmetered households[2]				Metered households
	1992-93	1993-94	1994-95	1995-96	1995-96
North West	134	135	136	144	116
Northumbrian	139	141	139	149	130
Yorkshire	127	128	132	137	124
Severn Trent	127	127	128	140	133
Anglian	146	145	146	155	128
Thames	153	157	162	159	148
Southern	146	150	155	164	134
Wessex	130	130	144	150	120
South West	142	142	148	163	136
Welsh	140	141	142	150	127

1 See Introduction to chapter.
2 Excluding underground supply pipe leakage.

Source: OFWAT

11.4 Rivers and canals: by chemical quality[1], 1988-1990 and 1993-1995

Percentages and kilometres

	1988-1990[2]					1993-1995[2]				
	Quality (percentages)				Total length surveyed (=100%)	Quality (percentages)				Total length surveyed (=100%)
	Good	Fair	Poor	Bad	(kms)	Good	Fair	Poor	Bad	(kms)
Environment Agency Regions[3]										
Northumbria and Yorkshire	58	24	14	4	4,250	62	24	12	1	5,960
North West	42	31	20	7	3,190	54	30	13	2	5,750
Severn Trent	34	46	18	2	5,700	45	46	8	1	6,590
Anglian	18	63	17	2	4,560	39	48	12	1	4,810
Thames	37	46	16	1	3,530	49	45	6	-	3,800
Southern	44	44	11	1	2,180	56	36	7	1	2,220
South Western	64	29	5	1	6,720	75	21	3	-	6,060
England	44	40	14	3	30,140	55	35	9	1	35,180
Wales	79	16	3	1	4,020	91	7	2	-	5,040
Northern Ireland	44	51	4	1	1,680	45	43	12	0	2,350

1 Based on the chemical quality grade of the General Quality Assessment (GQA) scheme. See Technical notes.
2 Average of three years data combined.
3 In England and Wales. The boundaries of the Environment Agency Regions are based on river catchment areas and not county borders. In particular, the figures shown for Wales are for the Environment Agency Welsh Region, the boundary of which does not coincide with the boundary of Wales. See map on page 214 and Technical notes.

Source: Environment Agency; Department of the Environment, Northern Ireland

11.5 Water pollution incidents: by type, 1995[1]

Numbers

	Industrial		Sewage and water related[3]		Agricultural		Other		Total		Number of prose-cutions[4]
	All	Major[2]	All	Major[2]	All	Major[2]	All	Major[2]	All	Major[2]	
Environment Agency Regions[5]											
United Kingdom	5,818	141	7,864	82	3,704	142	11,209	133	28,595	498	442
Northumbria & Yorkshire	539	13	1,013	10	220	7	804	6	2,576	36	35
North West	948	10	1,223	7	312	6	1,234	5	3,717	28	45
Severn Trent	749	10	1,175	6	371	2	1,964	10	4,259	28	50
Anglian	399	5	557	7	212	1	988	2	2,156	15	27
Thames	330	2	487	6	115	0	1,040	4	1,972	12	29
Southern	239	6	328	1	123	3	545	2	1,235	12	19
South Western	711	8	1,469	7	975	6	1,403	14	4,558	35	62
England	3,915	54	6,252	44	2,328	25	7,978	43	20,473	166	267
Wales[5]	848	8	905	4	392	7	845	14	2,990	33	35
Scotland	674	52	..	..	334	37	1,744	76	2,752	165	40
Northern Ireland	381	27	707	34	650	73	642	0	2,380	134	100

1 Data relate to substantiated reports of pollution only. Figures for Scotland relate to the financial year 1995-96.
2 Major incidents are those corresponding to Category 1 in the Environment Agency's pollution incidents classification scheme. For Northern Ireland major incidents also correspond to Category 2. For Scotland the term 'significant incidents' is used. See Technical notes.
3 Not summarised separately for Scotland - included in other sectors.
4 For England and Wales total prosecutions include cases concluded and prosecutions outstanding. Prosecutions concluded relate to cases which had been brought to court by 31 March 1996. In Scotland, this figure relates to the number of incidents referred to the Procurator Fiscal.
5 In England and Wales. The boundaries of the Environment Agency Regions are based on river catchment areas and not county borders. In particular, the figures shown for Wales are for the Environment Agency Welsh Region, the boundary of which does not coincide with the boundary of Wales. See map on page 214 and Technical notes.
Source: Environment Agency; Scottish Environment Protection Agency; Department of the Environment, Northern Ireland

11.6 Bathing Water - compliance with EC Bathing Water Directive[1] coliform standards[2]: by coastal region

Numbers and percentages

	Identified bathing waters (numbers)					Percentage complying during the bathing season[3]				
	1992	1993	1994	1995	1996	1992	1993	1994	1995	1996
Environment Agency Regions[4]										
United Kingdom	455	457	457	464	472	79	80	82	89	90
North West	33	33	33	33	33	33	39	73	45	61
Northumbria[5]	34	34	34	34	34	59	74	85	97	85
Yorkshire[5]	22	22	22	22	22	91	95	91	91	91
Anglian	33	33	33	34	35	94	85	82	88	97
Thames	3	3	3	3	3	100	100	67	100	67
Southern	67	67	67	67	69	76	87	79	93	90
Wessex[5]	39	42	42	42	42	92	83	95	95	98
South West[5, 6]	134	133	133	134	138	87	80	83	95	91
England	365	367	367	369	376	79	79	83	89	89
Wales[4]	51	51	51	56	57	76	82	76	88	91
Scotland	23	23	23	23	23	65	78	70	83	91
Northern Ireland	16	16	16	16	16	94	94	94	94	100

1 76/160/EEC.
2 At least 95 per cent of samples must have counts not exceeding the mandatory limit values for total faecal coliforms.
3 The bathing season is from mid-May to end-September in England and Wales, but is shorter in Scotland and Northern Ireland.
4 In England and Wales. The boundaries of the Environment Agency Regions are based on river catchment areas and not county borders. In particular, the figures shown for Wales are for the Environment Agency Welsh Region, the boundary of which does not coincide with the boundary of Wales. See map on page 214 and Technical notes.
5 In 1993, the Northumbria and Yorkshire regions amalgamated, as did the Wessex and South West regions. Data for these regions are shown on the old basis for consistency.
6 The decrease in the number of identified bathing waters in 1993 and 1994 was due to the closure of Lyme Regis Church Beach for engineering works.
Source: Environment Agency; Scottish Environment Protection Agency; Department of the Environment, Northern Ireland

11.7   Critical loads for acidity of soil vegetation and freshwaters[1]

Areas[2] where critical loads for acidity of soil vegetation are exceeded by annual mean total nitrogen and non-marine sulphur deposition, 1992-1994

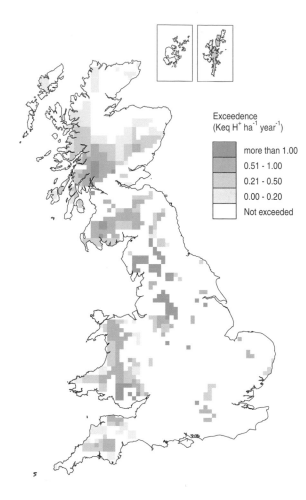

Exceedence
(Keq H$^+$ ha^{-1} year^{-1})

- more than 1.00
- 0.51 - 1.00
- 0.21 - 0.50
- 0.00 - 0.20
- Not exceeded

Areas[3] where critical loads for acidity of freshwaters are exceeded by annual mean total non-marine sulphur and nitrogen deposition, 1989-199

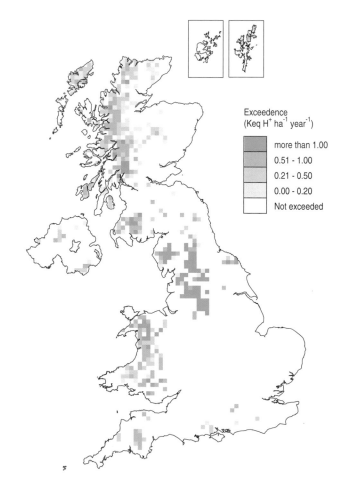

Exceedence
(Keq H$^+$ ha^{-1} year^{-1})

- more than 1.00
- 0.51 - 1.00
- 0.21 - 0.50
- 0.00 - 0.20
- Not exceeded

1 See Technical notes.
2 Areas of at least 20 square kilometres.
3 Areas of at least 10 square kilometres.

Source: Institute of Terrestial Ecology; National Environmental Technology Centre

11.8 Atmospheric pollution[1,2]

	Black smoke				Sulphur dioxide			
	Micrograms per cubic metre			Percentage change 1975-76 to 1995-96	Micrograms per cubic metre			Percentage change 1975-76 to 1995-96
	1975-76	1985-86	1995-96		1975-76	1985-86	1995-96	
Newcastle	228	89	54	-76	260	95	56	-78
Manchester	269	80	75	-72	319	105	62	-81
Barnsley	380	171	69	-82	323	166	171	-47
Mansfield Woodhouse	381	198	89	-77	226	214	108	-52
Stoke-on-Trent	456	119	44	-90	330	127	82	-75
Norwich	156	51	53	-66	133	51	115	-14
Stepney	185	31	48	-74	592	249	85	-86
Slough	113	62	39	-65	219	72	37	-83
Plymouth[3]	105	56	..	..	421	43	..	..
Cardiff	161	44	24	-85	180	71	36	-80
Glasgow	154	100	35	-77	190	81	46	-76
Belfast	335	98	74	-78	226	201	217	-4

1 One site chosen for each UK statistical region.
2 Figures shown are for 98th percentile daily mean concentrations ie the level which is exceeded by the highest 2 per cent of daily mean concentrations during the year.
3 Site out of service during 1995-96.

Source: National Environmental Technology Centre

11.9 Ground level ozone levels[1], 1990-1995

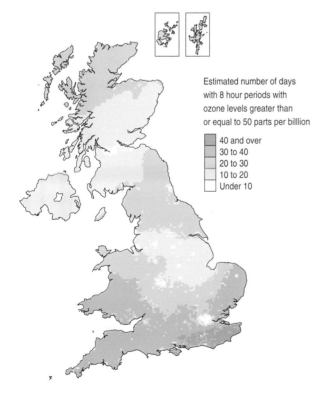

Estimated number of days with 8 hour periods with ozone levels greater than or equal to 50 parts per billlion

- 40 and over
- 30 to 40
- 20 to 30
- 10 to 20
- Under 10

1 See Technical notes.

Source: National Environmental Technology Centre

11.10 Radon affected areas[1], 1996

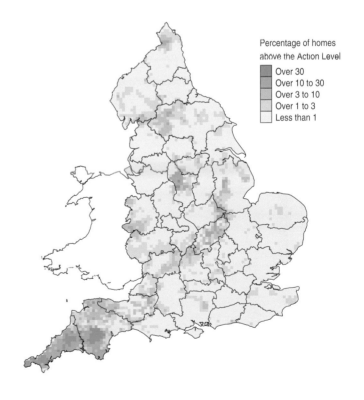

Percentage of homes above the Action Level

- Over 30
- Over 10 to 30
- Over 3 to 10
- Over 1 to 3
- Less than 1

1 Estimated proportion of homes exceeding the Action Level of 200 Bq/m[3] in each 5km square. See Technical notes.

Source: National Radiological Protection Board

11.11 Listed buildings[1], 1996

Numbers and rates

	Listed buildings (numbers)	Listed buildings per 10 sq km
United Kingdom	435,700	18
North East	12,000	14
North West (GOR) and Merseyside	24,600	17
North West (GOR)	21,900	16
Merseyside	2,800	42
Yorkshire and the Humber	30,500	20
East Midlands	29,100	19
West Midlands	33,500	26
Eastern	57,200	30
London	16,700	106
South East (GOR)	74,300	39
South West	87,600	37
England	365,500	28
Wales	18,800	9
Scotland	42,800	5
Northern Ireland	8,600	6

1 Entries on the list. An entry can cover more than one building.

Source: Department of National Heritage

11.12 Designated areas[1], 1996[2]

	National Parks		Areas of Outstanding Natural Beauty[3]		Green Belt land		Designated Heritage Coasts length (km)
	Area (sq km)	Percentage of total area in region	Area (sq km)	Percentage of total area in region	Area (sq km)	Percentage of total area in region	
Standard Statistical Regions							
North	3,620	23	2,260	15	465	3	128
North West	100	1	780	11	2,417	3	0
Yorkshire & Humberside	3,150	20	920	6	2,496	16	82
East Midlands	920	6	520	3	615	4	0
West Midlands	200	2	1,270	10	2,458	19	.
East Anglia	0	0	910	7	261	2	121
South East	0	0	6,620	24	6,058	22	72
South West	1,650	7	7,120	30	787	3	638
England	9,630	7	20,390	16	15,557	12	1,041
Wales	4,130	19	830	4	.	.	496
Scotland	.	.	10,020	13	1,550	2	.
Northern Ireland	.	.	2,850	20	2,266	17	.

1 See Technical notes. Some areas may be in more than one category.
2 At 31 March.
3 National Scenic Areas in Scotland.

Source: Department of the Environment

11.13 Protected areas[1], as at 31 December 1996

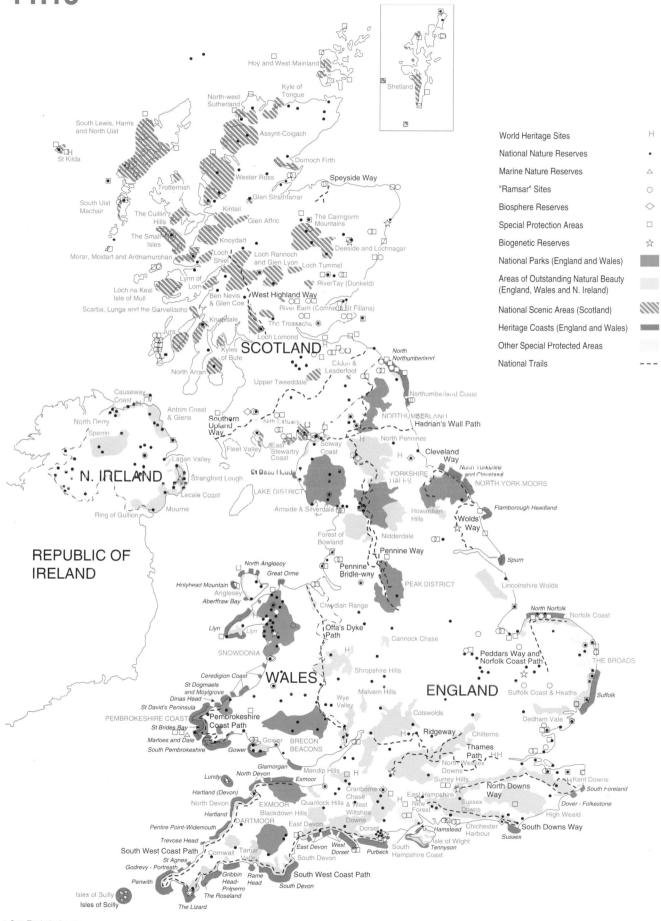

Legend:

World Heritage Sites	H
National Nature Reserves	•
Marine Nature Reserves	△
"Ramsar" Sites	○
Biosphere Reserves	◇
Special Protection Areas	□
Biogenetic Reserves	☆
National Parks (England and Wales)	
Areas of Outstanding Natural Beauty (England, Wales and N. Ireland)	
National Scenic Areas (Scotland)	
Heritage Coasts (England and Wales)	
Other Special Protected Areas	
National Trails	- - -

1 See Technical notes.

Source: Countryside Commission; English Nature; Department of National Heritage; Institute of Terrestial Ecology; Department of the Environment; Countryside Council for Wales; Scottish Natural Heritage; Department of the Environment, Northern Ireland

11.14 Previous use of land changing to urban use in 1992[1]

	Previous use (percentages)						All changes to urban uses (=100%) (hectares)	All changes to urban uses (hectares per 100,000 population[4])
	Rural uses			Urban uses				
	Agriculture	Other rural uses	All rural uses	Previously developed[2]	Vacant land not previously developed[3]	All urban uses		
North East	27	8	34	51	14	66	865	33
North West (GOR) and Merseyside	20	9	29	62	9	71	1,970	29
North West (GOR)	23	7	31	61	8	69	1,585	29
Merseyside	7	15	22	69	9	78	385	27
Yorkshire and the Humber	28	8	36	55	9	64	1,590	32
East Midlands	53	9	62	32	6	38	1,430	35
West Midlands	41	5	46	46	8	54	1,400	26
Eastern	36	10	46	47	8	54	1,605	31
London	3	6	9	89	3	91	690	10
South East (GOR)	36	11	47	44	10	53	2,245	29
South West	44	10	54	40	7	46	1,200	25
England	33	9	42	50	8	58	12,995	27

1 The information relates only to map changes recorded by the Ordnance Survey between 1992 and 1996 for which the year of change is judged to be 1992. See Technical notes.
2 Previously developed urban land is land which was previously in residential, transport and utilities, industrial and commercial, or community uses, or was previously developed vacant land.
3 Land in built-up areas which has not been developed previously and which is not currently used for agriculture.
4 Based on mid-1992 population estimates.

Source: Department of the Environment

12 Regional accounts

Gross domestic product

London and the South East (GOR) together account for nearly a third of UK GDP.

(Table 12.1)

Only in London was GDP per head over £12,000 in 1995; it was lowest in Wales and in Northern Ireland at about £8,400.

(Table 12.1)

GDP per head relative to the UK average increased significantly between 1991 and 1995 in the West Midlands, while that for Wales and the Yorkshire and Humber region decreased.

(Chart 12.2)

Income from employment was the source of around 66 per cent of GDP in London and 65 per cent in Scotland in 1995 compared with 60 per cent in Wales and the South West.

(Table 12.3)

Nearly a third of GDP in the West Midlands, but only an eighth in London, came from manufacturing in 1995, the highest and lowest proportions.

(Table 12.4)

More than two fifths of London's GDP in 1995 was generated by financial and business services compared with less than a fifth in Northern Ireland, Wales, the North and the East Midlands.

(Table 12.4)

Household income/ disposable income

Households in Northern Ireland, Wales, the North East and the North West benefited most from the redistributive effects of the tax and benefit system in 1995, whilst those in London and the South East contributed the most.

(Table 12.6)

Personal income/ disposable income

Personal income per head in 1995 was more than 15 per cent below the UK average in Wales and the North East, while in London it was 25 per cent above the UK average.

(Table 12.7)

Personal disposable income per head in 1995 was highest in London and the South East (GOR), at around £10,500 and £9,600 respectively, and lowest in Wales at £7,400.

(Table 12.7)

Consumers' expenditure

London had the highest consumers' expenditure per head, at over £9,000 per person in 1995, while Wales had the lowest, at under £6,700.

(Table 12.8)

Introduction

The regional accounts provide a breakdown of the main components of the national accounts into sub-national areas. The national accounts are published each year in the ONS' *Blue Book - United Kingdom National Accounts*. This chapter covers estimates for regions; county estimates of GDP and household income can be found in the sub-regional chapter for England. Estimates for Government Office Regions (GOR) are presented where possible throughout the chapter. Figures for GDP by industry groups, consumers' expenditure and gross domestic fixed capital formation have not been calculated on this basis because they require data which are not yet available on the GOR classification. A detailed analysis of the figures can be found in a series of articles in the ONS' publication *Economic Trends* (most recently January/February and June 1997 editions).

Wales, Scotland, Northern Ireland and the regions of England differ in size, character, industrial structure and economic performance. The South East (GOR) has the largest population - nearly 8 million - and the largest GDP at just under £90 billion in 1995. At the other extreme, Northern Ireland with a population of 1.6 million has a GDP of around £14 billion. The wide variation in the size of the regions makes it difficult to compare the regions' economic performance using cash totals; comparisons are therefore usually made in terms of amounts per head of population. However, it is important to note that the growth in totals can differ from growth per head where the population has increased or decreased. Furthermore the level per head is determined both by the working population's incomes and by the proportion who do not work. In Northern Ireland, for example, households have a high proportion of children: over a quarter of the population was aged under 16 in 1995 compared with about a fifth in most regions. This depresses income and expenditure per head in Northern Ireland relative to other regions. Ideally the age structure of the population should be taken into account when comparing figures on a per head basis.

UK GDP is defined as the sum of all incomes earned from productive activity in the United Kingdom. Regional GDP should thus be defined as the sum of incomes earned from productive activity in the region, so that the income of commuters should be included in the region where they work. However the estimates of regional GDP presented here are not compiled on this basis; they include regional estimates of income from employment on a residence basis, because this is the basis of the more reliable data source (the 1 per cent sample of Department of Social Security records). This has a significant effect on the estimates for London, for the South East (GOR) and for the Eastern region, but is assumed not to introduce any significant distortion for the other regions.

Estimates of GDP by region are at factor cost. They measure the income of factors of production and exclude taxes on expenditure such as VAT, but include subsidies. Regional accounts are only available in current prices which means that increases over time reflect inflation as well as real growth. Trends in totals per head cannot be analysed easily without deflating the data. However, there are no sub-national price indices, which could be used to remove the effect of inflation from the figures. Comparisons of trends can only therefore be based on either the difference between regional increases at current prices or on movements in levels relative to the UK average. Both approaches would be misleading if the rate of inflation in any region were different from the national average.

The regional accounts, although calculated as reliably as possible, cannot be regarded as accurate to the last digit shown. They are based partly on sample surveys and the quality of the results therefore varies according to sample size. This means that results for areas with smaller populations such as the Isle of Wight are likely to be less precise than those for more populous areas. An assessment of the quality of the regional and county estimates was published in *Economic Trends*, November 1990.

12.1 Gross domestic product[1], factor cost: current prices

	1985	1986	1987	1988	1989	1990	1991	1992	1993	1994	1995
£ million											
United Kingdom	307,902	328,272	360,675	401,428	441,759	478,886	496,253	518,132	548,025	579,177	604,259
North East	11,875	12,507	13,708	15,143	16,758	17,949	18,802	19,876	20,811	21,697	22,635
North West (GOR) &											
Merseyside	33,584	36,778	40,042	44,667	48,290	51,667	53,192	55,344	58,493	61,589	63,861
Yorkshire and the Humber	23,598	26,081	28,262	31,126	34,394	37,134	38,690	40,026	41,918	44,085	46,099
East Midlands	19,695	21,615	23,875	26,540	29,756	31,951	33,468	34,865	36,746	38,810	40,935
West Midlands	24,424	26,724	29,380	33,263	36,736	40,266	41,412	43,497	45,614	48,204	51,200
Eastern	27,852	30,968	33,883	38,502	42,865	46,251	47,672	49,805	51,999	55,519	57,784
London	42,399	47,204	52,212	58,214	64,281	69,836	72,477	75,762	81,197	84,075	87,608
South East (GOR)	40,839	45,738	50,596	58,206	64,229	70,021	72,397	74,869	79,657	85,031	88,130
South West	21,673	24,183	26,760	30,247	33,440	36,391	38,016	39,993	42,141	44,344	46,641
England	245,940	271,797	298,719	335,907	370,749	401,465	416,128	434,037	458,575	483,353	504,893
Wales	11,993	13,531	15,086	17,117	18,802	20,272	20,900	21,431	22,338	23,878	24,618
Scotland	25,207	27,268	29,813	32,986	36,206	40,128	42,094	44,547	46,917	49,548	50,713
Northern Ireland	6,304	6,988	7,533	8,364	9,249	10,191	11,138	11,722	12,463	13,216	13,868
United Kingdom *less* Continental Shelf and statistical discrepancy	289,444	319,584	351,151	394,374	435,006	472,056	490,259	511,737	540,293	569,995	594,091
Continental Shelf	18,458	8,688	9,524	7,054	6,753	6,830	5,994	6,395	7,732	9,182	10,348
Statistical discrepancy (income adjustment)	-	-	-	-	-	-	-	-	-	-	-180
As a percentage of											
United Kingdom *less* Continental Shelf and statistical discrepancy											
United Kingdom	100.0	100.0	100.0	100.0	100.0	100.0	100.0	100.0	100.0	100.0	100.0
North East	4.1	3.9	3.9	3.8	3.9	3.8	3.8	3.9	3.9	3.8	3.8
North West (GOR) &											
Merseyside	11.6	11.5	11.4	11.3	11.1	10.9	10.8	10.8	10.8	10.8	10.7
Yorkshire and the Humber	8.2	8.2	8.0	7.9	7.9	7.9	7.9	7.8	7.0	7.7	7.8
East Midlands	6.8	6.8	6.8	6.7	6.8	6.8	6.8	6.8	6.8	6.0	6.9
West Midlands	8.4	8.4	8.4	8.4	8.4	8.5	8.4	8.5	8.4	8.5	8.6
Eastern	9.6	9.7	9.6	9.8	9.9	9.8	9.7	9.7	9.6	9.7	9.7
London	14.6	14.8	14.9	14.8	14.8	14.8	14.8	14.8	15.0	14.8	14.7
South East (GOR)	14.1	14.3	14.4	14.8	14.8	14.8	14.8	14.6	14.7	14.9	14.8
South West	7.5	7.6	7.6	7.7	7.7	7.7	7.8	7.8	7.8	7.8	7.9
England	85.0	85.0	85.1	85.2	85.2	85.0	84.9	84.8	84.9	84.8	85.0
Wales	4.1	4.2	4.3	4.3	4.3	4.3	4.3	4.2	4.1	4.2	4.1
Scotland	8.7	8.5	8.5	8.4	8.3	8.5	8.6	8.7	8.7	8.7	8.5
Northern Ireland	2.2	2.2	2.1	2.1	2.1	2.2	2.3	2.3	2.3	2.3	2.3
£ per head											
United Kingdom *less* Continental Shelf and statistical discrepancy	5,106	5,621	6,160	6,900	7,584	8,201	8,481	8,822	9,285	9,761	10,134
North East	4,554	4,808	5,276	5,841	6,461	6,909	7,225	7,619	7,967	8,314	8,689
North West (GOR) &											
Merseyside	4,893	5,367	5,850	6,531	7,042	7,525	7,725	8,033	8,474	8,923	9,255
Yorkshire and the Humber	4,809	5,316	5,761	6,326	6,950	7,483	7,765	8,002	8,360	8,772	9,166
East Midlands	5,055	5,516	6,062	6,691	7,450	7,960	8,294	8,583	9,000	9,460	9,926
West Midlands	4,702	5,143	5,634	6,363	7,009	7,670	7,865	8,242	8,623	9,104	9,649
Eastern	5,600	6,179	6,715	7,582	8,419	9,046	9,257	9,623	10,013	10,628	10,991
London	6,244	6,938	7,678	8,598	9,455	10,191	10,519	10,973	11,712	12,068	12,503
South East (GOR)	5,494	6,104	6,716	7,675	8,443	9,163	9,428	9,708	10,296	10,922	11,231
South West	4,801	5,303	5,811	6,499	7,152	7,753	8,058	8,426	8,838	9,247	9,663
England	5,213	5,741	6,290	7,052	7,755	8,365	8,632	8,972	9,449	9,924	10,324
Wales	4,268	4,799	5,325	5,998	6,553	7,044	7,228	7,394	7,686	8,197	8,440
Scotland	4,907	5,323	5,831	6,476	7,104	7,865	8,242	8,715	9,163	9,654	9,873
Northern Ireland	4,047	4,460	4,782	5,300	5,843	6,412	6,955	7,243	7,637	8,050	8,410

1 See Technical notes.

Source: Office for National Statistics

12.2 Gross domestic product per head

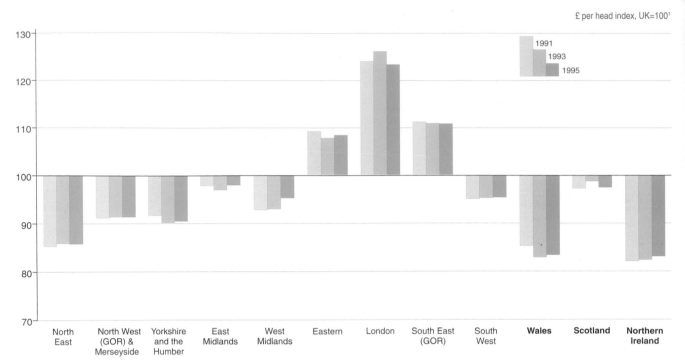

£ per head index, UK=100[1]

1991
1993
1995

1 United Kingdom *less* Continental Shelf and statistical discrepancy.

Source: Office for National Statistics

12.3 Factor incomes in the gross domestic product[1], factor cost: current prices, 1995

£ million

	Income from employment	Income from self-employment	Gross trading profits and surpluses	*Less* stock appreciation	Rent[2]	Gross domestic product
United Kingdom	377,895	67,685	96,274	4,902	67,487	604,259
North East	14,243	2,091	4,314	230	2,217	22,635
North West (GOR) & Merseyside	40,576	5,942	11,174	624	6,792	63,861
Yorkshire and the Humber	29,153	5,421	7,143	443	4,825	46,099
East Midlands	25,448	4,885	6,809	404	4,196	40,935
West Midlands	32,978	5,334	8,491	559	4,957	51,200
Eastern	36,840	7,339	7,650	410	6,364	57,784
London	57,625	9,127	8,701	474	12,628	87,608
South East (GOR)	56,568	10,328	11,327	601	10,508	88,130
South West	28,073	6,929	6,146	378	5,871	46,641
England	321,503	57,397	71,756	4,122	58,358	504,893
Wales	14,780	2,797	4,743	232	2,530	24,618
Scotland	32,892	5,604	7,518	413	5,111	50,713
Northern Ireland	8,720	1,887	1,901	127	1,487	13,868
Continental Shelf	..	..	10,356	8	..	10,348
Statistical discrepancy (income adjustment)	..	..	..	..	..	-180

1 See Technical notes.
2 Including imputed charges for consumption of non-trading capital.

Source: Office for National Statistics

12.4　Gross domestic product by industry groups[1], factor cost: current prices

£ million

Standard Statistical Regions	North 1991	North 1995	North West (SSR) 1991	North West (SSR) 1995	Yorkshire and Humberside 1991	Yorkshire and Humberside 1995	East Midlands 1991	East Midlands 1995
Agriculture, hunting, forestry and fishing	440	552	469	657	753	1,011	933	1,195
Mining, quarrying inc oil and gas extraction	550	240	131	82	893	346	1,016	346
Manufacturing[2]	6,519	8,403	13,787	16,098	10,076	11,852	9,254	12,175
Electricity, gas, water	541	792	1,382	1,617	1,280	1,208	1,089	1,179
Construction	1,673	1,602	2,932	2,970	2,543	2,664	2,195	2,277
Distribution, hotels and catering; repairs	3,025	3,405	7,252	8,615	6,091	7,085	4,839	6,047
Transport, storage and communication	1,727	1,887	4,053	5,043	2,950	3,756	2,294	2,797
Financial & business services, etc[3]	4,171	5,082	10,143	13,496	7,018	9,994	6,352	8,124
Public administration and defence[4]	1,489	1,806	2,665	3,241	2,271	2,881	1,708	2,048
Education, social work and health services	2,916	3,696	5,958	7,587	4,787	5,939	3,645	4,830
Other services	781	947	1,712	2,075	1,285	1,549	964	1,150
Adjustment for financial services	-537	-765	-1,784	-2,632	-1,257	-2,187	-820	-1,234
Total	23,294	27,648	48,699	58,848	38,690	46,099	33,468	40,934

	West Midlands 1991	West Midlands 1995	East Anglia 1991	East Anglia 1995	South East (SSR) 1991	South East (SSR) 1995	Greater London 1991	Greater London 1995
Agriculture, hunting, forestry and fishing	827	1,079	929	1,150	1,243	1,593	49	59
Mining, quarrying inc oil and gas extraction	362	160	107	151	440	737	179	230
Manufacturing[2]	12,142	16,001	3,773	4,938	27,416	33,393	9,505	11,380
Electricity, gas, water	1,084	1,516	458	643	4,082	3,972	1,447	1,235
Construction	2,588	2,582	1,259	1,161	10,858	10,497	3,750	3,468
Distribution, hotels and catering; repairs	5,984	7,294	2,610	2,907	25,701	30,565	10,438	12,670
Transport, storage and communication	2,817	3,448	1,742	2,187	18,450	22,324	8,641	9,996
Financial & business services, etc[3]	8,479	10,907	3,792	4,905	57,198	76,268	27,986	37,780
Public administration and defence[4]	2,304	2,578	1,277	1,370	12,436	14,094	4,772	5,652
Education, social work and health services	4,791	6,032	1,929	2,533	18,950	23,206	7,930	9,417
Other services	1,307	1,663	636	739	7,628	9,972	3,779	5,133
Adjustment for financial services	-1,272	-2,060	-706	-980	-9,661	-14,811	-5,999	-9,411
Total	41,412	51,200	17,807	21,709	174,739	211,812	72,477	87,608

	Rest of the South East 1991	Rest of the South East 1995	South West 1991	South West 1995	England 1991	England 1995	Wales 1991	Wales 1995
Agriculture, hunting, forestry and fishing	1,194	1,534	1,234	1,730	6,827	8,968	492	604
Mining, quarrying inc oil and gas extraction	261	507	387	686	3,885	2,749	228	209
Manufacturing[2]	17,912	22,014	7,366	8,988	90,333	111,849	5,839	6,930
Electricity, gas, water	2,635	2,737	1,423	1,724	11,338	12,651	582	860
Construction	7,108	7,029	2,608	2,693	26,655	26,446	1,248	1,295
Distribution, hotels and catering; repairs	15,263	17,895	5,831	6,834	61,332	72,752	2,990	3,271
Transport, storage and communication	9,809	12,329	2,557	3,073	36,589	44,515	1,431	1,590
Financial & business services, etc[3]	29,212	38,488	8,686	11,898	105,839	140,674	3,440	4,499
Public administration and defence[4]	7,664	8,442	3,715	4,113	27,865	32,139	1,568	1,819
Education, social work and health services	11,019	13,789	4,515	5,769	47,491	59,591	2,866	3,487
Other services	3,849	4,839	1,312	1,572	15,624	19,667	700	837
Adjustment for financial services	-3,662	-5,399	-1,617	-2,440	-17,654	-27,109	-490	-783
Total	102,262	124,204	38,016	46,641	416,126	504,892	20,901	24,618

	Scotland 1991	Scotland 1995	Northern Ireland 1991	Northern Ireland 1995	United Kingdom[5] 1991	United Kingdom[5] 1995
Agriculture, hunting, forestry and fishing	1,160	1,646	486	678	8,965	11,896
Mining, quarrying inc oil and gas extraction	1,044	1,187	53	82	5,210	4,227
Manufacturing[2]	8,483	10,173	2,240	2,707	106,895	131,658
Electricity, gas, water	1,110	1,868	358	408	13,387	15,787
Construction	2,951	3,310	651	763	31,505	31,815
Distribution, hotels and catering; repairs	6,010	6,876	1,415	1,807	71,756	84,706
Transport, storage and communication	3,572	4,030	598	700	42,190	50,835
Financial & business services, etc[3]	8,223	10,664	1,698	2,387	119,199	158,224
Public administration and defence[4]	3,181	3,692	1,642	1,860	34,257	39,510
Education, social work and health services	6,199	7,583	1,815	2,310	58,371	72,972
Other services	1,632	2,160	431	590	18,387	23,255
Adjustment for financial services	-1,470	-2,477	-249	-425	-19,864	-30,794
Total	42,094	50,713	11,138	13,868	490,258	594,091

1 Gross domestic product is shown for each industry after deducting stock appreciation. See Technical notes.
2 Definition of manufacturing as revised in SIC 1992.
3 Financial intermediation, real estate, renting, business activities, including rent on dwellings.
4 Public administration, national defence and compulsory social security.
5 The total excludes production from the Continental Shelf.

Source: Office for National Statistics

12.5 Household disposable income: by county[1], 1994

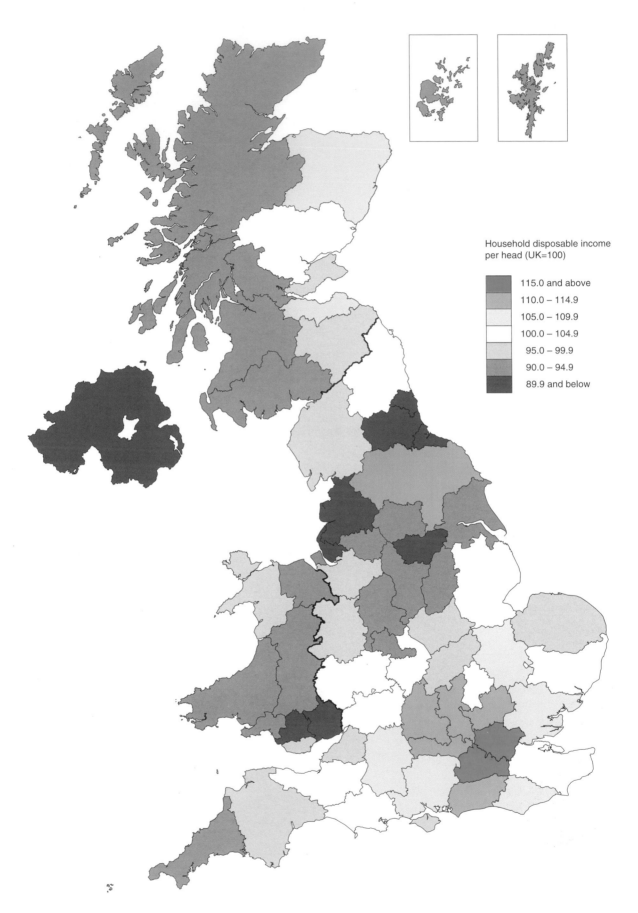

Household disposable income
per head (UK=100)

- 115.0 and above
- 110.0 – 114.9
- 105.0 – 109.9
- 100.0 – 104.9
- 95.0 – 99.9
- 90.0 – 94.9
- 89.9 and below

1 Local authority regions in Scotland; Northern Ireland is not sub-divided. For England, the figures underlying this map can be found in Table 14.7.

Source: Office for National Statistics

12.6 Household income and disposable household income

	1985	1990	1991	1992	1993	1994	1995
Household income							
£ million							
United Kingdom	287,633	471,444	501,703	530,998	546,605	566,645	598,654
North East	11,875	18,163	19,877	21,201	21,757	21,917	22,799
North West (GOR) & Merseyside	32,725	51,868	55,194	58,087	59,353	61,180	64,347
Yorkshire and the Humber	23,236	37,279	39,770	42,224	43,396	44,832	47,048
East Midlands	19,120	31,160	33,158	34,829	36,200	37,698	40,197
West Midlands	23,693	39,433	42,210	44,776	45,843	47,727	51,199
Eastern	26,880	45,785	48,334	50,955	51,707	54,428	57,475
London	40,552	67,819	72,102	75,301	78,793	80,929	86,501
South East (GOR)	41,599	69,906	73,524	77,291	80,424	85,058	89,710
South West	23,545	38,538	40,989	43,746	44,571	46,017	48,764
England	243,224	399,950	425,157	448,411	462,045	479,786	508,042
Wales	12,435	20,612	22,063	23,430	23,712	24,903	25,758
Scotland	25,386	40,313	42,998	46,848	47,950	48,459	50,542
Northern Ireland	6,590	10,569	11,486	12,309	12,897	13,496	14,312
£ per head							
United Kingdom	5,074	8,190	8,679	9,154	9,393	9,704	10,215
North East	4,555	6,991	7,638	8,127	8,329	8,398	8,752
North West (GOR) & Merseyside	4,768	7,554	8,016	8,431	8,599	8,864	9,326
Yorkshire and the Humber	4,735	7,512	7,982	8,441	8,655	8,922	9,355
East Midlands	4,907	7,763	8,217	8,575	8,866	9,190	9,747
West Midlands	4,561	7,511	8,016	8,484	8,667	9,014	9,649
Eastern	5,405	8,955	9,386	9,846	9,957	10,421	10,932
London	5,972	9,897	10,465	10,906	11,365	11,615	12,345
South East (GOR)	5,596	9,148	9,575	10,022	10,395	10,927	11,432
South West	5,216	8,210	8,688	9,217	9,348	9,590	10,103
England	5,155	8,334	8,819	9,269	9,520	9,850	10,389
Wales	4,425	7,162	7,631	8,083	8,158	8,549	8,831
Scotland	4,942	7,901	8,419	9,166	9,365	9,442	9,840
Northern Ireland	4,230	6,660	7,172	7,605	7,904	8,221	8,679
Disposable household income							
£ per head							
United Kingdom	4,050	6,622	7,075	7,524	7,808	8,027	8,417
North East	3,705	5,844	6,452	6,879	7,118	7,136	7,466
North West (GOR) & Merseyside	3,845	6,210	6,638	7,093	7,287	7,427	7,882
Yorkshire and the Humber	3,838	6,213	6,635	7,086	7,270	7,400	7,867
East Midlands	3,874	6,364	6,765	7,124	7,438	7,574	8,146
West Midlands	3,688	6,130	6,638	7,030	7,273	7,545	8,061
Eastern	4,190	7,112	7,517	7,943	8,175	8,529	8,875
London	4,775	7,669	8,146	8,583	9,129	9,378	9,703
South East (GOR)	4,357	7,187	7,564	7,991	8,402	8,774	9,035
South West	4,221	6,710	7,187	7,671	7,842	8,060	8,473
England	4,108	6,704	7,149	7,580	7,878	8,118	8,511
Wales	3,607	6,012	6,438	6,878	6,983	7,303	7,559
Scotland	3,920	6,502	7,015	7,685	7,912	7,885	8,296
Northern Ireland	3,497	5,645	6,214	6,518	6,871	7,046	7,532
£ per head, United Kingdom = 100							
United Kingdom	100.0	100.0	100.0	100.0	100.0	100.0	100.0
North East	91.5	88.3	91.2	91.4	91.2	88.9	88.7
North West (GOR) & Merseyside	95.0	93.8	93.8	94.3	93.3	92.5	93.6
Yorkshire and the Humber	94.8	93.8	93.8	94.2	93.1	93.3	93.5
East Midlands	95.7	96.1	95.6	94.7	95.3	94.4	96.8
West Midlands	91.1	92.6	93.8	93.4	93.1	94.0	95.8
Eastern	103.5	107.4	106.2	105.6	104.7	106.3	105.4
London	117.9	115.8	115.1	114.1	116.9	116.8	115.3
South East (GOR)	107.6	108.5	106.9	106.2	107.6	109.3	107.3
South West	104.2	101.3	101.6	101.9	100.4	100.4	100.7
England	101.4	101.2	101.0	100.7	100.9	101.1	101.1
Wales	89.1	90.8	91.0	91.4	89.4	91.0	89.8
Scotland	96.8	98.2	99.1	102.1	101.3	98.2	98.6
Northern Ireland	86.4	85.2	87.8	86.6	88.0	87.8	89.5

Source: Office for National Statistics

12.7 Personal income and disposable personal income[1]

	1985	1990	1991	1992	1993	1994	1995
Personal income							
£ million							
United Kingdom	307,081	485,175	516,732	547,929	572,125	596,929	633,237
North East	12,518	18,569	20,299	21,607	22,390	22,818	23,914
North West (GOR) & Merseyside	35,316	53,978	57,174	60,177	62,419	64,823	68,271
Yorkshire and the Humber	24,922	38,544	41,183	43,592	45,423	47,441	49,891
East Midlands	20,597	32,307	34,227	35,731	37,720	39,617	42,377
West Midlands	25,848	41,508	44,509	47,235	48,779	50,962	54,363
Eastern	27,789	44,778	47,189	49,685	51,126	53,861	57,081
London	44,041	71,133	75,851	79,758	85,067	88,134	94,676
South East (GOR)	44,724	72,572	76,273	80,959	85,344	90,744	97,072
South West	24,370	38,113	40,803	43,819	45,284	46,792	49,640
England	260,125	411,501	437,509	462,564	483,552	505,191	537,286
Wales	13,053	20,795	22,333	23,587	24,212	25,493	26,463
Scotland	26,879	41,914	44,800	48,735	50,502	51,564	53,922
Northern Ireland	7,024	10,965	12,088	13,042	13,859	14,680	15,566
£ per head							
United Kingdom	5,417	8,429	8,939	9,446	9,832	10,222	10,805
North East	4,801	7,148	7,800	8,283	8,572	8,744	9,180
North West (GOR) & Merseyside	5,146	7,861	8,304	8,734	9,043	9,392	9,894
Yorkshire and the Humber	5,078	7,767	8,265	8,714	9,059	9,441	9,920
East Midlands	5,286	8,049	8,482	8,797	9,239	9,658	10,276
West Midlands	4,976	7,907	8,453	8,950	9,222	9,625	10,245
Eastern	5,587	8,758	9,163	9,600	9,845	10,312	10,857
London	6,486	10,380	11,009	11,552	12,270	12,649	13,512
South East (GOR)	6,017	9,497	9,933	10,498	11,031	11,657	12,370
South West	5,399	8,120	8,649	9,232	9,498	9,751	10,284
England	5,513	8,574	9,075	9,561	9,963	10,372	10,987
Wales	4,645	7,226	7,724	8,138	8,330	8,751	9,073
Scotland	5,233	8,214	8,772	9,535	9,863	10,047	10,498
Northern Ireland	4,509	6,899	7,548	8,059	8,493	8,942	9,440
Personal disposable income							
£ per head							
United Kingdom	4,294	6,567	7,028	7,504	7,873	8,143	8,573
North East	3,858	5,713	6,276	6,713	6,997	7,092	7,420
North West (GOR) & Merseyside	4,101	6,224	6,616	7,046	7,339	7,576	7,971
Yorkshire and the Humber	4,074	6,183	6,617	7,020	7,357	7,626	7,978
East Midlands	4,158	6,325	6,705	7,005	7,443	7,718	8,206
West Midlands	3,982	6,235	6,718	7,182	7,447	7,738	8,217
Eastern	4,285	6,592	6,978	7,373	7,651	8,003	8,376
London	5,194	7,853	8,408	8,920	9,622	9,873	10,513
South East (GOR)	4,683	7,218	7,607	8,157	8,638	9,088	9,589
South West	4,313	6,353	6,830	7,384	7,635	7,785	8,192
England	4,365	6,644	7,090	7,549	7,939	8,222	8,678
Wales	3,736	5,781	6,316	6,690	6,851	7,184	7,400
Scotland	4,132	6,526	7,041	7,740	8,020	8,101	8,415
Northern Ireland	3,691	5,767	6,389	6,847	7,285	7,639	8,027
£ per head, United Kingdom = 100							
United Kingdom	100.0	100.0	100.0	100.0	100.0	100.0	100.0
North East	89.8	87.0	89.3	89.5	88.9	87.1	86.6
North West (GOR) & Merseyside	95.5	94.8	94.1	93.9	93.2	93.0	93.0
Yorkshire and the Humber	94.9	94.2	94.2	93.5	93.4	93.7	93.1
East Midlands	96.8	96.3	95.4	93.4	94.5	94.8	95.7
West Midlands	92.7	95.0	95.6	95.7	94.6	95.0	95.8
Eastern	99.8	100.4	99.3	98.3	97.2	98.3	97.7
London	120.9	119.6	119.6	118.9	122.2	121.3	122.6
South East (GOR)	109.0	109.9	108.2	108.7	109.7	111.6	111.9
South West	100.4	96.7	97.2	98.4	97.0	95.6	95.6
England	101.7	101.2	100.9	100.6	100.8	101.0	101.2
Wales	87.0	88.0	89.9	89.2	87.0	88.2	86.3
Scotland	96.2	99.4	100.2	103.2	101.9	99.5	98.2
Northern Ireland	85.9	87.8	90.9	91.2	92.5	93.8	93.6

1 See Technical notes.

12.8 Consumers' expenditure[1]

	1985	1986	1987	1988	1989[2]	1990[2]	1991[2]	1992[2]	1993[2]	1994[2]	1995[2]
£ million											
United Kingdom	217,485	241,553	265,290	299,449	327,363	347,527	365,469	383,490	406,399	427,276	447,247
North	10,465	11,828	12,744	14,080	15,324	16,232	17,379	18,520	19,830	20,477	21,114
North West (SSR)	22,681	25,322	28,140	31,732	34,555	36,628	38,511	40,033	42,583	45,150	47,440
Yorkshire and Humberside	16,817	18,428	20,351	23,140	25,387	26,611	28,281	30,639	33,273	34,985	36,315
East Midlands	13,750	14,964	16,557	18,915	21,493	23,425	24,445	25,332	26,997	28,865	30,804
West Midlands	18,099	19,790	21,907	25,113	27,902	29,621	30,996	31,657	33,431	36,409	38,364
East Anglia	7,475	8,471	9,200	10,443	11,482	12,094	12,902	13,533	13,904	14,443	15,141
South East (SSR)	77,478	86,688	94,901	106,518	115,777	121,634	127,071	134,073	141,975	148,691	155,656
Greater London	31,615	35,715	39,376	44,525	48,438	50,663	52,220	54,779	58,135	60,474	63,244
Rest of the South East	45,863	50,972	55,525	61,992	67,339	70,971	74,851	79,294	83,841	88,217	92,412
South West	17,164	19,566	21,989	24,674	26,753	28,674	30,267	31,193	32,341	33,360	34,678
England	183,930	205,056	225,791	254,615	278,672	294,919	309,851	324,980	344,334	362,381	379,512
Wales	9,888	10,753	11,568	13,134	14,541	15,811	16,872	17,647	18,205	18,556	19,477
Scotland	18,771	20,180	21,894	24,817	26,558	28,503	29,842	31,489	34,055	35,865	37,035
Northern Ireland[3]	4,896	5,563	6,037	6,883	7,592	8,294	8,904	9,373	9,805	10,475	11,222
£ per head											
United Kingdom	3,837	4,249	4,654	5,239	5,707	6,038	6,322	6,611	6,984	7,317	7,631
North	3,386	3,832	4,133	4,572	4,970	5,257	5,621	5,976	6,392	6,606	6,821
North West (SSR)	3,555	3,977	4,425	4,995	5,427	5,744	6,021	6,256	6,641	7,041	7,401
Yorkshire and Humberside	3,427	3,756	4,148	4,703	5,130	5,363	5,676	6,125	6,636	6,961	7,220
East Midlands	3,529	3,819	4,204	4,769	5,381	5,836	6,058	6,236	6,612	7,036	7,470
West Midlands	3,484	3,808	4,201	4,804	5,324	5,642	5,887	5,998	6,320	6,876	7,230
East Anglia	3,803	4,251	4,570	5,134	5,617	5,876	6,197	6,479	6,640	6,859	7,132
South East (SSR)	4,496	5,007	5,464	6,122	6,633	6,931	7,205	7,573	7,990	8,320	8,653
Greater London	4,656	5,250	5,790	6,577	7,125	7,393	7,579	7,934	8,385	8,680	9,026
Rest of the South East	4,392	4,849	5,255	5,833	6,320	6,635	6,965	7,343	7,737	8,000	8,415
South West	3,802	4,201	4,775	5,301	5,722	6,109	6,415	6,572	6,783	6,956	7,184
England	3,898	4,331	4,766	5,045	5,829	6,145	6,427	6,717	7,095	7,440	7,760
Wales	3,519	3,814	4,083	4,603	5,068	5,494	5,835	6,088	6,263	6,370	6,678
Scotland	3,654	3,939	4,282	4,872	5,211	5,586	5,843	6,161	6,651	6,988	7,210
Northern Ireland[3]	3,143	3,551	3,833	4,362	4,796	5,218	5,560	5,792	6,008	6,381	6,806
£ per head United Kingdom = 100											
United Kingdom	100.0	100.0	100.0	100.0	100.0	100.0	100.0	100.0	100.0	100.0	100.0
North	88.3	90.2	88.8	87.3	87.1	87.1	88.9	90.4	91.5	90.3	89.4
North West (SSR)	92.7	93.6	95.1	95.3	95.1	95.1	95.2	94.6	95.1	96.2	97.0
Yorkshire and Humberside	89.3	88.4	89.1	89.8	89.9	88.8	89.8	92.6	95.0	95.1	94.6
East Midlands	92.0	89.9	90.3	91.0	94.3	96.7	95.8	94.3	94.7	96.2	97.9
West Midlands	90.8	89.6	90.3	91.7	93.3	93.5	93.1	90.7	90.5	94.0	94.7
East Anglia	99.1	100.0	98.2	98.0	98.4	97.3	98.0	98.0	95.1	93.7	93.5
South East (SSR)	117.2	117.8	117.4	116.9	116.2	114.8	114.0	114.6	114.4	113.7	113.4
Greater London	121.4	123.6	124.4	125.5	124.8	122.5	119.9	120.0	120.1	118.6	118.3
Rest of the South East	114.5	114.1	112.9	111.3	110.7	109.9	110.2	111.1	110.8	110.6	110.3
South West	99.1	101.0	102.6	101.2	100.3	101.2	101.5	99.4	97.1	95.1	94.1
England	101.6	101.9	102.2	102.0	102.1	101.8	101.7	101.6	101.6	101.7	101.7
Wales	91.7	89.8	87.7	87.9	88.8	91.0	92.3	92.1	89.7	87.1	87.5
Scotland	95.2	92.7	92.0	93.0	91.3	92.5	92.4	93.2	95.2	95.5	94.5
Northern Ireland[3]	81.9	83.6	82.4	83.3	84.0	86.4	87.9	87.6	86.0	87.2	89.2

1 See Technical notes.
2 Domestic rates are treated as part of consumers' expenditure. Community Charge which was introduced in Scotland from 1989 and in England and Wales from 1990, and the Council Tax which replaced it from 1993, are deductions in the calculation of personal disposable income and hence not part of consumers' expenditure. There are therefore discontinuities in the regional and national series after 1988/1989.
3 Domestic rates continue in Northern Ireland. There is therefore no discontinuity in the Northern Ireland series. However it is not comparable with those for the regions of Great Britain after 1988/1989.

Source: Office for National Statistics

12.9 Consumers' expenditure[1]: by broad function, 1995

£ million

	Food, drink and tobacco	Clothing and footwear	Housing and fuel	Household goods and services	Vehicles, transport and comm-unications	Recreation	Other goods and services	Consumers' expend-iture in the UK[2]	Total consumers' expend-iture[3]
Standard Statistical Regions									
United Kingdom	86,860	25,801	87,706	27,806	77,803	40,526	92,585	439,087	447,247
North	4,657	1,277	4,010	1,269	3,342	1,846	3,950	20,352	21,114
North West (SSR)	9,778	2,661	8,942	3,070	8,384	3,933	9,240	46,008	47,440
Yorkshire and Humberside	7,418	2,000	6,829	2,369	5,720	3,253	7,449	35,038	36,315
East Midlands	6,021	1,720	5,882	1,931	5,392	2,793	6,091	29,829	30,804
West Midlands	7,617	1,900	7,129	2,233	6,886	3,640	7,619	37,024	38,364
East Anglia	2,937	762	3,107	1,041	2,510	1,537	3,148	15,041	15,141
South East (SSR)	27,358	9,367	31,978	9,724	29,195	14,062	34,191	155,875	155,656
Greater London	11,144	4,418	13,048	3,974	12,062	5,704	15,684	66,034	63,244
Rest of the South East	16,214	4,949	18,930	5,751	17,133	8,358	18,506	89,842	92,412
South West	6,618	1,942	7,624	1,980	5,112	3,444	7,133	33,853	34,678
England	72,404	21,630	75,500	23,618	66,542	34,509	78,819	373,022	379,512
Wales	4,004	1,046	3,880	1,159	3,301	1,779	3,638	18,808	19,477
Scotland	8,127	2,350	6,328	2,238	6,185	3,338	7,901	36,466	37,035
Northern Ireland[4]	2,325	776	1,998	791	1,775	899	2,227	10,791	11,222

1 See Technical notes.
2 Expenditure by UK households and foreign residents in the United Kingdom.
3 Expenditure by UK consumers, including private non-profit making bodies serving persons and UK households abroad but excluding expenditure in the United Kingdom by foreign residents.
4 Domestic rates which are levied in Northern Ireland are treated as part of consumers' expenditure. Council Tax levied in Great Britain is treated as a deduction from income, and is therefore not part of consumers' expenditure. These series are therefore not comparable with those for the regions of Great Britain.

Source: Office for National Statistics

12.10 Gross domestic fixed capital formation: by selected industry groups, 1994

£ million

	Agriculture forestry and fishing	Energy, mining and water[1]	Manufacturing[2]	Transport and com-munication[3]	Dwellings	Total of industries shown
Standard Statistical Regions						
United Kingdom	930	9,042	13,534	10,423	21,124	55,053
North	51	380	876	296	1,109	2,711
North West (SSR)	44	737	1,564	850	2,277	5,473
Yorkshire and Humberside	83	600	1,296	780	1,676	4,434
East Midlands	78	417	1,041	608	1,700	3,845
West Midlands	76	489	1,749	758	1,906	4,978
East Anglia	74	252	483	262	840	1,911
South East (SSR)	98	1,333	3,357	4,682	5,994	15,464
South West	129	426	936	730	1,847	4,068
England	634	4,634	11,302	8,965	17,349	42,884
Wales	79	497	766	355	1,018	2,715
Scotland	102	474	1,137	807	2,146	4,665
Northern Ireland	115	94	329	296	611	1,444
Continental shelf[4]	.	3,342	.	.	.	3,342

1 Includes extraction of mineral oil and natural gas, mining and quarrying, electricity, gas and water.
2 Definition of manufacturing as revised in SIC 1992.
3 Excluding sea and air transport.
4 Oil and gas extraction only.

Source: Office for National Statistics

13 Industry and Agriculture

Gross domestic product
The West Midlands, the North East and the East Midlands derived the highest proportion of their GDP from production and the lowest proportion from services of all the regions in 1995.
(Chart 13.1)

Northern Ireland derived a greater percentage of its GDP from agriculture than any other region in 1995.
(Chart 13.13)

Businesses
Over 24 per cent of individual businesses in Leicestershire were involved in production while nearly 90 per cent in the City of Edinburgh were involved in services, higher proportions than in any other county or unitary authority in Great Britain.
(Chart 13.3)

London and Northern Ireland were the only two regions where there was a net increase during 1995 in the number of enterprises registered for VAT.
(Table 13.9)

Manufacturing
On average, factories in London are smaller than elsewhere in the United Kingdom and those in the North East bigger.
(Table 13.2)

The level of gross value added in manufacturing in 1994 ranged from £23,790 per person employed in Northern Ireland to £33,450 in London.
(Table 13.4)

Assisted Areas
Almost two thirds of expenditure on preferential assistance to industry in Great Britain in 1995-96 went to Assisted Areas in Wales and Scotland.
(Table 13.7)

Research and Development
Expenditure on Research and Development in 1995 ranged from nearly 4 per cent of GDP in the Eastern region to less than 1 per cent in Wales and Northern Ireland.
(Table 13.11)

Tourism
Over a sixth of spending by UK tourists in 1995 was in the West Country, while more than half the spending by overseas residents was in London.
(Table 13.12)

Livestock
The South West and Scotland each account for around 18 per cent of the cattle in the United Kingdom, the Yorkshire and Humber region accounts for 24 per cent of the pigs and Wales for 26 per cent of the sheep.
(Table 13.18)

Introduction

S ome of the tables and charts in this chapter cover production industries, while others cover manufacturing. Production includes manufacturing industries, the construction industry, mining and quarrying, and the electricity, gas and water utilities. Charts 13.1 and 13.3 show information relating to both the production and the services sectors. In previous editions of *Regional Trends* these items featured manufacturing rather than production. This change has been made so that the industrial coverage of the charts is 100 per cent when the companion agricultural items - Charts 13.13 and 13.14 - are included. A more detailed breakdown of what is included in the production, services and agriculture sectors can be found in the Technical notes.

The percentage of gross domestic product (GDP) derived from production and services is shown in Chart 13.1 and the percentage of GDP derived from agriculture in Chart 13.13. It can be seen from the first chart that the service industries heavily outweigh the production industries in their contribution to GDP. Agriculture, although small in its contribution to overall GDP, is important in some regions, notably Northern Ireland, the South West and Scotland. This picture is also borne out by data from the Inter-Departmental Business Register (IDBR).

The IDBR is the ONS' structured list of business units for the selection, mailing and grossing of statistical inquiries. It comprises 1.9 million enterprises which represent nearly 99 per cent of economic activity, but only those registered for VAT (around 1.5 million enterprises) are included in the items in *Regional Trends*. Businesses generally register for VAT giving their Head Office address, but they may have individual local units, for example shops or factories, in other regions. Taking a large chain of department stores as an illustration, on a legal unit basis the data relating to this company are included in the region where the head office is located; on a local unit basis each branch's data are included in the region where the branch is located. Information from the IDBR is provided for the first time at local unit level in Table 13.2 and Chart 13.3. The information on agricultural units in Chart 13.14 remains at legal unit level as local unit data are not yet collected. However, it is believed that these figures would not differ greatly from those on a local unit basis.

Table 13.2 shows manufacturing units by employment sizeband. It can be seen from this table that in the United Kingdom as a whole over 90 per cent of factories have fewer than 50 employees; this is broadly the picture in every region. Another way of looking at the size of businesses is through their turnover. The IDBR indicates that some 80 per cent of production enterprises had a turnover of less than £500,000 in 1996; in services the proportion was about 86 per cent while in agriculture it was 95 per cent. This clearly highlights the importance of small businesses in the United Kingdom

Data on projects which have successfully attracted inward investment appear in Table 13.6. It should be noted that these figures are based on information provided to the Invest in Britain Bureau of the Department of Trade and Industry by companies at the time of the announcement of the decision to invest. There is no requirement to notify the department, and so the figures include only those projects where the Invest in Britain Bureau or its regional partners were involved, or which have come to their notice. They also take no account of subsequent developments; for example, if a company goes bankrupt several years later.

Some areas of Great Britain are classified as Development or Intermediate Assisted Areas and are thus eligible for assistance from the UK government. Eligibility depends on various factors, the principal being the level of unemployment. The Assisted Area map, last revised in August 1993, was included in *Regional Trends 31*. Information on the regional allocation of European Union Structural Funds is given in Table 13.8. These Funds are allocated according to specific objectives, details of which can be found in the Technical notes.

13.1 Percentage of gross domestic product[1] derived from production and services, 1995

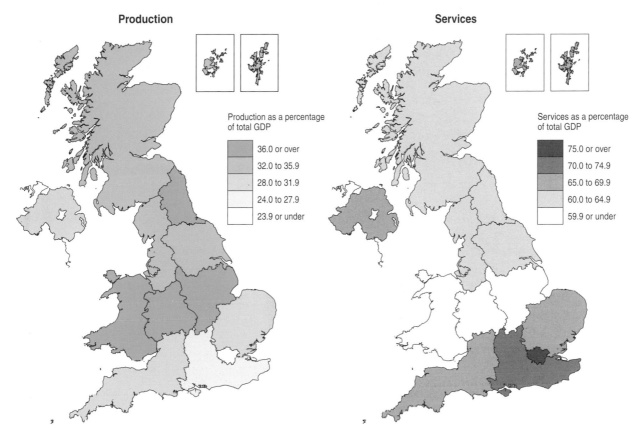

Production

Production as a percentage of total GDP

- 36.0 or over
- 32.0 to 35.9
- 28.0 to 31.9
- 24.0 to 27.9
- 23.9 or under

Services

Services as a percentage of total GDP

- 75.0 or over
- 70.0 to 74.9
- 65.0 to 69.9
- 60.0 to 64.9
- 59.9 or under

1 Factor cost at current prices. See Technical notes.

Source: Office for National Statistics

13.2 Manufacturing[1] industry local units[2]: by employment sizeband, 1996

Percentages and thousands

	Percentage of manufacturing local units with an employment size[3] of								Total manufacturing local units (=100%) (thousands)
	1-9	10-19	20-49	50-99	100-199	200-499	500-999	1,000 or over	
United Kingdom	69.4	13.0	9.5	3.9	2.3	1.5	0.4	0.1	180.4
North East	60.5	14.7	12.0	5.1	3.8	2.7	0.9	0.2	5.2
North West (GOR) & Merseyside	64.9	14.6	10.6	4.6	2.9	1.8	0.4	0.2	19.6
North West (GOR)	64.6	14.7	10.5	4.7	3.0	1.8	0.4	0.2	16.9
Merseyside	66.7	13.9	11.3	3.8	2.4	1.5	0.4	0.2	2.7
Yorkshire and the Humber	64.6	13.7	11.2	5.0	3.0	1.8	0.6	0.2	15.2
East Midlands	65.3	13.8	11.0	4.8	2.8	1.8	0.4	0.1	16.2
West Midlands	65.5	14.4	10.9	4.5	2.6	1.5	0.4	0.2	21.6
Eastern	72.3	12.2	8.7	3.4	1.8	1.2	0.3	0.1	17.9
London	78.8	11.1	6.3	2.0	1.0	0.6	0.1	0.1	23.5
South East (GOR)	74.2	11.5	8.0	3.1	1.7	1.0	0.3	0.1	24.5
South West	73.0	11.8	7.9	3.5	2.0	1.4	0.3	0.1	14.6
England	69.9	12.9	9.3	3.8	2.2	1.4	0.4	0.1	158.3
Wales	66.6	12.5	9.8	4.7	3.3	2.2	0.6	0.2	6.8
Scotland	63.9	14.1	11.5	4.8	3.0	1.8	0.7	0.2	11.1
Northern Ireland	67.3	13.5	10.1	3.8	2.9	1.9	0.4	0.1	4.2

1 Based on SIC 1992 Section D.
2 Includes local units in VAT-based enterprises only.
3 Includes paid full and part-time employees and working proprietors.

Source: Inter-Departmental Business Register, Office for National Statistics

13.3 Production and service industry[1] local units as a percentage of total local units, 1996

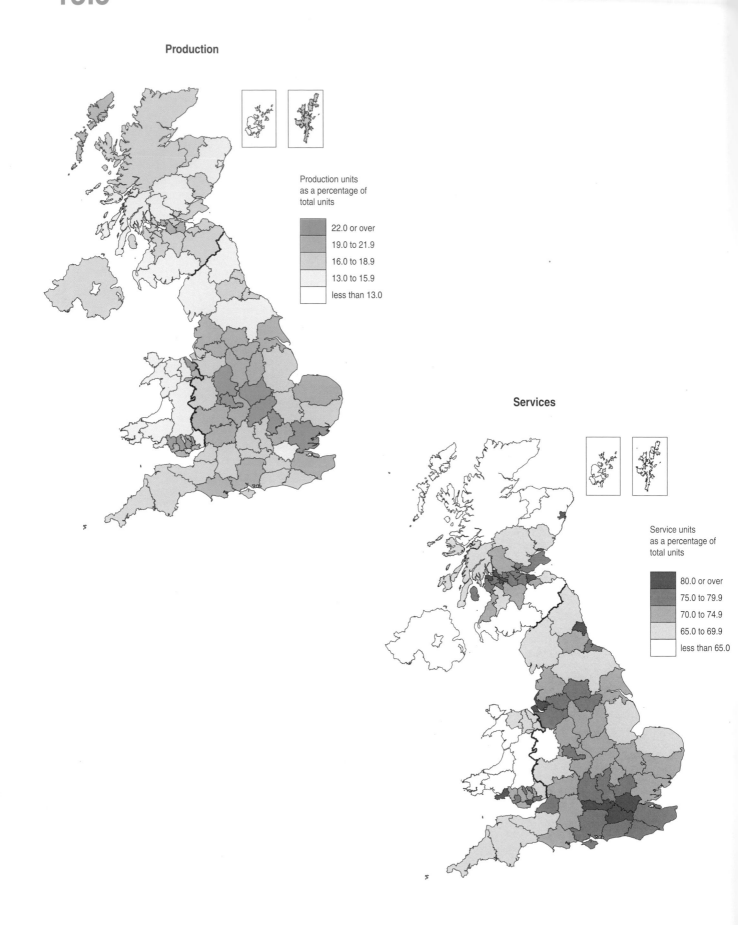

Production

Production units
as a percentage of
total units

22.0 or over
19.0 to 21.9
16.0 to 18.9
13.0 to 15.9
less than 13.0

Services

Service units
as a percentage of
total units

80.0 or over
75.0 to 79.9
70.0 to 74.9
65.0 to 69.9
less than 65.0

1 See Technical notes.

Source: Inter-Departmental Business Register, Office for National Statistics

13.4 Net capital expenditure and gross value added in manufacturing, 1991 and 1994[1]

| | Net capital expenditure | | | | Gross value added | | | | | |
| | £ million | | As a percentage of UK | | £ million | | As a percentage of UK | | £ per person employed | |
	1991	1994	1991	1994	1991	1994	1991	1994	1991	1994
United Kingdom	13,100	13,723	*100.0*	*100.0*	105,606	123,115	*100.0*	*100.0*	23,274	28,969
North East	819	624	*6.3*	*4.5*	4,935	6,080	*4.7*	*4.9*	24,340	32,236
North West (GOR) and Merseyside	1,904	1,957	*14.5*	*14.3*	14,937	17,420	*14.1*	*14.1*	24,494	31,020
North West (GOR)	1,611	1,673	*12.3*	*12.2*	13,014	15,088	*12.3*	*12.3*	24,788	31,003
Merseyside	293	284	*2.2*	*2.1*	1,923	2,332	*1.8*	*1.9*	22,674	31,130
Yorkshire and the Humber	1,216	1,279	*9.3*	*9.3*	9,534	11,137	*9.0*	*9.0*	21,466	26,209
East Midlands	1,207	1,051	*9.2*	*7.7*	9,109	11,068	*8.6*	*9.0*	20,953	26,117
West Midlands	1,311	1,659	*10.0*	*12.1*	12,322	14,060	*11.7*	*11.4*	20,237	24,857
Eastern	950	1,191	*7.3*	*8.7*	8,912	11,164	*8.4*	*9.1*	22,702	30,406
London	1,305	950	*10.0*	*6.9*	9,696	10,364	*9.2*	*8.4*	27,760	33,452
South East (GOR)	1,296	1,728	*9.9*	*12.6*	12,643	14,419	*12.0*	*11.7*	26,436	32,267
South West	714	937	*5.5*	*6.8*	7,182	8,410	*6.8*	*6.8*	21,775	27,352
England	10,723	11,376	*81.9*	*82.9*	89,269	104,151	*84.5*	*84.6*	23,186	28,951
Wales	837	791	*6.4*	*65.8*	5,545	6,579	*5.2*	*5.3*	25,207	31,570
Scotland	1,205	1,237	*9.2*	*9.0*	8,485	9,803	*8.0*	*8.0*	23,947	29,218
Northern Ireland	334	319	*2.6*	*2.3*	2,308	2,583	*2.2*	*2.1*	20,405	23,790

1 Based on SIC 1992. See Technical notes.

Source: Annual Sample Inquiry Into Production, Office for National Statistics

13.5 Gross value added in manufacturing: by size of local unit, 1994[1]

Percentages and £ million

| | Percentage of gross value added by number employed[2] | | | | | | | Total (=100%) (£ million) |
	1-24	25-49	50-99	100-199	200-499	500-999	1,000 or over	
United Kingdom	*14.2*	*8.6*	*11.1*	*13.9*	*20.7*	*12.5*	*18.8*	123,115
North East	*8.8*	*6.3*	*8.2*	*12.7*	*25.2*	*16.7*	*22.0*	6,080
North West (GOR) and Merseyside	*11.1*	*7.1*	*10.2*	*12.7*	*19.6*	*11.1*	*28.1*	17,420
North West (GOR)	*10.9*	*7.1*	*10.4*	*13.1*	*19.1*	*10.2*	*29.3*	15,088
Merseyside	*12.6*	*7.5*	*9.4*	*10.3*	*22.4*	*17.3*	*20.5*	2,332
Yorkshire and the Humber	*13.3*	*9.6*	*12.8*	*15.3*	*20.5*	*11.6*	*16.9*	11,137
East Midlands	*13.6*	*8.8*	*12.2*	*15.3*	*23.6*	*13.7*	*12.8*	11,068
West Midlands	*14.7*	*9.7*	*11.4*	*14.8*	*19.0*	*9.8*	*20.5*	14,060
Eastern	*15.6*	*9.4*	*11.0*	*13.8*	*17.9*	*15.3*	*17.1*	11,164
London	*20.6*	*9.9*	*11.7*	*11.8*	*19.4*	*7.9*	*18.7*	10,394
South East (GOR)	*16.6*	*8.9*	*11.6*	*13.6*	*20.9*	*12.5*	*16.0*	14,419
South West	*15.9*	*8.8*	*13.4*	*15.8*	*22.2*	*11.2*	*12.8*	8,410
England	*14.6*	*8.8*	*11.4*	*13.9*	*20.5*	*11.9*	*18.9*	104,151
Wales	*9.6*	*6.0*	*9.0*	*14.2*	*24.9*	*14.7*	*21.5*	6,579
Scotland	*12.5*	*8.3*	*9.9*	*13.3*	*19.6*	*18.4*	*17.9*	9,803
Northern Ireland	*20.1*	*8.8*	*9.4*	*15.8*	*22.5*	*8.8*	*14.5*	2,583

1 Based on SIC 1992. See Technical notes.
2 Average numbers employed during the year, including full and part-time employees and working proprietors.

Source: Annual Sample Inquiry Into Production, Office for National Statistics

13.6 Direct inward investment[1] project successes[2]

Numbers

DTI Regions[3]	Manufacturing					Non-manufacturing				
	1986	1991	1993	1994	1995	1986	1991	1993	1994	1995
United Kingdom	236	276	284	360	233	125	86	104	112	111
North East	26	20	30	37	37	7	12	5	9	9
North West	27	59	21	41	17	10	16	7	15	8
Yorkshire and the Humber	13	19	37	12	27	1	3	13	7	12
East Midlands	9	6	11	22	6	6	2	9	14	11
West Midlands	37	34	49	59	49	40	17	19	15	14
East[4]	..	5	4	7	6	..	7	8	7	7
South East[4]	22	19	8	15	0	43	13	9	15	34
South West	8	3	11	30	9	4	3	0	3	0
England	142	165	171	223	151	111	73	70	85	95
Wales	45	68	43	48	30	6	6	10	12	4
Scotland	33	27	56	72	40	6	5	24	13	11
Northern Ireland	16	16	14	17	12	2	2	0	2	1

1 See Introduction to chapter.
2 A project success is defined as a case where an overseas company specifies an interest and successfully completes investment in a UK company.
3 See map on page 215.
4 Prior to 1990, figures for the East are included with those for the South East.

Source: Invest in Britain Bureau, Department of Trade and Industry

13.7 Government expenditure on regional preferential assistance to industry

£ million

DTI Regions[1]	1988-89	1989-90	1990-91	1991-92	1992-93	1993-94	1994-95	1995-96
Great Britain[2]	615.7	539.3	497.3	427.8	364.0	394.4	368.9	343.0
North East	134.1	117.0	85.0	63.8	48.3	52.7	38.4	46.4
North West	82.3	74.3	57.5	49.5	36.8	40.3	32.4	24.3
of which								
Merseyside	..	..	..	..	..	..	15.0	13.0
Yorkshire & Humberside	50.2	32.4	29.4	18.2	13.7	35.6	23.0	19.7
East Midlands	8.8	9.5	5.5	2.6	1.2	1.9	5.2	7.3
West Midlands	26.2	19.9	18.0	8.7	10.8	14.4	14.7	14.2
East	.	.	.	.	.	-	0.7	2.1
South East	.	.	.	.	.	-	1.5	5.9
of which								
London	.	.	.	.	.	-	0.6	1.7
South West	14.7	10.7	9.0	8.3	8.2	9.5	9.4	7.7
England	316.3	263.8	204.4	151.1	119.0	154.4	125.3	127.6
Wales	148.2	131.7	133.7	153.9	140.6	118.8	109.2	98.0
Scotland	151.2	143.8	159.2	122.8	104.4	121.2	134.4	117.4
Northern Ireland[2]	138.3	127.1	132.1	138.0	105.6	117.6	132.9	131.2

1 See map on page 215.
2 The system of assistance available in Northern Ireland is not comparable with that operating in Great Britain, and thus UK figures are not produced. See Technical notes.

Source: Department of Trade and Industry; Department of Economic Development, Northern Ireland

13.8 Allocation of EU Structural Funds[1]

Million ECUs[2]

	Objective 1[3]			Objective 2[3]			Objective 5b[3]		
	1996	1997	1998	1996	1997	1998	1996	1997	1998
United Kingdom	376	402	436	749	784	810	147	149	149
North East	.	.	.	108	112	115	5	6	6
North West (GOR) and Merseyside	130	139	151	124	135	140	5	6	6
North West (GOR)	.	.	.	124	135	140	5	6	6
Merseyside	130	139	151	.	.	.	.	.	.
Yorkshire and the Humber	.	.	.	109	115	119	9	8	8
East Midlands	.	.	.	28	31	32	12	12	12
West Midlands	.	.	.	130	139	143	7	7	7
Eastern	.	.	.	.	.	.	11	11	11
London	.	.	.	26	31	32	.	.	.
South East (GOR)	.	.	.	5	5	6	.	.	.
South West	.	.	.	10	11	12	39	40	40
England	130	139	151	540	579	599	88	90	90
Wales	.	.	.	66	67	69	33	33	33
Scotland	50	53	57	143	138	142	26	26	26
Northern Ireland	196	210	228	.	.	.	.	.	.

1 Only allocations resulting from the Commission's Single Programming Documents are shown. Allocations resulting from Community Initiatives, the value of which is about 8 per cent of the total Objective 1, 2 and 5b allocations, are not included because not all of these can be allocated to the Government Office Regions in the table.
2 At 1994 prices. The average exchange rate in 1996 was £1.00 = 1.229 ECUs.
3 See Technical notes.

Source: Department of Trade and Industry

13.9 Business registrations and deregistrations[1]

Thousands and percentages

	1994						1995					
	Re-gist-rations	De-regist-rations	Net change	Regist-ration rates[2]	De-regist-ration rates[2]	End-year stock	Re-gist-rations	De-regist-rations[3]	Net change	Regist-ration rates[2]	De-regist-ration rates[2]	End-year stock
United Kingdom	173.1	174.4	-1.3	10.7	10.8	1,611.4	165.8	175.1	-9.3	10.3	10.9	1,602.1
North East	4.5	4.8	-0.3	10.4	11.1	43.4	4.1	5.1	-1.0	9.5	11.7	42.4
North West (GOR) and Merseyside	16.9	18.2	-1.2	10.5	11.3	159.9	16.1	18.2	-2.1	10.1	11.4	157.8
North West (GOR)	14.4	15.5	-1.2	10.3	11.2	137.6	13.6	15.4	-1.7	9.9	11.2	135.8
Merseyside	2.6	2.7	-0.1	11.4	11.8	22.4	2.5	2.9	-0.4	11.0	12.8	22.0
Yorkshire and the Humber	11.9	12.7	-0.8	9.8	10.5	120.6	11.3	13.5	-2.2	9.3	11.2	118.3
East Midlands	11.2	11.2	-	10.1	10.1	110.4	10.8	11.7	-0.9	9.8	10.6	109.6
West Midlands	14.1	14.3	-0.2	10.3	10.5	136.7	13.6	14.8	-1.3	9.9	10.8	135.4
Eastern	16.4	17.0	-0.5	10.4	10.8	156.9	16.1	16.8	-0.7	10.2	10.7	156.2
London	34.0	30.3	3.7	14.1	12.5	245.2	33.5	29.4	4.1	13.7	12.0	249.2
South East (GOR)	28.0	28.1	-0.1	11.7	11.7	239.8	26.5	27.6	-1.1	11.0	11.5	238.6
South West	14.5	15.8	-1.3	9.6	10.5	149.5	13.0	15.8	-2.8	8.7	10.6	146.7
England	151.5	152.4	-0.9	11.1	11.2	1,362.3	144.9	152.9	-8.1	10.6	11.2	1,354.3
Wales	6.4	7.7	-1.3	8.2	9.8	77.3	6.0	7.2	-1.2	7.8	9.3	76.1
Scotland	11.6	11.5	0.2	9.8	9.7	118.9	11.2	12.0	-0.7	9.4	10.1	118.1
Northern Ireland	3.5	2.8	0.7	6.7	5.3	52.9	3.7	3.0	0.7	6.9	5.6	53.6

1 Enterprises registered for VAT. This table is therefore not directly comparable with data published in previous editions of *Regional Trends* which were based on VAT legal units. An enterprise is defined as a legal unit, person or group of people producing goods or services under their own control and with their own legal identity. A branch or office of a larger organisation is not in itself an enterprise. There may be more than one VAT unit within an enterprise. See Technical notes. Figures include adjustments to allow for the effects of changes introduced in the 1993 budget.
2 Registrations and deregistrations during the year as a percentage of the stock figure at the end of the previous year.
3 Figures include an adjustment to allow for the change to the partial exemption rule.

Source: Department of Trade and Industry

13.10 Construction: value at current prices of contractors' output[1]

£ million and percentages

	Total work (£ million)						Of which new work (percentages)					
	1991	1992	1993	1994	1995	1996	1991	1992	1993	1994	1995	1996
Standard Statistical Regions												
Great Britain	47,389	43,735	42,797	45,870	48,942	51,806	57.8	55.9	54.3	54.0	53.9	53.7
North	2,058	1,946	1,863	2,139	2,186	2,506	59.6	57.4	56.4	58.5	56.9	61.5
North West (SSR)	4,273	3,984	4,117	4,576	5,072	5,362	54.2	54.4	55.2	55.0	55.4	54.0
Yorkshire and Humberside	3,673	3,566	3,468	3,703	3,862	4,292	54.0	54.6	52.9	53.3	50.2	52.1
East Midlands	3,060	2,934	3,019	3,301	3,446	3,820	56.5	54.9	56.4	56.5	55.2	56.9
West Midlands	3,937	3,730	3,716	4,039	4,157	4,397	56.6	55.5	52.4	52.7	51.8	50.5
East Anglia	1,895	1,801	1,786	1,977	2,064	1,994	58.8	55.0	50.7	52.7	52.9	51.0
South East (SSR)	18,576	15,617	14,970	15,598	16,690	17,932	60.0	54.9	52.7	51.6	52.0	52.1
Greater London	7,690	6,296	5,646	6,118	6,917	7,437	65.0	59.8	55.0	55.8	57.8	59.4
Rest of the South East	10,886	9,321	9,325	9,481	9,773	10,495	56.4	51.6	51.2	48.8	47.8	46.9
South West	3,846	3,914	3,781	4,055	4,317	4,192	51.6	54.7	54.6	54.4	54.0	49.0
England	41,319	37,492	36,720	39,389	41,794	44,496	57.4	55.0	53.5	53.4	53.0	52.8
Wales	1,959	2,082	1,826	2,172	2,377	2,327	58.0	61.0	56.0	59.9	61.2	58.1
Scotland	4,111	4,161	4,251	4,310	4,771	4,983	61.2	61.4	60.5	57.1	58.3	59.8

1 Output of contractors, including estimates of unrecorded output by small firms and self-employed workers, classified to construction in SIC 1992. For new work, figures relate to the region in which the site is located; for repair and maintenance, figures are for the region in which the reporting unit is based.

Source: Department of the Environment

13.11 Expenditure on Research & Development, 1995

£ million and percentages

	R&D performed within					
	Businesses	Percentage of regional GDP	Government[1]	Percentage of regional GDP	Higher education institutions	Percentage of regional GDP
United Kingdom	9,379	1.3	2,076	0.3	2,695	0.4
North East	230	0.9	16	0.1	91	0.3
North West (GOR) and Merseyside	1,121	1.5	82	0.1	223	0.3
North West (GOR)	993	1.5	71	0.1	162	0.2
Merseyside	128	1.5	11	0.1	60	0.7
Yorkshire and the Humber	279	0.5	46	0.1	209	0.4
East Midlands	615	1.3	65	0.1	142	0.3
West Midlands	663	1.1	179	0.3	149	0.2
Eastern	2,024	3.0	261	0.4	195	0.3
London	881	0.9	281	0.3	669	0.7
South East (GOR)	2,301	2.2	674	0.7	404	0.4
South West	777	1.4	249	0.5	122	0.2
England	8,890	1.5	1,852	0.3	2,205	0.4
Wales	96	0.3	31	0.1	102	0.4
Scotland	332	0.6	175	0.3	336	0.6
Northern Ireland	61	0.4	18	0.1	52	0.3

1 Figures include estimates of NHS and local authorities' R&D.

Source: Office for National Statistics

13.12 Value of tourism[1]

£ million

	1993		1994		1995	
	UK residents[2]	Overseas residents[3]	UK residents[2]	Overseas residents[3]	UK residents[2]	Overseas residents[3]
Tourist Board Regions						
United Kingdom	12,430	9,256	14,495	9,820	12,775	11,989
Northumbria	310	134	355	131	370	201
Cumbria	350	52	425	53	410	53
North West	860	302	1,090	395	1,060	382
Yorkshire & Humberside	825	248	1,110	220	850	281
East Midlands	715	204	835	188	710	237
Heart of England	740	385	1,050	378	715	468
East Anglia	1,035	401	1,175	390	960	566
London	875	4,850	1,105	5,281	880	6,508
Southern	1,070	654	1,145	590	1,100	769
South East England	685	657	900	639	725	772
West Country	2,195	391	2,455	399	2,220	459
England	9,650	8,294	11,650	8,671	10,000	10,698
Wales	945	173	1,075	190	1,045	203
Scotland	1,420	659	1,310	768	1,300	865
Northern Ireland	147	81	152	90	165	106

1 Tourist Board Regions. See map on page 215. Although these regions are the same as those shown in previous editions of *Regional Trends* the presentation order is different and now follows the north to south geography of the Government Office Regions.
2 The United Kingdom figures include the value of tourism in the Channel Islands, the Isle of Man, and a small amount where the region was unknown.
3 The England figures include the value of tourism in the Channel Islands, the Isle of Man, and a small amount where the region was unknown. The United Kingdom figures also include an amount which cannot be allocated to an individual country. The Northern Ireland figures include the value of tourism created by visitors from the Republic of Ireland.

Source: British Tourist Authority; International Passenger Survey, Office for National Statistics; Northern Ireland Tourist Board

13.13 Percentage of gross domestic product[1] derived from agriculture[2], 1995

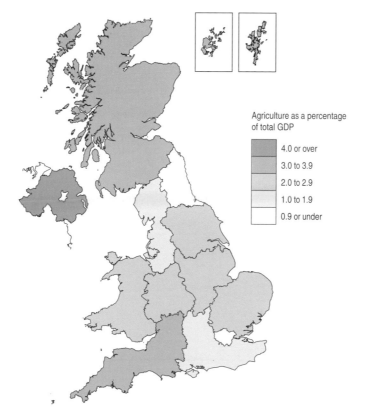

Agriculture as a percentage of total GDP

- 4.0 or over
- 3.0 to 3.9
- 2.0 to 2.9
- 1.0 to 1.9
- 0.9 or under

1 Factor cost at current prices. See Technical notes.
2 Gross domestic product for the agricultural industry includes income from related activities such as riding stables and bed and breakfast.

Source: Office for National Statistics

13.14 Agricultural legal units as a percentage of total legal units, 1996[1]

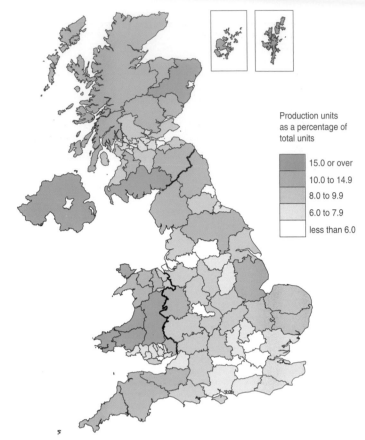

Production units
as a percentage of
total units

- 15.0 or over
- 10.0 to 14.9
- 8.0 to 9.9
- 6.0 to 7.9
- less than 6.0

1 The figures include only those enterprises that are registered for VAT. Some smaller holdings will therefore not be included. See Technical notes.

Source: Inter-Departmental Business Register, Office for National Statistics

13.15 Agricultural holdings[1]: by area of crops and grass[2], 1991 and 1995

Percentages and numbers

	1991					1995				
	Nil[3]	Under 10 hectares	10-49.9 hectares	50 hectares or over	Total holdings (=100%) (numbers)	Nil[3]	Under 10 hectares	10-49.9 hectares	50 hectares or over	Total holdings (=100%) (numbers)
Standard Statistical Regions										
United Kingdom	5.3	25.1	39.9	29.7	240,941	4.9	25.4	39.9	29.8	234,918
North	4.2	16.3	36.9	42.6	11,605	3.9	18.0	35.6	42.5	11,474
North West (SSR)	6.4	30.3	42.1	21.2	12,199	5.2	30.2	43.0	21.6	11,395
Yorkshire and Humberside	4.9	24.9	35.4	34.8	16,853	4.3	25.4	36.3	34.0	16,193
East Midlands	3.7	22.8	36.5	37.0	16,583	3.4	23.9	37.0	35.7	16,256
West Midlands	4.5	26.8	38.0	30.6	19,403	3.9	26.7	39.4	30.0	18,761
East Anglia	5.3	27.8	30.0	36.8	12,417	5.1	28.0	30.4	36.5	11,675
South East (SSR)	7.5	32.5	30.8	29.3	26,202	7.2	31.9	32.4	28.5	24,938
South West	4.0	25.6	41.1	29.2	35,704	3.5	26.2	41.4	28.9	35,417
England	5.1	26.4	36.6	31.9	150,966	4.5	26.7	37.3	31.4	146,109
Wales	7.0	22.5	45.0	25.5	29,710	5.3	22.0	45.6	27.1	28,076
Scotland	7.0	23.0	32.0	38.0	30,902	8.0	26.0	30.0	36.0	32,796
Northern Ireland	3.1	22.7	60.4	13.8	29,363	2.3	22.0	59.4	16.3	27,937

1 Figures exclude estimates for minor holdings which contribute less than 1 per cent of the total crops and grass area. See Technical notes.
2 Hectares of crops and grass only at June of each year.
3 'Nil' means holdings without crops and grass (ie consisting only of rough grazing, woodland or other land).

Source: Ministry of Agriculture, Fisheries and Food; Welsh Office; The Scottish Office Agriculture, Environment and Fisheries Department; Department of Agriculture, Northern Ireland

13.16 Agricultural land use[1], June 1992 and 1995

Percentages and thousand hectares

	Percentage of agricultural land in 1992 covered by				Total area on agri-cultural holdings (thousand hectares) (= 100%) 1992	Percentage of agricultural land in 1995 covered by				Total area on agri-cultural holdings (thousand hectares) (= 100%) 1995
	Total arable land[2]	All grass five years old and over (incl-uding sole right rough grazing)	Set aside land[3]	All other land on agri-cultural holdings including woodland[4]		Total arable land[2]	All grass five years old and over (incl-uding sole right rough grazing)	Set aside land	All other land on agri-cultural holdings including woodland[4]	
Standard Statistical Regions										
United Kingdom	38.2	57.3	0.9	3.7	17,281	34.8	57.3	3.7	4.2	17,158
North	26.9	70.1	0.5	2.6	1,042	23.9	70.8	2.3	3.0	1,041
North West (SSR)	31.3	65.6	0.4	2.5	450	29.5	65.8	1.7	3.0	441
Yorkshire and Humberside	57.8	38.9	0.6	2.7	1,108	51.8	39.1	6.0	3.2	1,095
East Midlands	71.0	25.2	1.2	2.7	1,240	64.0	24.7	8.0	3.3	1,233
West Midlands	52.2	43.1	0.9	3.8	968	48.4	42.8	4.6	4.3	955
East Anglia	82.8	10.3	1.5	5.3	1,013	74.3	10.8	8.9	6.0	1,015
South East (SSR)	63.8	26.0	3.1	7	1,690	57.3	26.1	8.9	7.8	1,668
South West	40.9	53.5	1.4	4.3	1,823	38.0	53.5	3.6	4.9	1,819
England	54.4	40.1	1.4	4.2	9,423	49.2	40.2	5.8	4.7	9,364
Wales	15.1	81.3	0.2	3.4	1,509	13.9	82.0	0.4	3.8	1,499
Scotland	18.8	77.9	0.5	2.7	5,297	17.2	77.5	1.5	3.8	5,253
Northern Ireland	23.3	72.6	..	4.1	1,052	23.8	73.3	0.2	2.8	1,043

1 Data include estimates for minor holdings except for Scotland and the regions of England. As a result the sum of the English regions is not equal to the national total. See Technical notes
2 Crops, bare fallow and all grass under five years old.
3 The figure shown against the United Kingdom is for Great Britain.
4 In Great Britain this includes farm roads, yards, buildings (except glasshouses), ponds and derelict land. In Northern Ireland it includes land under bog, water, roads, buildings etc and wasteland not used for agriculture.

Source: Ministry of Agriculture, Fisheries and Food; Welsh Office; The Scottish Office Agriculture, Environment and Fisheries Department; Department of Agriculture for Northern Ireland

13.17 Areas and estimated yields of selected crops[1], 1990-1994[2] and 1995

Thousand hectares and tonnes per hectare

	Areas (thousand hectares)						Estimated yields (tonnes per hectare)					
	Wheat		Barley		Rape (for oilseed)[3]		Wheat		Barley		Rape (for oilseed)	
	1990-1994	1995	1990-1994	1995	1990-1994	1995	1990-1994	1995	1990-1994	1995	1990-1994[4]	1995
Standard Statistical Regions												
United Kingdom	1,926	1,859	1,295	1,192	406	354	7.1	7.7	5.4	5.7	2.8	2.8
North	70	70	67	61	22	19	7.6	8.4	5.6	6.3	..	..
North West (SSR)	23	23	27	26	4	3	6.7	7.3	5.1	5.1	..	..
Yorkshire and Humberside	246	236	136	127	48	40	7.6	8.1	6.0	6.2	..	..
East Midlands	373	363	122	110	83	73	7.2	7.9	5.6	5.8	..	..
West Midlands	146	143	92	82	25	21	6.8	7.0	5.2	5.7	..	..
East Anglia	327	319	158	143	40	32	7.4	7.9	5.6	5.9	..	..
South East (SSR)	431	410	172	154	100	86	6.9	7.3	5.5	5.7	..	..
South West	178	167	143	134	25	26	6.6	7.2	5.2	5.4	..	..
England	1,796	1,732	920	837	348	300	7.1	7.7	5.5	5.8	2.8	2.9
Wales	12	11	35	32	1	2	6.4	7.5	4.8	4.7	2.8	2.9
Scotland	111	108	303	290	56	52	7.7	8.3	5.2	5.7	2.9	2.7
Northern Ireland	7	6	37	33	1	0	6.7	7.8	4.4	5.2	2.5	2.9

1 Figures for England, Wales and Northern Ireland include estimates for minor holdings; figures for English regions exclude minor holdings hence their sum may be less than the England total. Figures for Scotland exclude minor holdings. See Technical notes.
2 Five year average.
3 Excludes crops grown on Set-Aside scheme land.
4 The figure for Wales is the average of 1992 and 1994 only.

Source: Ministry of Agriculture, Fisheries and Food; Welsh Office; The Scottish Office Agriculture, Environment and Fisheries Department; Department of Agriculture for Northern Ireland

13.18 Livestock on agricultural holdings, June 1995[1]

Thousands

	Cattle and calves			Sheep and lambs	Pigs	Poultry	
	Total herd[2]	Dairy cows	Beef cows			Total fowls[3]	Total laying flock[4]
Standard Statistical Regions							
United Kingdom	11,733	2,602	1,805	42,771	7,534	125,981	31,692
North	885	168	159	5,063	198	3,459	541
North West (SSR)	598	238	37	1,078	277	6,746	2,193
Yorkshire and Humberside	646	146	89	2,597	1,797	7,460	2,065
East Midlands	624	138	76	1,628	628	13,634	4,584
West Midlands	911	261	98	2,852	401	13,098	3,387
East Anglia	198	34	34	288	1,456	12,496	2,107
South East (SSR)	723	175	93	2,007	770	16,635	5,528
South West	2,112	649	199	4,095	799	16,615	4,786
England	6,747	1,811	800	19,850	6,341	90,355	25,331
Wales	1,337	294	219	11,191	91	6,252	1,015
Scotland	2,057	225	508	9,259	554	14,884	2,250
Northern Ireland	1,592	271	278	2,470	548	14,490	3,096

1 Figures for England, Wales and Northern Ireland include minor holdings; figures for English regions exclude minor holdings and hence their sum may be less than the England total. Figures for Scotland exclude minor holdings. See Technical notes.
2 Includes bulls, in-calf heifers and fattening cattle and calves.
3 Excludes ducks, geese and turkeys.
4 Excludes growing pullets (from day-old to point of lay).

Source: Ministry of Agriculture, Fisheries and Food; Welsh Office; The Scottish Office Agriculture, Environment and Fisheries Department; Department of Agriculture for Northern Ireland

13.19 Agricultural gross domestic fixed capital formation[1]

£ million

	Plant and machinery			Vehicles			Buildings and works			Total		
	1981	1986	1995	1981	1986	1995	1981	1986	1995	1981	1986	1995
Standard Statistical Regions												
United Kingdom	516	592	1,178	105	106	284	475	427	526	1,096	1,125	1,987
North	29	34	61	7	7	17	20	20	30	55	61	108
North West (SSR)	26	24	53	6	5	15	19	14	26	51	43	93
Yorkshire and Humberside	55	55	101	13	11	28	39	32	49	108	97	178
East Midlands	43	70	141	11	11	28	20	28	48	74	108	217
West Midlands	56	49	96	7	7	19	53	21	49	117	77	164
East Anglia	41	65	132	10	10	26	20	26	45	71	100	203
South East (SSR)	58	90	169	15	14	34	27	36	58	100	140	260
South West	89	82	162	12	11	32	84	34	83	185	128	277
England	397	469	915	80	75	199	283	210	388	760	754	1,501
Wales	33	35	73	8	8	31	44	41	47	84	84	152
Scotland	59	56	127	10	14	22	79	76	51	148	145	200
Northern Ireland	27	33	63	7	10	32	69	100	39	103	143	134

1 See Technical notes.

Source: Ministry of Agriculture, Fisheries and Food; Welsh Office; The Scottish Office Agriculture, Environment and Fisheries Department; Department of Agriculture for Northern Ireland

14 Sub-regions of England

Government Office Regions and counties in England

14.1 Area and population: by district, 1995

	Area (sq km)	Persons per sq km	Population (thousands) Males	Females	Total	Total population percentage change 1981-1995	Total Period Fertility Rate (TPFR)[1]	Standardised Mortality Ratio (UK=100) (SMR)[2]	Percentage of population aged Under 5	5-15	16 up to pension age[3]	Pension age[3] or over
UNITED KINGDOM	242,910	241	28,727	29,878	58,606	*4.0*	1.71	100	*6.5*	*14.1*	*61.2*	*18.2*
ENGLAND	130,423	375	24,008	24,896	48,903	*4.4*	1.71	98	*6.6*	*14.0*	*61.2*	*18.2*
NORTH EAST	8,592	303	1,272	1,333	2,605	*-1.2*	1.67	110	*6.3*	*14.4*	*60.7*	*18.5*
Cleveland#	597	937	274	285	559	*-2.0*	1.79	112	*6.9*	*15.7*	*60.5*	*16.9*
Hartlepool	94	982	45	47	92	*-2.9*	1.94	111	*6.9*	*15.3*	*59.9*	*17.9*
Langbaurgh-on-Tees	245	577	69	72	141	*-6.3*	1.82	111	*6.6*	*15.3*	*60.0*	*18.1*
Middlesbrough	54	2,738	72	75	148	*-2.0*	1.81	115	*7.2*	*16.2*	*60.4*	*16.3*
Stockton-on-Tees	204	874	87	91	178	*2.4*	1.68	110	*6.9*	*15.8*	*61.2*	*16.1*
Durham	2,429	250	298	310	608	*-0.6*	1.64	111	*6.2*	*14.1*	*61.0*	*18.6*
Chester-le-Street	68	818	27	28	55	*5.0*	1.58	112	*6.2*	*13.4*	*63.6*	*16.8*
Darlington	197	510	49	52	101	*2.0*	1.82	107	*6.7*	*14.2*	*60.0*	*19.1*
Derwentside	271	323	43	45	88	*-1.0*	1.70	122	*6.2*	*13.8*	*60.5*	*19.5*
Durham	187	480	44	45	90	*2.1*	1.32	95	*5.4*	*13.7*	*64.5*	*16.4*
Easington	145	668	47	49	97	*-4.8*	1.79	119	*7.0*	*15.0*	*59.4*	*18.5*
Sedgefield	217	418	45	46	91	*-2.9*	1.71	116	*6.4*	*14.6*	*60.8*	*18.2*
Teesdale	840	29	12	12	24	*-2.4*	1.72	99	*5.5*	*12.3*	*59.8*	*22.5*
Wear Valley	505	125	30	33	63	*-1.7*	1.67	112	*5.8*	*14.1*	*59.6*	*20.5*
Northumberland	5,026	61	150	157	307	*2.7*	1.67	106	*5.8*	*13.9*	*60.6*	*19.7*
Alnwick	1,079	29	15	16	31	*7.1*	1.59	101	*5.4*	*13.7*	*58.8*	*22.0*
Berwick-upon-Tweed	972	27	13	14	26	*1.0*	1.59	94	*4.8*	*12.8*	*57.8*	*24.6*
Blyth Valley	70	1,144	39	41	80	*3.3*	1.74	120	*6.4*	*14.6*	*63.2*	*15.8*
Castle Morpeth	619	80	24	26	50	*-0.3*	1.43	101	*4.8*	*13.8*	*60.9*	*20.6*
Tynedale	2,219	26	28	30	58	*6.7*	1.67	101	*5.7*	*14.2*	*59.4*	*20.7*
Wansbeck	67	932	30	32	62	*-0.6*	1.77	110	*6.4*	*13.5*	*60.3*	*19.8*
Tyne and Wear	540	2,093	551	580	1,131	*-2.1*	1.63	110	*6.3*	*14.1*	*60.7*	*18.8*
Gateshead	143	1,409	98	103	202	*-5.4*	1.64	115	*6.1*	*13.4*	*61.1*	*19.3*
Newcastle-upon-Tyne	112	2,533	139	144	283	*-0.3*	1.52	109	*6.4*	*13.3*	*62.3*	*18.0*
North Tyneside	84	2,317	93	101	194	*-2.3*	1.68	102	*6.0*	*13.8*	*59.5*	*20.7*
South Tyneside	64	2,444	76	80	156	*-3.5*	1.77	107	*6.3*	*14.8*	*58.5*	*20.4*
Sunderland	138	2,149	144	152	296	*-0.5*	1.66	113	*6.6*	*15.1*	*61.0*	*17.3*
NORTH WEST (GOR) & MERSEYSIDE	14,165	487	3,376	3,524	6,900	*-0.6*	1.72	107	*6.6*	*14.6*	*60.6*	*18.2*
NORTH WEST (GOR)	13,510	405	2,687	2,786	5,473	*1.0*	1.74	106	*6.6*	*14.6*	*60.7*	*18.1*
Cheshire	2,331	420	481	497	978	*4.9*	1.69	100	*6.4*	*14.4*	*61.6*	*17.6*
Chester	448	268	59	61	120	*2.8*	1.66	93	*6.0*	*13.7*	*60.9*	*19.4*
Congleton	211	406	42	44	86	*7.1*	1.63	94	*5.6*	*14.2*	*62.0*	*18.2*
Crewe and Nantwich	430	264	56	57	114	*15.3*	1.58	105	*6.8*	*13.9*	*62.0*	*17.3*
Ellesmere Port and Neston	87	934	40	41	81	*-1.9*	1.69	94	*6.5*	*14.9*	*61.0*	*17.5*
Halton	74	1,669	61	63	123	*0.0*	1.81	115	*7.0*	*16.7*	*61.3*	*15.0*
Macclesfield	525	289	74	78	152	*1.3*	1.62	94	*5.7*	*13.2*	*61.3*	*19.8*
Vale Royal	380	302	56	58	115	*2.8*	1.78	98	*6.3*	*14.7*	*60.9*	*18.1*
Warrington	176	1,068	93	95	188	*10.7*	1.73	104	*6.8*	*14.4*	*62.6*	*16.3*
Cumbria	6,824	72	240	250	490	*1.9*	1.61	102	*6.0*	*13.5*	*60.1*	*20.4*
Allerdale	1,258	76	47	49	96	*0.2*	1.73	105	*6.1*	*13.4*	*60.0*	*20.4*
Barrow-in-Furness	78	921	35	36	72	*-2.2*	1.79	107	*7.0*	*14.0*	*60.8*	*18.2*
Carlisle	1,040	100	50	53	104	*2.5*	1.55	102	*6.2*	*13.6*	*60.2*	*20.1*
Copeland	738	96	35	35	71	*-3.0*	1.63	112	*5.9*	*14.9*	*61.4*	*17.8*
Eden	2,156	22	24	24	48	*10.6*	1.45	98	*5.7*	*12.9*	*60.6*	*20.9*
South Lakeland	1,554	65	48	52	100	*5.8*	1.47	92	*5.2*	*12.4*	*58.5*	*23.9*
Greater Manchester	1,286	2,005	1,268	1,310	2,578	*-1.6*	1.75	110	*6.9*	*14.9*	*61.0*	*17.2*
Bolton	140	1,900	131	135	265	*1.2*	1.76	107	*6.9*	*15.0*	*60.9*	*17.2*
Bury	99	1,835	90	92	182	*3.0*	1.73	106	*6.5*	*14.6*	*61.9*	*16.9*
Manchester	116	3,726	213	220	433	*-6.5*	1.71	124	*7.9*	*15.7*	*60.4*	*16.0*
Oldham	141	1,560	108	112	220	*-0.6*	2.05	109	*7.3*	*15.7*	*60.4*	*16.6*
Rochdale	160	1,301	102	106	208	*-0.3*	1.89	114	*7.5*	*15.8*	*60.2*	*16.5*
Salford	97	2,382	114	116	231	*-6.7*	1.73	113	*7.0*	*14.2*	*60.2*	*18.6*
Stockport	126	2,307	142	149	291	*0.0*	1.63	94	*6.1*	*14.1*	*61.0*	*18.7*
Tameside	103	2,148	109	112	222	*1.4*	1.81	119	*6.9*	*14.8*	*61.0*	*17.2*
Trafford	106	2,068	107	111	218	*-1.5*	1.67	95	*6.4*	*14.3*	*60.8*	*18.4*
Wigan	199	1,558	153	157	310	*-0.2*	1.65	112	*6.6*	*14.4*	*62.8*	*16.3*

14.1 (continued)

	Area (sq km)	Persons per sq km	Population (thousands)			Total population percentage change 1981-1995	Total Period Fertility Rate (TPFR)[1]	Standardised Mortality Ratio (UK=100) (SMR)[2]	Percentage of population aged			
			Males	Females	Total				Under 5	5-15	16 up to pension age[3]	Pension age[3] or over
Lancashire	3,070	465	697	729	1,426	2.9	1.76	105	6.5	14.5	59.9	19.1
Blackburn	137	1,024	69	71	140	-1.6	2.25	111	8.2	16.8	59.0	16.0
Blackpool	35	4,400	74	79	154	3.0	1.60	111	6.0	12.1	59.5	22.4
Burnley	111	811	44	46	90	-3.2	1.97	112	7.3	16.1	58.6	18.0
Chorley	203	478	48	49	97	5.2	1.72	97	6.1	14.6	62.9	16.3
Fylde	166	450	36	39	75	8.0	1.63	96	5.1	11.8	57.2	26.0
Hyndburn	73	1,098	39	41	80	0.9	2.20	114	7.5	15.3	59.2	18.0
Lancaster	576	236	66	70	136	8.8	1.53	99	5.8	13.6	59.9	20.6
Pendle	169	503	42	44	85	-1.2	1.98	102	7.1	15.9	58.8	18.2
Preston	142	944	67	68	134	6.2	1.66	116	7.1	14.8	61.2	16.9
Ribble Valley	584	89	26	26	52	-3.6	1.54	95	5.1	13.8	61.1	20.0
Rossendale	138	474	32	33	65	0.6	1.90	110	6.9	15.1	60.9	17.1
South Ribble	113	913	50	53	103	6.5	1.54	98	6.2	14.7	61.9	17.1
West Lancashire	338	326	54	56	110	2.6	1.69	104	6.2	15.2	61.6	17.0
Wyre	284	367	50	54	104	5.0	1.60	101	5.4	13.3	56.3	25.0
MERSEYSIDE	655	2,178	690	737	1,427	-6.2	1.68	110	6.5	14.8	59.9	18.7
Knowsley	97	1,582	75	79	154	-11.5	1.93	127	7.5	17.0	59.5	15.9
Liverpool	113	4,173	229	242	471	-8.9	1.63	121	6.7	14.8	61.0	17.5
Sefton	153	1,903	139	152	291	-3.1	1.58	111	5.9	14.2	58.5	21.3
St Helens	133	1,349	88	91	180	-5.5	1.65	99	6.3	14.1	62.0	17.6
Wirral	159	2,088	159	173	332	-2.7	1.73	103	6.3	14.7	58.8	20.2
YORKSHIRE AND THE HUMBER	15,411	326	2,474	2,556	5,029	2.3	1.75	101	6.6	14.2	60.9	18.3
Humberside#	3,508	253	437	452	889	3.7	1.75	102	6.4	14.5	60.3	18.8
Beverley	404	296	58	61	120	11.8	1.56	94	5.6	13.4	61.0	20.0
Boothferry	646	101	32	33	65	7.9	1.74	106	6.2	13.9	61.2	18.7
Cleethorpes	164	432	35	36	71	3.1	1.73	100	6.3	14.8	59.9	19.0
East Yorkshire	1,043	86	44	46	90	19.6	1.86	95	5.6	13.2	58.6	22.7
Glanford	580	126	37	37	73	9.5	1.70	104	5.7	13.6	62.2	18.4
Great Grimsby	28	3,183	44	46	90	-3.5	1.86	104	7.2	16.1	58.7	18.0
Holderness	538	98	26	27	53	13.3	1.50	103	5.2	14.6	61.9	18.3
Kingston upon Hull	71	3,759	133	136	269	-1.9	1.76	106	7.3	14.0	60.6	17.3
Scunthorpe	34	1,766	29	30	60	-10.2	2.15	101	7.2	16.1	57.7	18.9
North Yorkshire#	8,309	88	355	375	731	7.9	1.67	91	5.8	13.4	60.3	20.5
Craven	1,179	43	24	27	51	6.6	1.73	89	5.5	14.0	57.0	23.5
Hambleton	1,311	64	41	43	84	11.8	1.78	86	6.0	13.5	61.7	18.8
Harrogate	1,333	113	72	78	150	6.7	1.55	97	5.8	13.1	60.8	20.3
Richmondshire	1,319	35	23	23	46	6.6	1.80	80	6.5	13.7	62.4	17.4
Ryedale	1,597	59	46	48	94	9.5	1.62	82	5.3	13.1	59.3	22.3
Scarborough	817	133	52	57	109	6.5	1.79	95	5.5	13.1	57.0	24.3
Selby	725	127	46	47	92	15.6	1.84	92	5.9	14.3	62.4	17.4
York	29	3,543	51	54	104	2.3	1.52	93	6.1	13.0	61.8	19.1
South Yorkshire	1,559	836	645	659	1,304	-1.0	1.72	105	6.5	13.8	61.1	18.5
Barnsley	328	691	111	115	227	0.4	1.76	113	6.6	14.0	61.0	18.4
Doncaster	581	504	145	148	293	0.7	1.88	106	6.7	14.9	60.2	18.2
Rotherham	283	905	126	129	256	1.2	1.74	106	6.7	14.6	61.3	17.4
Sheffield	367	1,439	262	266	529	-3.5	1.62	101	6.3	12.7	61.7	19.3
West Yorkshire	2,034	1,035	1,037	1,069	2,106	1.9	1.80	102	6.9	14.6	61.2	17.3
Bradford	366	1,318	238	245	483	3.8	2.06	105	7.6	16.1	59.6	16.7
Calderdale	363	532	94	99	193	0.2	1.86	107	6.8	14.5	60.6	18.1
Kirklees	410	946	190	197	388	2.8	1.87	102	6.9	14.7	61.2	17.2
Leeds	562	1,291	358	367	725	1.0	1.64	96	6.5	13.7	62.0	17.7
Wakefield	333	953	157	160	317	1.0	1.72	108	6.7	14.4	61.8	17.1
EAST MIDLANDS	15,627	264	2,038	2,086	4,124	7.0	1.68	98	6.4	14.1	61.2	18.3
Derbyshire	2,629	364	474	484	958	4.8	1.70	102	6.4	13.6	61.3	18.7
Amber Valley	265	434	57	58	115	5.0	1.70	97	5.6	13.0	61.8	19.6
Bolsover	160	443	35	36	71	-0.2	1.75	108	6.6	13.0	60.3	20.2
Chesterfield	66	1,528	50	51	101	3.0	1.60	115	6.3	13.0	61.1	19.6
Derby	78	2,972	115	117	232	6.7	1.72	100	7.1	14.3	60.6	18.1
Derbyshire Dales	795	87	34	35	69	2.1	1.58	92	5.3	12.9	60.5	21.3
Erewash	109	976	53	54	107	3.0	1.82	104	6.7	13.8	61.2	18.2
High Peak	540	163	43	45	88	6.6	1.67	105	6.6	14.5	62.0	16.9
North East Derbyshire	277	359	49	50	99	3.2	1.71	102	5.9	13.3	61.6	19.2
South Derbyshire	338	225	38	38	76	11.3	1.64	104	6.0	14.0	63.3	16.8

14.1 (continued)

	Area (sq km)	Persons per sq km	Population (thousands)			Total population percentage change 1981-1995	Total Period Fertility Rate (TPFR)[1]	Standardised Mortality Ratio (UK=100) (SMR)[2]	Percentage of population aged			
			Males	Females	Total				Under 5	5-15	16 up to pension age[3]	Pension age[3] or over
Leicestershire	2,551	362	458	465	923	7.5	1.69	94	6.6	14.5	61.9	17.0
Blaby	130	653	43	43	85	10.3	1.75	91	6.6	13.8	63.4	16.2
Charnwood	279	553	77	77	154	10.2	1.57	87	5.9	14.0	63.1	17.0
Harborough	593	122	36	36	72	17.4	1.61	85	6.2	14.7	61.9	17.2
Hinckley and Bosworth	297	328	48	49	98	10.7	1.77	89	6.1	13.8	62.4	17.8
Leicester	73	4,033	146	149	296	4.5	1.71	103	7.7	15.5	60.6	16.2
Melton	481	97	23	23	46	6.7	1.80	88	6.5	13.8	61.8	17.9
North West Leicestershire	279	300	42	42	84	5.8	1.69	95	6.0	14.2	61.8	18.0
Oadby and Wigston	24	2,263	26	27	53	0.3	1.79	93	5.8	13.9	61.8	18.5
Rutland	394	88	17	18	35	4.9	1.46	88	5.5	14.8	62.5	17.3
Lincolnshire	5,921	103	299	313	612	10.6	1.67	96	5.8	13.5	59.3	21.4
Boston	362	150	27	28	54	3.1	1.64	88	5.6	13.0	59.2	22.2
East Lindsey	1,760	70	59	63	122	16.1	1.73	96	5.3	12.6	56.5	25.5
Lincoln	36	2,361	41	43	84	10.1	1.77	98	6.9	13.8	60.9	18.5
North Kesteven	922	92	42	43	85	5.8	1.58	92	5.8	13.1	59.6	21.4
South Holland	742	96	35	36	71	14.1	1.63	100	5.1	12.3	59.1	23.5
South Kesteven	943	125	57	60	117	19.4	1.61	95	6.2	14.7	60.8	18.3
West Lindsey	1,156	67	38	39	78	-0.2	1.78	104	5.6	14.5	59.6	20.2
Northamptonshire	2,367	253	296	303	599	12.5	1.73	96	6.8	15.0	61.7	16.5
Corby	80	652	26	27	52	-0.5	1.87	108	7.1	16.3	60.7	15.9
Daventry	666	97	32	32	65	11.7	1.74	89	6.5	14.5	62.8	16.2
East Northamptonshire	510	138	35	35	70	13.0	1.67	98	6.3	14.8	61.2	17.7
Kettering	233	342	39	41	80	11.8	1.74	97	6.8	14.0	61.5	17.7
Northampton	81	2,349	93	96	190	19.4	1.72	98	7.2	15.1	62.0	15.8
South Northamptonshire	634	117	37	37	74	14.6	1.63	89	6.3	15.6	62.2	16.0
Wellingborough	163	418	34	35	68	5.4	1.77	93	6.7	14.9	61.1	17.3
Nottinghamshire	2,160	478	510	522	1,032	3.8	1.65	100	6.4	14.0	61.5	18.1
Ashfield	110	994	54	55	109	2.3	1.77	99	6.3	13.8	61.8	18.2
Bassetlaw	637	167	53	54	107	3.6	1.76	98	6.3	13.6	61.8	18.3
Broxtowe	81	1,383	55	57	112	7.3	1.50	96	5.9	13.3	62.9	17.9
Gedling	120	928	55	57	111	2.9	1.60	99	5.9	13.5	62.0	18.6
Mansfield	77	1,322	50	51	102	1.6	1.74	109	6.5	14.9	60.4	18.1
Newark and Sherwood	651	160	51	53	104	3.3	1.66	104	6.0	14.1	60.9	18.9
Nottingham	75	3,804	140	144	284	2.0	1.65	103	7.4	14.4	61.0	17.3
Rushcliffe	409	252	51	52	103	10.9	1.57	93	5.7	13.6	62.2	18.6
WEST MIDLANDS	13,004	408	2,621	2,686	5,306	2.3	1.79	103	6.7	14.5	60.9	18.0
Hereford and Worcester	3,923	177	341	353	694	9.1	1.74	96	6.1	13.9	60.8	19.2
Bromsgrove	220	388	42	43	85	-3.4	1.71	108	5.7	13.1	61.9	19.4
Hereford	20	2,437	24	25	50	3.3	1.84	95	6.8	14.2	59.0	19.9
Leominster	933	44	20	21	41	9.6	1.96	89	5.7	12.9	58.0	23.3
Malvern Hills	899	102	45	47	92	7.6	1.57	95	5.2	13.8	58.0	23.0
Redditch	54	1,436	39	39	78	15.1	1.93	93	7.1	16.3	63.0	13.6
South Herefordshire	904	60	27	28	55	17.1	1.67	94	6.1	14.2	58.3	21.4
Worcester	33	2,737	45	46	91	18.1	1.74	88	6.9	13.6	62.6	16.9
Wychavon	664	160	52	54	106	12.5	1.72	98	5.8	13.5	60.7	20.0
Wyre Forest	195	497	48	49	97	5.8	1.66	96	6.0	14.0	62.3	17.8
Shropshire	3,488	120	208	212	420	10.3	1.75	96	6.3	14.3	61.1	18.3
Bridgnorth	633	80	25	25	50	-0.0	1.70	103	5.3	13.3	62.5	18.9
North Shropshire	679	80	27	27	54	6.2	1.74	94	5.9	13.5	59.6	21.0
Oswestry	256	136	17	18	35	10.1	1.62	98	5.9	14.0	59.3	20.8
Shrewsbury and Atcham	602	159	47	49	96	9.1	1.63	88	6.3	13.9	60.4	19.4
South Shropshire	1,027	39	20	20	40	16.4	1.65	79	5.1	13.1	58.1	23.7
The Wrekin	290	498	72	73	145	15.3	1.90	107	7.3	15.6	62.8	14.3
Staffordshire	2,715	389	524	532	1,056	3.7	1.66	105	6.2	14.2	62.2	17.4
Cannock Chase	79	1,150	46	45	91	6.5	1.77	112	6.7	14.8	63.6	15.0
East Staffordshire	390	257	50	51	100	4.2	1.84	100	6.8	14.4	60.5	18.3
Lichfield	329	284	46	47	93	4.9	1.73	111	5.9	13.5	64.1	16.5
Newcastle-under-Lyme	211	583	60	63	123	2.1	1.62	104	5.7	14.1	60.9	19.3
South Staffordshire	408	255	52	53	104	7.0	1.55	94	5.6	14.0	63.7	16.7
Stafford	599	206	61	62	123	5.1	1.53	92	5.8	13.7	62.3	18.2
Staffordshire Moorlands	576	165	47	48	95	-1.1	1.55	113	5.4	13.6	62.2	18.9
Stoke-on-Trent	93	2,743	126	128	254	0.8	1.65	111	6.7	14.1	61.0	18.2
Tamworth	31	2,341	36	36	72	10.7	1.76	113	7.2	17.0	64.0	11.9

14.1 *(continued)*

	Area (sq km)	Persons per sq km	Population (thousands)			Total population percentage change 1981-1995	Total Period Fertility Rate (TPFR)[1]	Standardised Mortality Ratio (UK=100) (SMR)[2]	Percentage of population aged			
			Males	Females	Total				Under 5	5-15	16 up to pension age[3]	Pension age[3] or over
Warwickshire	1,979	252	246	252	499	4.5	1.66	100	6.1	13.8	62.0	18.2
North Warwickshire	285	216	31	31	61	2.5	1.63	104	6.4	14.1	62.8	16.7
Nuneaton and Bedworth	79	1,507	59	60	119	4.5	1.81	118	6.6	15.0	62.2	16.2
Rugby	356	245	43	44	87	-0.6	1.74	102	6.4	14.1	61.5	18.0
Stratford-on-Avon	977	113	54	57	110	9.7	1.55	87	5.3	12.5	62.0	20.1
Warwick	282	428	59	61	121	4.8	1.59	94	5.7	13.3	61.7	19.3
West Midlands (Met. County)	899	2,934	1,301	1,336	2,637	-1.3	1.87	106	7.2	14.9	60.2	17.8
Birmingham	265	3,833	502	515	1,017	-0.3	1.95	106	7.7	15.5	59.8	17.0
Coventry	97	3,145	150	154	304	-5.0	1.82	107	7.0	15.0	59.9	18.1
Dudley	98	3,190	155	158	312	3.9	1.79	104	6.4	13.6	61.7	18.3
Sandwell	86	3,430	144	150	294	-5.2	1.90	113	7.1	14.6	59.5	18.8
Solihull	179	1,136	99	104	203	2.3	1.69	91	6.2	14.3	61.5	18.1
Walsall	106	2,484	130	133	263	-1.8	1.91	109	6.9	14.8	60.6	17.7
Wolverhampton	69	3,552	120	124	244	-4.8	1.82	106	7.1	14.8	59.4	18.7
EASTERN	19,120	275	2,591	2,667	5,257	8.3	1.71	93	6.5	13.9	61.2	18.4
Bedfordshire	1,236	442	272	274	546	7.0	1.85	96	7.3	15.1	62.7	14.9
Bedford	477	287	68	69	137	2.6	1.83	95	6.3	14.3	62.1	17.2
Luton	43	4,184	91	90	181	10.0	2.09	101	8.5	16.2	62.2	13.2
Mid Bedfordshire	503	231	58	58	116	11.4	1.62	92	6.9	14.3	64.0	14.8
South Bedfordshire	213	521	55	56	111	3.4	1.69	93	6.9	15.0	63.2	14.9
Cambridgeshire	3,400	204	344	349	694	17.7	1.60	91	6.6	13.9	63.0	16.5
Cambridge	41	2,821	58	57	115	13.7	1.15	78	5.4	10.6	68.1	15.9
East Cambridgeshire	655	99	32	33	65	20.3	1.00	89	6.1	13.8	61.0	19.0
Fenland	540	144	39	40	79	18.6	1.92	100	6.4	13.0	59.0	21.6
Huntingdonshire	923	162	74	76	150	19.0	1.62	91	7.2	15.0	63.7	14.1
Peterborough	333	479	79	80	159	18.8	1.84	100	7.5	15.5	61.5	15.5
South Cambridgeshire	902	140	63	64	126	16.0	1.68	85	6.2	14.4	62.8	16.6
Essex	3,675	429	773	805	1,578	6.4	1.70	95	6.4	13.7	61.1	18.7
Basildon	110	1,479	80	83	163	6.7	1.97	95	7.0	15.1	61.3	16.6
Braintree	612	204	62	63	125	11.1	1.62	96	6.5	14.2	62.3	17.0
Brentwood	149	482	35	37	72	0.9	1.35	100	5.8	12.7	62.1	19.4
Castle Point	45	1,896	42	43	85	-1.7	1.62	93	5.7	13.8	62.7	17.7
Chelmsford	342	457	77	79	156	12.1	1.54	84	6.4	14.3	63.5	15.9
Colchester	334	453	74	77	151	9.3	1.70	89	6.6	13.5	63.0	16.8
Epping Forest	340	350	58	61	119	1.7	1.71	94	6.2	12.5	61.9	19.4
Harlow	30	2,423	36	37	73	-8.3	1.84	98	7.0	14.6	60.8	17.6
Maldon	360	151	27	27	54	12.4	1.92	100	6.2	14.6	61.4	17.9
Rochford	169	440	37	39	76	3.3	1.73	89	6.0	14.0	60.8	19.3
Southend-on-Sea	42	4,099	82	89	171	8.6	1.59	100	6.5	12.9	59.0	21.7
Tendring	337	390	62	69	132	14.7	1.75	95	5.5	12.0	52.7	29.7
Thurrock	164	803	65	66	132	3.3	1.84	104	7.5	14.5	62.9	15.2
Uttlesford	641	107	34	35	68	9.0	1.76	86	6.2	14.4	62.7	16.7
Hertfordshire	1,639	617	500	512	1,011	4.5	1.71	91	6.8	14.0	62.0	17.2
Broxbourne	52	1,575	41	42	82	3.0	1.53	83	6.4	13.9	63.3	16.4
Dacorum	212	633	66	68	134	2.8	1.85	93	6.8	14.6	61.5	17.2
East Hertfordshire	477	257	61	61	123	12.0	1.75	98	6.5	13.6	64.6	15.3
Hertsmere	98	969	46	49	95	7.0	1.59	97	6.9	14.0	59.9	19.2
North Hertfordshire	375	306	57	58	115	5.8	1.71	93	6.5	14.0	61.4	18.1
St Albans	161	804	64	66	130	3.4	1.75	82	6.5	13.2	63.4	16.9
Stevenage	26	2,929	38	38	76	1.9	1.81	103	7.9	16.2	60.6	15.3
Three Rivers	89	946	41	43	84	3.6	1.51	79	5.9	13.6	61.5	19.0
Watford	21	3,605	38	39	77	3.5	1.78	99	7.9	13.9	63.4	14.8
Welwyn Hatfield	127	747	47	48	95	1.1	1.75	92	6.8	13.9	60.1	19.3
Norfolk	5,372	144	378	394	772	9.9	1.69	91	5.8	12.9	59.0	22.2
Breckland	1,305	86	55	57	112	15.8	1.79	90	6.1	13.5	58.4	22.0
Broadland	552	204	55	57	112	14.7	1.55	94	5.6	12.9	60.5	21.0
Great Yarmouth	174	511	43	46	89	9.2	1.89	99	6.3	13.7	58.0	22.1
Kings Lynn and West Norfolk	1,429	92	64	67	131	7.5	1.85	95	5.9	12.8	57.9	23.4
North Norfolk	965	99	47	49	96	14.9	1.60	86	5.0	12.2	55.4	27.4
Norwich	39	3,247	62	65	127	0.5	1.49	88	6.3	12.6	62.0	19.1
South Norfolk	908	116	52	53	105	10.7	1.75	85	5.4	13.0	60.3	21.4

14.1 *(continued)*

	Area (sq km)	Persons per sq km	Population (thousands)			Total population percentage change 1981-1995	Total Period Fertility Rate (TPFR)[1]	Standardised Mortality Ratio (UK=100) (SMR)[2]	Percentage of population aged			
			Males	Females	Total				Under 5	5-15	16 up to pension age[3]	Pension age[3] or over
Suffolk	3,798	173	323	334	657	9.2	1.73	91	6.4	14.2	59.3	20.1
Babergh	595	133	39	40	79	6.5	1.87	84	5.1	14.4	60.1	20.4
Forest Heath	374	180	34	34	67	28.1	1.38	89	8.3	16.7	61.6	13.3
Ipswich	39	2,895	56	58	114	-5.0	1.95	98	7.0	14.3	58.9	19.8
Mid Suffolk	871	91	40	40	80	12.5	1.91	87	6.0	14.1	59.6	20.3
St Edmundsbury	657	142	46	47	93	6.8	1.71	96	6.3	13.1	62.3	18.4
Suffolk Coastal	892	130	57	59	116	19.7	1.57	86	6.1	14.4	58.0	21.5
Waveney	370	291	52	56	108	7.7	1.81	96	6.0	13.2	56.2	24.5
LONDON (GOR)	1,578	4,440	3,432	3,575	7,007	3.0	1.73	98	7.2	13.3	64.0	15.5
Barking and Dagenham	34	4,535	75	79	155	2.1	1.93	108	8.0	15.0	58.0	19.0
Barnet	89	3,492	152	161	312	5.8	1.60	88	6.8	13.4	62.9	16.9
Bexley	61	3,633	108	113	220	1.5	1.72	94	6.8	14.0	61.7	17.5
Brent	44	5,553	122	123	245	-3.5	1.84	99	7.6	14.0	64.9	13.5
Bromley	152	1,933	142	151	293	-1.7	1.71	89	6.2	12.6	61.5	19.7
Camden	22	8,512	90	95	185	3.3	1.48	102	6.2	10.7	67.8	15.2
City of London	3	1,901	3	2	5	-3.7	1.43	71	5.0	6.3	67.7	21.0
City of Westminster	22	9,059	96	99	195	3.7	1.28	90	5.4	8.8	70.0	15.9
Croydon	87	3,821	162	169	331	3.1	1.72	96	7.1	13.9	63.8	15.1
Ealing	55	5,269	145	147	292	3.5	1.78	98	7.4	13.4	65.1	14.1
Enfield	81	3,221	128	133	261	0.1	2.02	89	7.4	13.7	62.1	16.9
Greenwich	48	4,433	103	109	211	-2.0	1.89	103	7.6	15.3	60.9	16.2
Hackney	20	9,958	95	99	194	4.9	2.07	108	8.7	15.0	63.7	12.6
Hammersmith and Fulham	16	9,665	74	82	156	3.2	1.34	106	6.5	10.2	69.7	13.5
Haringey	30	7,045	106	108	213	3.0	1.80	108	7.6	12.9	66.9	12.6
Harrow	51	4,134	103	107	210	5.6	1.64	89	6.7	14.0	63.0	16.3
Havering	118	1,962	113	118	231	-4.6	1.61	96	5.9	13.7	61.2	19.2
Hillingdon	110	2,224	121	124	245	5.1	1.70	91	7.0	13.5	63.3	16.3
Hounslow	58	3,538	102	102	204	0.1	1.87	93	7.4	13.9	64.0	14.7
Islington	15	11,726	85	90	175	5.1	1.61	108	7.2	12.7	66.0	14.0
Kensington and Chelsea	12	12,891	74	79	154	9.9	1.23	89	5.7	9.3	71.0	14.0
Kingston upon Thames	38	3,733	69	71	140	4.3	1.56	94	6.3	12.5	64.3	16.9
Lambeth	27	9,596	128	134	262	3.5	1.64	110	7.8	13.1	66.3	12.8
Lewisham	35	6,901	115	124	240	1.4	1.75	110	7.7	13.7	63.4	15.2
Merton	38	4,726	88	91	179	6.9	1.66	89	7.1	12.6	64.3	16.0
Newham	36	6,281	114	114	228	7.3	2.46	116	9.7	17.1	60.9	12.2
Redbridge	56	4,025	111	116	227	-0.9	1.82	93	7.0	14.0	61.9	17.1
Richmond-upon-Thames	55	3,179	85	91	176	8.6	1.52	87	6.2	11.6	64.8	17.4
Southwark	29	8,066	114	118	232	6.3	1.97	106	8.4	13.6	63.6	14.4
Sutton	43	4,019	85	90	174	2.5	1.71	92	7.0	13.4	62.1	17.5
Tower Hamlets	20	8,755	87	86	173	19.0	2.42	117	8.9	17.3	59.9	13.9
Waltham Forest	40	5,578	108	113	221	1.6	1.53	101	8.2	13.8	63.0	15.0
Wandsworth	35	7,600	128	137	265	1.2	1.90	104	6.8	10.0	68.9	14.3
SOUTH EAST (GOR)	19,096	411	3,847	4,000	7,847	8.3	1.70	92	6.4	13.8	61.1	18.7
Berkshire	1,259	622	392	391	783	12.7	1.70	95	6.9	14.4	64.3	14.5
Bracknell Forest	109	984	54	53	108	27.2	1.65	93	7.5	14.9	65.2	12.4
Newbury	704	203	71	72	143	16.3	1.68	94	6.5	15.0	63.8	14.7
Reading	40	3,503	72	70	141	2.9	1.64	92	7.0	13.3	64.5	15.2
Slough	27	3,984	54	55	109	12.0	1.88	109	8.1	15.1	63.0	13.8
Windsor and Maidenhead	198	706	70	70	140	3.5	1.60	97	6.1	13.4	63.5	17.0
Wokingham	179	793	72	70	142	21.4	1.79	85	6.7	15.0	65.3	13.0
Buckinghamshire	1,877	355	330	335	666	16.7	1.71	92	6.9	14.9	63.6	14.6
Aylesbury Vale	903	170	76	77	154	14.5	1.78	97	7.0	14.7	64.0	14.3
Chiltern	196	471	45	47	92	2.0	1.63	77	5.8	14.3	61.9	18.1
Milton Keynes	309	625	96	97	193	53.1	1.75	97	7.7	16.5	64.3	11.5
South Buckinghamshire	145	435	31	32	63	0.8	1.64	97	6.2	13.3	61.6	18.9
Wycombe	325	506	82	82	164	4.3	1.65	89	6.8	14.3	64.1	14.9
East Sussex	1,795	407	347	384	731	9.9	1.61	91	5.7	12.6	57.3	24.5
Brighton	58	2,677	77	79	156	4.5	1.40	92	5.6	11.7	63.5	19.3
Eastbourne	44	2,007	41	48	89	14.3	1.55	90	5.6	11.5	54.0	29.0
Hastings	30	2,779	39	44	83	9.2	1.96	99	6.6	14.2	57.0	22.3
Hove	24	3,848	43	48	92	4.7	1.50	105	5.5	10.9	60.5	23.1
Lewes	292	301	42	46	88	11.4	1.86	90	5.7	13.7	54.6	26.0
Rother	511	171	40	47	87	14.0	1.73	85	5.1	12.4	50.1	32.4
Wealden	836	163	65	71	136	14.3	1.69	83	5.8	14.0	56.6	23.6

14.1 *(continued)*

	Area (sq km)	Persons per sq km	Population (thousands)			Total population percentage change 1981-1995	Total Period Fertility Rate (TPFR)[1]	Standardised Mortality Ratio (UK=100) (SMR)[2]	Percentage of population aged			
			Males	Females	Total				Under 5	5-15	16 up to pension age[3]	Pension age[3] or over
Hampshire	3,779	428	799	818	1,617	8.5	1.69	94	6.4	14.0	61.8	17.8
Basingstoke and Deane	634	233	73	74	147	11.7	1.83	95	7.1	14.6	64.2	14.0
East Hampshire	515	213	53	56	110	19.8	1.68	89	6.4	15.1	61.6	16.9
Eastleigh	80	1,395	55	56	111	19.8	1.75	91	6.7	14.6	62.9	15.8
Fareham	74	1,381	50	53	103	15.2	1.58	89	5.6	14.0	61.3	19.1
Gosport	25	2,959	35	39	75	-4.0	1.74	99	7.2	15.2	59.9	17.7
Hart	215	391	43	41	84	20.3	1.67	91	6.1	14.3	66.3	13.4
Havant	55	2,133	57	61	118	2.0	1.71	94	5.9	15.1	58.5	20.4
New Forest	753	224	82	87	169	16.0	1.69	92	5.7	12.9	57.1	24.4
Portsmouth	40	4,718	96	94	190	-0.7	1.69	101	6.6	12.7	62.6	18.1
Rushmoor	39	2,209	44	43	86	-0.9	1.75	104	7.7	13.9	65.4	13.0
Southampton	50	4,284	107	106	214	1.8	1.62	100	6.6	13.4	62.3	17.8
Test Valley	637	166	52	53	106	12.9	1.59	89	6.2	14.6	62.8	16.4
Winchester	661	158	51	54	104	12.3	1.62	87	5.6	13.8	61.0	19.6
Isle of Wight UA[4]	380	329	60	65	125	6.0	1.82	92	5.2	13.1	55.5	26.3
Medina[4]	117	610	35	37	71	5.2	..	..	5.6	13.3	57.5	23.5
South Wight[4]	263	204	25	28	54	6.9	..	..	4.7	12.7	52.7	29.9
Kent	3,735	415	758	793	1,551	4.5	1.77	96	6.5	14.1	60.4	19.0
Ashford	581	166	47	49	96	10.8	1.71	94	6.6	14.2	60.5	18.6
Canterbury	309	437	65	70	135	10.5	1.54	92	5.5	13.1	58.3	23.2
Dartford	73	1,147	42	42	84	2.9	1.81	111	6.6	13.3	63.6	16.5
Dover	315	341	52	55	107	3.7	1.82	94	6.4	13.9	58.3	21.4
Gillingham	32	2,952	48	48	96	-0.8	1.77	103	6.8	15.7	62.8	14.7
Gravesham	99	933	45	47	92	-3.2	1.88	97	6.9	14.5	61.1	17.6
Maidstone	393	354	68	71	139	0.5	1.70	91	6.3	14.1	62.5	17.1
Rochester-upon-Medway	160	904	71	73	144	0.4	1.81	110	7.6	11.9	63.0	14.5
Sevenoaks	368	298	54	56	110	0.1	1.78	88	6.3	14.2	60.6	18.9
Shepway	357	272	46	51	97	12.7	1.64	92	6.2	13.1	57.6	23.1
Swale	373	316	59	59	118	7.1	1.94	101	6.8	14.9	61.2	17.3
Thanet	103	1,213	59	66	125	2.8	1.89	101	5.9	13.5	54.4	20.2
Tonbridge and Malling	240	434	52	52	104	6.4	1.75	92	6.9	14.1	62.5	16.5
Tunbridge Wells	332	311	50	54	103	4.9	1.73	87	6.1	14.0	60.6	19.3
Oxfordshire	2,606	230	299	299	598	10.4	1.58	87	6.7	13.9	63.3	16.1
Cherwell	589	223	65	67	131	20.3	1.55	92	7.7	15.1	62.8	14.4
Oxford	46	2,957	68	67	135	3.4	1.22	92	5.7	12.3	66.5	15.4
South Oxfordshire	679	182	61	62	123	5.3	1.86	81	6.9	14.3	61.8	17.0
Vale of White Horse	579	196	57	56	113	9.3	1.85	79	6.3	14.4	62.4	10.9
West Oxfordshire	714	134	48	48	96	17.3	1.68	91	7.0	13.4	62.6	17.1
Surrey	1,677	623	512	533	1,044	2.9	1.72	88	6.2	13.3	61.8	18.7
Elmbridge	97	1,264	59	63	122	8.6	1.65	84	6.4	13.5	61.7	18.4
Epsom and Ewell	34	2,031	34	35	69	-0.2	1.67	84	5.9	13.0	61.4	19.7
Guildford	271	462	62	63	125	0.2	1.61	80	6.1	13.1	62.5	18.3
Mole Valley	258	307	39	41	79	2.4	1.74	93	5.7	12.2	60.2	21.9
Reigate and Banstead	129	919	58	61	119	1.4	1.91	95	6.3	13.5	60.9	19.3
Runnymede	78	971	37	38	76	3.9	1.63	89	6.2	12.1	62.6	19.0
Spelthorne	57	1,582	44	45	89	-3.6	1.80	85	6.2	12.0	62.8	19.0
Surrey Heath	95	863	41	41	82	8.0	1.67	94	6.8	14.7	64.6	13.9
Tandridge	250	308	37	40	77	-1.2	1.66	87	5.9	14.1	60.2	19.7
Waverley	345	334	56	59	115	2.8	1.86	89	6.0	14.0	59.7	20.3
Woking	64	1,420	45	46	90	10.2	1.72	87	6.8	14.0	63.3	15.9
West Sussex	1,988	368	351	381	731	9.8	1.65	89	5.8	13.2	57.7	23.3
Adur	42	1,398	28	30	58	-0.2	1.95	90	5.8	13.0	56.0	25.2
Arun	221	617	64	72	136	14.9	1.61	91	5.2	11.7	53.4	29.7
Chichester	786	132	48	56	104	5.3	1.52	87	5.5	12.7	55.3	26.5
Crawley	44	2,083	45	47	92	12.0	1.65	97	7.2	14.3	62.2	16.3
Horsham	530	219	57	59	116	15.8	1.66	84	6.3	14.4	60.3	18.9
Mid Sussex	333	379	62	64	126	9.2	1.64	87	5.6	14.3	61.9	18.2
Worthing	32	3,033	46	53	99	6.5	1.64	92	5.5	12.0	54.5	28.0

Regional Trends 32, © Crown copyright 1997

14.1 *(continued)*

	Area (sq km)	Persons per sq km	Population (thousands)			Total population percentage change 1981-1995	Total Period Fertility Rate (TPFR)[1]	Standardised Mortality Ratio (UK=100) (SMR)[2]	Percentage of population aged			
			Males	Females	Total				Under 5	5-15	16 up to pension age[3]	Pension age[3] or over
SOUTH WEST	23,829	203	2,357	2,470	4,827	10.2	1.67	90	5.9	13.4	59.4	21.2
Avon#	1,332	737	484	498	982	5.8	1.65	91	6.3	13.3	61.7	18.7
Bath	29	2,969	41	44	85	1.0	1.36	85	5.3	12.0	61.1	21.6
Bristol	110	3,657	198	202	401	-0.1	1.58	96	6.6	13.2	62.3	17.9
Kingswood	48	1,931	45	47	92	9.2	1.78	83	6.6	13.8	61.3	18.3
Northavon	449	313	71	70	141	18.8	1.91	86	7.1	13.5	65.0	14.3
Wansdyke	322	247	39	41	80	2.9	1.70	88	5.6	13.6	60.1	20.8
Woodspring	375	490	89	95	184	12.8	1.70	90	5.5	13.6	59.1	21.8
Cornwall and the Isles of Scilly	3,559	136	234	249	483	13.2	1.73	93	5.5	13.7	58.0	22.8
Caradon	664	120	39	41	79	17.2	1.78	94	5.5	14.4	59.0	21.1
Carrick	461	183	40	44	85	11.7	1.75	92	5.4	13.4	56.6	24.7
Kerrier	473	188	43	46	89	6.3	1.71	98	5.9	13.7	58.8	21.6
North Cornwall	1,190	65	38	40	78	20.0	1.62	94	5.7	13.7	57.6	23.0
Penwith	304	198	29	31	60	10.8	1.86	87	5.0	12.8	57.4	24.9
Restormel	452	200	44	46	90	14.8	1.70	94	5.5	13.9	58.7	21.9
Isles of Scilly	15	127	1	1	2	-0.5	2.59	53	5.1	17.7	55.7	21.5
Devon	6,703	158	512	547	1,059	9.6	1.62	90	5.7	13.3	58.4	22.7
East Devon	814	152	58	66	124	14.8	1.68	79	4.9	11.7	53.1	30.3
Exeter	47	2,267	52	54	107	5.9	1.51	93	5.8	13.1	62.4	18.8
Mid Devon	915	72	32	34	66	12.4	1.84	85	5.9	14.3	58.7	21.1
North Devon	1,086	79	42	44	86	9.5	1.71	94	5.8	13.3	57.9	23.1
Plymouth	80	3,230	128	130	257	1.6	1.52	101	6.3	13.9	62.0	17.8
South Hams	887	89	38	41	79	18.6	1.72	89	5.5	13.5	57.8	23.1
Teignbridge	674	170	55	59	115	19.7	1.74	86	5.5	12.8	56.5	25.1
Torbay	63	1,971	58	66	124	9.6	1.61	88	5.4	12.5	55.6	26.6
Torridge	979	56	27	28	55	13.1	1.64	93	5.7	14.6	56.8	22.9
West Devon	1,160	40	23	24	47	9.1	1.81	88	5.2	14.1	57.9	22.8
Dorset	2,653	256	327	352	679	13.4	1.57	87	5.4	12.5	57.0	25.0
Bournemouth	46	3,484	76	85	161	12.2	1.44	93	5.3	11.1	57.8	25.8
Christchurch	50	854	20	23	43	12.5	1.73	78	4.8	10.8	51.0	33.4
East Dorset	354	230	39	42	82	18.1	1.54	72	4.5	12.4	55.7	27.4
North Dorset	609	93	28	29	57	16.0	1.61	86	5.6	14.4	57.1	22.9
Poole	65	2,145	67	72	139	15.4	1.65	89	6.1	13.1	58.6	22.2
Purbeck	404	111	22	23	45	10.8	1.61	94	5.5	13.1	58.5	22.9
West Dorset	1,082	83	43	47	90	12.1	1.66	82	5.2	13.1	54.6	27.1
Weymouth and Portland	42	1,505	31	32	63	8.4	1.58	97	6.1	13.6	59.9	20.4
Gloucestershire	2,653	208	273	280	553	9.2	1.73	92	6.2	13.7	60.4	19.7
Cheltenham	47	2,286	52	54	107	3.7	1.58	91	5.8	12.9	60.9	20.4
Cotswold	1,165	70	40	42	81	15.7	1.56	84	5.9	13.2	59.0	21.8
Forest of Dean	526	143	37	38	75	2.9	1.80	102	5.8	13.6	60.5	20.1
Gloucester	41	2,611	53	53	106	5.6	1.93	101	7.5	14.8	60.7	17.0
Stroud	461	233	53	55	107	11.7	1.79	93	6.0	14.2	59.8	20.0
Tewkesbury	414	184	38	38	76	20.0	1.70	84	6.0	13.5	61.3	19.2
Somerset	3,452	139	235	246	481	11.7	1.74	89	5.9	13.9	58.2	21.9
Mendip	739	133	48	50	99	9.7	1.71	95	6.2	15.4	59.1	19.4
Sedgemoor	564	179	50	51	101	12.4	1.75	90	5.9	13.7	58.6	21.8
South Somerset	462	213	48	51	99	11.7	1.66	92	5.7	14.0	58.5	21.9
Taunton Deane	959	157	74	77	150	13.0	1.76	85	6.1	13.7	58.5	21.8
West Somerset	727	45	15	17	32	9.7	1.99	85	5.4	11.4	52.2	31.1
Wiltshire	3,476	170	293	298	591	12.5	1.75	93	6.6	14.1	61.6	17.7
Kennet	957	78	38	37	75	13.8	1.86	85	6.6	14.0	61.7	17.7
North Wiltshire	768	158	61	61	122	15.9	1.81	89	7.0	13.8	62.7	16.4
Salisbury	1,004	110	53	58	111	7.9	1.56	93	5.9	14.2	59.7	20.2
Thamesdown	230	755	87	87	174	14.6	1.76	100	6.9	14.5	62.7	15.9
West Wiltshire	517	212	54	56	110	9.5	1.80	92	6.3	14.0	60.3	19.4

14.1 *(continued)*

	Area (sq km)	Persons per sq km	Population (thousands)			Total population percentage change 1981-1995	Total Period Fertility Rate (TPFR)[1]	Standardised Mortality Ratio (UK=100) (SMR)[2]	Percentage of population aged			
			Males	Females	Total				Under 5	5-15	16 up to pension age[3]	Pension age[3] or over
New local government structure with effect from 1 April 1996												
Former County of Cleveland												
Hartlepool UA	94	982	45	47	92	-3	1.94	111	6.9	15.3	59.9	17.9
Middlesbrough UA	54	2,738	72	75	148	-2	1.81	115	7.2	16.2	60.4	16.3
Redcar & Cleveland UA	245	577	69	72	141	-6	1.82	111	6.6	15.3	60.0	18.1
Stockton-on-Tees UA	204	874	87	901	178	2	1.68	110	6.9	15.8	61.2	16.1
Former County of Humberside												
East Riding of Yorkshire	2415	128	151	158	308	14	1.66	98	5.6	13.7	60.5	20.3
Kingston upon Hull UA	71	3,759	133	136	268	-2	1.76	106	7.3	14.8	60.6	17.3
North East Lincolnshire	192	835	78	82	160	-1	1.80	102	6.8	15.5	59.2	18.5
North Lincolnshire UA	838	181	75	77	152	1	1.89	102	6.3	14.6	60.4	18.8
Former County of North Yorkshire												
York UA	271	643	85	89	174	5	1.52	92	5.7	13.2	61.7	19.4
North Yorkshire	8,038	69.2	270	286	556	9	1.73	91	5.8	13.5	59.9	20.8
Former County of Avon												
Bath and North East Somerset UA	351	469	80	84	165	2	1.51	87	5.4	12.8	60.6	21.2
Bristol UA	110	3,657	198	202	401	-0	1.50	96	6.6	13.2	62.3	17.9
North Somerset UA	375	490	89	94	184	13	1.70	90	5.5	13.6	59.1	21.8
South Gloucestershire UA	497	469	116	116	233	15	1.86	84	6.9	13.6	63.5	15.9

\# New local government structure came into effect on 1 April 1996.

1 The Total Period Fertility Rate (TPFR) measures the average number of children which would be born if women were to experience the age-specific fertility rates of the year in question throughout their child-bearing life

2 Adjusted for the age structure of the population. See Technical notes to the Population chapter.

3 Pension age is 60 for women and 65 for men.

4 The Isle of Wight became a Unitary Authority on 1 April 1995.

Source: Office for National Statistics

14.2   Vital and social statistics: by county

	Live births[1] per 1,000 population		Deaths[1] per 1,000 population		Perinatal mortality rate[2]	Infant mortality rate[3]	Percentage of live births outside marriage	Children looked after by LAs per 1,000 population aged under 18
	1981	1995	1981	1995	1993-1995	1993-1995	1995	1995[4]
United Kingdom	13.0	12.5	11.7	10.9	8.9	6.2	*34*	..
England	12.8	12.5	11.6	10.8	8.8	6.2	*34*	4.4
North East	13.0	11.8	12.2	11.6	9.8	6.6	*41*	..
Cleveland#	14.4	12.7	10.8	10.6	8.6	5.7	*46*	4.1
Durham	12.6	11.4	12.4	11.9	8.4	5.4	*38*	4.7
Northumberland	12.3	10.8	13.0	12.1	11.1	7.5	*32*	4.1
Tyne & Wear	12.6	11.8	12.5	11.8	10.3	7.5	*43*	..
North West (GOR) and Merseyside	13.0	12.2	12.5	11.6	8.9	6.4	*40*	..
North West (GOR)	13.0	12.3	12.5	11.5	9.2	6.6	40	..
Cheshire	12.7	11.7	10.7	10.4	8.0	6.3	*32*	2.5
Cumbria	11.7	10.7	12.8	12.2	8.6	6.2	*32*	4.0
Greater Manchester	13.5	12.8	12.4	11.3	9.8	6.8	*41*	5.2
Lancashire	12.7	12.1	13.7	12.2	9.0	6.8	*37*	5.2
Merseyside	13.2	12.0	12.4	12.2	7.8	5.5	*47*	..
Yorkshire and the Humber	12.7	12.5	12.0	11.1	9.3	7.3	*37*	5.2
Humberside#	12.6	12.0	11.4	11.3	9.1	6.8	*42*	6.1
North Yorkshire#	11.1	11.3	12.5	11.4	7.8	5.7	*27*	2.5
South Yorkshire	12.2	12.3	11.5	11.4	9.7	8.4	*40*	..
West Yorkshire	13.6	13.2	12.4	10.6	9.6	7.3	*35*	..
East Midlands	12.8	12.0	11.1	10.6	8.8	6.4	*34*	4.0
Derbyshire	12.5	12.0	11.9	11.3	7.6	5.7	*34*	4.5
Leicestershire	13.6	12.4	10.0	9.6	9.4	6.7	*30*	3.1
Lincolnshire	11.8	11.0	11.9	11.9	8.8	6.3	*32*	3.5
Northamptonshire	13.5	12.5	10.5	9.7	8.9	7.0	*34*	4.1
Nottinghamshire	12.4	12.0	11.3	10.7	9.5	6.5	*39*	4.4
West Midlands	13.0	12.6	10.9	10.8	10.2	7.1	*35*	4.6
Hereford & Worcs.	12.3	11.6	10.8	11.0	9.7	6.0	*30*	4.0
Shropshire	12.3	11.8	10.7	10.4	8.1	5.5	*33*	3.9
Staffordshire	13.0	11.6	10.6	10.7	9.1	6.7	*34*	4.4
Warwickshire	12.1	11.4	10.1	10.7	9.0	5.5	*29*	4.5
West Midlands (Met. county)	13.4	13.7	11.2	11.0	11.1	7.9	*37*	..
Eastern	12.9	12.3	10.4	10.3	9.7	6.6	*29*	..
Bedfordshire	15.6	14.3	9.0	8.6	10.2	6.5	*28*	3.7
Cambridgeshire	13.6	12.3	9.8	9.1	6.3	5.2	*26*	4.5
Essex	12.8	12.1	10.7	10.7	8.0	5.3	*31*	3.9
Hertfordshire	12.4	12.8	9.5	9.4	7.5	4.8	*26*	2.6
Norfolk	11.5	11.0	12.1	12.1	7.5	5.5	*32*	3.4
Suffolk	12.6	11.9	11.2	11.2	7.1	4.7	*30*	2.6
London	13.5	14.9	11.4	9.5	9.5	6.4	*33*	5.3

14.2 *(continued)*

	Live births[1] per 1,000 population		Deaths[1] per 1,000 population		Perinatal mortality rate[2] 1993-1995	Infant mortality rate[3] 1993-1995	Percentage of live births outside marriage 1995	Children looked after by LAs per 1,000 population aged under 18 1995[4]
	1981	1995	1981	1995				
South East (GOR)	12.3	12.2	11.2	10.7	7.8	5.0	*29*	..
Berkshire	13.9	13.6	8.9	8.4	7.7	4.8	*26*	3.7
Buckinghamshire	13.8	12.9	8.6	8.3	8.1	5.8	*26*	..
East Sussex	10.0	10.8	16.4	14.6	7.7	5.0	*36*	4.9
Hampshire	13.0	12.3	10.1	10.2	7.7	5.0	*30*	2.8
Isle of Wight	9.6	10.0	14.8	14.9	8.4	6.1	*42*	4.0
Kent	12.6	12.3	11.9	11.2	8.5	5.3	*34*	..
Oxfordshire	12.7	12.2	9.1	8.6	6.7	3.5	*24*	3.4
Surrey	11.1	12.3	10.7	10.3	7.2	4.4	*22*	..
West Sussex	11.2	11.1	13.7	13.2	7.5	5.4	*26*	4.5
South West	11.5	11.3	12.4	11.8	7.8	5.4	*31*	4.1
Avon#	12.0	12.2	11.2	10.4	7.8	5.5	*32*	4.4
Cornwall#	11.4	10.4	13.4	12.8	9.2	6.2	*33*	3.8
Devon	11.1	10.6	13.7	12.7	7.1	5.7	*33*	4.9
Dorset	10.1	10.1	14.2	13.6	7.1	5.4	*32*	4.0
Gloucestershire	11.8	11.9	11.2	11.0	9.2	5.3	*30*	3.2
Somerset	11.4	11.0	12.4	11.9	7.9	5.0	*29*	3.6
Wiltshire	12.8	12.7	10.7	9.9	7.4	4.7	*27*	3.5

New local government structure with effect from 1 April 1996

Former County of Cleveland

Hartlepool UA	..	13.7	..	11.1	..	..	*50*	..
Middlesbrough UA	..	13.6	..	10.5	..	..	*50*	..
Redcar & Cleveland UA	..	12.0	..	11.3	..	..	*45*	..
Stockton-on-Tees UA	..	12.0	..	9.9	..	..	*40*	..

Former County of Humberside

East Riding of Yorkshire UA	..	10.2	..	11.8	..	..	*30*	..
Kingston upon Hull UA	..	13.6	..	10.9	..	..	*53*	..
North East Lincolnshire UA	..	12.4	..	11.2	..	..	*47*	..
North Lincolnshire UA	..	12.4	..	11.0	..	..	*37*	..

Former County of North Yorkshire

York UA	..	11.1	..	10.8	..	..	*33*	..
North Yorkshire	..	11.3	..	11.6	..	..	*25*	..

Former County of Avon

Bath and North East Somerset UA	..	10.2	..	11.3	..	..	*28*	..
Bristol UA	..	12.6	..	10.6	..	..	*40*	..
North Somerset UA	..	10.4	..	12.5	..	..	*31*	..
South Gloucestershire UA	..	14.0	..	8.0	..	..	*24*	..

New local government structure came into effect on 1 April 1996.
1 Births are on the basis of year of occurrence in England and Wales and year of registration in Scotland and Northern Ireland. Deaths relate to year of registration.
2 Still births and deaths of infants under 1 week of age per 1,000 live and still births, 3 year average.
3 Deaths of infants under 1 year of age per 1,000 live births, 3 year average.
4 At 31 March. Under 18 mid-1994 population estimates used. In some cases figures are estimates which take account of missing or incomplete data.

Source: Office for National Statistics; Department of Health

14.3 Education: by county

	Day nursery places per 1,000 population aged under 5 years[1] March 1995	Children under 5 in education[2] (percentages) Jan. 1996	Pupil/teacher ratio 1995/96 (numbers)		Pupils and students participating in post-compulsory education[3]		Pupils in last year of compulsory schooling[4,5] 1994/95 with		Average A/AS level points score[5,6] 1994/95
			Primary schools	Secondary schools	1985/86	1994/95	No graded results	5 or more A*-Cs at GCSE	
United Kingdom	..	53	22.7	16.1	..	80	7.7	41.9	15.9
England	48.5	54	23.2	16.6	62	79	7.8	40.4	15.9
North East	32.9	82	23.7	17.1	55	71	10.5	34.9	15.5
Cleveland#	41.8	97	24.1	16.8	58	74	11.8	33.6	18.0
Durham	24.9	80	24.0	17.5	55	66	9.6	34.4	15.3
Northumberland	15.5	77	24.6	18.5	58	72	6.9	42.8	16.1
Tyne & Wear	36.7	77	23.1	16.5	52	71	11.3	33.5	14.9
North West (GOR) and Merseyside	57.9	65	23.7	16.6	65	74	9.1	39.2	17.3
North West (GOR)	63.2	63	23.8	16.7	64	74	8.4	40.5	18.0
Cheshire	60.8	55	24.0	17.0	72	82	5.3	46.8	17.6
Cumbria	41.8	61	23.2	16.9	65	76	7.0	43.5	18.3
Greater Manchester	58.6	70	23.7	16.4	61	71	10.3	36.6	17.4
Lancashire	80.5	54	24.1	17.0	62	73	7.9	41.7	19.1
Merseyside	40.9	75	23.3	16.2	70	75	11.7	34.4	15.7
Yorkshire and the Humber	39.3	67	23.8	17.0	58	75	9.8	36.3	16.6
Humberside#	32.7	63	24.7	17.2	55	72	9.8	33.8	15.4
North Yorkshire#	..	52	23.6	16.3	67	85	4.9	50.2	20.5
South Yorkshire	22.6	66	23.7	17.2	58	73	11.1	33.9	16.3
West Yorkshire	48.9	73	23.5	17.0	57	75	10.6	34.3	15.6
East Midlands	46.2	53	24.1	16.8	62	75	7.5	39.6	15.9
Derbyshire	44.3	63	25.3	17.0	65	79	6.4	39.8	17.1
Leicestershire	53.0	40	23.3	17.1	64	77	7.3	39.7	15.2
Lincolnshire	48.1	50	23.6	15.9	63	72	6.7	44.8	18.4
Northamptonshire	49.8	52	23.4	17.0	62	78	6.4	40.0	14.6
Nottinghamshire	38.6	59	24.3	16.7	59	72	9.8	36.0	14.8
West Midlands	55.8	61	23.5	16.7	63	79	8.6	37.7	16.2
Hereford & Worcs.	74.4	28	23.2	17.7	65	81	6.7	43.0	16.1
Shropshire	56.3	41	24.3	16.5	70	87	5.4	45.6	16.3
Staffordshire	57.2	60	24.9	17.6	62	72	7.3	38.7	16.6
Warwickshire	54.2	51	23.6	16.8	71	83	5.9	43.8	17.5
West Midlands (Met. county)	51.2	73	23.0	16.1	60	78	10.6	33.7	15.7
Eastern	30.3	41	22.7	16.5	59	81	5.9	44.1	15.6
Bedfordshire	4.6	51	23.0	17.8	64	82	5.3	39.3	16.2
Cambridgeshire	..	43	23.9	17.2	62	79	6.2	44.5	15.0
Essex	43.7	31	22.6	16.7	54	77	6.4	42.8	16.6
Hertfordshire	..	56	22.3	15.7	66	92	5.8	47.9	15.4
Norfolk	25.6	37	22.3	15.6	57	79	6.8	43.2	15.0
Suffolk	..	34	22.3	16.5	58	77	4.0	45.8	14.5
London	62.0	58	21.6	15.8	61	81	9.1	36.8	14.5

Regional Trends 32, © Crown copyright 1997

14.3 *(continued)*

	Day nursery places per 1,000 population aged under 5 years[1] March 1995	Children under 5 in education[2] (percentages) Jan. 1996	Pupil/teacher ratio 1995/96 (numbers)		Pupils and students participating in post-compulsory education[3]		Pupils in last year of compulsory schooling[4,5] 1994/95 with		Average A/AS level points score[5,6] 1994/95
			Primary schools	Secondary schools	1985/86	1994/95	No graded results	5 or more A*-Cs at GCSE	
South East (GOR)	45.9	36	23.0	16.7	66	84	6.0	46.0	16.1
Berkshire	55.0	37	23.3	16.3	67	88	5.8	48.3	16.0
Buckinghamshire	43.0	34	23.6	17.1	67	77	5.9	49.1	18.0
East Sussex	62.7	43	22.7	16.0	66	83	7.7	41.9	13.7
Hampshire	31.9	37	22.8	16.6	66	87	5.2	46.0	14.8
Isle of Wight	20.1	42	23.2	18.1	67	84	5.8	39.1	15.2
Kent	66.3	39	23.9	16.4	61	82	6.4	41.9	16.4
Oxfordshire	55.6	27	23.3	17.9	70	79	7.3	45.8	15.0
Surrey	28.4	41	22.0	16.6	72	85	5.5	49.3	15.8
West Sussex	28.1	25	22.5	16.6	67	84	4.9	51.0	15.1
South West	49.2	38	23.6	17.1	64	82	4.9	45.7	15.7
Avon#	51.6	53	23.3	16.3	63	81	6.5	41.2	14.1
Cornwall	29.3	48	23.6	17.5	67	81	3.3	46.3	13.9
Devon	37.9	29	24.0	17.0	64	78	5.2	43.2	15.8
Dorset	54.6	38	23.9	17.5	55	90	4.6	48.8	18.1
Gloucestershire	82.8	32	23.4	17.6	67	82	4.6	49.4	16.2
Somerset	48.1	38	23.2	18.0	72	84	4.0	47.7	15.9
Wiltshire	42.9	28	23.4	16.8	65	79	4.6	48.4	16.0

\# New local government structure came into effect on 1 April 1996.

1 Local authority provided and registered day nurseries only. A small number of places provided by facilities exempt from registration are excluded. Population data used are mid-1994 estimates.

2 Figures relate to pupils in maintained nursery and primary schools as a percentage of the three and four year old population.

3 1985/86 rates refer to full and part-time pupils and students aged 16 in maintained institutions as a percentage of 15 year old pupils in maintained schools one year earlier; 1994/95 rates refer to pupils and students aged 16 in education as a percentage of the 16 year old population (ages measured at the beginning of the academic year).

4 Pupils in their last year of compulsory schooling as a percentage of the school population of the same age.

5 Figures relate to maintained schools only, hence they are not directly comparable with those in Table 4.0 which include independent schools and further education institutions.

6 Figure for United Kingdom relates to England and Wales average

Source: Department of Health; Department for Education and Employment

14.4 Housing and households: by district

| | Housing starts 1995[1] (numbers) | | | Households 1995 | | | | | Local authority tenants: | |
	Private enterprise	Housing associations local authorities etc	Stock of dwellings[2] 1995 (thousands)	All households (thousands)	Average household size (numbers)	Lone parents[3] as a percentage of all households	One-person households as a percentage of all households	Households receiving Housing Benefit as a percentage of all households	average weekly unrebated rent per dwelling (£) April 1996[4]	Council Tax (£) April 1996[5]
UNITED KINGDOM	141,445	35,384	24,430	23,922.4	2.41	..	28.2	19.5	..	.
ENGLAND	111,242	26,056	20,367	20,026.9	2.41	5.5	28.4	18.8	39.96	646
NORTH EAST	5,316	918	1,101	1,076.2	2.39	6.4	29.2	26.8	33.30	724
Cleveland#	1,395	293	229	224.3	2.47	7.4	27.5	26.4	37.27	763
Hartlepool	250	57	38	37.0	2.46	6.8	27.5	29.8	35.24	837
Langbaurgh-on-Tees	193	105	60	57.7	2.42	6.5	27.5	23.7	37.14	640
Middlesbrough	238	91	59	58.1	2.51	9.9	28.1	32.2	40.86	854
Stockton-on-Tees	715	38	72	71.5	2.47	6.3	27.1	22.1	35.04	749
Durham	1,354	210	255	249.5	2.40	5.6	27.7	23.7	34.82	689
Chester-le-Street	328	0	23	23.1	2.37	4.4	26.6	20.1	32.23	623
Darlington	219	72	43	41.7	2.37	5.6	30.1	19.5	33.33	660
Derwentside	142	45	37	36.1	2.39	6.1	27.7	26.2	37.83	706
Durham	166	42	35	35.5	2.48	5.2	26.8	19.5	35.36	642
Easington	142	0	41	39.3	2.43	6.3	28.0	31.4	35.93	747
Sedgefield	151	0	38	37.3	2.40	6.1	26.2	25.7	32.79	728
Teesdale	35	51	11	10.1	2.37	2.6	29.0	13.5	32.75	656
Wear Valley	128	0	27	26.4	2.36	6.1	27.3	25.7	35.19	715
Northumberland	781	61	133	125.9	2.39	4.4	27.4	19.2	31.13	679
Alnwick	46	38	14	12.8	2.37	4.3	26.1	17.8	31.75	686
Berwick-upon-Tweed	59	0	13	11.6	2.25	3.2	33.4	17.3	28.26	687
Blyth Valley	..	..	34	33.0	2.41	5.1	26.8	23.1	29.28	664
Castle Morpeth	110	12	20	19.5	2.42	3.6	26.1	13.6	33.32	680
Tynedale	85	8	25	23.3	2.42	3.9	28.1	13.1	36.28	679
Wansbeck	166	0	27	25.7	2.41	5.0	26.4	25.3	30.55	691
Tyne and Wear	1,786	354	484	476.6	2.35	7.0	31.2	30.7	31.74	737
Gateshead	258	39	88	86.0	2.32	6.2	31.1	30.6	32.16	781
Newcastle-upon-Tyne	180	77	122	120.6	2.32	7.7	34.4	33.4	34.52	771
North Tyneside	711	64	87	84.1	2.28	6.0	31.1	26.2	28.28	786
South Tyneside	338	2	67	66.2	2.33	7.5	31.8	32.6	27.87	709
Sunderland	332	161	120	119.6	2.45	7.1	27.8	30.1	33.03	652
NORTH WEST (GOR) & MERSEYSIDE	15,738	4,955	2,874	2,802.9	2.43	6.6	29.0	22.5	37.27	745
NORTH WEST (GOR)	12,583	3,409	2,285	2,229.6	2.42	6.2	28.7	20.7	36.23	721
Cheshire	3,153	410	400	395.3	2.45	5.1	26.3	15.3	32.33	676
Chester	312	29	51	50.0	2.36	5.2	29.6	16.1	34.77	672
Congleton	425	0	38	34.1	2.48	3.2	24.5	9.5	33.31	665
Crewe and Nantwich	373	86	44	46.1	2.45	4.6	26.1	13.7	34.50	675
Ellesmere Port and Neston	..	..	33	32.3	2.49	5.8	23.8	15.7	26.87	690
Halton	..	..	48	47.7	2.56	8.2	24.5	28.0	30.64	647
Macclesfield	437	46	65	63.1	2.37	4.0	27.4	9.9	36.36	670
Vale Royal	607	113	47	45.6	2.50	4.2	24.6	13.6	34.37	691
Warrington	762	108	76	76.4	2.43	5.3	27.1	15.8	29.94	692
Cumbria	1,045	303	216	204.0	2.36	4.0	28.9	16.2	36.71	711
Allerdale	155	38	42	39.5	2.39	3.8	29.5	19.1	35.86	699
Barrow-in-Furness	42	18	31	30.2	2.36	5.1	28.5	18.0	41.98	735
Carlisle	256	51	44	43.3	2.36	4.4	29.0	17.5	34.51	733
Copeland	133	157	30	28.7	2.43	5.2	27.2	20.7	34.04	692
Eden	204	0	21	19.7	2.38	2.9	26.5	10.4	46.99	704
South Lakeland	258	39	47	42.6	2.29	2.8	30.8	10.5	36.55	701
Greater Manchester	5,059	1,824	1,079	1,053.3	2.42	7.2	29.7	25.7	37.22	746
Bolton	..	..	110	107.6	2.44	5.9	28.6	21.3	34.18	736
Bury	381	95	75	73.8	2.43	5.3	27.7	14.4	35.93	652
Manchester	549	699	188	178.5	2.39	12.6	34.9	52.2	43.35	838
Oldham	452	40	91	89.4	2.44	7.1	28.8	22.2	32.24	771
Rochdale	629	108	86	83.3	2.46	7.4	28.7	22.3	35.44	727
Salford	613	57	101	96.2	2.37	7.9	32.8	33.4	38.19	814
Stockport	258	253	120	120.4	2.39	5.0	28.6	15.6	31.65	803
Tameside	253	99	93	90.3	2.43	6.0	27.4	20.3	35.33	756
Trafford	292	117	89	89.0	2.42	5.8	29.1	14.4	36.62	592
Wigan	831	16	127	124.9	2.46	5.2	26.2	19.1	30.60	700

Regional Trends 32, © Crown copyright 1997

14.4 *(continued)*

	Housing starts 1995[1] (numbers)		Stock of dwellings[2] 1995 (thousands)	Households 1995					Local authority tenants: average weekly unrebated rent per dwelling (£) April 1996[4]	Council Tax (£) April 1996[5]
	Private enterprise	Housing associations local authorities etc		All households (thousands)	Average household size (numbers)	Lone parents[3] as a percentage of all households	One-person households as a percentage of all households	Households receiving Housing Benefit as a percentage of all households		
Lancashire	3,326	872	590	577.0	2.42	5.8	28.4	16.9	35.80	716
Blackburn	380	226	57	54.3	2.54	7.6	28.1	23.6	40.41	776
Blackpool	99	79	66	65.4	2.25	5.4	32.6	21.5	33.63	666
Burnley	212	69	39	36.3	2.43	7.8	28.1	21.1	37.15	747
Chorley	..	..	39	38.3	2.49	5.2	23.7	13.1	28.13	686
Fylde	183	11	33	31.8	2.26	3.3	30.8	10.3	31.61	690
Hyndburn	228	6	34	32.4	2.44	6.6	28.1	18.2	38.49	751
Lancaster	274	138	55	55.7	2.38	6.1	29.8	16.5	34.85	690
Pendle	111	65	37	34.7	2.43	6.0	29.8	15.8	35.81	754
Preston	415	58	54	53.5	2.46	6.9	31.3	21.5	35.91	749
Ribble Valley	283	2	22	20.1	2.49	3.2	26.7	7.1	31.68	699
Rossendale	57	12	28	26.3	2.44	5.8	27.0	18.8	35.98	764
South Ribble	309	167	41	40.7	2.51	4.7	23.1	9.1	0.00	690
West Lancashire	217	0	42	43.3	2.51	6.4	24.7	18.6	34.60	714
Wyre	270	39	44	44.1	2.33	3.9	29.1	9.5	0.00	695
MERSEYSIDE	3,155	1,546	589	573.3	2.45	8.4	29.3	29.2	41.02	847
Knowsley	758	227	60	58.2	2.62	12.8	24.1	38.9	43.83	795
Liverpool	765	431	200	190.6	2.43	10.2	32.6	39.8	40.23	1,006
Sefton	440	46	118	72.3	2.47	6.1	25.4	23.7	39.22	755
St Helens	..	..	73	116.4	2.44	6.1	29.0	19.1	38.37	781
Wirral	349	142	139	135.7	2.40	7.1	29.3	21.9	43.53	792
YORKSHIRE AND THE HUMBER	11,073	2,645	2,085	2,064.0	2.40	5.5	28.4	18.1	31.40	667
Humberside#	2,485	370	371	362.0	2.42	5.6	27.4	..	31.41	744
Beverley[6]	858	7	49	48.5	2.44	3.2	26.1	..	.	.
Boothferry	139	5	28	26.4	2.45	4.3	23.2	..	,	.
Cleethorpes	175	22	29	28.5	2.45	5.1	24.9	..	.	.
East Yorkshire	359	0	00	37.4	2.36	3.9	27.1	..	.	.
Glanford	273	37	30	29.6	2.44	3.9	22.8	..	.	.
Great Grimsby	20	05	38	38.4	2.42	8.0	28.1	..	.	.
Holderness	150	42	21	21.0	2.47	3.6	22.9	..	.	.
Kingston upon Hull	399	209	112	110.1	2.41	7.6	31.6	33.8	.	.
Scunthorpe	72	13	25	24.0	2.46	7.0	27.4	..	.	.
North Yorkshire#	2,055	480	313	300.5	2.37	4.0	27.9	5.4	38.63	587
Craven	179	1	23	21.1	2.37	4.0	29.0	10.6	38.69	598
Hambleton	251	55	34	32.9	2.50	3.2	24.4	10.6	0.00	510
Harrogate	533	18	63	62.0	2.34	3.8	28.6	..	41.65	626
Richmondshire	46	46	19	18.0	2.43	3.8	25.1	10.2	37.68	589
Ryedale	423	138	41	38.6	2.39	2.6	25.4	..	0.00	621
Scarborough	232	106	50	46.7	2.26	4.8	31.0	18.3	37.87	583
Selby	333	50	38	36.7	2.48	3.5	23.7	..	36.82	583
York	66	66	45	44.6	2.29	5.8	32.7	..	.	.
South Yorkshire	2,501	333	538	539.2	2.39	5.5	28.1	24.8	29.22	674
Barnsley	538	35	93	91.6	2.45	5.3	25.2	24.6	28.56	629
Doncaster	678	66	119	118.6	2.44	5.8	25.7	21.8	28.26	604
Rotherham	608	95	103	103.8	2.44	5.4	25.7	22.5	26.36	688
Sheffield	717	124	223	225.2	2.32	5.4	31.6	27.6	31.09	725
West Yorkshire	4,032	1,462	862	862.3	2.41	6.0	29.3	21.5	32.07	665
Bradford	968	466	188	188.2	2.53	6.8	28.6	20.9	34.63	647
Calderdale	292	115	82	80.6	2.37	5.5	29.4	17.9	32.88	733
Kirklees	830	131	160	158.2	2.43	5.9	29.0	18.6	36.37	760
Leeds	1,218	562	301	305.4	2.35	6.2	31.1	23.8	30.03	637
Wakefield	733	191	131	129.9	2.42	5.0	26.4	23.2	30.62	593
EAST MIDLANDS	11,549	1,984	1,707	1,674.5	2.43	4.9	26.3	11.9	34.06	665
Derbyshire	2,809	467	402	393.6	2.41	4.4	26.7	16.8	31.34	681
Amber Valley	..	..	49	47.5	2.40	3.3	25.5	13.2	33.31	680
Bolsover	238	82	31	28.8	2.45	3.7	24.2	20.7	28.75	721
Chesterfield	108	66	44	43.1	2.32	4.0	30.0	22.5	29.87	667
Derby	..	..	96	95.5	2.40	6.1	29.3	20.6	32.56	665
Derbyshire Dales	164	29	30	28.2	2.42	2.8	26.0	9.5	32.75	687
Erewash	284	29	45	44.2	2.39	4.7	26.3	15.3	30.05	667
High Peak	322	0	36	35.5	2.44	4.3	26.5	13.7	36.28	693
North East Derbyshire	216	80	41	40.9	2.41	3.9	24.4	15.9	28.44	712
South Derbyshire	465	0	31	29.9	2.51	3.6	23.0	12.1	33.47	673

Regional Trends 32, © Crown copyright 1997

14.4 (continued)

	Housing starts 1995[1] (numbers)		Stock of dwellings[2] 1995 (thousands)	Households 1995					Local authority tenants: average weekly unrebated rent per dwelling (£) April 1996[4]	Council Tax (£) April 1996[5]
	Private enterprise	Housing associations local authorities etc		All households (thousands)	Average household size (numbers)	Lone parents[3] as a percentage of all households	One-person households as a percentage of all households	Households receiving Housing Benefit as a percentage of all households		
Leicestershire	2,088	268	365	363.4	2.51	5.0	25.9	15.4	36.08	635
Blaby	351	16	35	33.3	2.53	3.4	20.5	6.5	31.13	627
Charnwood	365	12	59	61.1	2.50	4.0	25.6	10.9	32.15	617
Harborough	311	10	29	28.5	2.50	2.9	24.0	8.5	40.02	619
Hinckley and Bosworth	281	0	40	39.6	2.44	3.2	24.5	9.3	35.87	587
Leicester	191	208	114	114.5	2.55	8.0	30.4	27.9	37.91	686
Melton[6]	43	0	19	18.8	2.45	3.5	24.3	10.7	32.42	616
North West Leicestershire	284	16	34	33.5	2.49	3.7	24.5	13.0	33.63	635
Oadby and Wigston	113	6	21	20.7	2.54	3.7	21.9	7.5	31.38	627
Rutland	77	0	13	13.4	2.50	4.9	23.3	9.8	41.15	632
Lincolnshire	2,413	306	264	253.9	2.37	4.0	26.0	15.7	33.45	622
Boston	245	0	24	22.7	2.35	3.8	26.9	19.2	34.16	629
East Lindsey	358	84	55	51.5	2.33	3.4	26.5	15.0	35.25	612
Lincoln	172	40	37	36.5	2.27	6.1	32.2	27.0	31.76	625
North Kesteven	397	84	36	34.6	2.39	3.6	22.3	11.1	33.89	632
South Holland	300	16	31	29.7	2.36	2.8	24.3	11.7	33.60	637
South Kesteven	617	68	49	47.7	2.44	4.6	24.9	13.8	33.55	605
West Lindsey	195	40	33	31.3	2.44	3.8	24.7	13.3	33.25	635
Northamptonshire	2,292	495	248	239.4	2.47	5.0	25.0	15.8	36.60	628
Corby	96	48	22	20.3	2.56	8.9	21.6	25.8	33.13	617
Daventry	506	147	27	25.6	2.50	3.3	22.8	11.2	34.60	609
East Northamptonshire	310	27	29	28.2	2.47	3.5	24.1	13.1	36.68	640
Kettering	219	43	34	32.4	2.44	4.4	25.8	14.5	36.36	626
Northampton	569	103	79	76.3	2.45	5.7	27.3	18.3	39.24	671
South Northamptonshire	290	55	29	29.0	2.52	3.1	22.7	9.3	40.53	655
Wellingborough	236	47	29	27.7	2.44	6.2	25.9	17.1	33.11	500
Nottinghamshire	1,947	448	428	424.2	2.40	5.7	27.2	20.3	33.98	728
Ashfield	240	8	46	44.4	2.43	4.4	25.3	17.8	33.27	721
Bassetlaw	306	86	44	43.3	2.42	4.0	24.8	17.7	36.04	722
Broxtowe	157	7	46	46.7	2.38	4.6	26.2	12.4	31.51	716
Gedling	204	28	47	46.0	2.40	3.6	25.9	11.0	31.28	711
Mansfield	314	65	43	41.4	2.44	5.5	25.5	22.1	36.22	693
Newark and Sherwood	207	22	43	42.1	2.44	4.5	24.9	16.3	34.15	766
Nottingham	250	179	118	118.1	2.36	9.2	31.5	33.7	33.67	769
Rushcliffe	255	6	41	42.1	2.41	3.7	26.4	9.4	35.09	681
WEST MIDLANDS	10,982	2,137	2,147	2,116.5	2.48	5.5	26.8	20.2	36.79	656
Hereford and Worcester	2,772	374	288	279.9	2.44	4.3	24.9	14.2	35.53	584
Bromsgrove	304	19	37	34.1	2.46	3.8	21.8	8.9	33.05	574
Hereford	37	28	21	20.4	2.40	6.4	28.1	22.8	32.72	578
Leominster	175	105	17	16.4	2.47	2.8	24.4	13.9	0.00	565
Malvern Hills	306	17	37	37.2	2.41	3.1	26.0	11.8	0.00	573
Redditch	167	55	31	30.2	2.56	6.4	22.3	20.0	37.48	620
South Herefordshire	361	0	23	21.8	2.44	3.0	24.8	11.1	37.13	581
Worcester	603	24	37	37.7	2.38	5.4	27.2	16.4	35.39	583
Wychavon	690	8	44	43.0	2.44	3.6	24.5	11.3	0.00	579
Wyre Forest	131	118	40	39.1	2.45	4.5	25.7	15.1	36.10	601
Shropshire	1,344	230	174	167.7	2.47	4.5	25.4	16.6	37.80	636
Bridgnorth[6]	40	0	21	20.1	2.45	3.9	24.3	12.9	36.18	611
North Shropshire	113	22	23	21.5	2.48	2.4	24.9	13.4	32.22	637
Oswestry	169	1	15	14.3	2.39	3.7	28.2	16.1	33.13	625
Shrewsbury and Atcham	216	29	39	38.9	2.41	4.7	28.7	14.3	33.59	611
South Shropshire	117	57	17	16.4	2.40	2.9	24.7	12.7	0.00	620
The Wrekin	676	116	59	56.5	2.54	6.1	23.3	22.1	42.05	672
Staffordshire	2,567	441	426	419.3	2.49	4.3	24.5	15.5	35.03	599
Cannock Chase	..	..	36	35.3	2.56	4.8	21.8	18.1	39.16	633
East Staffordshire	..	..	41	39.9	2.49	3.4	24.8	13.7	32.47	611
Lichfield	264	33	37	36.3	2.53	3.5	21.2	10.7	36.67	594
Newcastle-under-Lyme	207	13	50	49.8	2.45	3.8	27.4	14.3	29.74	590
South Staffordshire	180	59	41	48.0	2.51	3.7	23.8	9.8	36.18	529
Stafford	358	6	49	41.4	2.49	3.6	21.7	13.6	34.51	586
Staffordshire Moorlands	218	26	39	37.6	2.49	3.1	22.9	8.7	33.75	594
Stoke-on-Trent	397	237	104	103.4	2.44	5.6	27.9	22.2	35.46	645
Tamworth	283	8	28	27.8	2.59	6.0	21.2	19.7	38.48	572

14.4 (continued)

	Housing starts 1995[1] (numbers)		Stock of dwellings[2] 1995 (thousands)	Households 1995					Local authority tenants: average weekly unrebated rent per dwelling (£) April 1996[4]	Council Tax (£) April 1996[5]
	Private enterprise	Housing associations local authorities etc		All households (thousands)	Average household size (numbers)	Lone parents[3] as a percentage of all households	One-person households as a percentage of all households	Households receiving Housing Benefit as a percentage of all households		
Warwickshire	1,232	85	205	202.8	2.43	4.2	25.9	13.8	35.90	673
North Warwickshire	202	11	25	24.5	2.49	4.0	24.7	14.2	32.93	714
Nuneaton and Bedworth	135	45	48	47.3	2.50	4.9	23.8	16.3	32.71	706
Rugby	98	15	36	35.6	2.42	4.8	25.8	13.4	36.22	676
Stratford-on-Avon	413	14	46	45.6	2.40	2.9	26.8	11.0	37.59	649
Warwick	384	0	50	49.8	2.38	4.6	27.7	14.2	39.53	654
West Midlands (Met. County)	3,067	1,007	1,054	1,046.7	2.49	6.7	28.7	25.5	37.42	704
Birmingham	644	509	397	401.9	2.50	8.2	31.4	28.0	39.28	749
Coventry	432	28	124	122.6	2.44	7.6	29.8	22.5	35.41	809
Dudley	405	24	125	126.1	2.46	4.1	25.5	19.3	35.32	637
Sandwell	670	114	122	117.0	2.49	5.6	28.4	31.6	40.72	679
Solihull	341	21	81	80.8	2.49	5.2	24.2	14.2	39.46	626
Walsall	383	157	104	101.9	2.55	5.3	24.8	24.6	31.02	588
Wolverhampton	195	153	101	96.3	2.51	7.1	28.5	29.9	35.86	725
EASTERN	17,190	3,467	2,194	2,141.5	2.42	4.4	26.5	13.0	41.32	600
Bedfordshire	1,271	498	219	217.8	2.48	4.9	25.9	15.2	42.99	643
Bedford	257	103	57	56.2	2.41	4.7	28.3	15.7	36.14	634
Luton	255	218	71	71.1	2.53	6.4	26.4	18.9	42.43	651
Mid Bedfordshire	526	115	47	46.1	2.48	3.0	24.2	10.2	41.06	617
South Bedfordshire	224	48	45	44.4	2.48	4.7	24.0	13.6	45.04	671
Cambridgeshire	2,306	480	280	281.1	2.43	4.6	26.4	15.2	40.42	554
Cambridge	109	115	42	48.5	2.30	6.1	34.7	17.4	40.87	604
East Cambridgeshire	488	88	27	26.4	2.44	2.3	24.2	12.9	0.00	540
Fenland	251	34	35	32.9	2.37	3.0	26.0	16.1	39.72	578
Huntingdonshire	589	128	61	58.9	2.50	4.6	22.3	11.3	39.48	538
Peterborough	397	35	60	64.7	2.44	0.4	27.5	22.3	39.96	565
South Cambridgeshire	474	80	49	49.7	2.50	2.8	23.3	9.3	42.13	517
Essex	5,365	1,107	658	642.8	2.42	4.4	26.4	15.5	42.48	609
Basildon	1,344	445	68	65.7	2.47	5.5	25.4	21.0	39.56	652
Braintree	628	6	51	50.8	2.44	4.2	25.8	16.5	41.78	604
Brentwood	47	26	29	28.9	2.44	3.2	26.3	10.0	48.56	585
Castle Point	94	0	35	33.7	2.52	3.4	22.2	8.3	52.78	637
Chelmsford	96	37	63	63.0	2.46	3.7	25.2	11.5	44.29	606
Colchester	363	138	62	60.3	2.45	5.2	25.7	15.6	42.53	613
Epping Forest	453	31	49	48.7	2.42	3.7	26.1	13.7	46.07	598
Harlow	384	24	31	29.7	2.44	6.0	26.8	27.3	39.94	705
Maldon	..	..	23	21.5	2.50	3.1	24.5	12.3	0.00	581
Rochford	275	47	31	30.1	2.50	3.5	23.5	9.5	43.21	598
Southend-on-Sea	107	131	73	74.2	2.26	5.5	32.1	19.1	44.63	574
Tendring	244	73	61	57.2	2.25	3.3	31.7	13.7	40.32	597
Thurrock	854	49	55	51.9	2.51	5.6	23.3	19.7	41.23	605
Uttlesford	110	38	28	27.1	2.50	3.2	24.1	10.8	45.07	592
Hertfordshire	3,398	499	409	406.7	2.45	4.3	26.3	14.9	44.23	595
Broxbourne	230	52	33	32.5	2.52	3.5	22.7	12.0	52.09	559
Dacorum	252	78	55	55.2	2.42	4.6	27.3	15.1	40.27	575
East Hertfordshire	640	115	49	48.7	2.49	3.0	24.6	10.9	46.49	576
Hertsmere	181	58	37	37.5	2.47	4.4	25.2	13.3	44.50	592
North Hertfordshire	329	0	47	47.3	2.40	3.9	27.9	16.8	44.93	585
St Albans	144	185	51	51.6	2.45	3.8	26.8	10.9	46.27	593
Stevenage	331	40	32	30.3	2.49	6.5	24.4	25.8	46.14	626
Three Rivers	..	..	32	33.3	2.47	3.8	25.6	12.4	45.68	610
Watford	658	4	32	31.4	2.43	5.7	29.5	18.1	43.87	666
Welwyn Hatfield	270	32	40	38.8	2.43	4.4	28.3	18.2	40.35	612
Norfolk	2,861	429	346	324.2	2.34	4.3	27.3	16.8	36.40	591
Breckland	515	140	48	46.3	2.39	3.9	25.2	12.4	0.00	577
Broadland	688	21	48	45.2	2.44	2.9	22.2	8.4	0.00	575
Great Yarmouth	170	31	39	37.3	2.34	4.9	28.8	23.4	34.31	578
Kings Lynn and West Norfolk	455	63	61	54.5	2.37	3.5	26.5	15.5	35.34	587
North Norfolk	478	14	48	40.6	2.29	3.4	28.8	14.4	37.39	588
Norwich	163	145	56	56.8	2.20	7.1	34.4	30.0	36.47	641
South Norfolk	369	15	46	43.5	2.40	3.5	24.1	11.1	39.72	587

14.4 *(continued)*

	Housing starts 1995[1] (numbers)		Stock of dwellings[2] 1995 (thousands)	Households 1995					Local authority tenants: average weekly unrebated rent per dwelling (£) April 1996[4]	Council Tax (£) April 1996[5]
	Private enterprise	Housing associations local authorities etc		All households (thousands)	Average household size (numbers)	Lone parents[3] as a percentage of all households	One-person households as a percentage of all households	Households receiving Housing Benefit as a percentage of all households		
Suffolk	1,989	454	282	268.9	2.40	*4.0*	*26.5*	*15.8*	38.74	610
Babergh	213	57	34	32.4	2.41	*3.5*	*24.6*	*14.2*	41.61	598
Forest Heath	153	0	24	25.6	2.56	*5.2*	*23.8*	*10.8*	37.21	566
Ipswich	202	87	50	48.0	2.35	*5.9*	*29.7*	*23.0*	37.38	671
Mid Suffolk	341	13	34	32.0	2.45	*2.6*	*24.3*	*11.3*	41.48	608
St Edmundsbury	407	155	39	37.9	2.40	*3.5*	*24.5*	*14.4*	39.67	597
Suffolk Coastal	455	26	50	47.3	2.41	*2.9*	*27.2*	*12.0*	35.39	608
Waveney	218	116	49	45.7	2.32	*4.3*	*28.4*	*20.0*	36.58	594
LONDON	7,676	3,531	2,994	2,962.7	2.33	*7.4*	*33.0*	*27.6*	52.72	616
Barking and Dagenham	..	..	61	62.1	2.48	*6.9*	*28.9*	*29.6*	39.71	576
Barnet	511	188	125	125.0	2.46	*5.3*	*29.7*	*16.3*	52.11	637
Bexley	73	0	91	89.6	2.45	*4.7*	*25.4*	*13.3*	53.02	584
Brent	58	12	102	98.1	2.47	*9.2*	*30.4*	*33.9*	66.92	456
Bromley	257	106	127	124.1	2.34	*4.5*	*29.5*	*13.3*	42.72	540
Camden	262	99	88	85.1	2.07	*7.7*	*44.1*	*39.4*	56.22	779
City of London	9	0	3	2.8	1.70	*2.8*	*56.6*	*47.7*	55.04	450
City of Westminster	330	275	103	94.2	1.95	*5.4*	*48.3*	*28.2*	64.47	295
Croydon	145	199	134	135.3	2.41	*6.7*	*28.4*	*19.2*	62.03	593
Ealing	51	44	114	118.5	2.43	*6.6*	*31.9*	*23.1*	58.95	532
Enfield	612	244	111	105.6	2.45	*5.7*	*28.1*	*18.5*	51.92	617
Greenwich	113	109	90	87.3	2.39	*9.4*	*31.4*	*45.1*	50.56	763
Hackney	..	..	83	83.3	2.31	*12.4*	*36.2*	*49.3*	54.79	855
Hammersmith and Fulham	83	2	74	74.9	2.05	*8.4*	*40.9*	*31.3*	53.70	725
Haringey	64	172	91	93.2	2.27	*9.9*	*35.4*	*42.3*	57.54	780
Harrow	83	21	80	81.7	2.54	*4.5*	*26.2*	*13.8*	64.68	580
Havering	158	48	94	92.6	2.47	*4.3*	*25.1*	*12.8*	44.59	595
Hillingdon	..	..	98	99.2	2.44	*4.9*	*27.7*	*15.8*	63.18	593
Hounslow	786	12	86	82.2	2.45	*5.9*	*29.4*	*22.3*	49.76	662
Islington	..	..	78	78.9	2.17	*10.9*	*38.6*	*42.8*	55.99	853
Kensington and Chelsea	77	255	80	77.3	1.92	*6.7*	*48.1*	*23.4*	67.02	511
Kingston upon Thames	583	50	58	58.4	2.37	*4.0*	*31.6*	*12.7*	61.15	596
Lambeth	81	602	116	119.9	2.15	*12.8*	*37.2*	*35.2*	49.84	665
Lewisham	..	..	106	105.2	2.26	*10.8*	*32.6*	*34.9*	46.73	629
Merton	..	..	77	75.4	2.36	*5.5*	*29.6*	*16.7*	52.56	647
Newham	..	..	87	86.1	2.64	*10.4*	*29.4*	*45.7*	43.72	594
Redbridge	392	70	94	89.9	2.50	*4.5*	*28.6*	*15.1*	66.06	581
Richmond-upon-Thames	336	11	75	78.4	2.21	*4.0*	*35.7*	*12.4*	52.92	712
Southwark	..	..	111	103.8	2.21	*12.0*	*37.6*	*43.1*	50.12	731
Sutton	622	128	111	73.4	2.35	*4.9*	*29.9*	*14.5*	50.97	597
Tower Hamlets	..	..	72	69.5	2.45	*10.7*	*36.5*	*48.2*	44.97	646
Waltham Forest	172	127	92	92.7	2.37	*7.7*	*32.3*	*26.0*	46.38	738
Wandsworth	163	0	118	119.1	2.19	*7.6*	*35.4*	*25.7*	59.64	434
SOUTH EAST (GOR)	19,662	3,756	3,219	3,192.3	2.41	*4.3*	*27.2*	*14.1*	46.06	603
Berkshire	1,879	161	300	310.9	2.48	*4.4*	*25.5*	*13.3*	49.88	606
Bracknell Forest	698	0	41	42.1	2.51	*4.9*	*23.7*	*13.5*	42.69	551
Newbury	..	..	54	55.8	2.53	*3.6*	*23.5*	*10.0*	41.95	611
Reading	..	..	54	59.4	2.35	*5.9*	*30.5*	*19.9*	56.60	696
Slough	168	6	41	42.7	2.54	*6.6*	*27.2*	*21.3*	50.35	539
Windsor and Maidenhead	161	0	55	56.5	2.44	*3.1*	*26.9*	*10.3*	0.00	591
Wokingham	411	149	54	54.3	2.58	*2.9*	*20.9*	*6.0*	47.80	624
Buckinghamshire	2,273	515	277	263.0	2.50	*4.3*	*24.6*	*13.2*	42.11	612
Aylesbury Vale	590	0	61	60.0	2.50	*3.2*	*24.0*	*11.3*	43.48	599
Chiltern	138	11	46	36.5	2.49	*3.4*	*24.6*	*8.7*	0.00	613
Milton Keynes	1,186	373	81	77.2	2.48	*6.7*	*25.6*	*19.7*	37.22	657
South Buckinghamshire	144	48	26	25.2	2.46	*3.7*	*23.8*	*10.2*	35.81	560
Wycombe	181	69	63	64.1	2.54	*3.4*	*24.1*	*10.9*	50.60	604
East Sussex	1,712	174	331	321.0	2.22	*4.6*	*33.6*	*19.1*	44.56	622
Brighton	251	20	71	70.6	2.16	*5.7*	*36.4*	*27.6*	44.89	580
Eastbourne	..	..	41	39.9	2.14	*5.2*	*35.7*	*19.2*	43.51	639
Hastings	137	107	39	35.8	2.23	*6.3*	*34.6*	*28.1*	0.00	643
Hove	195	0	43	43.0	2.07	*4.8*	*39.4*	*21.9*	41.25	604
Lewes	187	8	40	37.8	2.27	*3.7*	*30.5*	*13.1*	46.96	633
Rother	169	30	40	37.7	2.24	*3.3*	*31.3*	*13.1*	51.63	619
Wealden	530	33	58	56.2	2.38	*3.2*	*27.1*	*8.6*	39.32	647

Regional Trends 32, © Crown copyright 1997

14.4 *(continued)*

	Housing starts 1995[1] (numbers)		Stock of dwellings[2] 1995 (thousands)	Households 1995					Local authority tenants: average weekly unrebated rent per dwelling (£) April 1996[4]	Council Tax (£) April 1996[5]
	Private enterprise	Housing associations local authorities etc		All households (thousands)	Average household size (numbers)	Lone parents[3] as a percentage of all households	One-person households as a percentage of all households	Households receiving Housing Benefit as a percentage of all households		
Hampshire	4,200	653	653	653.3	2.43	4.6	26.0	15.0	44.42	593
Basingstoke and Deane	299	77	58	58.2	2.51	4.2	22.9	13.0	0.00	578
East Hampshire	335	93	42	43.4	2.48	3.7	23.8	9.9	0.00	603
Eastleigh	310	21	45	44.6	2.48	3.9	22.6	11.0	0.00	593
Fareham	510	6	42	41.2	2.44	3.3	22.6	7.8	43.93	587
Gosport	431	49	32	30.5	2.40	6.6	25.6	16.7	48.84	610
Hart	202	55	32	32.4	2.53	3.3	21.2	6.5	61.46	595
Havant	197	134	49	47.5	2.45	5.1	24.8	9.0	0.00	614
New Forest	384	24	72	70.7	2.34	3.4	27.0	10.9	49.98	609
Portsmouth	134	54	78	78.8	2.35	6.5	30.8	27.3	44.71	572
Rushmoor	202	49	33	33.6	2.47	4.7	23.9	14.2	76.12	581
Southampton	596	0	87	89.3	2.36	6.2	31.1	24.9	40.17	592
Test Valley	358	41	42	41.9	2.47	3.9	23.7	11.6	46.93	574
Winchester	253	63	41	41.1	2.47	3.1	26.9	12.8	45.99	600
Isle of Wight UA[7]	314	73	58	52.5	2.30	4.1	29.5	..	39.37	640
Medina[7]	.	.	..	29.8	2.32	4.6	29.7	..	.	.
South Wight[7]	.	.	..	22.7	2.27	3.4	29.1	..	.	.
Kent	2,946	1,146	642	627.3	2.43	4.4	26.6	16.2	47.22	598
Ashford	463	110	39	30.0	2.44	4.4	25.7	15.5	49.86	584
Canterbury	187	20	54	55.0	2.39	4.4	29.0	15.0	47.66	611
Dartford	294	14	34	33.4	2.46	3.9	25.0	14.7	47.71	612
Dover	126	90	45	44.3	2.36	4.7	29.3	19.0	49.78	611
Gillingham	154	60	39	37.8	2.51	5.0	24.7	13.5	42.05	584
Gravesham	98	57	38	36.7	2.50	5.0	24.8	18.8	47.02	661
Maidstone	335	95	56	55.2	2.49	3.9	24.3	13.2	48.26	634
Rochester-upon-Medway	146	125	60	57.2	2.50	5.0	24.0	18.0	0.00	515
Sevenoaks	220	131	44	43.6	2.49	3.4	25.1	11.6	0.00	609
Shepway	170	97	43	41.6	2.28	5.3	31.0	18.3	42.95	631
Swale	210	145	48	46.6	2.50	4.4	23.6	17.2	35.04	564
Thanet	131	8	57	53.7	2.26	5.4	31.9	23.8	45.53	640
Tonbridge and Malling	156	13	42	40.9	2.52	3.7	23.2	12.6	0.00	612
Tunbridge Wells	97	154	42	42.3	2.38	3.3	29.5	13.5	..	598
Oxfordshire	1,959	168	230	233.8	2.51	4.4	25.5	13.3	43.70	604
Cherwell	553	53	50	51.1	2.53	4.9	23.2	12.2	40.80	587
Oxford	305	0	48	52.6	2.48	6.6	32.0	22.7	41.46	680
South Oxfordshire	598	96	50	48.1	2.52	3.7	24.1	10.4	51.16	615
Vale of White Horse	178	23	44	44.0	2.54	2.7	23.0	9.1	0.00	578
West Oxfordshire	364	11	38	37.9	2.48	3.7	23.9	10.3	43.00	553
Surrey	2,574	384	424	421.9	2.42	3.4	26.8	10.2	49.99	590
Elmbridge	331	0	50	49.6	2.44	3.9	27.4	10.5	51.37	617
Epsom and Ewell	80	69	27	27.0	2.44	3.3	27.9	7.7	46.71	582
Guildford	316	4	50	50.3	2.42	3.8	26.9	11.9	52.05	598
Mole Valley	141	18	33	33.2	2.35	2.3	27.9	9.6	44.11	569
Reigate and Banstead	273	91	50	48.2	2.40	3.0	27.2	11.0	50.44	596
Runnymede	224	91	29	30.9	2.39	3.0	27.8	10.8	55.62	528
Spelthorne	119	85	39	37.7	2.35	3.0	27.0	10.7	0.00	592
Surrey Heath	315	10	31	31.8	2.54	3.9	21.7	7.2	0.00	591
Tandridge	159	29	31	30.3	2.47	2.8	26.4	8.6	39.98	597
Waverley	222	0	47	46.3	2.44	3.6	27.4	10.8	48.09	604
Woking	378	74	36	36.7	2.43	4.0	26.1	10.8	56.31	575
West Sussex	1,805	482	315	308.6	2.32	3.7	29.5	12.7	46.77	615
Adur	22	40	26	24.7	2.33	3.8	29.4	13.9	44.04	654
Arun	183	51	62	60.4	2.19	3.3	31.8	13.4	54.14	628
Chichester	55	20	46	44.1	2.29	3.5	29.6	12.9	43.54	603
Crawley	..	..	37	36.7	2.48	5.7	24.8	18.1	44.10	615
Horsham	..	..	48	47.6	2.41	3.0	26.8	10.4	53.04	603
Mid Sussex	455	97	51	50.7	2.43	3.4	26.5	9.2	0.00	614
Worthing	49	82	45	44.3	2.15	3.9	36.7	13.2	44.19	610

14.4 (continued)

| | Housing starts 1995[1] (numbers) | | Stock of dwellings[2] 1995 (thousands) | Households 1995 | | | | Households receiving Housing Benefit as a percentage of all households | Local authority tenants: average weekly unrebated rent per dwelling (£) April 1996[4] | Council Tax (£) April 1996[5] |
	Private enterprise	Housing associations local authorities etc		All households (thousands)	Average household size (numbers)	Lone parents[3] as a percentage of all households	One-person households as a percentage of all households			
SOUTH WEST	12,056	2,663	2,046	1,996.2	2.37	4.4	27.8	15.1	40.84	625
Avon#	2,114	499	404	406.0	2.38	4.9	28.2	12.2	40.20	730
Bath	49	36	36	36.9	2.26	5.0	32.9	..	.	.
Bristol	..	..	165	169.3	2.33	6.4	31.5	22.7	.	.
Kingswood	144	22	38	36.9	2.48	3.9	23.7	..	.	.
Northavon	890	70	56	55.9	2.49	3.7	23.0	..	.	.
Wansdyke	241	25	33	31.9	2.46	2.7	23.4	..	.	.
Woodspring	469	103	76	75.2	2.38	3.7	26.4	14.8	.	.
Cornwall and the Isles of Scilly	830	309	213	199.1	2.37	4.5	27.1	17.8	40.22	614
Caradon	170	6	35	32.5	2.40	4.4	24.6	15.0	40.69	608
Carrick	180	121	38	35.5	2.32	3.9	28.7	17.5	38.17	629
Kerrier	107	20	38	36.2	2.40	4.9	25.9	17.2	41.20	617
North Cornwall	147	56	35	32.0	2.37	4.2	26.9	18.1	40.74	617
Penwith	48	67	29	25.4	2.30	5.0	29.1	21.5	0.00	614
Restormel[6]	105	21	38	36.7	2.38	4.4	27.8	18.4	40.53	600
Isles of Scilly	2	2	1	0.7	2.51	6.1	22.0	15.2	40.73	433
Devon	2,620	520	455	440.2	2.34	4.6	28.6	17.3	37.86	591
East Devon	393	42	55	53.7	2.23	3.6	30.2	11.2	36.95	572
Exeter	..	..	42	44.3	2.34	5.2	31.6	19.7	36.00	562
Mid Devon	240	67	28	27.0	2.42	3.4	26.3	14.9	39.29	585
North Devon	259	43	38	35.5	2.34	4.2	27.9	17.2	45.75	582
Plymouth	248	154	103	105.2	2.39	6.3	27.7	22.8	33.61	650
South Hams	264	64	38	32.7	2.36	3.2	26.7	13.8	47.26	586
Teignbridge	513	33	50	47.8	2.33	3.4	27.9	13.2	40.73	589
Torbay	350	45	56	53.0	2.25	5.6	31.9	20.6	43.29	568
Torridge	143	26	24	22.1	2.45	3.6	25.7	15.2	33.35	546
West Devon	108	4	20	19.0	2.38	3.6	26.8	12.8	45.03	603
Dorset	1,844	341	299	288.6	2.29	3.9	29.7	14.7	42.98	585
Bournemouth	256	156	72	70.5	2.18	5.0	33.9	21.7	44.17	580
Christchurch	148	0	21	19.6	2.17	3.5	32.0	11.4	0.00	569
East Dorset	220	31	34	34.4	2.34	2.8	24.6	7.3	48.31	603
North Dorset	269	20	24	23.3	2.40	3.8	27.5	32.7	0.00	576
Poole	355	6	60	58.0	2.35	3.9	28.5	4.1	43.21	588
Purbeck	134	43	20	18.4	2.39	2.5	26.7	27.0	48.75	573
West Dorset	313	31	41	38.3	2.29	2.7	30.6	12.5	0.00	592
Weymouth and Portland	132	54	27	26.1	2.31	5.5	29.2	10.4	37.41	582
Gloucestershire	1,110	303	232	227.8	2.39	4.1	27.6	14.4	44.04	597
Cheltenham	78	75	47	46.5	2.24	5.1	34.1	16.1	45.60	598
Cotswold	178	103	35	33.7	2.39	2.9	27.2	12.4	51.56	596
Forest of Dean	163	23	32	30.1	2.47	2.9	24.5	13.8	39.95	629
Gloucester	252	23	44	43.0	2.42	5.8	27.1	18.3	43.41	575
Stroud	215	65	44	43.4	2.44	3.7	25.7	13.4	44.54	648
Tewkesbury	228	0	31	31.2	2.41	3.3	24.5	10.9	36.81	520
Somerset	1,210	345	201	197.5	2.39	3.9	27.4	15.9	41.74	629
Mendip	321	0	40	39.3	2.47	3.9	27.6	15.4	41.40	639
Sedgemoor	219	202	42	41.7	2.39	4.1	26.3	15.6	42.88	625
South Somerset	341	83	62	61.6	2.41	3.3	26.6	11.7	42.77	641
Taunton Deane	252	46	41	40.9	2.36	4.8	28.9	6.6	37.57	602
West Somerset	79	14	16	13.9	2.24	2.8	29.4	64.9	50.17	636
Wiltshire	2,328	346	243	237.0	2.45	4.1	24.5	14.1	42.93	604
Kennet	247	124	30	28.9	2.52	3.4	23.3	13.3	0.00	579
North Wiltshire	688	57	49	47.6	2.50	4.1	22.3	11.7	0.00	622
Salisbury	251	32	45	44.5	2.42	3.8	25.5	14.9	49.80	590
Thamesdown	857	91	73	71.0	2.42	5.0	24.8	15.6	36.74	620
West Wiltshire	399	41	47	44.9	2.40	3.5	26.2	14.1	48.49	595

14.4 *(continued)*

| | Housing starts 1995[1] (numbers) | | Stock of dwellings[2] 1995 (thousands) | Households 1995 | | | | | Local authority tenants: average weekly unrebated rent per dwelling (£) April 1996[4] | Council Tax (£) April 1996[5] |
	Private enterprise	Housing associations local authorities etc		All households (thousands)	Average household size (numbers)	Lone parents[3] as a percentage of all households	One-person households as a percentage of all households	Households receiving Housing Benefit as a percentage of all households		
New local government structure with effect from 1 April 1996										
Former County of Cleveland										
Hartlepool UA	250	57	38	37.0	2.46	*6.8*	*27.5*	*29.8*	35.24	837
Middlesbrough UA	238	91	59	58.1	2.51	*9.9*	*28.1*	*32.2*	40.86	854
Redcar & Cleveland UA	193	105	60	57.7	2.42	*6.5*	*27.5*	*23.7*	37.14	640
Stockton-on-Tees UA	715	38	72	71.5	2.47	*6.3*	*27.1*	*22.1*	35.04	749
Former County of Humberside										
East Riding of Yorkshire UA	..	..	..	125.4	2.42	*3.6*	*25.4*	..	32.01	742
Kingston upon Hull UA	..	..	..	110.1	2.41	*7.6*	*31.6*	..	31.18	655
North East Lincolnshire UA	..	..	..	64.9	2.44	*6.7*	*26.7*	..	32.05	735
North Lincolnshire UA	..	..	..	61.4	2.44	*5.2*	*24.6*	..	30.90	887
Former County of North Yorkshire										
York UA	..	..	..	72.9	2.35	*4.7*	*29.6*	..	38.57	581
North Yorkshire	..	..	..	227.7	2.37	*3.8*	*27.4*	..	..	589
Former County of Avon										
Bath and North East Somerset UA	..	..	..	68.7	2.35	*3.9*	*28.5*	..	39.92	673
Bristol UA	..	..	..	169.3	2.33	*6.4*	*31.5*	*22.7*	38.19	871
North Somerset UA	..	..	..	75.2	2.38	*3.7*	*26.4*	*14.8*	47.43	616
South Gloucestershire UA	..	..	..	92.8	2.49	*3.8*	*23.3*	..	42.32	653

\# New local government structure came into effect on 1 April 1996.
1 District figures do not always add to county totals; see Technical notes.
2 The figures for housing stock at local authority level shown in this table are derived using different methods from the regional stock figures shown in Table 6.1. This has led to small
   discrepancies between the two sets of figures. The figures in Table 6.1 provide the definitive regional estimates.
3 Lone parents with dependent children only.
4 Some local authorities have nil housing stock following large scale voluntary transfers to Housing Associations.
5 See Technical notes.
6 Figures for housing starts represent a partial local authority response only.
7 The Isle of Wight became a Unitary Authority on 1 April 1995.

Source: Department of the Environment

14.5 Labour market statistics[1]: by county

	In employment		ILO unemploy-ment rate June 1995-May 1996[2] (per-centages)	Average gross weekly full-time earnings, April 1996 (£)						
				Males			Females			
					10 per cent earned			10 per cent earned		All persons total
	Total Spring 1996[2,3] (thousands)	Manufacturing Spring 1996[2] (percentages)		Total	Less than	More than	Total	Less than	More than	
United Kingdom	26,219	*19.3*	*8.5*	389.9	188.1	628.8	282.3	146.0	447.8	350.3
England	22,131	*19.4*	*8.4*	396.2	190.1	641.2	286.6	148.1	455.9	356.0
North East	1,058	*22.1*	*10.5*	347.7	179.8	550.0	252.4	136.0	409.4	314.1
Cleveland#	222	*22.7*	*14.0*	366.6	193.0	602.2	231.1	120.0	386.7	330.1
Durham	259	*25.1*	*9.1*	340.5	177.4	517.6	244.0	137.4	405.1	305.9
Northumberland	143	*17.5*	*7.9*	327.4	168.5	520.8	242.1	129.2	386.7	290.8
Tyne & Wear	434	*21.5*	*12.1*	346.2	180.0	545.0	264.5	144.0	422.4	316.2
North West (GOR) & Merseyside	2,952	*22.1*	*8.8*	367.8	189.7	598.0	264.2	143.9	424.0	329.6
North West (GOR)	2,420	*23.1*	*7.8*	369.0	186.7	595.0	262.4	143.6	421.9	330.5
Cheshire	448	*21.8*	*7.7*	398.6	199.7	640.5	265.5	136.5	424.5	354.3
Cumbria	224	*23.8*	*7.0*	366.1	190.0	591.4	249.4	136.2	412.4	323.6
Greater Manchester	1,112	*22.5*	*8.9*	366.2	186.2	600.7	268.7	148.5	426.1	329.5
Lancashire	636	*25.0*	*6.4*	350.7	179.6	555.8	251.1	140.0	403.9	315.6
Merseyside	532	*17.5*	*13.0*	361.7	183.5	567.9	271.3	144.8	437.7	325.4
Yorkshire and the Humber	2,223	*21.9*	*8.3*	350.7	180.0	547.1	252.5	136.7	410.6	316.4
Humberside#	390	*24.1*	*8.8*	360.0	185.0	556.6	243.5	132.0	414.1	322.7
North Yorkshire#	336	*17.1*	*5.9*	340.9	175.1	545.8	240.2	130.3	398.0	306.4
South Yorkshire	532	*21.7*	*10.7*	344.9	182.6	532.6	243.3	131.8	393.2	308.8
West Yorkshire	964	*22.8*	*7.6*	353.0	178.7	555.3	263.0	144.2	418.0	320.8
East Midlands	1,926	*26.4*	*7.2*	352.9	181.9	548.9	248.7	137.4	406.4	317.9
Derbyshire	442	*28.6*	*8.2*	355.3	180.8	536.4	253.9	137.4	421.9	325.6
Leicestershire	458	*31.1*	*6.5*	358.6	181.4	552.7	252.5	137.4	419.6	321.1
Lincolnshire	284	*19.2*	*7.1*	338.5	187.5	539.6	233.0	129.6	421.5	303.7
Northamptonshire	302	*25.7*	*5.1*	373.0	200.0	564.0	257.0	150.1	398.7	331.7
Nottinghamshire	439	*24.3*	*8.3*	340.1	170.5	548.3	243.7	137.8	390.2	306.8
West Midlands	2,348	*27.4*	*8.8*	360.1	187.6	558.5	256.9	140.4	421.9	324.3
Hereford & Worcs.	350	*22.7*	*7.1*	345.6	179.7	545.0	253.7	138.9	421.9	311.2
Shropshire	199	*23.5*	*6.8*	337.4	172.8	527.5	232.5	133.9	394.9	302.4
Staffordshire	501	*28.3*	*6.7*	339.1	186.0	523.9	252.7	141.2	431.3	308.9
Warwickshire	237	*24.8*	*5.9*	369.9	190.6	562.5	255.9	134.0	431.9	329.1
West Midlands (Met. county)	1,060	*29.8*	*11.3*	371.6	191.3	574.6	262.6	142.7	421.9	334.4
Eastern	2,527	*18.4*	*7.0*	382.3	193.7	613.0	279.9	148.7	443.0	345.7
Bedfordshire	271	*21.3*	*8.3*	410.5	207.0	643.4	298.2	155.5	447.0	368.6
Cambridgeshire	347	*21.1*	*6.7*	378.2	195.7	604.8	282.6	151.8	447.0	342.6
Essex	738	*17.9*	*7.2*	383.4	190.3	611.3	280.1	152.9	432.2	346.0
Hertfordshire	513	*15.8*	*6.4*	417.7	201.5	690.9	301.8	162.5	480.2	374.0
Norfolk	356	*19.1*	*7.8*	339.8	183.0	549.6	252.3	134.4	405.6	310.0
Suffolk	302	*17.7*	*5.9*	350.0	187.1	551.6	254.6	138.9	421.9	318.9
London	3,110	*10.3*	*11.6*	514.3	221.2	872.8	364.9	192.3	559.9	454.3

14.5 *(continued)*

	In employment		ILO unemployment rate June 1995-May 1996[2] (percentages)	Average gross weekly full-time earnings, April 1996 (£)						
				Males			Females			All persons total
	Total Spring 1996[2,3] (thousands)	Manufacturing Spring 1996[2] (percentages)			10 per cent earned			10 per cent earned		
				Total	Less than	More than	Total	Less than	More than	
South East (GOR)	3,772	*16.4*	*6.2*	412.7	188.7	597.0	292.7	156.3	455.3	367.4
Berkshire	408	*18.3*	*4.5*	479.6	209.6	779.3	320.9	166.8	492.5	420.9
Buckinghamshire	344	*21.5*	*6.0*	442.3	213.0	726.9	298.5	160.0	499.0	391.2
East Sussex	318	*11.3*	*9.4*	346.0	174.5	556.7	289.6	156.8	447.2	322.5
Hampshire	764	*19.3*	*6.6*	391.0	190.0	630.0	277.4	154.3	431.1	349.5
Isle of Wight	47	*12.6*	*11.9*	318.7	157.0	457.5	..	..	..	296.8
Kent	737	*15.2*	*7.5*	381.3	187.8	590.9	271.2	144.3	426.8	339.1
Oxfordshire	302	*16.4*	*4.2*	399.5	194.8	645.7	289.3	154.8	440.6	357.6
Surrey	523	*13.3*	*4.7*	458.1	201.5	758.3	317.7	171.2	499.7	405.5
West Sussex	329	*14.7*	*6.3*	408.9	193.7	671.6	299.0	158.9	468.4	365.1
South West	2,216	*16.8*	*7.1*	364.8	179.2	582.0	261.1	140.0	421.9	326.5
Avon#	476	*16.3*	*7.2*	381.2	192.5	599.8	269.9	148.8	421.3	342.6
Cornwall	202	*11.3*	*8.6*	303.4	159.1	479.9	224.6	118.0	384.4	271.2
Devon	442	*16.7*	*8.3*	328.5	162.3	537.4	247.3	134.5	414.3	297.3
Dorset	285	*13.5*	*6.7*	370.7	177.5	625.7	267.2	141.6	432.4	328.6
Gloucestershire	267	*19.3*	*6.6*	386.0	191.9	605.3	267.5	149.4	414.3	344.6
Somerset	226	*20.0*	*6.8*	348.1	176.5	556.4	261.5	138.5	447.0	317.9
Wiltshire	317	*19.8*	*5.0*	399.0	198.9	626.1	274.9	146.5	447.0	354.0

New local government structure with effect from 1 April 1996

Former County of Cleveland

Hartlepool UA	34	*22.5*	*17.3*	..	..	..	..	..	..	..
Middlesbrough UA	50	*14.7*	*19.8*	360.4	193.8	614.8	..	..	..	327.5
Redcar & Cleveland UA	56	*21.7*	*12.0*	401.4	227.8	565.8	..	..	..	370.0
Stockton-on-Tees UA	73	*22.5*	*14.1*	367.6	106.5	592.9	209.2	120.9	322.6	329.8

Former County of Humberside

East Riding of Yorkshire UA	138	*18.9*	*4.7*	354.0	189.6	556.6	244.8	126.8	444.8	319.7
Kingston upon Hull UA	109	*20.9*	*9.9*	343.4	172.8	547.7	257.8	144.9	418.1	314.1
North East Lincolnshire UA	70	*31.8*	*10.9*	367.7	180.0	536.9	..	..	..	327.0
North Lincolnshire UA	70	*25.9*	*10.4*	388.5	192.2	571.8	220.0	121.4	327.4	336.9

Former County of North Yorkshire

York UA	87	*16.9*	*..*	302.9	186.3	595.9	240.6	134.7	386.9	317.7
North Yorkshire	263	*15.5*	*6.6*	333.3	173.7	537.0	240.0	130.0	398.6	302.3

Former County of Avon

Bath and North East Somerset UA	81	*18.8*	*..*	373.5	191.0	629.2	..	..	..	334.7
Bristol UA	182	*12.3*	*9.8*	377.9	185.0	601.9	274.0	152.4	418.3	339.1
North Somerset UA	85	*11.4*	*..*	362.9	181.8	549.6	249.8	133.5	421.9	321.0
South Gloucestershire UA	122	*21.9*	*4.6*	395.2	217.3	594.7	262.5	152.6	415.5	358.6

New local government structure came into effect on 1 April 1996.
1 See Technical notes to the Labour market chapter. In some cases sample sizes are too small to provide reliable estimates.
2 Figures for Unitary Authorities relate to the period March 1995 to February 1996. Not adjusted to take account of seasonal influences.
3 Includes those on Government-supported employment and training schemes and unpaid family workers.

Source: Office for National Statistics

14.6 Labour market[1] and economic statistics: by district

| | Economically active[2] 1995-96 (percentages) | Claimant unemployed January 1997 | | | Income Support bene-ficiaries[4] Nov. 1995 (percentages) | Businesses registered for VAT 1995 | | Stock of businesses 1994 (numbers) |
		Total (thousands)	Of which females (percentages)	Of which long-term unemployed[3] (percentages)		Registration rates[5] (percentages)	Deregistration rates[5] (percentages)	
UNITED KINGDOM	62.8	1,907.8	23.3	36.2	..	10.3	10.9	1,611,400
ENGLAND	63.0	1,554.9	23.6	36.6	14	10.6	11.2	1,362,333
NORTH EAST	58.5	107.3	20.0	38.6	18	9.5	11.7	43,364
Cleveland#	60.1	27.9	19.6	40.1	20	9.1	13.3	8,191
Hartlepool	58.6	4.7	18.1	38.7	22	8.0	14.2	1,345
Langbaurgh-on-Tees	60.0	6.7	19.0	39.8	19	8.1	11.5	1,945
Middlesbrough	58.8	8.3	19.3	41.4	23	9.9	13.5	1,958
Stockton-on-Tees	62.1	8.3	21.3	39.8	17	9.8	14.1	2,942
Durham	59.0	19.7	19.3	31.8	15	9.1	11.0	11,028
Chester-le-Street	61.6	1.7	19.1	33.8	12	10.5	12.5	778
Darlington	64.4	4.0	19.3	34.2	15	9.6	11.7	2,099
Derwentside	54.9	3.2	19.4	33.3	17	7.7	11.4	1,447
Durham	62.7	2.5	21.8	28.2	11	10.7	11.6	1,350
Easington	48.7	2.8	16.9	30.5	19	7.3	12.5	1,171
Sedgefield	64.3	2.5	19.9	26.0	15	11.9	12.8	1,542
Teesdale	60.5	0.6	22.0	30.7	9	6.6	6.0	1,190
Wear Valley	55.7	2.5	18.4	35.7	19	7.7	9.6	1,452
Northumberland	60.9	10.5	23.2	34.8	12	8.3	9.4	7,581
Alnwick	56.0	1.0	23.9	36.8	13	7.3	6.8	1,075
Berwick-upon-Tweed	61.7	0.9	24.9	20.0	12	6.9	9.1	1,117
Blyth Valley	65.0	3.1	24.1	32.4	15	11.5	13.4	1,026
Castle Morpeth	61.7	1.3	23.2	35.0	9	7.7	9.5	1,339
Tynedale	61.4	1.3	26.6	31.4	9	7.1	7.4	2,295
Wansbeck	57.2	2.8	19.8	42.7	14	12.0	14.8	728
Tyne and Wear	56.7	49.3	19.8	41.3	20	10.4	12.4	16,564
Gateshead	58.1	7.6	19.1	39.3	19	11.7	12.0	3,216
Newcastle-upon-Tyne	57.2	13.7	19.8	47.3	20	9.9	12.3	5,018
North Tyneside	54.5	7.7	21.9	36.7	18	9.3	12.2	2,800
South Tyneside	55.2	7.6	20.3	39.9	21	10.7	11.5	1,848
Sunderland	57.6	12.7	18.5	39.5	21	10.7	13.8	3,683
NORTH WEST (GOR) & MERSEYSIDE	59.9	230.6	21.8	33.2	17	10.1	11.4	159,911
NORTH WEST (GOR)	61.2	160.9	21.9	29.2	15	9.9	11.2	137,555
Cheshire	63.0	24.1	23.2	27.5	12	10.3	10.5	26,171
Chester	63.2	2.9	23.3	28.4	11	10.5	10.1	3,609
Congleton	65.0	1.4	26.7	25.3	8	9.4	11.5	2,862
Crewe and Nantwich	63.2	2.6	23.2	26.4	11	9.3	8.7	2,764
Ellesmere Port and Neston	58.4	2.3	21.8	23.9	13	11.5	12.9	1,352
Halton	57.3	5.3	22.1	32.0	20	9.9	11.8	1,855
Macclesfield	62.3	2.4	23.3	23.3	8	10.0	9.9	6,316
Vale Royal	64.3	2.8	24.0	27.7	11	10.0	11.2	3,192
Warrington	67.5	4.4	23.7	26.9	11	11.8	10.7	4,220
Cumbria	63.2	15.8	22.6	32.1	12	6.4	8.1	16,419
Allerdale	66.3	3.7	22.5	38.0	13	5.8	7.5	3,243
Barrow-in-Furness	61.4	3.0	17.7	32.8	18	10.6	14.1	1,131
Carlisle	65.6	3.3	23.9	30.7	11	7.5	8.6	3,010
Copeland	62.1	3.2	21.4	37.3	15	6.1	9.3	1,562
Eden	66.9	0.8	33.1	20.3	7	4.1	5.6	3,041
South Lakeland	58.4	1.9	25.7	18.1	7	6.8	7.9	4,433
Greater Manchester	59.6	83.7	21.4	31.9	18	11.2	12.0	58,770
Bolton	60.6	7.1	18.2	24.5	16	10.4	13.3	5,876
Bury	64.6	3.9	24.1	21.2	14	10.8	12.9	4,295
Manchester	51.3	24.2	21.2	39.3	29	12.8	11.4	10,196
Oldham	63.6	7.0	22.0	29.3	17	9.5	11.6	4,538
Rochdale	61.9	7.0	21.2	27.1	19	10.2	12.2	4,428
Salford	54.0	7.2	19.9	33.1	20	11.8	11.6	4,482
Stockport	62.6	6.1	21.2	29.0	11	10.6	12.4	8,056
Tameside	62.5	6.4	22.9	30.3	16	11.4	12.7	4,731
Trafford	60.3	5.5	22.8	32.0	13	12.5	11.8	6,153
Wigan	61.2	9.5	22.4	30.4	14	10.4	11.0	6,013

14.6 *(continued)*

	Economically active[2] 1995-96 (percentages)	Claimant unemployed January 1997			Income Support bene-ficiaries[4] Nov. 1995 (percentages)	Businesses registered for VAT 1995		Stock of businesses 1994 (numbers)
		Total (thousands)	Of which females (percentages)	Of which long-term unemployed[3] (percentages)		Registration rates[5] (percentages)	Deregistration rates[5] (percentages)	
Lancashire	62.1	37.3	21.8	23.2	14	9.2	11.6	36,196
Blackburn	60.5	4.2	18.4	21.2	19	9.9	13.0	3,036
Blackpool	54.8	6.4	21.2	20.3	18	8.3	13.5	3,271
Burnley	62.8	1.8	21.2	15.0	17	9.7	13.1	1,922
Chorley	63.8	2.2	23.0	22.8	10	9.9	11.4	2,678
Fylde	59.3	1.0	25.2	13.4	10	9.1	12.3	1,980
Hyndburn	67.9	1.7	22.9	15.8	14	9.4	12.5	1,939
Lancaster	56.8	4.6	22.4	30.7	15	7.5	11.2	3,294
Pendle	60.0	1.8	21.0	17.3	16	8.8	11.6	2,224
Preston	62.9	4.5	19.9	30.8	18	10.5	11.8	3,306
Ribble Valley	71.6	0.6	26.2	16.0	6	7.7	8.9	2,121
Rossendale	68.8	1.1	20.8	16.0	13	11.1	12.3	1,961
South Ribble	68.9	1.8	25.4	22.5	8	9.5	11.3	2,417
West Lancashire	62.5	3.3	23.9	31.0	15	9.4	9.6	3,025
Wyre	62.2	2.3	22.9	20.7	11	8.2	10.9	3,021
MERSEYSIDE	54.9	69.7	21.5	42.3	24	11.0	12.8	22,356
Knowsley	49.6	8.4	20.1	43.7	31	11.3	13.4	1,604
Liverpool	50.7	28.8	21.4	47.1	30	12.1	12.2	7,551
Sefton	58.6	11.5	22.1	36.8	11	10.3	14.0	5,250
St Helens	58.0	6.4	21.4	38.5	29	9.9	11.6	2,887
Wirral	58.4	14.7	22.0	37.7	19	10.5	12.8	5,063
YORKSHIRE AND THE HUMBER	61.9	176.6	22.1	33.9	15	9.3	11.2	120,579
Humberside#	60.6	34.7	21.6	31.4	16	8.6	11.2	21,471
Beverley	..	2.4	26.9	22.9	7	8.4	12.7	2,929
Boothferry	..	2.1	24.3	29.4	15	7.3	10.6	2,419
Cleethorpes	..	2.8	22.4	27.4	17	8.3	11.5	1,406
East Yorkshire	..	2.8	24.2	32.3	11	6.5	8.6	3,370
Glanford	..	1.8	24.4	30.6	11	9.7	10.7	2,144
Great Grimsby	..	5.0	18.0	34.9	21	10.4	12.7	1,980
Holderness	..	1.5	26.1	28.7	12	7.1	10.5	1,663
Kingston upon Hull	..	13.7	19.9	32.6	24	10.3	12.4	4,516
Scunthorpe	..	2.5	20.4	33.1	18	9.0	11.2	1,045
North Yorkshire#	65.8	16.8	27.3	29.0	9	7.4	9.3	26,960
Craven	..	0.7	26.2	17.8	8	6.8	7.3	2,708
Hambleton	..	1.5	28.6	27.7	7	6.5	7.8	3,987
Harrogate	..	2.6	31.6	26.7	8	8.3	10.5	6,040
Richmondshire	..	0.7	33.6	23.0	7	6.3	8.3	2,037
Ryedale	..	1.6	29.4	29.0	7	6.6	8.1	3,751
Scarborough	..	4.0	25.8	30.3	15	6.7	11.1	3,288
Selby	..	2.3	26.8	29.4	8	8.4	9.5	2,931
York	..	3.5	23.5	32.7	13	10.0	11.1	2,209
South Yorkshire	57.9	55.4	21.0	36.5	18	10.3	11.6	23,362
Barnsley	57.5	8.2	20.0	28.0	17	10.5	12.2	3,854
Doncaster	59.0	13.2	20.1	34.0	18	10.5	12.7	5,163
Rotherham	60.2	10.9	19.7	35.2	17	10.5	11.4	4,227
Sheffield	56.4	23.2	22.5	41.6	18	10.1	10.8	10,118
West Yorkshire	63.6	69.7	22.0	34.2	15	10.2	12.1	48,787
Bradford	62.4	17.1	21.6	35.8	18	10.3	12.6	10,671
Calderdale	67.0	5.9	23.7	31.6	14	10.2	11.7	5,600
Kirklees	66.2	11.6	22.7	29.6	14	9.6	11.7	9,705
Leeds	63.3	24.1	21.8	37.4	14	10.6	12.3	16,713
Wakefield	60.2	11.0	21.7	30.8	14	10.2	11.4	6,098
EAST MIDLANDS	63.8	118.8	23.3	34.1	13	9.8	10.6	110,443
Derbyshire	64.5	29.2	22.5	34.2	13	9.3	10.5	23,591
Amber Valley	65.3	2.7	23.9	33.1	10	9.2	10.3	3,095
Bolsover	60.8	2.6	17.6	38.4	15	11.3	11.6	1,217
Chesterfield	64.6	3.9	21.5	33.7	16	10.1	12.0	2,126
Derby	62.7	9.3	22.0	37.7	17	10.5	12.6	4,090
Derbyshire Dales	66.6	1.1	28.9	29.2	7	7.0	7.3	3,483
Erewash	66.6	3.1	22.9	30.2	12	10.4	10.2	2,423
High Peak	63.9	2.0	23.1	27.1	10	8.4	8.9	2,752
North East Derbyshire	63.1	2.8	23.0	32.7	12	9.0	11.5	2,441
South Derbyshire	69.6	1.8	25.4	32.6	9	9.6	11.1	1,964

14.6 *(continued)*

| | Economically active[2] 1995-96 (percentages) | Claimant unemployed January 1997 | | | Income Support bene-ficiaries[4] Nov. 1995 (percentages) | Businesses registered for VAT 1995 | | Stock of businesses 1994 (numbers) |
		Total (thousands)	Of which females (percentages)	Of which long-term unemployed[3] (percentages)		Registration rates[5] (percentages)	Deregistration rates[5] (percentages)	
Leicestershire	64.9	21.1	24.4	34.1	12	10.5	11.0	26,626
Blaby	74.3	1.2	27.7	29.0	7	10.2	9.9	2,233
Charnwood	64.9	2.8	26.6	30.1	8	9.6	10.7	4,111
Harborough	72.3	0.7	25.7	25.7	7	10.3	11.1	2,977
Hinckley and Bosworth	72.6	1.3	27.4	20.5	7	10.2	10.6	3,148
Leicester	55.3	11.5	22.5	39.4	21	12.4	12.5	7,472
Melton	77.9	0.7	32.0	21.6	7	8.0	8.1	1,633
North West Leicestershire	65.7	1.7	22.2	33.9	10	9.4	9.8	2,509
Oadby and Wigston	66.9	0.9	29.6	27.0	8	8.5	12.3	1,324
Rutland	61.3	0.3	26.2	20.2	5	10.5	11.0	1,220
Lincolnshire	63.7	17.5	25.5	27.3	12	8.0	9.4	19,811
Boston	66.7	1.5	21.5	20.7	12	8.9	9.4	1,871
East Lindsey	60.6	4.5	26.8	20.2	15	6.9	8.6	4,553
Lincoln	66.1	4.3	21.9	39.2	19	10.3	13.3	1,697
North Kesteven	61.2	1.7	27.4	28.9	10	7.4	8.8	2,468
South Holland	59.8	1.2	27.1	19.4	9	5.8	8.2	2,936
South Kesteven	66.0	2.3	27.9	24.5	10	10.4	10.3	3,691
West Lindsey	66.7	2.1	27.8	29.1	12	7.6	9.2	2,595
Northamptonshire	67.7	13.0	24.9	32.0	11	10.5	10.8	17,974
Corby	60.7	1.5	22.6	32.3	14	10.5	12.5	971
Daventry	71.7	1.1	31.3	20.8	7	10.1	9.6	2,786
East Northamptonshire	65.2	1.1	24.8	25.1	8	8.5	10.1	2,329
Kettering	68.6	1.7	24.4	35.1	11	10.2	12.3	1,999
Northampton	67.9	5.2	23.3	35.8	13	11.7	11.4	4,499
South Northamptonshire	70.7	0.9	30.4	28.8	7	9.5	10.0	2,992
Wellingborough	67.0	1.6	25.5	30.0	12	11.8	10.4	2,398
Nottinghamshire	60.1	38.0	21.7	37.8	15	10.4	10.9	22,441
Ashfield	62.8	3.9	20.3	38.3	14	7.8	11.3	2,044
Bassetlaw	62.9	3.8	22.5	32.8	13	10.0	11.7	2,670
Broxtowe	62.6	2.8	26.7	32.3	10	11.5	12.6	2,106
Gedling	67.6	3.1	25.0	34.7	10	10.3	11.6	2,309
Mansfield	54.5	3.8	19.8	31.8	15	10.9	11.0	1,748
Newark and Sherwood	60.3	2.8	22.6	29.0	12	9.7	9.6	2,899
Nottingham	53.8	15.5	20.1	44.0	23	11.4	11.0	5,977
Rushcliffe	65.9	2.3	25.6	34.6	8	10.6	9.5	2,687
WEST MIDLANDS	62.7	165.9	23.7	38.0	15	9.9	10.8	136,687
Hereford and Worcester	67.7	16.4	27.1	29.6	10	8.7	10.1	24,769
Bromsgrove	70.5	1.9	27.2	34.7	8	9.1	11.0	2,753
Hereford	55.8	1.8	27.7	19.9	12	9.9	10.3	1,294
Leominster	70.6	0.9	28.2	28.6	9	5.5	7.5	2,577
Malvern Hills	69.2	1.7	26.1	28.3	9	7.7	8.9	3,945
Redditch	68.9	2.4	28.1	36.1	13	10.6	12.1	2,009
South Herefordshire	69.0	1.1	27.8	23.5	9	6.8	9.2	2,793
Worcester	65.7	2.4	24.7	32.5	11	10.8	12.8	2,156
Wychavon	69.5	1.9	30.3	25.1	8	9.4	9.8	4,456
Wyre Forest	66.5	2.3	25.4	30.9	12	9.7	11.3	2,785
Shropshire	65.9	8.4	23.9	26.1	12	8.5	9.1	14,216
Bridgnorth	71.7	0.8	23.9	28.3	8	7.8	10.0	2,174
North Shropshire	60.9	0.9	26.5	23.1	10	8.0	8.0	2,461
Oswestry	61.5	0.9	28.5	27.1	14	9.1	8.9	1,268
Shrewsbury and Atcham	68.2	1.8	22.5	27.5	11	8.7	8.1	2,985
South Shropshire	51.7	0.8	24.6	29.8	9	6.5	6.9	2,162
The Wrekin	69.4	3.3	22.7	24.4	14	10.3	11.8	3,166
Staffordshire	65.4	25.3	24.2	28.8	12	9.5	10.3	26,306
Cannock Chase	72.2	2.5	23.4	30.4	12	11.0	11.3	2,284
East Staffordshire	63.4	3.0	24.9	30.8	11	8.7	8.9	2,991
Lichfield	64.9	1.6	28.4	25.8	8	9.4	10.5	2,955
Newcastle-under-Lyme	63.3	2.8	23.8 ·	30.2	10	9.1	11.1	2,501
South Staffordshire	71.8	2.3	26.4	33.6	9	11.0	10.0	2,682
Stafford	71.0	2.4	24.8	24.1	9	8.9	10.3	3,462
Staffordshire Moorlands	61.6	1.7	28.2	25.0	9	7.0	8.9	3,289
Stoke-on-Trent	59.2	7.3	21.1	29.4	16	10.8	11.3	4,652
Tamworth	72.2	1.9	25.2	25.3	14	9.5	10.0	1,491

14.6 (continued)

	Economically active[2] 1995-96 (percentages)	Claimant unemployed January 1997			Income Support bene-ficiaries[4] Nov. 1995 (percentages)	Businesses registered for VAT 1995		Stock of businesses 1994 (numbers)
		Total (thousands)	Of which females (percentages)	Of which long-term unemployed[3] (percentages)		Registration rates[5] (percentages)	Deregistration rates[5] (percentages)	
Warwickshire	62.0	10.0	26.4	30.1	10	10.1	10.3	15,870
North Warwickshire	59.6	1.2	25.2	26.6	9	9.1	10.1	2,023
Nuneaton and Bedworth	60.3	3.0	24.7	30.2	13	10.4	11.4	2,326
Rugby	62.3	1.9	28.5	28.3	10	9.8	9.9	2,569
Stratford-on-Avon	62.2	1.6	29.4	32.5	7	9.8	9.2	5,021
Warwick	64.1	2.2	25.1	31.7	10	11.1	11.4	3,930
West Midlands (Met. County)	59.9	105.9	22.8	43.3	20	11.0	12.0	55,526
Birmingham	57.7	47.9	22.5	45.5	23	11.3	11.6	21,053
Coventry	59.7	10.8	22.1	41.0	19	10.9	12.5	5,346
Dudley	65.3	9.3	24.7	40.3	15	10.1	12.3	7,664
Sandwell	59.2	12.7	23.4	45.2	21	10.9	12.2	6,394
Solihull	64.3	5.2	26.1	39.6	10	12.4	12.8	4,375
Walsall	59.5	9.9	22.1	41.1	19	9.4	10.8	5,716
Wolverhampton	59.5	10.1	21.5	39.3	21	11.7	13.6	4,979
EASTERN	65.4	130.8	24.7	33.0	11	10.2	10.7	156,907
Cambridgeshire	67.9	15.1	25.7	30.8	10	10.0	9.7	21,677
Cambridge	63.2	2.7	25.5	39.7	9	10.9	10.1	2,998
East Cambridgeshire	74.3	1.1	27.7	29.9	8	7.6	8.1	2,731
Fenland	63.4	2.3	25.9	30.1	13	8.6	8.6	2,678
Huntingdonshire	72.4	2.5	28.1	27.1	8	10.6	9.8	4,926
Peterborough	63.4	5.1	23.7	28.3	15	12.5	11.5	3,379
South Cambridgeshire	72.0	1.5	26.6	31.6	6	9.3	9.5	4,964
Bedfordshire	71.1	13.6	25.3	33.9	12	10.6	11.4	15,563
Bedford	69.8	3.7	26.7	32.2	12	9.6	11.0	3,948
Luton	68.5	6.2	23.3	39.4	16	11.7	12.3	3,889
Mid Bedfordshire	74.8	1.7	29.4	28.4	7	10.9	10.1	4,227
South Bedfordshire	73.1	2.0	25.8	25.1	9	10.3	12.4	3,498
Essex	62.6	42.9	24.1	35.5	12	10.7	11.2	43,478
Basildon	64.0	5.2	24.0	33.2	15	11.3	12.0	3,862
Braintree	64.9	2.8	25.4	32.7	11	10.2	9.8	4,019
Brentwood	66.1	1.2	24.1	30.4	7	13.0	10.6	2,304
Castle Point	62.3	2.4	24.7	37.2	14	11.2	13.3	2,173
Chelmsford	71.0	3.3	26.2	31.1	8	10.4	9.7	4,197
Colchester	63.5	3.5	23.6	27.4	11	10.4	10.9	4,108
Epping Forest	65.3	2.7	26.7	39.6	10	11.4	12.6	4,033
Harlow	66.0	2.3	25.8	39.5	16	11.2	10.3	1,403
Maldon	59.2	1.3	22.5	34.7	9	8.8	10.1	2,260
Rochford	60.3	1.8	25.6	33.5	11	9.8	10.5	2,066
Southend-on-Sea	55.9	7.2	22.5	43.9	17	12.2	13.6	3,973
Tendring	46.4	4.0	21.9	33.5	15	9.5	11.0	3,154
Thurrock	64.9	4.3	23.4	35.8	15	11.0	12.4	2,537
Uttlesford	71.5	0.8	29.3	29.9	7	9.7	9.5	3,387
Hertfordshire	69.1	18.3	24.3	34.0	9	11.6	11.7	32,842
Broxbourne	65.1	2.1	26.2	41.6	11	10.1	10.7	2,250
Dacorum	68.1	2.3	23.1	32.4	8	12.1	12.7	4,551
East Hertfordshire	71.4	1.7	28.0	33.6	7	11.9	10.4	4,756
Hertsmere	68.3	1.6	25.6	36.4	10	12.4	12.7	3,096
North Hertfordshire	71.1	2.2	24.8	31.8	10	9.2	10.2	4,262
St Albans	70.9	1.6	25.0	26.5	7	12.6	12.5	4,620
Stevenage	74.0	2.3	21.4	35.6	14	15.0	12.9	1,525
Three Rivers	64.3	1.2	22.2	36.0	7	10.6	11.9	2,585
Watford	68.9	1.8	22.3	35.7	12	11.7	11.5	2,535
Welwyn Hatfield	67.6	1.5	24.9	29.0	10	11.1	12.4	2,662
Norfolk	61.6	23.6	24.9	29.9	13	8.0	9.8	23,593
Breckland	65.4	2.6	27.7	29.0	11	8.0	10.1	3,589
Broadland	60.1	2.0	28.0	25.8	8	8.1	9.8	3,183
Great Yarmouth	58.5	4.9	24.2	28.2	18	7.4	11.1	2,426
Kings Lynn and West Norfolk	64.2	3.6	25.0	28.4	12	6.4	9.4	4,265
North Norfolk	57.5	2.5	25.9	27.0	14	6.6	8.1	3,248
Norwich	60.9	5.8	21.6	35.1	19	12.3	10.6	3,030
South Norfolk	63.3	2.3	27.9	31.0	8	8.1	9.9	3,852

14.6 *(continued)*

	Economically active[2] 1995-96 (percentages)	Claimant unemployed January 1997			Income Support bene- ficiaries[4] Nov. 1995 (percentages)	Businesses registered for VAT 1995		Stock of businesses 1994 (numbers)
		Total (thousands)	Of which females (percentages)	Of which long-term unemployed[3] (percentages)		Registration rates[5] (percentages)	Deregistration rates[5] (percentages)	
Suffolk	64.0	17.4	24.5	31.1	11	9.6	9.4	19,754
Babergh	60.0	1.5	24.7	31.0	11	10.2	9.5	2,971
Forest Heath	61.9	1.0	26.2	33.2	8	12.7	11.0	1,911
Ipswich	66.0	4.1	21.3	33.9	16	12.0	11.8	2,322
Mid Suffolk	66.0	1.4	28.8	26.0	8	7.9	8.1	3,342
St Edmundsbury	68.4	2.1	26.2	28.5	10	9.5	8.5	2,984
Suffolk Coastal	62.7	2.4	24.0	28.7	9	8.6	9.2	3,496
Waveney	62.0	4.8	25.1	32.0	15	8.1	9.2	2,729
LONDON (GOR)	63.8	315.8	26.0	44.0	19	13.7	12.0	245,183
Barking and Dagenham	60.5	5.8	22.5	41.7	22	18.8	12.3	2,196
Barnet	62.4	8.9	27.8	38.0	14	14.1	13.9	10,510
Bexley	68.4	6.5	25.8	40.5	11	11.7	13.4	4,459
Brent	66.1	14.9	26.1	43.8	26	14.1	14.6	7,626
Bromley	62.9	7.6	25.0	41.4	10	11.6	12.8	7,912
Camden	65.2	10.4	29.5	44.7	23	12.9	10.0	16,044
City of London	..	0.1	26.5	41.6	12	9.5	6.4	11,631
City of Westminster[6]	57.5	7.2	29.6	36.4	19	15.0	10.1	32,328
Croydon	66.7	12.2	25.4	43.9	15	12.2	12.6	8,238
Ealing	62.8	10.8	25.8	41.8	19	13.9	13.3	8,334
Enfield	65.1	10.7	25.4	44.6	18	13.0	13.0	5,771
Greenwich	59.6	11.5	24.5	44.0	23	13.2	13.4	3,572
Hackney	55.4	17.2	25.6	51.4	37	17.4	15.6	6,066
Hammersmith and Fulham	66.9	9.1	29.0	47.0	21	14.1	11.2	6,732
Haringey	58.7	15.6	26.1	47.1	31	16.2	15.5	5,565
Harrow	68.3	5.1	27.1	37.4	12	13.2	14.4	6,110
Havering	65.0	5.4	23.8	32.9	12	11.1	13.0	5,184
Hillingdon	63.0	5.7	25.7	37.9	12	12.3	12.0	6,730
Hounslow	67.3	7.5	24.5	36.1	17	13.0	11.9	6,415
Islington	63.8	12.9	28.4	52.8	29	14.2	11.5	8,797
Kensington and Chelsea	57.6	6.2	32.8	48.5	16	14.1	11.0	9,523
Kingston upon Thames	69.5	3.0	26.9	34.5	10	11.7	11.7	4,491
Lambeth	70.0	19.0	27.0	44.6	27	14.7	12.5	5,782
Lewisham	68.4	15.2	24.6	48.6	24	13.9	12.5	4,048
Merton	68.3	5.9	25.6	39.8	13	13.9	12.2	4,884
Newham	57.9	14.5	27.7	44.6	34	16.3	14.5	3,647
Redbridge	60.3	7.9	26.1	41.1	15	15.4	16.2	5,108
Richmond-upon-Thames	65.9	3.7	29.2	39.6	8	13.9	11.1	7,154
Southwark	59.6	15.8	25.8	45.6	29	13.3	12.3	6,457
Sutton	66.8	4.1	25.8	36.4	11	11.3	12.2	4,678
Tower Hamlets	53.3	12.6	20.6	44.1	36	15.2	11.9	6,684
Waltham Forest	63.1	11.2	24.6	45.0	23	13.2	14.7	4,326
Wandsworth	68.6	12.1	27.3	44.8	17	14.0	11.6	8,181
SOUTH EAST (GOR)	65.7	173.2	23.6	33.9	10	11.0	11.5	239,763
Berkshire	69.4	13.5	22.7	32.4	9	12.7	11.9	25,942
Bracknell Forest	71.3	1.4	22.8	25.3	8	15.7	12.7	2,793
Newbury	75.5	1.7	26.1	26.8	6	11.5	10.9	5,607
Reading	66.5	3.5	20.4	33.5	13	12.3	12.1	3,751
Slough	65.0	3.5	21.7	38.6	15	14.3	13.7	2,777
Windsor and Maidenhead	66.5	2.0	24.9	35.4	6	12.6	11.7	6,185
Wokingham	70.4	1.3	23.8	22.8	5	12.1	11.6	4,829
Buckinghamshire	70.1	11.2	23.7	30.2	8	11.6	11.6	25,228
Aylesbury Vale	74.4	2.4	24.6	32.3	8	11.4	10.4	5,627
Chiltern	68.0	1.0	23.5	33.7	6	11.1	10.9	3,975
Milton Keynes	71.9	4.4	24.1	24.7	12	14.0	12.7	5,182
South Buckinghamshire	60.4	0.8	26.2	35.5	5	10.9	12.0	3,316
Wycombe	69.3	2.5	21.4	34.9	8	10.4	12.0	7,128
East Sussex	60.5	25.7	24.9	43.2	14	10.9	12.5	20,542
Brighton	62.1	9.7	26.0	49.1	20	13.0	13.1	3,796
Eastbourne	57.9	2.4	24.0	32.0	13	9.9	13.6	1,772
Hastings	61.5	3.8	21.3	40.4	20	9.7	13.7	1,757
Hove	56.8	4.2	26.7	46.4	18	14.4	15.4	2,380
Lewes	63.6	2.1	22.2	42.5	10	10.3	12.0	2,577
Rother	51.7	1.9	23.7	38.8	11	9.5	12.4	2,830
Wealden	65.6	1.7	27.5	29.3	7	9.4	10.4	5,429

14.6 *(continued)*

	Economically active[2] 1995-96 (percentages)	Claimant unemployed January 1997			Income Support bene- ficiaries[4] Nov. 1995 (percentages)	Businesses registered for VAT 1995		Stock of businesses 1994 (numbers)
		Total (thousands)	Of which females (percentages)	Of which long-term unemployed[3] (percentages)		Registration rates[5] (percentages)	Deregistration rates[6] (percentages)	
Hampshire	65.6	35.4	22.6	32.8	10	11.2	11.0	42,542
Basingstoke and Deane	73.8	2.1	24.9	33.9	7	11.7	11.4	4,481
East Hampshire	67.4	1.6	27.5	26.4	8	10.9	10.4	4,139
Eastleigh	63.0	1.6	25.1	27.9	7	12.4	12.3	2,760
Fareham	69.3	1.7	24.5	27.6	7	11.5	11.3	2,626
Gosport	54.4	1.9	25.7	26.6	10	11.7	13.0	1,009
Hart	67.9	0.6	25.8	23.9	5	10.7	9.5	2,942
Havant	61.7	3.3	20.2	33.6	14	12.5	12.2	2,230
New Forest	59.8	3.0	25.5	27.5	9	9.5	10.4	5,213
Portsmouth	66.5	7.5	21.1	40.6	16	12.5	11.6	3,323
Rushmoor	72.6	1.3	24.3	21.9	8	12.1	11.0	2,136
Southampton	61.3	8.1	19.5	36.8	17	11.1	12.7	4,085
Test Valley	69.8	1.3	25.7	23.0	6	11.1	10.5	3,727
Winchester	69.1	1.4	23.1	27.1	7	10.4	9.4	3,870
Isle of Wight UA	57.9	5.7	26.3	34.9	15	7.6	10.0	3,183
Medina	..	3.1	25.3	37.6	..	9.2	10.7	1,639
South Wight	..	2.6	27.6	31.7	..	5.9	9.3	1,543
Kent	65.5	46.9	22.8	34.1	13	10.4	12.1	40,843
Ashford	67.1	2.5	21.8	33.5	11	9.2	10.1	3,164
Canterbury	54.7	3.8	22.0	39.3	12	10.5	12.1	3,172
Dartford	71.4	2.5	24.0	39.1	12	10.9	10.4	1,947
Dover	65.0	3.8	20.3	33.0	13	9.2	12.5	2,208
Gillingham	69.0	2.8	25.3	29.4	14	12.0	13.0	1,631
Gravesham	71.5	3.4	25.0	34.4	14	12.4	12.3	1,910
Maidstone	66.0	3.0	24.5	28.1	10	9.9	12.5	4,497
Rochester-upon-Medway	68.2	5.1	23.6	27.7	14	13.2	12.9	3,024
Sevenoaks	63.7	2.1	25.0	34.4	8	10.4	11.1	4,228
Shepway	59.1	3.9	20.2	36.9	16	8.8	13.6	2,361
Swale	65.3	4.0	23.4	38.5	16	9.5	12.5	2,912
Thanet	61.0	5.8	20.7	39.7	20	10.4	13.9	2,226
Tonbridge and Malling	72.7	2.0	25.7	27.4	9	10.2	12.3	3,415
Tunbridge Wells	67.1	1.9	22.5	30.0	9	10.1	12.0	4,088
Oxfordshire	70.4	9.1	26.1	30.3	8	10.9	10.4	19,443
Cherwell	77.6	1.8	25.7	25.4	8	10.8	10.3	4,225
Oxford	63.2	3.5	24.8	36.4	11	10.3	10.4	2,680
South Oxfordshire	70.0	1.5	26.4	29.2	6	11.8	10.3	5,208
Vale of White Horse	70.1	1.2	28.2	24.2	6	11.3	10.9	3,595
West Oxfordshire	71.6	1.1	28.1	27.1	6	9.5	10.0	3,734
Surrey	64.9	13.5	24.4	28.9	7	11.0	11.3	40,003
Elmbridge	68.3	1.6	26.2	34.8	6	11.7	12.3	5,206
Epsom and Ewell	58.4	1.0	23.7	28.0	7	11.8	13.2	1,997
Guildford	66.1	1.6	24.4	29.5	7	10.9	9.9	4,582
Mole Valley	59.9	0.8	23.3	24.6	7	10.1	9.2	3,494
Reigate and Banstead	63.3	1.7	23.1	25.7	8	10.0	12.2	4,226
Runnymede	67.1	1.1	26.1	31.7	7	10.8	11.0	2,838
Spelthorne	66.7	1.6	25.7	33.0	8	12.2	11.6	3,292
Surrey Heath	71.2	0.9	23.5	21.0	6	12.0	10.6	3,212
Tandridge	62.4	1.0	24.8	30.2	8	9.9	11.9	3,147
Waverley	63.3	1.2	23.2	29.4	6	10.4	10.0	4,890
Woking	66.2	0.9	22.7	23.5	7	11.6	13.2	3,119
West Sussex	62.5	12.1	24.0	29.8	9	10.2	11.4	22,038
Adur	56.8	1.2	24.8	34.4	11	10.0	12.5	1,364
Arun	56.5	2.7	23.8	28.0	11	10.2	11.3	3,475
Chichester	59.8	1.6	24.4	27.6	8	9.1	10.4	4,261
Crawley	65.6	2.0	23.5	30.1	10	12.8	12.5	1,931
Horsham	68.3	1.3	26.5	25.8	6	9.6	11.0	4,534
Mid Sussex	68.8	1.5	24.6	30.8	7	10.6	11.0	4,303
Worthing	59.6	1.9	21.1	33.0	11	10.8	13.4	2,170

14.6 (continued)

	Economically active[2] 1995-96 (percentages)	Claimant unemployed January 1997			Income Support bene- ficiaries[4] Nov. 1995 (percentages)	Businesses registered for VAT 1995		Stock of businesses 1994 (numbers)
		Total (thousands)	Of which females (percentages)	Of which long-term unemployed[3] (percentages)		Registration rates[5] (percentages)	Deregistration rates[5] (percentages)	
SOUTH WEST	62.6	135.8	25.3	31.6	12	8.7	10.6	149,496
Avon#	65.7	29.1	24.5	35.0	13	10.4	11.3	26,213
Bath	..	3.1	25.6	35.3	12	10.2	12.1	2,579
Bristol	..	15.8	22.8	37.3	17	12.0	11.1	10,369
Kingswood	..	1.9	26.9	31.3	9	8.9	11.9	1,855
Northavon	..	2.4	27.6	29.1	8	9.5	10.7	3,813
Wansdyke	..	1.6	29.7	29.4	8	9.0	9.3	2,546
Woodspring	..	4.3	25.4	32.9	11	9.4	12.3	5,051
Cornwall and the Isles of Scilly	56.4	19.5	27.3	27.2	15	6.5	9.9	17,144
Caradon	57.9	2.4	28.3	26.8	12	6.4	10.6	2,778
Carrick	55.7	3.4	25.6	26.5	14	8.7	10.5	3,028
Kerrier	63.0	3.6	24.4	30.6	16	6.0	10.1	2,687
North Cornwall	60.2	2.8	28.4	30.6	14	5.4	8.1	3,723
Penwith	51.3	3.2	28.0	26.7	19	6.7	11.1	2,046
Restormel	49.7	4.1	29.4	23.4	15	6.7	10.5	2,726
Isles of Scilly	..	-	54.8	6.5	3	1.3	3.8	157
Devon	58.1	33.8	25.0	32.2	13	7.8	10.8	33,293
East Devon	52.0	2.4	25.6	24.1	8	7.0	10.1	4,193
Exeter	68.2	3.3	22.5	32.8	14	10.9	12.7	2,448
Mid Devon	64.4	1.2	28.0	31.0	9	7.1	7.7	3,317
North Devon	58.8	2.8	28.2	29.9	14	7.3	9.3	3,627
Plymouth	55.7	11.2	24.2	35.4	15	10.2	15.5	3,754
South Hams	63.5	2.0	27.5	28.2	11	6.7	10.0	3,582
Teignbridge	54.0	2.9	24.3	29.7	13	8.7	11.6	3,915
Torbay	56.7	5.4	23.5	30.4	20	9.4	14.9	3,175
Torridge	57.1	1.8	28.7	37.4	14	4.7	7.6	2,765
West Devon	61.0	1.0	27.2	36.3	10	6.0	8.2	2,517
Dorset	57.7	16.8	23.6	32.0	11	9.2	11.1	20,330
Bournemouth	54.0	6.0	21.3	38.3	17	11.6	13.9	4,124
Christchurch	43.7	0.9	24.2	28.5	10	10.1	11.7	1,267
East Dorset	57.0	1.2	29.4	29.6	8	8.2	9.9	2,896
North Dorset	60.3	0.7	29.6	18.1	8	6.9	8.3	2,262
Poole	61.6	3.2	21.8	33.8	11	10.7	11.8	3,599
Purbeck	57.8	0.9	24.0	29.5	9	8.0	9.5	1,406
West Dorset	61.5	1.6	27.9	27.0	9	7.2	9.1	3,648
Weymouth and Portland	62.3	2.3	24.0	24.4	13	10.4	15.6	1,128
Gloucestershire	68.3	12.8	25.8	33.3	10	9.2	10.2	18,367
Cheltenham	69.1	3.0	23.7	36.2	10	11.0	11.4	3,041
Cotswold	65.2	1.0	28.3	26.3	6	8.4	8.9	3,900
Forest of Dean	58.2	1.9	27.4	29.4	12	8.9	10.1	2,835
Gloucester	71.5	3.5	23.3	38.3	15	9.7	11.5	2,280
Stroud	71.1	2.1	28.8	29.8	9	8.4	9.5	3,894
Tewkesbury	72.4	1.3	28.2	29.7	8	9.0	10.6	2,416
Somerset	63.4	12.2	26.4	30.8	11	7.9	9.3	17,004
Mendip	69.0	2.7	28.3	30.9	11	7.9	9.5	3,820
Sedgemoor	61.0	2.9	24.5	27.9	12	8.8	9.6	3,415
South Somerset	61.3	2.8	27.4	30.3	14	7.3	8.8	5,262
Taunton Deane	68.0	2.6	24.3	33.9	8	8.2	9.8	3,097
West Somerset	51.0	1.1	28.6	32.5	12	7.8	9.4	1,410
Wiltshire	70.3	11.6	25.9	27.6	9	9.7	10.8	17,144
Kennet	75.1	1.2	28.0	29.3	7	9.5	11.3	2,582
North Wiltshire	71.8	2.1	28.7	27.3	8	9.2	9.9	4,162
Salisbury	67.3	1.9	24.2	22.7	8	8.4	10.0	3,485
Thamesdown	71.8	4.1	24.6	29.0	12	11.9	12.2	3,734
West Wiltshire	66.5	2.3	26.2	28.6	9	9.5	10.7	3,180

14.6 *(continued)*

	Economically active[2] 1995-96 (percentages)	Claimant unemployed January 1997			Income Support bene-ficiaries[4] Nov. 1995 (percentages)	Businesses registered for VAT 1995		Stock of businesses 1994 (numbers)
		Total (thousands)	Of which females (percentages)	Of which long-term unemployed[3] (percentages)		Registration rates[5] (percentages)	Deregistration rates[5] (percentages)	
New local government structure with effect from 1 April 1996								
Former County of Cleveland								
Hartlepool UA	58.6	4.7	18.1	38.7	..	..	..	..
Middlesbrough UA	58.8	8.3	19.3	41.4	..	..	..	..
Redcar & Cleveland UA	60.0	6.7	19.0	39.8	..	..	..	..
Stockton-on-Tees UA	62.1	8.3	21.3	39.8	..	..	..	..
Former County of Humberside								
East Riding of Yorkshire UA	59.1	8.3	25.5	28.3	..	..	..	..
Kingston upon Hull UA	57.2	13.7	19.9	32.6	..	..	..	..
North East Lincolnshire UA	64.6	7.8	19.9	32.2	..	..	..	..
North Lincolnshire UA	65.6	4.8	21.9	31.8	..	..	..	..
Former County of North Yorkshire								
York UA	65.6	4.5	24.4	31.1	..	..	..	..
North Yorkshire	65.9	12.3	28.3	28.2	..	..	..	..
Former County of Avon								
Bath and North East Somerset UA	64.2	4.7	26.7	33.3	..	..	..	..
Bristol UA	65.3	15.8	22.8	37.3	..	..	..	..
North Somerset UA	62.3	4.3	25.4	32.9	..	..	..	..
South Gloucestershire UA	69.8	4.3	27.3	30.1	..	..	..	..

\# New local government structure came into effect on 1 April 1996.
1 See Technical notes to the Labour market chapter.
2 Economic activity rate of persons aged 16 or over. Data are from the Labour Force Survey and relate to the period March 1995 to February 1996.
3 Persons who have been unemployed for 12 months or more as a percentage of all claimants.
4 Claimants and their partners aged 16 or over as a percentage of the population aged 16 or over. Data are from the Income Support Quarterly Statistical Enquiry.
5 Registrations/deregistrations during 1995 as a percentage of the end-1994 stock figure.
6 Figure for economically active includes the City of London.

Source: Office for National Statistics; Department of Social Security; Department of Trade and Industry

14.7 Regional accounts: by county

| | Gross domestic product[1,2] | | | | Household income 1994 | | Disposable household income 1994 | |
| | 1991 | | 1993 | | | | | |
	£ million	£ per head index (UK=100)	£ million	£ per head index (UK=100)	£ million	£ per head index (UK=100)	£ million	£ per head index (UK=100)
United Kingdom	489,905	100.0	539,014	100.0	566,645	100.0	468,707	100.0
England	415,844	101.8	457,480	101.8	479,786	101.5	395,394	101.1
North East	18,817	85.3	20,758	85.8	21,917	86.5	18,621	88.9
Cleveland#	4,236	89.3	4,631	89.4	4,679	86.1	3,999	89.0
Durham	4,021	78.3	4,353	77.4	4,929	83.6	4,165	85.4
Northumberland	1,957	75.3	2,163	76.0	3,007	100.7	2,524	102.2
Tyne & Wear	8,603	89.8	9,611	91.2	9,301	84.5	7,933	87.2
North West (GOR) and Merseyside	53,143	91.1	58,296	91.2	61,180	91.3	51,262	92.5
North West (GOR)	44,003	95.5	48,204	95.3	49,087	92.5	40,912	93.2
Cheshire	8,484	103.6	9,930	110.3	9,611	101.5	7,772	99.2
Cumbria	4,497	108.5	4,775	105.2	4,600	96.7	3,874	98.5
Greater Manchester	20,043	92.0	21,880	91.6	22,437	89.7	19,017	91.9
Lancashire	10,978	91.9	11,620	88.3	12,438	90.0	10,249	89.7
Merseyside	9,140	74.4	10,092	75.6	12,093	86.9	10,350	89.9
Yorkshire and the Humber	38,749	91.8	41,765	89.9	44,832	91.9	37,635	93.3
Humberside#	7,079	95.2	7,703	94.0	7,706	89.3	6,496	91.0
North Yorkshire#	6,190	101.6	6,831	102.2	7,641	108.4	6,412	110.0
South Yorkshire	8,961	81.2	9,246	76.4	10,751	84.9	9,165	87.5
West Yorkshire	16,519	93.5	17,984	92.4	18,734	91.8	15,562	92.1
East Midlands	33,463	97.8	36,556	96.7	37,698	94.7	31,070	94.4
Derbyshire	7,254	90.8	7,707	87.5	8,309	89.8	6,889	90.0
Leicestershire	7,910	104.4	8,783	104.2	8,573	96.4	6,997	95.1
Lincolnshire	4,590	91.6	5,148	92.4	5,865	99.8	4,951	101.9
Northamptonshire	5,116	102.9	5,783	105.5	5,681	98.4	4,574	95.8
Nottinghamshire	8,592	99.4	9,135	95.9	9,269	92.7	7,659	92.6
West Midlands	41,431	92.8	45,602	93.1	47,727	92.9	39,948	94.0
Hereford & Worcs.	5,020	86.4	5,769	89.6	6,900	101.6	5,740	102.2
Shropshire	3,150	90.3	3,545	92.4	3,914	96.9	3,222	96.4
Staffordshire	7,500	84.3	7,802	79.9	9,481	92.7	7,892	93.2
Warwickshire	4,132	99.7	4,536	99.2	5,010	104.0	4,061	101.9
West Midlands (Met. county)	21,630	97.1	23,951	98.2	22,422	87.9	19,034	90.2
Eastern	42,142	96.6	46,027	95.7	54,428	107.4	44,549	106.3
Bedfordshire	4,551	100.9	4,922	98.5	5,583	105.9	4,575	104.9
Cambridgeshire	6,134	108.2	7,008	110.8	7,140	107.1	5,845	106.0
Essex	10,970	83.7	12,182	84.3	16,645	109.3	13,609	108.0
Hertfordshire	8,843	105.5	9,282	100.2	11,516	118.0	9,200	114.0
Norfolk	6,129	95.2	6,629	93.5	7,326	98.2	6,103	98.9
Suffolk	5,514	99.5	6,005	100.3	6,218	98.7	5,216	100.1
London	83,660	143.3	92,922	144.7	80,929	119.7	65,339	116.8

14.7 *(continued)*

| | Gross domestic product[1,2] | | | | Household income 1994 | | Disposable household income 1994 | |
| | 1991 | | 1993 | | | | | |
	£ million	£ per head index (UK=100)	£ million	£ per head index (UK=100)	£ million	£ per head index (UK=100)	£ million	£ per head index (UK=100)
South East (GOR)	66,521	102.2	73,389	102.4	85,058	112.6	68,296	109.3
Berkshire	8,376	131.3	9,436	133.4	8,822	118.2	6,816	110.4
Buckinghamshire	6,121	113.0	6,632	109.9	7,601	119.0	5,930	112.2
East Sussex	4,627	76.3	4,996	74.7	7,410	105.1	6,166	105.7
Hampshire	13,842	103.3	15,226	103.1	17,041	109.4	13,847	107.4
Isle of Wight	791	73.9	785	67.9	1,141	94.3	989	98.8
Kent	11,992	92.1	12,459	87.4	15,237	101.5	12,544	101.1
Oxfordshire	5,284	107.3	6,265	115.5	6,701	117.0	5,413	114.3
Surrey	9,574	109.3	10,995	114.4	13,107	129.7	10,097	120.8
West Sussex	5,914	98.0	6,595	99.2	7,998	114.1	6,494	112.0
South West	37,918	94.8	42,164	95.5	46,017	98.8	38,674	100.4
Avon#	8,614	105.3	9,604	106.5	9,330	98.2	7,737	98.5
Cornwall	2,878	71.6	3,146	71.2	4,132	88.8	3,605	93.6
Devon	7,597	86.3	8,436	86.8	9,755	95.4	8,326	98.5
Dorset	5,184	92.6	5,656	91.5	6,387	97.8	5,409	100.1
Gloucestershire	4,658	101.9	5,198	103.2	5,519	103.5	4,582	103.9
Somerset	3,596	90.6	3,996	91.0	4,648	100.2	3,914	102.0
Wiltshire	5,392	111.3	6,129	113.5	6,244	109.8	5,101	108.4

New local government structure came into effect on 1 April 1996.

1 The GDP data in this table are consistent with the national figures published in the ONS' *United Kingdom National Accounts (Blue Book) 1995*. They therefore differ from the data contained in Chapter 12 which are consistent with the 1996 edition of the *Blue Book*. Figures for United Kingdom exclude the Continental Shelf which in 1993 was £7,720 million.

2 See Technical notes to both this table and the Regional accounts chapter.

Source: Office for National Statistics

15 Sub-regions of Wales

Unitary Authorities in Wales

Isle of
Anglesey

Conwy

Flintshire

Denbighshire

Wrexham

Gwynedd

Ceredigion

Powys

1 Merthyr Tydfil
2 Blaenau Gwent
3 Torfaen

Pembrokeshire

Carmarthenshire

Monmouthshire

Neath
Port
Talbot

2

Swansea

Rhondda,
Cynon,
Taff

1

Caerphilly

3

Bridgend

Newport

Cardiff

The Vale of
Glamorgan

Regional Trends 32, © Crown copyright 1997

15.1 Area and population, 1995

	Area (sq km)	Persons per sq km	Population (thousands)			Total population percentage change 1981-1995	Total Period Fertility Rate (TPFR)[1]	Standardisd Mortality Ratio (UK=100) (SMR)[2]	Percentage of population aged			
			Males	Females	Total				Under 5	5-15	16 up to pension age[3]	Pension age[3] or over
United Kingdom	242,910	241	28,727	29,878	58,606	4.0	1.71	100	6.5	14.1	61.2	18.2
Wales	20,779	140	1,426	1,491	2,917	3.5	1.78	103	6.3	14.4	59.3	19.9
Blaenau Gwent	109	674	36	37	73	-3.4	2.00	112	6.9	14.7	58.9	19.5
Bridgend	246	531	63	67	131	3.4	1.83	107	6.4	14.5	59.9	19.2
Caerphilly	278	611	83	87	170	-1.1	1.75	115	6.9	15.6	60.1	17.4
Cardiff	140	2,209	152	158	309	7.3	1.87	96	7.0	14.7	60.8	17.5
Carmarthenshire	2,395	71	82	87	170	2.6	1.76	104	5.5	13.7	57.7	23.1
Ceredigion	1,795	39	35	36	70	12.9	1.55	97	5.3	12.8	60.4	21.6
Conwy	1,130	98	53	59	111	11.0	1.78	91	5.5	12.8	55.1	26.5
Denbighshire	844	109	44	48	92	5.4	1.80	93	6.3	13.3	56.4	24.1
Flintshire	438	333	72	74	146	4.8	1.70	103	6.5	14.3	62.1	17.1
Gwynedd	2,548	46	57	61	118	5.2	1.82	93	6.0	13.6	58.4	22.0
Isle of Anglesey	714	94	33	34	67	-1.2	1.69	103	6.1	14.8	57.7	21.4
Merthyr Tydfil	111	529	29	30	59	-3.1	1.91	118	7.0	16.2	58.3	18.6
Monmouthshire	850	101	42	44	86	10.6	1.64	93	5.8	14.1	60.1	20.0
Neath Port Talbot	442	316	68	72	140	-2.2	1.74	106	6.1	14.4	58.5	21.0
Newport	190	722	67	70	137	3.5	1.93	104	7.0	15.2	59.2	18.5
Pembrokeshire	1,590	71	56	58	114	5.4	1.82	102	6.1	14.7	58.3	20.9
Powys	5,196	24	61	62	122	8.3	1.82	98	5.8	13.7	58.5	22.1
Rhondda, Cynon, Taff	424	566	118	122	240	0.6	1.75	110	6.4	14.9	60.4	18.3
Swansea	378	610	113	118	231	0.6	1.69	104	5.8	14.0	59.7	20.5
Torfaen	126	716	44	46	90	-0.3	2.05	110	6.9	15.0	59.5	18.5
The Vale of Glamorgan	335	354	58	61	119	4.7	1.89	102	6.4	15.3	59.3	19.1
Wrexham	498	248	60	64	123	3.4	1.69	105	6.1	14.8	60.2	18.9

1 The Total Period Fertility Rate (TPFR) measures the average number of children which would be born if women were to experience the age-specific fertility rates of the year in question throughout their child bearing life

2 Adjusted for the age structure of the population. See Technical notes to the Population chapter.

3 Pension age is 60 for women and 65 for men.

Source: Office for National Statistics; Welsh Office

15.2 Vital and social statistics

	Live births[1] per 1,000 population		Deaths[1] per 1,000 population		Perinatal mortality rate[2]	Infant mortality rate[3]	Percentage of live births outside marriage	Children looked after by LAs per 1,000 population aged under 18
	1991	1995	1991	1995	1993-1995	1993-1995	1995	1995[4]
United Kingdom	13.7	12.5	11.2	10.9	8.9	6.2	*34*	..
Wales	13.2	11.8	11.8	12.1	8.5	5.9	*38*	4.4
Blaenau Gwent	14.8	12.0	12.5	12.8	7.0	6.0	*47*	3.5
Bridgend	13.3	12.1	11.6	12.0	10.9	5.9	*41*	4.2
Caerphilly	14.2	12.7	10.0	11.4	8.1	5.7	*44*	5.4
Cardiff	14.8	13.4	10.8	10.1	9.2	6.0	*39*	7.0
Carmarthenshire	11.3	10.6	13.1	13.9	10.9	7.3	*34*	4.7
Ceredigion	10.8	9.5	12.6	12.6	6.4	6.4	*33*	3.8
Conwy	11.8	10.3	15.6	15.3	6.2	4.8	*37*	1.8
Denbighshire	12.6	11.0	13.9	13.9	8.6	3.8	*40*	2.3
Flintshire	13.4	12.0	10.5	10.4	9.0	6.9	*31*	2.1
Gwynedd	12.2	11.5	13.0	12.2	7.9	3.9	*36*	..
Isle of Anglesey	12.2	11.9	11.6	12.9	4.9	5.3	*36*	..
Merthyr Tydfil	14.7	13.0	11.6	12.4	10.6	7.0	*47*	5.8
Monmouthshire	11.8	10.5	11.1	11.2	7.3	5.1	*27*	1.8
Neath Port Talbot	12.4	11.1	13.2	12.9	7.6	4.3	*38*	4.3
Newport	12.4	13.1	10.6	11.2	9.5	6.4	*44*	5.6
Pembrokeshire	13.0	11.1	11.2	12.0	9.0	5.8	*34*	3.9
Powys	12.0	11.0	12.4	12.8	7.7	5.6	*29*	2.4
Rhondda, Cynon, Taff	13.4	12.1	11.6	12.5	8.7	4.3	*42*	4.5
Swansea	12.5	11.2	11.8	12.5	8.8	7.1	*38*	5.0
Torfaen	14.3	13.8	11.4	11.6	8.1	7.1	*40*	3.3
The Vale of Glamorgan	13.4	12.1	11.5	11.5	7.2	4.7	*34*	6.2
Wrexham	13.1	11.7	11.2	11.7	7.1	9.1	*39*	3.8

1 Births are on the basis of year of occurrence in England and Wales and year of registration in Scotland and Northern Ireland. Deaths relate to year of registration.
2 Still births and deaths of infants under 1 week of age per 1,000 live and still births, 3 year average.
3 Deaths of infants under 1 year of age per 1,000 live births, 3 year average.
4 At 31 March. Under 18 mid-1994 population estimates used.

Source: Office for National Statistics; Welsh Office

Regional Trends 32, © Crown copyright 1997

15.3 Education

	Day nursery places per 1,000 population aged under 5 years[1] March 1996	Children under 5 in education[2] (percent-ages) Dec. 1995	Pupil/teacher ratio 1995/96 (numbers)		Pupils in last year of compulsory schooling[3,4] 1994/95 with		Average A/AS level points score[4,5] 1994/95
			Primary schools	Secondary schools	No graded results	5 or more A*-Cs at GCSE	
United Kingdom	..	53	22.7	16.1	8	42	15.9
Wales	46.3	73	22.5	16.0	11	40	14.9
Blaenau Gwent	6.3	75	23.4	15.9	14	28	11.7
Bridgend	18.3	65	24.2	15.8	17	37	14.5
Caerphilly	..	69	23.9	15.9	13	33	12.7
Cardiff	68.4	65	22.3	16.4	13	40	15.7
Carmarthenshire	33.6	74	19.9	16.7	9	46	15.4
Ceredigion	54.2	57	19.0	15.6	9	55	16.3
Conwy	85.6	65	23.3	15.8	9	46	14.0
Denbighshire	110.1	77	23.9	16.6	10	39	15.4
Flintshire	72.5	79	25.2	17.0	5	44	14.7
Gwynedd	..	47	21.0	14.4	10	42	15.4
Isle of Anglesey	13.9	55	21.5	16.0	8	42	15.2
Merthyr Tydfil	..	85	23.5	15.2	17	29	12.1
Monmouthshire	35.8	54	24.1	16.5	8	49	15.7
Neath Port Talbot	18.0	90	20.1	15.8	12	33	13.4
Newport	..	76	24.8	16.5	14	35	14.5
Pembrokeshire	33.8	69	20.4	15.6	6	44	15.1
Powys	..	57	20.6	14.8	6	50	16.1
Rhondda, Cynon, Taff	19.3	85	23.7	15.9	13	33	13.4
Swansea	41.5	92	21.5	15.9	10	42	16.6
Torfaen		74	24.2	16.4	10	37	16.8
The Vale of Glamorgan	50.0	72	22.1	16.2	11	44	15.6
Wrexham	66.4	85	24.2	16.7	12	40	13.6

1 Local authority provided and registered day nurseries only. A small number of places provided by facilities exempt from registration are excluded. Population data used are mid-1995 estimates.

2 Figures relate to pupils in maintained nursery and primary schools as a percentage of the three and four year old population.

3 Pupils in their last year of compulsory schooling as a percentage of the school population of the same age.

4 Figures relate to maintained schools only, hence they are not directly comparable with those in Table 4.6 which include independent schools and further education institutions.

5 Figure for United Kingdom relates to England and Wales average.

Source: Welsh Office

15.4 Housing

	Housing starts 1996[1] (numbers)		Stock of dwellings 1996 (thousands)	Local authority tenants: average weekly unrebated rent per dwelling (£) April 1996	Council Tax (£) April 1996[2]
	Private enterprise	Housing associations, local authorities etc			
United Kingdom	141,445	35,384	22,430	..	.
Wales	5,302	1,643	1,232	37.2	462
Blaenau Gwent	64	44	32	37.1	428
Bridgend	256	5	55	37.2	500
Caerphilly	586	133	69	39.2	467
Cardiff	572	319	123	42.5	425
Carmarthenshire	264	26	74	35.4	553
Ceredigion	70	32	30	38.6	510
Conwy	171	63	51	34.9	401
Denbighshire	144	69	38	31.8	459
Flintshire	236	128	58	34.2	500
Gwynedd	106	30	56	34.4	481
Isle of Anglesey	50	-	31	34.4	417
Merthyr Tydfil	42	50	25	35.7	495
Monmouthshire	265	49	34	41.1	409
Neath Port Talbot	205	71	61	35.5	543
Newport	259	48	57	40.7	391
Pembrokeshire	254	64	51	34.8	436
Powys	275	90	54	34.8	434
Rhondda, Cynon, Taff	412	49	101	36.3	495
Swansea	392	265	94	37.1	455
Torfaen	88	50	38	42.9	438
The Vale of Glamorgan	372	12	48	41.9	435
Wrexham	219	46	53	31.6	489

1 April to December 1996 only.
2 See Technical notes.

Source: Welsh Office

15.5 Labour market[1] statistics

| | Economically active 1995-96[2,3] (percentages) | In employment | | ILO unemployment rate 1995-96[3,5] (percentages) | Claimant unemployed January 1997 | | | Average gross weekly full-time earnings, all persons, April 1996 (£) |
		Total 1995-96[3,4] (thousands)	Manufacturing 1995-96[3,5] (percentages)		Total (thousands)	Of which females (percentages)	Of which long-term unemployed[6] (percentages)	
United Kingdom	62.8	26,172	19.1	8.6	1,907.8	23.3	36.2	350.3
Wales	57.5	1,192	21.6	8.8	96.4	21.9	32.7	313.1
Blaenau Gwent	56.2	30	41.2	..	2.7	19.0	35.5	255.1
Bridgend	64.9	58	29.5	10.9	3.4	21.9	28.1	..
Caerphilly	54.5	68	28.9	..	5.7	18.9	34.3	296.2
Cardiff	63.3	136	16.6	8.8	11.4	20.4	36.6	332.9
Carmarthenshire	53.0	65	18.2	9.3	5.4	23.8	32.1	303.7
Ceredigion	60.0	32	..	..	1.9	25.2	25.8	..
Conwy	56.8	48	..	..	3.8	23.9	35.7	..
Denbighshire	55.8	33	..	..	3.2	23.4	32.7	..
Flintshire	59.9	66	32.4	..	3.5	23.2	27.7	334.1
Gwynedd	57.0	49	11.8	10.9	5.5	24.1	33.6	275.5
Isle of Anglesey	52.9	24	..	..	3.2	22.7	39.9	..
Merthyr Tydfil	57.2	24	29.6	..	2.2	18.0	44.5	..
Monmouthshire	56.5	35	17.4	..	1.9	26.8	31.5	..
Neath Port Talbot	50.7	50	31.6	12.4	4.3	20.1	29.6	338.9
Newport	63.7	62	25.2	..	5.3	21.9	36.0	331.2
Pembrokeshire	58.3	43	16.9	14.0	5.3	22.8	31.2	..
Powys	62.3	56	21.3	..	2.3	30.0	25.0	275.8
Rhondda, Cynon, Taff	56.3	94	26.3	9.6	7.6	20.0	31.2	306.7
Swansea	51.9	81	16.8	12.4	7.7	20.5	31.3	298.6
Torfaen	61.3	42	27.3	..	2.9	22.3	30.2	323.0
The Vale of Glamorgan	56.3	51	12.8	..	3.8	22.4	29.1	326.5
Wrexham	54.0	46	31.2	..	3.4	23.2	29.1	..

1 See Technical notes to the Labour market chapter. In some cases sample sizes are too small to provide reliable estimates.
2 Economic activity rate of persons aged 16 or over. Data are from the Labour Force Survey.
3 Figures relate to the period March 1995 to February 1996.
4 Includes those on Government-supported employment and training schemes and unpaid family workers.
5 Not adjusted to take account of seasonal influences.
6 Persons who have been unemployed for 12 months or more as a percentage of all claimants.

Source: Office for National Statistics

16 Sub-regions of Scotland

New Councils in Scotland

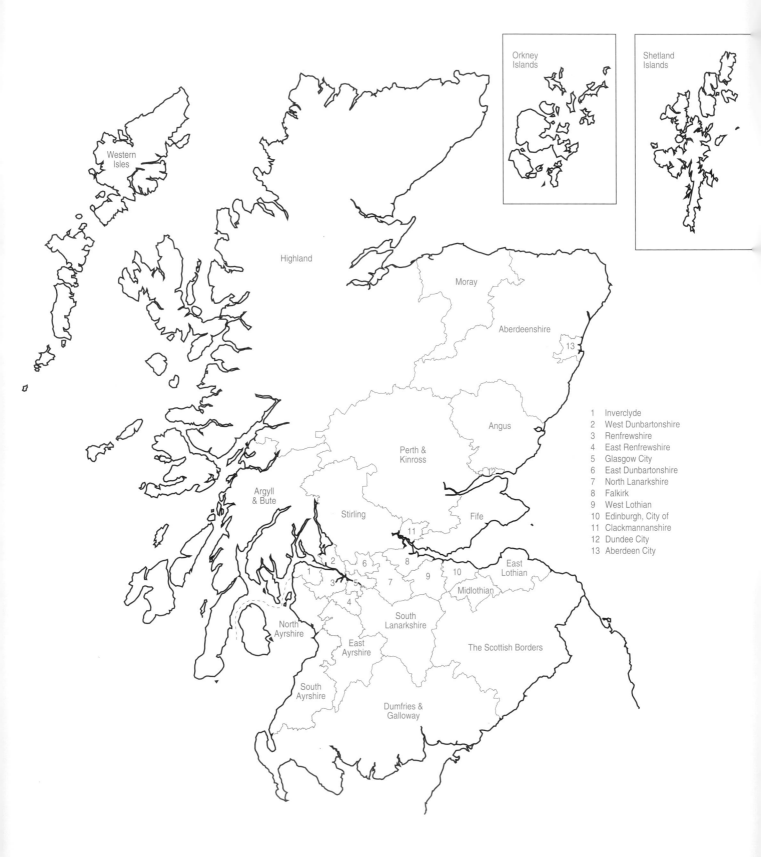

Orkney Islands

Shetland Islands

Western Isles

Highland

Moray

Aberdeenshire

13

Angus

Perth & Kinross

Argyll & Bute

Stirling

Fife

11

2   6   8
1   3   5   9   10   East Lothian

7   Midlothian

4   South Lanarkshire

North Ayrshire

East Ayrshire

The Scottish Borders

South Ayrshire

Dumfries & Galloway

1   Inverclyde
2   West Dunbartonshire
3   Renfrewshire
4   East Renfrewshire
5   Glasgow City
6   East Dunbartonshire
7   North Lanarkshire
8   Falkirk
9   West Lothian
10 Edinburgh, City of
11 Clackmannanshire
12 Dundee City
13 Aberdeen City

16.1 Area and population, 1995

	Area (sq km)	Persons per sq km	Population (thousands) Males	Females	Total	Total population percentage change 1981 1995	Total population percentage change 1991-1995	Total Period Fertility Rate (TPFR)[1]	Standardisd Mortality Ratio (UK=100) (SMR)[2]	Under	55-15	16 up to pension age[3]	Pension age[3] or over
United Kingdom	242,910	241	28,727	29,878	58,606	4.0	1.4	1.71	100	6.5	14.1	61.2	18.2
Scotland	78,133	66	2,489	2,647	5,137	-0.8	0.6	1.55	115	6.3	13.9	62.0	17.8
Aberdeen City	186	1,179	107	112	219	3.1	1.9	1.29	109	5.9	12.2	64.9	17.0
Aberdeenshire	6,318	36	113	114	227	19.9	4.7	1.68	102	6.7	15.5	62.7	15.2
Angus	2,181	51	55	57	112	5.8	2.9	1.67	110	6.2	13.8	60.7	19.3
Argyll and Bute	6,930	13	45	47	91	0.4	-2.5	1.77	108	5.7	13.8	59.7	20.8
Clackmannanshire	157	312	24	25	49	1.2	0.9	1.86	108	6.7	14.6	62.0	16.6
Dumfries and Galloway	6,439	23	72	76	148	1.6	0.1	1.75	101	6.0	13.7	59.2	21.1
Dundee City	65	2,318	72	79	151	-11.0	-3.3	1.53	112	6.1	13.1	61.1	19.7
East Ayrshire	1,252	98	59	64	123	-3.3	-0.9	1.67	117	6.5	14.4	60.9	18.2
East Dunbartonshire	172	647	54	57	111	1.3	0.5	1.64	97	5.9	14.4	63.5	16.2
East Lothian	678	129	43	45	88	8.6	3.2	1.76	108	6.5	13.5	60.3	19.6
East Renfrewshire	173	510	43	46	88	9.9	2.4	1.63	101	6.4	14.7	62.0	16.9
Edinburgh, City of	262	1,706	216	232	448	0.4	1.8	1.31	106	5.8	11.4	64.7	18.0
Falkirk	299	477	69	74	143	-1.6	-0.2	1.53	118	6.4	13.6	62.7	17.4
Fife	1,323	266	171	181	352	2.9	0.6	1.59	108	6.2	14.4	61.4	18.1
Glasgow City	175	3,533	295	324	618	-13.2	-2.1	1.48	138	6.5	13.2	62.0	18.3
Highland	25,784	8	102	106	208	6.9	2.1	1.74	111	6.3	14.9	60.8	18.0
Inverclyde	162	548	43	46	89	-12.3	-3.2	1.69	132	6.3	14.6	60.6	18.5
Midlothian	356	224	39	41	80	-4.4	-0.4	1.65	120	6.4	14.3	62.9	16.3
Moray	2,238	39	44	44	87	4.4	3.5	1.82	111	6.7	14.5	61.1	17.8
North Ayrshire	884	158	67	72	140	1.6	0.3	1.65	116	6.4	15.0	61.0	17.5
North Lanarkshire	474	690	159	168	327	-4.4	0.6	1.61	126	6.5	15.0	62.7	15.8
Orkney Islands	992	20	10	10	20	3.6	1.6	1.97	109	6.3	15.3	60.1	18.3
Perth and Kinross	5,311	25	64	69	133	9.0	4.1	1.57	106	5.8	13.8	59.6	20.8
Renfrewshire	261	682	86	92	178	-3.6	0.0	1.50	120	6.4	14.1	62.6	16.9
Scottish Borders, The	4,734	22	51	55	106	4.9	2.0	1.71	103	5.9	13.2	59.2	21.7
Shetland Islands	1,438	16	12	11	23	-12.4	2.4	1.85	106	7.3	15.9	61.8	15.0
South Ayrshire	1,202	95	55	60	115	1.2	0.9	1.44	112	5.6	13.7	59.9	20.8
South Lanarkshire	1,771	174	149	159	307	-0.8	1.0	1.52	124	6.4	14.6	62.6	16.4
Stirling	2,196	37	40	43	82	2.5	1.0	1.54	100	5.7	13.8	62.6	17.9
West Dunbartonshire	162	594	46	50	96	-9.0	-1.4	1.62	123	6.6	15.2	60.4	17.8
West Lothian	425	352	74	76	150	7.4	2.2	1.70	121	6.9	15.1	64.8	13.1
Western Isles	3,134	9	14	15	29	-7.9	-1.2	1.74	114	5.7	15.0	58.7	20.6

1 The Total Period Fertility Rate (TPFR) measures the average number of children which would be born if women were to experience the age-specific fertility rates of the year in question throughout their child-bearing life
2 Adjusted for the age structure of the population. See Technical notes to the Population chapter.
3 Pension age is 60 for women and 65 for men.

Source: Office for National Statistics; General Register Office for Scotland

16.2 Vital and social statistics

	Live births[1] per 1,000 population		Deaths[1] per 1,000 population		Perinatal mortality rate[2]	Infant mortality rate[3]	Percentage of live births outside marriage
	1991	1995	1991	1995	1993-1995	1993-1995	1995
United Kingdom	13.7	12.5	11.2	10.9	8.9	6.2	*34*
Scotland	13.1	11.7	12.0	11.8	8.2	6.3	*34*
Aberdeen City	12.5	10.8	10.8	10.9	9.0	5.4	*33*
Aberdeenshire	13.5	11.9	9.6	9.4	7.5	4.2	*22*
Angus	12.3	11.2	12.9	12.9	9.5	4.4	*30*
Argyll and Bute	13.0	11.1	12.7	13.8	10.6	5.6	*29*
Clackmannanshire	13.7	13.0	10.1	10.6	10.4	8.5	*38*
Dumfries and Galloway	12.1	11.1	13.1	11.9	8.3	8.4	*30*
Dundee City	12.9	11.5	12.4	12.4	8.2	7.2	*47*
East Ayrshire	13.9	11.9	11.9	11.9	8.1	4.2	*38*
East Dunbartonshire	12.4	11.3	8.7	8.6	11.1	5.4	*17*
East Lothian	13.1	12.4	12.6	12.3	7.5	6.2	*27*
East Renfrewshire	13.0	11.4	9.5	10.0	8.0	6.2	*16*
Edinburgh, City of	12.9	11.3	12.5	11.4	8.9	6.7	*32*
Falkirk	13.5	11.4	11.5	11.5	8.6	4.7	*33*
Fife	12.6	11.5	11.9	11.3	11.2	6.5	*33*
Glasgow City	14.3	12.6	14.4	14.3	8.2	8.1	*48*
Highland	13.0	11.6	11.5	11.7	14.3	5.8	*30*
Inverclyde	12.9	12.2	13.6	13.9	10.3	9.5	*40*
Midlothian	13.5	11.8	10.6	10.7	9.5	6.5	*32*
Moray	13.8	12.3	11.2	11.3	10.9	7.4	*23*
North Ayrshire	13.9	11.7	11.7	11.8	11.3	6.5	*37*
North Lanarkshire	13.6	12.3	11.1	11.1	4.2	6.6	*35*
Orkney Islands	12.1	11.6	11.8	11.9	8.4	4.2	*29*
Perth and Kinross	12.2	10.3	13.0	12.9	7.8	6.1	*30*
Renfrewshire	12.6	11.8	11.5	11.2	6.1	5.9	*37*
Scottish Borders, The	12.1	11.0	13.8	13.2	20.7	3.8	*28*
Shetland Islands	14.4	12.6	10.4	10.1	9.2	2.2	*30*
South Ayrshire	10.8	9.4	13.3	13.5	8.4	5.5	*32*
South Lanarkshire	13.3	11.4	10.5	11.2	12.3	5.9	*30*
Stirling	11.9	11.1	11.8	10.8	10.3	5.9	*32*
West Dunbartonshire	13.1	12.2	12.5	11.9	10.4	7.1	*40*
West Lothian	14.3	13.8	9.2	9.1	13.6	5.2	*32*
Western Isles	11.2	10.4	14.9	14.8	9.5	6.8	*20*

1 Births are on the basis of year of occurrence in England and Wales and year of registration in Scotland and Northern Ireland. Deaths relate to year of registration.
2 Still births and deaths of infants under 1 week of age per 1,000 live and still births, 3 year average.
3 Deaths of infants under 1 year of age per 1,000 live births, 3 year average.

Source: Office for National Statistics; General Register Office for Scotland

Regional Trends 32, © Crown copyright 1997

16.3 Education

	Day nursery places per 1,000 population aged under 5 years[1] Nov. 1994	Children under 5 in education[2] (percent-ages) Sept. 1995	Pupil/teacher ratio 1995/96 (numbers)		Pupils in last year of compulsory schooling[3] 1994/95 with	
			Primary schools	Secondary schools	No graded results	5 or more Grades 1-3 SCE Standard Grade (or equivalent)
United Kingdom	..	..	22.7	16.1	7.9	44.4
Scotland	59	36	19.5	12.9	6.4	51.3
Aberdeen City	79	43	19.7	12.9	..	54.9
Aberdeenshire	25	33	18.7	13.9	7.6	58.6
Angus	34	33	18.7	12.8	4.3	54.3
Argyll and Bute	49	8	17.3	12.6	3.8	54.1
Clackmannanshire	42	52	21.0	13.3	..	60.7
Dumfries and Galloway	8	42	18.8	11.9	5.2	59.1
Dundee City	112	58	18.7	11.8	4.6	46.9
East Ayrshire	26	47	20.8	12.9	14.1	43.8
East Dunbartonshire	50	6	22.1	13.9	..	65.9
East Lothian	33	54	20.0	13.0	19.6	41.4
East Renfrewshire	79	23	22.4	13.9	..	76.5
Edinburgh, City of	74	48	20.4	12.8	2.0	56.3
Falkirk	61	44	21.8	13.6	9.1	43.6
Fife	20	49	19.0	13.4	8.7	50.9
Glasgow City	92	53	19.0	12.2	15.3	39.1
Highland	33	16	17.3	12.0	3.5	56.4
Inverclyde	116	22	20.7	13.1	0.6	56.6
Midlothian	51	54	19.9	13.3	3.2	55.7
Moray	17	31	18.7	11.8	9.7	52.7
North Ayrshire	74	13	20.8	13.4	14.9	43.5
North Lanarkshire	64	23	20.2	13.3	7.1	42.3
Orkney Islands	6	40	15.2	10.9	3.1	71.4
Perth and Kinross	68	36	18.2	12.2	9.8	54.6
Renfrewshire	73	33	21.7	13.4	1.9	53.2
Scottish Borders, The	26	22	18.0	12.2	..	63.9
Shetland Islands	14	43	12.8	8.5	10.9	63.0
South Ayrshire	70	22	20.4	13.4	..	61.3
South Lanarkshire	69	15	20.7	13.7	6.5	49.1
Stirling	75	43	19.8	13.1	0.4	61.1
West Dunbartonshire	68	52	20.6	13.3	1.7	43.6
West Lothian	33	52	19.9	13.0	11.4	44.1
Western Isles	35	..	13.3	9.5	1.5	63.3

1 Social Work Provision only (local authority and registered); includes Day Nurseries, Children's Centres, Family Centres and Private Nursery Schools. Population data used mid-1994 estimates.
2 Figures relate to pupils in maintained nursery schools and departments only as a percentage of the three and four year old population.
3 Pupils in their last year of compulsory schooling as a percentage of the school population of the same age.

Source: The Scottish Office Home Department; The Scottish Office Education and Industry Department

16.4 Housing and households

	Housing starts 1995 (numbers)		Stock of dwellings 1995 (thousands)	Households 1995 (thousands)	Local authority tenants: average weekly unrebated rent per dwelling (£) April 1996	Council Tax (£) September 1996[1]
	Private enterprise	Housing associations, local authorities etc				
United Kingdom	141,445	35,384	24,430	23,922.4	..	.
Scotland	16,926	5,881	2,232	2,132.4	31.2	708
Aberdeen City	770	165	100	97.0	25.7	648
Aberdeenshire	1,065	286	92	87.7	28.9	591
Angus	269	106	48	45.8	23.2	659
Argyll and Bute	249	148	43	37.5	33.9	675
Clackmannanshire	146	64	21	19.8	27.2	692
Dumfries and Galloway	319	176	66	61.7	32.1	590
Dundee City	143	257	72	67.9	35.0	801
East Ayrshire	245	131	51	50.4	25.0	714
East Dunbartonshire	186	0	42	40.9	29.8	668
East Lothian	392	75	38	36.3	26.4	670
East Renfrewshire	347	39	34	33.7	26.9	621
Edinburgh, City of	1,271	491	206	198.6	40.6	812
Falkirk	561	64	61	58.9	26.2	624
Fife	1,056	421	152	144.5	28.5	694
Glasgow City	1,108	1,026	286	276.6	37.3	805
Highland	843	268	95	85.1	35.9	659
Inverclyde	242	86	39	36.9	31.2	762
Midlothian	200	126	32	30.7	22.3	718
Moray	496	122	37	34.3	27.3	608
North Ayrshire	427	223	60	57.3	28.9	660
North Lanarkshire	1,597	233	130	126.9	29.4	758
Orkney Islands	0	40	9	8.2	33.0	480
Perth and Kinross	616	322	59	54.5	27.1	699
Renfrewshire	944	163	77	73.8	28.9	738
Scottish Borders, The	209	104	49	45.6	28.1	558
Shetland Islands	108	40	10	9.0	34.3	443
South Ayrshire	503	75	49	47.1	30.6	731
South Lanarkshire	886	249	124	122.5	31.5	724
Stirling	432	126	34	32.5	32.8	678
West Dunbartonshire	337	180	42	39.8	32.3	812
West Lothian	865	61	61	59.4	26.5	678
Western Isles	94	14	13	11.5	35.9	550

1 See Technical notes.

Source: The Scottish Office Development Department

16.5 Labour market statistics[1]

	Claimant unemployed January 1997			Average gross weekly full-time earnings, all persons, April 1996 (£)
	Total (thousands)	Of which females (percentages)	Of which long-term unemployed[2] (percentages)	
United Kingdom	1,907.8	23.3	36.2	350.3
Scotland	185.6	22.1	30.2	324.9
Aberdeen City	4.9	21.5	25.4	397.6
Aberdeenshire	4.5	27.1	20.6	307.2
Angus	3.6	28.4	28.3	292.6
Argyll and Bute	3.4	28.9	30.3	287.6
Clackmannanshire	1.9	20.6	31.6	..
Dumfries and Galloway	5.2	25.7	30.6	282.9
Dundee City	7.7	20.7	36.8	307.3
East Ayrshire	5.7	20.9	33.8	287.5
East Dunbartonshire	2.5	22.8	28.0	..
East Lothian	2.3	20.5	24.5	..
East Renfrewshire	1.8	24.4	26.5	..
Edinburgh, City of	14.9	22.4	30.8	344.3
Falkirk	5.1	21.0	27.0	318.7
Fife	13.5	23.0	31.2	307.1
Glasgow City	31.6	19.7	36.4	323.4
Highland	9.6	26.2	26.2	285.8
Inverclyde	2.9	18.9	22.6	324.1
Midlothian	1.9	18.3	24.9	..
Moray	2.7	25.9	23.4	284.7
North Ayrshire	6.1	22.5	26.6	320.8
North Lanarkshire	12.6	10.0	29.0	331.1
Orkney Islands	-	28.5	26.9	..
Perth and Kinross	3.5	24.6	26.1	..
Renfrewshire	6.6	20.9	32.2	334.8
Scottish Borders, The	2.2	25.9	18.3	..
Shetland Islands	-	22.5	16.4	..
South Ayrshire	4.5	25.3	29.1	339.1
South Lanarkshire	10.3	20.6	32.1	321.1
Stirling	2.5	24.4	25.7	304.7
West Dunbartonshire	4.9	18.6	33.1	..
West Lothian	4.4	21.9	19.4	318.1
Western Isles	1.4	19.7	30.4	..

1 See Technical notes to the Labour market chapter. In some cases sample sizes are too small to provide reliable estimates.
2 Persons who have been unemployed for 12 months or more as a percentage of all claimants.

Source: Office for National Statistics

17 Sub-regions of Northern Ireland

Boards in Northern Ireland

Health and Social Services Boards

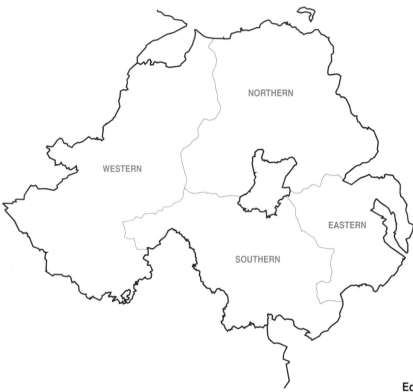

Education and Library Boards

17.1 Area and population: by Board[1] and district, 1995

	Area (sq km)	Persons per sq km	Population (thousands)			Total population percentage change 1981-1995	Total Period Fertility Rate (TPFR)[2]	Standardisd Mortality Ratio (UK=100) (SMR)[3]	Percentage of population aged			
			Males	Females	Total				Under 5	5-15	16 up to pension age[4]	Pension age[4] or over
United Kingdom	242,910	241	28,727	29,878	58,606	4.0	1.71	100	6.5	14.1	61.2	18.2
Northern Ireland	13,576	121	805	844	1,649	7.2	1.92	108	7.7	17.6	59.7	15.0
Eastern	1,751	381	320	347	668	4.5	1.73	..	7.3	16.3	59.6	16.8
Ards	380	175	..	..	67	15.4	..	..	..	..	..	..
Belfast	110	2,707	..	..	297	5.9	..	..	..	..	..	..
Castlereagh	85	746	..	..	63	4.4	..	..	..	..	..	..
Down	649	94	..	..	61	13.2	..	..	..	..	..	..
Lisburn	447	237	..	..	106	24.9	..	..	..	..	..	..
North Down	81	915	..	..	74	10.9	..	..	..	..	..	..
Northern	4,093	100	202	209	411	9.6	1.85	..	7.3	17.1	61.0	14.6
Antrim	421	115	..	..	49	5.7	..	..	..	..	..	..
Ballymena	630	91	..	..	58	4.9	..	..	..	..	..	..
Ballymoney	416	59	..	..	25	7.4	..	..	..	..	..	..
Carrickfergus	81	432	..	..	35	22.0	..	..	..	..	..	..
Coleraine	486	111	..	..	54	15.8	..	..	..	..	..	..
Cookstown	514	61	..	..	31	10.6	..	..	..	..	..	..
Larne	336	89	..	..	30	3.4	..	..	..	..	..	..
Magherafelt	564	66	..	..	37	13.5	..	..	..	..	..	..
Moyle	494	30	..	..	15	2.8	..	..	..	..	..	..
Newtownabbey	151	522	..	..	79	8.9	..	..	..	..	..	..
Southern	3,075	97	148	151	299	9.2	2.22	..	8.3	19.0	59.0	13.7
Armagh	671	78	..	..	53	6.7	..	..	..	..	..	..
Banbridge	451	83	..	..	37	24.3	..	..	..	..	..	..
Craigavon	282	277	..	..	78	6.5	..	..	..	..	..	..
Dungannon	772	61	..	..	47	6.8	..	..	..	..	..	..
Newry and Mourne	898	94	..	..	84	8.8	..	..	..	..	..	..
Western	4,658	58	135	137	271	8.7	2.21	..	8.4	20.4	58.8	12.4
Derry	1,600	32	..	..	55	5.4	..	..	..	..	..	..
Fermanagh	586	53	..	..	31	13.6	..	..	..	..	..	..
Limavady	381	270	..	..	103	14.5	..	..	..	..	..	..
Ömagh	1,130	42	..	..	47	5.2	..	..	..	..	..	..
Strabane	862	42	..	..	36	-0.3	..	..	..	..	..	..

1 Health and Social Services Board areas.
2 The Total Period Fertility Rate (TPFR) measures the average number of children which would be born if women were to experience the age-specific fertility rates of the year in question throughout their child-bearing life.
3 Adjusted for the age structure of the population. See Technical notes to the Population chapter.
4 Pension age is 60 for women and 65 for men.

Source: Northern Ireland Statistics and Research Agency; Office for National Statistics

17.2 Vital and social statistics: by Board[1]

	Live births[2] per 1,000 population		Deaths[2] per 1,000 population		Perinatal mortality rate[3]	Infant mortality rate[4]	Percentage of live births outside marriage	Children looked after by LAs per 1,000 pop. aged under 18
	1991	1995	1991	1995	1993-1995	1993-1995	1995	1995[5]
United Kingdom	13.7	12.5	11.2	10.9	8.9	6.2	34	..
Northern Ireland	16.5	14.5	9.4	9.3	9.6	6.8	23	4.6
Eastern	15.9	13.4	10.4	10.2	10.1	7.4	28	5.4
Northern	15.2	14.0	8.4	8.8	9.2	6.0	21	4.6
Southern	18.2	15.9	8.9	8.6	9.1	6.1	15	3.6
Western	17.9	16.3	8.7	8.5	9.7	7.0	24	4.0

1 Health and Social Services Board Areas.
2 Births are on the basis of year of occurrence in England and Wales and year of registration in Scotland and Northern Ireland. Deaths relate to year of registration.
3 Still births and deaths of infants under 1 week of age per 1,000 live and still births, 3 year average.
4 Deaths of infants under 1 year of age per 1,000 live births, 3 year average.
5 As at 31 March. Data relate to children in care excluding children home on trial. Legislation in Northern Ireland relating to children in care is different from that in the rest of the United Kingdom. Figures are not directly comparable with similar data in the England and Wales chapters.

Source: Northern Ireland Statistics and Research Agency; Department of Health and Social Services, Northern Ireland

17.3 Education: by Board[1]

	Day nursery places per 1,000 population aged under 5 years[2] March 1995	Pupil/teacher ratio 1995/96 (numbers)		Pupils in last year of compulsory schooling[3] 1994/95 with	
		Primary schools	Secondary schools	No graded results	5 or more A*-Cs at GCSE
United Kingdom	..	22.7	16.1	*7.9*	*44.4*
Northern Ireland	24.7	20.4	14.7	*4.4*	*51.3*
Belfast	..	19.5	14.6	*6.8*	*54.6*
South Eastern[4]	36.2	21.0	14.7	*4.7*	*50.1*
Southern	17.0	20.1	15.0	*3.3*	*50.1*
North Eastern	22.3	21.0	14.5		*48.8*
Western	11.5	20.5	14.7	*3.4*	*52.7*

1 Education and Library Boards, except for day nursery information which refers to Health and Social Services Board Areas.
2 Local authority provided and registered day nurseries only. A small number of places provided by facilities exempt from registration are excluded. Population data used are mid-1994 estimates.
3 Pupils in their last year of compulsory schooling as a percentage of the school population of the same age.
4 South Eastern figure for day nursery places includes Belfast.

Source: Department of Health and Social Services, Northern Ireland; Department of Education, Northern Ireland

17.4 Labour market statistics[1]: by district

	Economically active Spring 1996[2] (percentages)	Claimant unemployed January 1997		
		Total (thousands)	Of which females (percentages)	Of which long-term unemployed[3] (percentages)
United Kingdom	*62.4*	1,907.8	*23.3*	*36.2*
Northern Ireland	*59.0*	70.8	*20.9*	*54.3*
Antrim	*67.2*	1.4	*23.6*	*44.5*
Ards	*65.0*	2.1	*24.3*	*47.3*
Armagh	*63.4*	2.1	*23.2*	*56.6*
Ballymena	*58.0*	1.9	*25.0*	*50.7*
Ballymoney	*58.6*	1.1	*16.8*	*55.9*
Banbridge	*65.7*	0.9	*24.5*	*51.2*
Belfast	*52.7*	16.3	*19.0*	*53.9*
Carrickfergus	*63.2*	1.2	*24.1*	*48.2*
Castlereagh	*66.2*	1.8	*25.0*	*47.2*
Coleraine	*52.4*	2.5	*23.1*	*52.5*
Cookstown	*47.0*	1.5	*20.9*	*57.5*
Craigavon	*60.4*	2.5	*20.8*	*52.9*
Derry	*58.2*	6.2	*17.8*	*57.8*
Down	*67.5*	2.5	*26.0*	*48.0*
Dungannon	*61.0*	2.2	*20.7*	*59.6*
Fermanagh	*66.0*	2.8	*20.0*	*61.0*
Larne	*60.1*	1.1	*22.6*	*42.6*
Limavady	*64.3*	1.7	*20.1*	*56.0*
Lisburn	*60.0*	3.3	*23.2*	*50.9*
Magherafelt	*55.4*	1.5	*20.6*	*61.1*
Moyle	*63.5*	0.9	*17.6*	*59.0*
Newry and Mourne	*55.6*	4.5	*17.9*	*62.9*
Newtownabbey	*64.0*	2.3	*24.5*	*46.4*
North Down	*56.5*	2.2	*30.0*	*42.2*
Omagh	*60.2*	2.4	*19.4*	*61.6*
Strabane	*44.8*	2.1	*15.0*	*62.5*

1 See Technical notes to the Labour market chapter.
2 Economic activity rate of persons aged 16 or over. Data are from the Labour Force Survey.
3 Persons who have been unemployed for 12 months or more as a percentage of all claimants.

Source: Office for National Statistics; Department of Economic Development, Northern Ireland

Technical notes

REGIONAL CLASSIFICATION

Government Office Regions within England

Most of the statistics in *Regional Trends* are on the basis of the Government Office Regions (GORs) of England, together with Wales Scotland and Northern Ireland. Although Merseyside has a Government Office of its own, for statistical purposes it has not been adopted as a region in its own right. Wherever possible, however, figures for the two components of the North West and Merseyside region are given separately. Maps of the GORs are on pages 11 and 165.

Standard Statistical Regions

Prior to the introduction of the GORs, regional statistics were presented on the basis of the Standard Statistical Regions (SSRs) of the United Kingdom. A few tables in *Regional Trends 32* continue to be presented on this classification. The SSRs are shown in a map on page 214 and their relationship to the GORs is given in a table on page 10.

Sub-regions of England

The 46 counties and 366 districts of England in place prior to the current local government reorganisation are listed in the sub-regional statistics in Chapter 14. The relationship of the counties to the Government Office Regions is shown in the map on page 165. Also listed in Chapter 14 is the new local government structure which came into place on 1 April 1996.

Unitary Authorities of Wales

On 1 April 1996 the 8 counties and 37 districts of Wales were replaced by 22 Unitary Authorities. A map is given on page 198.

New Councils of Scotland

On 1 April 1996, the 10 LA regions and 56 districts of Scotland were replaced by 32 Unitary councils. A map is given on page 204.

Northern Ireland

The 26 districts of Northern Ireland are listed in Chapter 17. For some topics, they have been grouped into either the five Education and Library Boards or the four Health and Social Services Boards. For the claimant unemployment rates in Chart 5.22 the travel-to-work areas are used. The districts comprising the Education and Library Boards are as follows:

Board	Districts
Belfast	Belfast
South Eastern	Ards, Castlereagh, Down, Lisburn, North Down.
Southern	Armagh,Banbridge, Cookstown, Craigavon, Dungannon, Newry and Mourne.
North Eastern	Antrim, Ballymena, Ballymoney, Carrickfergus, Coleraine, Larne, Magherafelt, Moyle, Newtownabbey.
Western	Derry, Fermanagh, Limavady, Omagh, Strabane.

Health and Social Services Boards are as follows:

Northern	as North Eastern Education and Library Board but including Cookstown.
Eastern	as South Eastern Education and Library Board but including Belfast.
Southern	as Southern Education and Library Board but excluding Cookstown.
Western	as Western Education and Library Board.

Maps of the Boards are on page 210.

Other Regional Classifications

Maps of non-standard regions used in *Regional Trends* are shown on pages 214 and 215.

The UK Continental Shelf is treated as a separate region in Tables 12.1, 12.3 and 12.10 (see Technical notes to the Regional accounts chapter).

Standard Statistical Regions

ENGLAND

—— SSR boundary

Environment Agency regions

ENGLAND and WALES

—— Environment Agency region boundary

Regional Health Authority areas
(upto 31 March 1994)

ENGLAND

—— Health Authority boundary

Regional Health Authority areas
(from 1 April 1994 to 31 March 1996)

ENGLAND

—— Health Authority boundary

Department of Trade and Industry regions

Tourist Board regions

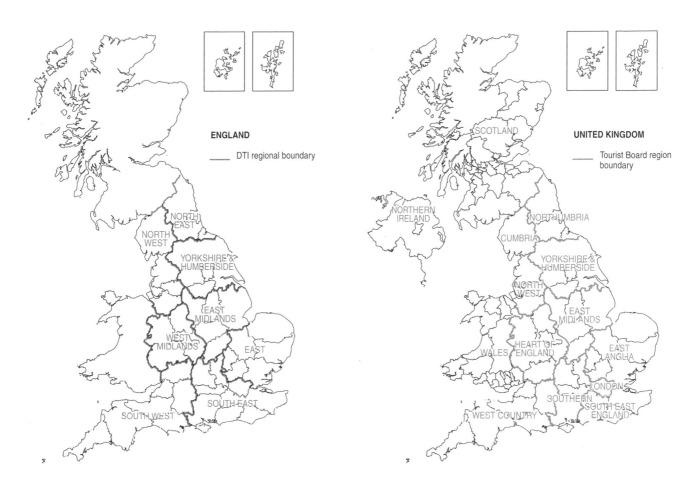

ENGLAND

——— DTI regional boundary

UNITED KINGDOM

——— Tourist Board region boundary

**CHAPTER 1:
REGIONAL PROFILES**

The Regional Profiles do not highlight much information from Chapter 7: Health due to the boundary differences between the GORs and the Regional Health Authority areas.

**CHAPTER 2:
EUROPEAN UNION
REGIONAL STATISTICS**
Table 2.3 Economic statistics

The data appearing in this section are based on information in the statistical yearbook *Regions* produced by EUROSTAT.

Employment statistics are derived from the annual Community Labour Force Survey (CLFS), which closely resembles national Labour Force Surveys. Since the survey is conducted on a sample basis, results relating to small regions should be treated with caution. The main statistical objectives of the CLFS are to divide the population of working age into three groups: persons in employment, unemployed persons and inactive persons (those not classified as employed or unemployed).

The above groups are used to derive the following measures: activity rates - the labour force as a percentage of the population of working age; employment/population ratios - persons in employment as a percentage of the population of working age; unemployment rates - unemployed persons as a percentage of the labour force.

The definitions of employment and unemployment used in the CLFS closely follow those adopted by the 13th International Conference of Labour Statisticians (ILO) and are as follows (further detail is available in the EUROSTAT publication *Labour Force Survey, Methods and Definitions*, 1992):

Employment: the employed comprise all persons above a specified age who during a specified brief period either one week or one day were in the following categories:
a) paid employment - at work or with a job but not at work ie temporarily absent but in receipt of a wage or salary;
b) self-employment - at work ie persons who during the reference period performed some work for profit or family gain, in cash or kind, or with an enterprise but not at work ie temporarily absent. (An 'enterprise' may be a business enterprise, a farm or a service undertaking.)

Unemployment: the unemployed comprise all persons above a specified age who, during the reference period, were:

a) without work - ie were not in paid employment or self-employment;

b) currently available for work - ie were available for paid employment or self-employment during the reference period;

c) seeking work - ie had taken specific steps in a specified recent period to seek paid employment or self-employment.

The type of employment is classified by *Economic activity* in accordance with the General Classification of Economic Activities in the European Communities (NACE): Agriculture (NACE code O), Industry (NACE codes 1 to 5) and Services (NACE codes 6 to 9).

Long-term unemployment: persons who have been unemployed for 12 or more consecutive months.

Table 2.3 Economic statistics and Chart 2.5 Gross domestic product

Purchasing Power Standard: a unit of measurement which expresses an identical volume of goods and services for each country taking account of differences in price levels.

Table 2.4 Agricultural statistics

Agricultural holdings/enterprise economic value: the 'gross margin' of an agricultural enterprise is defined as the monetary value of gross production from which corresponding specific costs are deducted. The 'Standard Gross Margin' (SGM) is the value of gross margin corresponding to the average situation in a given region for each agricultural characteristic eg crop production, livestock production. 'Gross production' is the sum of the value of the principal product(s) and of any secondary product(s). The values are calculated by multiplying production per unit (less any losses) by the farm-gate price, excluding VAT. Gross production also includes subsidies linked to products, to area and/or to livestock.

Basic data are collected in Member States from farm accounts, specific surveys or compiled from appropriate calculations for a reference period which covers three successive years or agricultural production years. The reference period is the same for all Member States. SGMs are first calculated in Member States national currencies and then converted into European currency units (ECUs) using the average exchange rates for the reference period.

CHAPTER 3: POPULATION AND HOUSEHOLDS

Tables 3.1, 3.3, 3.12 and 3.13 and Charts 3.2, 3.4-3.6 Resident population

The estimated population of an area includes all those usually resident in the area, whatever their nationality. HM Forces stationed outside the United Kingdom are excluded but foreign forces stationed here are included. Students are taken to be resident at their term-time address.

The population estimates for mid-1995 are based on the 1991 Census results (with allowance for Census under-enumeration) and take account of births, deaths and migration between 1991 and mid-1995. In Table 3.1 and Chart 3.2 annual growth rates are shown as geometric averages.

Table 3.7 Live births, deaths and natural increase in population

Numbers shown relate to calendar years. Crude birth/death rates and natural increase are affected by the age and gender structure of the population. For example, for any given levels of fertility and mortality, a population with a relatively high proportion of persons in the younger age-groups will have a higher crude birth-rate and a lower crude death-rate, and consequently a higher rate of natural increase, than a population with a higher proportion of elderly people.

Table 3.9 Death rates and standardised mortality ratios

The standardised mortality ratio (SMR) compares overall mortality in a region with that for the UK. The ratio expresses the number of deaths in a region as a percentage of the hypothetical number that would have occurred if the region's population had experienced the sex/age-specific rates of the UK in that year.

Table 3.10 Inter-regional movements

Estimates for internal population movements are counts of the transfers of NHS doctors' patients between Family Health Services Authorities (FHSAs) in England and Wales and Area Health Boards (AHBs) in Scotland and Northern Ireland. These transfers are recorded at the NHS Central Registers (NHSCRs) in Southport and Edinburgh and at the Central Services Agency in Belfast. The figures shown here have been adjusted to take account of differences in recorded cross-border flows between England and Wales, Scotland, and Northern Ireland.

These figures provide a detailed indicator of population movement within the United Kingdom. However, they should not be regarded as a perfect measure of migration as there is variation in the delay between a person moving and registering with a new doctor. Additionally, some moves may not result in a re-registration, ie individuals may migrate again before registering with a doctor. Conversely, there may be others who move and re-register several times in a year.

The NHSCR at Southport was computerised in 1990. Before 1990, the time lag was assumed to be three months between moving and the processing of data. (It was estimated that processing at NHSCR took two months.) Since computerisation, estimates of internal migration derived from the NHSCR are based on date of acceptance of the new patient by the FHSA (not previously available), and a one month time lag assumed.

Table 3.11 Migration

The first part of Table 3.11 shows a historical perspective for the yearly migrant data shown in Table 3.10. The international migration data, in the second part of the table, are derived from the International Passenger Survey (IPS), a continuous voluntary sample survey covering the principal air, sea and tunnel routes between the United Kingdom and overseas. Routes between the United Kingdom and the Irish Republic, and those between the Channel Islands, Isle of Man and the rest of the world are excluded. However, prior to 1988 data for the South East (GOR) include migration via the UK mainland between the Channel Islands and the Isle of Man and the rest of the world. Short-term visitors are not included as migrants in the IPS. However, some are granted extension of stay for a year or more, for example, persons applying for asylum after entering the United Kingdom. These are termed 'visitor switchers' and the effect of this group on the inflow into the country is partly balanced by visitor switchers leaving. IPS results shown in Table 3.11 appear to indicate a net inflow of 54 thousand to the United Kingdom in 1995. However if allowance is made for visitor switchers and movements to and from the Irish Republic, there was a net civilian inward migration of about 109 thousand.

The proportion of passengers sampled in the IPS varies between 0.1 and 5 per cent according to route and time of year. In view of the small number of migrants in the sample, it should be noted that the estimates of migration, in particular the differences between inflow and outflow, are subject to large sampling errors. As a rough guide, the standard error for an estimate of one thousand migrants is around 40 per cent, whilst that for an estimate of 40 thousand migrants reduces to about 10 per cent, but on occasions these standard errors can be higher. However, the structure of the sample is such that estimates based on the sampling of passengers on certain routes have much larger standard errors associated with them.

For demographic purposes, a migrant into the UK is defined as a person who has resided abroad for a year or more and states the intention to stay in the UK for a year or more, and vice versa for a migrant from the UK. Migrants, defined in this way were asked an additional group of questions which form the basis of these statistics.

Table 3.13 Area classification

An area classification has been produced after each of the 1971, 1981 and 1991 Censuses. It provides a simple indicator of the characteristics of areas, and of the similarity between areas. The classification brings areas into 'families', 'groups' and 'clusters' by measuring similarities in a range of variables covering demographic structure, household composition, housing, socio-economic character and employment.

Table 3.13 presents the proportion of the population within each region in each of the six 'family' types: Rural areas; Prospering areas characterised by low unemployment, high availability of cars, high proportions of people with higher educational qualifications and high proportions of people in Social Classes I and II; Maturer areas characterised by above average proportions of pensioners and indications of relative prosperity; Urban centres which share characteristics such as above average proportions of households without cars and people who travel to work by public transport; Mining and Industrial areas characterised by a tradition of mining and industry, by de-industrialisation, and by above national averages in 'deprivation' variables such as limiting long-term illness; and finally Inner London as a separate area because the dominant characteristics of the Inner London boroughs (well above average proportions of people in ethnic minority groups, one-person households, and people who travel to work by public transport) are not matched elsewhere.

Table 3.14 Social class

Based on the Labour Force Survey (see Technical notes to the Labour market chapter), the table gives percentages of economically active people aged 16 or over in each social class based on occupations. The method used is designed to group together as far as possible people with similar levels of occupational skills. The basis of the groupings is given in Volume 3, *Standard Occupational Classification*, HMSO, 1991.

The six occupational social classes in the classification are as follows:

I		Professional occupations (including doctors, solicitors, chemists, university professors and clergymen)
II		Managerial and technical occupations (including school teachers, computer programmers, personnel managers, nurses, actors and laboratory technicians)
III		Skilled occupations
	(N)	Non-manual (including typists, clerical workers, photographers, sales representatives and shop assistants)
	(M)	Manual (including cooks, bus drivers, railway guards, plasterers, bricklayers, hairdressers and carpenters)
IV		Partly skilled occupations (including bar staff, waitresses, gardeners and caretakers)
V		Unskilled occupations (including refuse collectors, messengers, lift attendants, cleaners and labourers).

For those in employment in the reference week of the survey, the occupation was that of their main job, and for the unemployed (on the ILO definition), their last occupation if they had done any paid work in the previous eight years.

Table 3.15 Ethnic group

The information on the ethnic group of each respondent to the Labour Force Survey is collected using the categories first used in the 1991 Census. Those classified as 'mixed/other' includes Chinese, some other Asians and those of mixed origin.

Tables 3.19 and 3.20 Household projections

The household projections are trend-based; they illustrate what would happen if past trends in household formation were to continue into the future. They are therefore not policy-based forecasts of what is expected to happen, but provide a starting point for policy decisions. The projections are heavily dependent on the assumptions involved, particularly international and internal migration, the marital status projections and the continuation of past trends in household formation.

CHAPTER 4: EDUCATION AND TRAINING

School classifications

Schools are generally classified according to the ages for which they cater, or the type of education they provide. Nursery education is for children below compulsory school age. Pupils in England and Wales generally undertake 6 of their 11 years of compulsory education in primary schools and 5 in secondary. Primary schools generally consist of infants' schools (for children up to age 7) and junior schools (for children age 7-11). In scotland, pupils undertake 7 years of compulsory education in primary and 4 in secondary. In Northern Ireland, pupils undertake 7 years of compulsory education at primary school and 5 at secondary. These differences in the length of time spent in the different stages of education need to be taken into account when making comparisons between countries. Special schools provide education for children with special educational needs who cannot be educated satisfactorily in an ordinary school.

United Kingdom educational establishments are administered and financed in one of three ways:

a. by local education authorities (LEAs), which form part of the structure of local government, partly through funds provided by central government;

b. by governing bodies which have a substantial degree of autonomy from public authorities but which receive grants from centrally financed funding bodies and from central government sources directly;

c. by the private sector, including individuals, companies and charitable institutions.

Types of school establishment falling within the categories typically have different names in England, Wales, Scotland and Northern Ireland. Therefore, to avoid confusion, standardised terms are used for the purposes of United Kingdom statistics:

a. Public sector or maintained - LEA maintained and grant-maintained (England and Wales)

- education authority, grant aided and self-governing (Scotland)

- controlled, controlled integrated, maintained, voluntary and grant-maintained integrated (Northern Ireland)

b. Non-maintained - independent including City Technology Colleges(England)

Academic years

Count dates for the various surveys of educational institutions on which most of the statistics are based differ between countries. The information collected on a particular date is taken as a proxy for the academic year as a whole.

Table 4.1 Pupils and teachers: by type of school

In England and Wales qualified teachers only are included for public sector schools. In Scotland and Northern Ireland all teachers employed in schools, other than in independent schools, are required to be qualified.

The pupil-teacher ratio in a school is the ratio of all pupils on the register to all teachers employed on the day of an annual count. Part-time teachers and part-time pupils are included on a full-time equivalent basis. The difference in the age at which pupils transfer from primary to secondary school affects the comparison of pupil-teacher ratios between Scotland and the rest of the United Kingdom.

Tables 4.6 and 4.7
Examination achievements

The main examination for pupils at the minimum school-leaving age in England, Wales and Northern Ireland is the General Certificate of Secondary Education (GCSE) - Scottish Certificate of Education (SCE) S (Standard) Grade in Scotland. The GCSE is awarded in eight grades, A* to G, while the SCE S Grade is awarded in seven levels, 1 to 7.

In Scotland, Standard courses begin in the third year and continue to the end of the fourth year. Each subject has a number of elements, some of which are internally assessed in school. The award for the subject as a whole is given on a 7 point scale at three levels: Credit (1 and 2), General (3 and 4) and Foundation (5 and 6). An award of 7 means that the course has been completed. Pupils who do not complete the course or do not sit all parts of the examination get 'no award'.

GCSE and equivalent figures relate to achievements by 16 year olds (year S4 in Scotland) at the end of the academic year and are shown as percentages of 16 year olds in school (year S4 in Scotland). That is, the achievements of pupils by the end of their last year of compulsory schooling: some may have been passed a year earlier.

GCE A levels are usually taken after a further two years of post-compulsory education, passes being graded from A to E. The SCE H (Higher) Grade requires only one year of post-compulsory study and for the more able candidates the range of subjects taken may be as wide as at S Grade.

GCE A level and equivalent figures for pupils aged between 17 and 19 at the end of the school year are shown as a percentage of the 18 year old population. This age spread in the examination result figures takes account of those pupils sitting examinations a year early or resitting them. Scottish Higher figures are based on the 17 year old population as Highers are normally taken one year earlier (in Year S5) than A levels, although they can resit them or take additional subjects in year S6. However the data for Scotland relate only to year S5 pupils' examination results. Figures for Northern Ireland are not available by gender.

Average GCE A/AS level points scores are shown in Table 4.6. Points scores are determined by totalling pupils' individual GCE A/AS results: GCE A-level grades A-E count as 10 to 2 points respectively; and GCE AS grades A-E count as 5 to 1 respectively.

In Wales, at below GCSE standard, the Certificate of Education examination is also available and is widely used by schools. Many pupils take Welsh as a first language at GCSE. In all countries pupils may sit non GCE/GCSE examinations such as BTEC (SCOTVEC in Scotland), City and Guilds, RSA and Pitman. A proportion of pupils who are recorded as achieving no GCSE, AS or A level qualification will have passed in one or more of these other examinations.

In Table 4.7 Mathematics figures exclude computing science (England) and computer studies and statistics (Wales) while 'Any science' in England and Wales includes double award, single award and individual science subjects. Double award science was introduced with the GCSEs in 1988. Success in double award science means that the pupil has achieved two GCSEs rather than just one pass with single science or the individual sciences of biology, physics and chemistry. The majority of 15 year olds now attempt GCSE double award science in preference to the single science subjects, although the individual sciences are still popular in the independent sector. There is no equivalent to double award science in Standard Grade.

Comparisons of examination results for England, Wales and Northern Ireland with those for Scotland are not straightforward because of the different education and examination systems. However, the following should be used as a guideline:

a.	5 or more GCSEs at grades A*-C	=	5 or more SCE Standard Grades at levels 1-3
b.	1-4 GCSEs at grades A*-C	=	1-4 SCE Standard Grades at levels 1-3
c.	GCSEs at grades D-G only	=	SCE Standard Grades at levels 4-7 only
d.	2 or more GCE A levels passes at A-E	=	3 or more SCE Higher Grade passes at A-C

Under the *Education Reform Act 1988* a National Curriculum has been progressively introduced into primary and secondary schools in England and Wales. This consists of mathematics, English and science (and Welsh in Welsh speaking schools in Wales) as core subjects with a modern language, history, geography, information technology, design and technology, music, art and physical education (and Welsh in non-Welsh speaking schools in Wales) as foundation subjects.

Statutory authorities have been set up for England and Wales to advise the government on the National Curriculum and promote curriculum development generally. Northern Ireland has it own common curriculum which is similar but not identical to the National Curriculum in England and Wales. In Scotland, though school curricula are the responsibility of education authorities and individual head teachers, in practice almost all 14 to 16 year olds study mathematics, English, science, a modern foreign language, a social subject, physical education, religious and moral education, technology and a creative and aesthetic subject.

Tables 4.8 and 4.9
Further education

These tables include home students on courses of further education (FE) in further education institutions. The FE sector includes all provision outside schools that is below higher education (HE) level. This ranges from courses in independent living skills for students with severe learning difficulties up to GCE A level, advanced GNVQ or GSVQ and level 3 NVQ or SVQ courses. There are also many students pursuing recreational courses not leading to a formal qualification. Students in England and Wales are counted once only, irrespective of the number of courses for which a student has enrolled. In Scotland and Northern Ireland, students enrolled in more than one course in unrelated subjects are counted for each of these courses with the exception of those on SCE S/GCSE and/or SCE H/GCE courses, who are counted once only irrespective of the number of levels/grades.

Students may be of any age from 16 upwards (no minimum age in Scotland), full or part-time. Full-time students aged under 19 are exempt from tuition fees and fully funded by the Further Education Funding Councils in England, the Further Education Funding Council of Wales, The Scottish Office Education and Industry Department in Scotland and the Department of Education, Northern Ireland. For other students tuition fees are payable, but may be remitted for students in receipt of certain social security benefits. In some cases discretionary grants may be available from LEAs.

Part-time day courses are mainly those organised for students released by their employers either for one or two days a week (or any part of a week in Scotland), or for a period (or periods) of block release.

Sandwich courses are those where periods of full-time study are broken by a period (or periods) of associated industrial training or experience, and where the total period (or periods) of full-time study over the whole course averages more than 19 weeks per academic year, (18 weeks in Scotland). Sandwich course students are classed as full-time students.

National Vocational Qualifications (NVQs) and Scottish Vocational Qualifications (SVQs) are occupational qualifications, available at five levels, and are based on up-to-date standards set by employers.

General National Vocational Qualifications (GNVQs) and General Scottish Vocational Qualifications (GSVQs) combine general and vocational education and are available at three levels:

Foundation	-	broadly equivalent to four GCSEs at grades D-G or four SCE Standard Grades at levels 4 to 7.
Intermediate	-	broadly equivalent to five GCSEs at grades A* to C or five SCE Standard Grades at levels 1 to 3.
Advanced	-	broadly equivalent to two GCE A levels, or three SCE Higher Grade passes; also known as vocational A levels .

Tables 4.10 and 4.11
Higher education

Higher education (HE) students are those on courses that are of a standard that is higher than GCE A level, the Higher Grade of the Scottish Certificate of Education, GNVQ/NVQ level 3 or the BTEC or SCOTVEC National Certificate or Diploma. Higher education in publicly funded institutions is funded by block grants from the three Higher Education Funding Councils (HEFCs) in Great Britain and the Department of Education, Northern Ireland (DENI). Some HE activity takes place in FE sector institutions, some of which is funded by the HEFCs and some by the FEFCs (The Scottish Office Education and Industry Department in Scotland). Most home students on full-time undergraduate courses are eligible for a mandatory award and top-up student loans.

Table 4.12 New awards made
by local education authorities

Discretionary awards can be made by LEAs under Section 2 of the *Education Act 1962* in respect of any course which is not designated for mandatory or certain postgraduate awards, including courses of FE and certain courses of HE. Awards made under Section 1(6) of the *Education Act 1962* may be made at the local education authority's discretion to students on designated courses who are personally ineligible to receive a mandatory award. In Scotland, student awards are administered by the Student Awards Agency for Scotland.

Table 4.13 Education expenditure by local education authorities

In Table 4.13 transport of pupils for England and Wales is allocated across the schools sectors. Continuing education includes expenditure on adult education centres, teacher and curriculum centres and on awards (fees and maintenance exclusive of parental contributions) to students normally resident within the local authority area prior to going to college. 'Other educational services' includes school catering services, school welfare, youth service and other facilities such as sports, outdoor activity and residential study centres, and educational research. For Scotland and Northern Ireland it also includes transport of pupils. Loan charges are excluded.

The proportion of post-compulsory education pupils in schools who attract higher levels of expenditure will vary between regions due to differences in staying-on rates at school as opposed to colleges of further education (including sixth form colleges).

Table 4.14 National Targets for Education and Training

Table 4.14 shows the proportions of people meeting the required qualification level for four of the National Targets for Education and Training. The Targets are split into two groups, Foundation learning and Lifetime learning. The Targets have been set using the competence-based National Vocational Qualifications (NVQs), Scottish Vocational Qualifications (SVQs), and their vocational and academic equivalents. It should be noted that the data in Table 4.14 relate to the region in which the person is resident, and not where they obtained the qualifications. This can lead to some distortion of the regional picture of educational standards; this is particularly relevant in Northern Ireland, as many qualified young people leave home to enter higher education or seek employment in Great Britain.

The four main quantifiable targets are:

Foundation learning
Target 1   -   by the year 2000, 85 per cent of young people to achieve 5 GCSE passes at grades A*-C, anIntermediate GNVQ or an NVQ level 2.

Target 3   -   by the year 2000, 60 per cent of young people to achieve 2 GCE A levels, or Advanced GNVQ or NVQ level 3.

Lifetime learning
Target 1   -   by the year 2000, 60 per cent of the workforce to be qualified to NVQ level 3, Advanced GNVQ or 2 GCE A level standard

Target 2   -   by the year 2000, 30 per cent of the workforce to have a vocational, professional, management or academic qualification at NVQ level 4 or above.

Tables 4.16 and 4.17 Training For Work (TfW), Youth Training (YT) and Modern Apprenticeship (MA)

TfW replaced Employment Training in Great Britain on 1 April 1993. It is a programme for the long-term unemployed (people unemployed for six months or more), locally planned and delivered to help people find and stay in employment. Training and Enterprise Councils in England and Wales and Local Enterprise Companies in Scotland are responsible for the planning and delivery of TfW.

YT aims to provide broad-based training mainly for 16 and 17 year olds and to provide better qualified young entrants into the labour market. Training and Enterprise Councils in England and Wales and Local Enterprise Companies in Scotland are responsible for the planning and delivery of YT.

MAs offer young people, mainly 16 to 19 year olds, a work-based training route to NVQ level 3 or higher. They aim to improve the supply of technical, craft and junior management skills through work-based training for young men and women entering the labour market. They cover core skills development and broad occupational knowledge, and have an off-the-job component appropriate for the particular sector of industry.

Leavers were followed up six months after they left TfW/YT. Response to the survey was generally low.

For Northern Ireland, figures relate mainly to the Jobskills programme but also include persons remaining on the Job Training Programme (JTP) and the Youth Training Programme (YTP) which had operated in Northern Ireland until April 1995 and which have now both been superseded by Jobskills. Jobskills is an integrated programme which focuses on the attainment of NVQs at level 2 and above in line with National Targets for Education and Training. For statistical purposes, young persons on Jobskills are classified as those who were under 18 years of age on joining the programme.

CHAPTER 5:
LABOUR MARKET

Tables and Charts 5.1-5.4,
5.6, 5.7, 5.9, 5.10, 5.12-5.15,
5.19, 5.21 and 5.25,
Labour Force Survey

The Labour Force Survey (LFS) is a sample survey of about 60 thousand private households in the United Kingdom each quarter, with questions also being asked about students living away from home in halls of residence; a sample of people living in NHS accommodation is also interviewed. It was conducted biennially from 1973, and annually from 1983. In Great Britain the survey has been conducted quarterly since Spring 1992, but in Northern Ireland the survey was carried out annually until the Winter of 1994/95, when a quarterly survey was introduced. For this reason the Spring quarter is used as the main reference period in *Regional Trends* although full Great Britain quarterly LFS data, together with key estimates for Northern Ireland, are published regularly by the Office for National Statistics in *Labour Market Trends* and the *LFS Quarterly Bulletin*.

The survey results are grossed up to give the correct population total and reflect the distributions by gender, age and region shown by the population figures. All LFS estimates since 1984 were re-weighted in 1995 to take into account revised population estimates following the 1991 Census of Population. Care should therefore be taken when comparing figures in this edition with those given in *Regional Trends 30* and earlier additions. Detailed accounts of the re-weighting exercise were published in the May 1995 *Employment Gazette* and the December 1995 *Labour Market Trends*.

All LFS estimates have been rounded to the nearest thousand, and those of less than 10,000 taken from one quarter's survey (and averages of four quarters of less than 6,000) are not given because they are likely to be subject to high sampling error and are therefore considered unreliable.

Estimates from the LFS relating to employees and self-employed cover those aged 16 or over and are based upon the respondents' own assessment of their employment status. Those on government-supported employment and training schemes comprise all people aged 16 or over who were at the time of interview participating in Youth Training, Community Industry, Training for Work or Employment Action, together with those on similar programmes administered by the Training and Enterprise Councils (TECs) in England and Wales or Local Enterprise Companies (LECs) in Scotland or the Training & Employment Agency (T&EA) in Northern Ireland. Other similar programmes such as the Youth Training Scheme were included when they were in operation. Unpaid family workers were only identified separately in the survey from Spring 1992.

Tables 5.1-5.4
The labour force and
economic activity rates

The *labour force* includes people aged 16 or over who are either in employment (whether employed, self-employed or on work-related government-supported employment and training schemes or unpaid family worker) or unemployed. The 'ILO definition' of unemployment counts as unemployed people without a job who were available to start work within two weeks and had either looked for work in the past four weeks or were waiting to start a job they had already obtained.

The most recent national (Great Britain) labour force projections were published in the February 1997 edition of *Labour Market Trends* and were based upon 1996 estimates of the labour force. However, the latest regional projections published in the August 1995 edition of *Employment Gazette* were based upon 1994 estimates and relate to Standard Statistical Regions.

Tables 5.5 and 5.8
Short-term Turnover and
Employment Surveys

Short-term surveys are used to monitor monthly and quarterly movements (monthly for the production sector, and quarterly for the rest of the economy). Estimates of the number of employees in employment for each period are derived by applying the movements obtained through the short-term surveys to the most recent annual level.

Samples of businesses are drawn from the business register each period, and although there is a large degree of overlap in the sample from period to period, a guaranteed number of new businesses are introduced each time. A stratified random sampling scheme ensures that each sample is representative of the businesses on the register. A total estimate of employment for all businesses on the register is made, based on the returns from the sampled businesses. Movements from period to period are then derived by looking at these total estimates.

Table 5.9 Self-employment

The data are based on the respondents' own assessment of their employment status.

Tables 5.10
Educational qualifications

Table 5.10 covers all people of working age (16-64 for males, 16-59 for females) who were economically active, either in employment or unemployed in accordance with the ILO definition. Please see notes to Tables 4.6 and 4.7.

Degree or equivalent includes graduate membership of a professional institute.

Higher education below degree includes: Diploma in Higher Education and Higher HND-HNC BTEC.

GCE 'A' level or equivalent includes: National OND-ONC BTEC, and SCE Higher Grade in Scotland.

GCE 'O' level equivalent includes: all GCSE qualifications and CSE grade 1, and SCE Standard Grade in Scotland.

Chart 5.11 Labour disputes

The chart shows rates per 1,000 employees of working days lost for all industries and services. The statistics relate only to disputes connected with terms and conditions of employment. Stoppages involving fewer than ten workers or lasting less than one day are excluded except where the aggregate of working days lost exceeded 100. When interpreting the figures the following points should be borne in mind:

i.   geographical variations in industrial structure affect overall regional comparisons;

ii.   a few large stoppages affecting a small number of firms may have a significant effect;

iii.   the number of working days lost and workers involved relate to persons both directly and indirectly involved at the establishments where the disputes occurred;

iv.   the regional figures involve a greater degree of estimation than the national figures as some large national stoppages cannot be disaggregated to a regional level and are only shown in the national figure.

Tables 5.16 and 5.17 New Earnings Survey

These tables contain some of the regional results of the New Earnings Survey 1996, fuller details of which are given for the Standard Statistical Regions in part E of the report *New Earnings Survey 1996* (The Stationery Office), published in November 1996. Results for Northern Ireland are published separately by the Department of Economic Development, Northern Ireland. The survey measured gross earnings of a 1 per cent sample of employees, most of whom were members of Pay-As-You-Earn (PAYE) schemes for a pay-period which included 17 April 1996. The earnings information collected was converted to a weekly basis where necessary, and to an hourly basis where normal basic hours were reported.

Figures are given where the number of employees reporting in the survey was ten or more and the standard error of average weekly earnings was 5 per cent or less. Gross earnings are measured before tax, National Insurance or other deductions. They include overtime pay, bonuses and other additions to basic pay but exclude any payments for earlier periods (e.g. back pay), most income in kind, tips and gratuities. All the results in this volume relate to full-time male and female employees on adult rates whose pay for the survey pay-period was not affected by absence. Employees were classified to the region in which they worked (or were based if mobile), and to manual or non-manual occupations on the basis of the Standard Occupational Classification (SOC). Part A of the report for Great Britain gives full details of definitions used in the survey.

Full-time employees are defined as those normally expected to work more than 30 hours per week, excluding overtime and main meal breaks (but 25 hours or more in the case of teachers) or, if their normal hours were not specified, as those regarded as full-time by the employer.

Chart 5.19 Redundancies

Estimates cover those people who reported that they had been made redundant during the three calendar months prior to the week in which the LFS interview was conducted. Information on redundancies was collected in the LFS in Northern Ireland for the first time in Spring 1995, but the number of people identified in the survey as having been made redundant in the three months prior to their interview is too small to gross up to a reliable estimate.

Tables and Charts 5.20-5.25 Unemployment statistics

Prior to 7 October 1996, figures in Tables and Charts 5.20 and 5.22-5.24 relate to persons claiming unemployment-related benefits (that is, Unemployment Benefit, Income Support or National Insurance credits) at an Employment Service Office on the day of the monthly count, who on that day were unemployed and satisfied the conditions for claiming benefit. The unemployment figures include disabled people, so long as they meet the eligibility criteria and are claiming unemployment-related benefits, but exclude students seeking vacation work and temporarily stopped workers.

From 7 October 1996, a new single benefit, the Jobseeker's Allowance (JSA), replaced Unemployment Benefit and Income Support for unemployed people. People who qualify for JSA through their National Insurance contributions are eligible for a personal allowance (known as contribution-based JSA) for a maximum of six months. People who do not qualify for contribution-based JSA, or whose needs are not met by it, are able to claim a means-tested allowance (known as income-based JSA) for themselves and their dependants for as long as they need it. All those eligible for and claiming for JSA, as well as those claiming National Insurance credits, continue to be included in the monthly claimant count.

National and regional unemployment rates are calculated by expressing the number of unemployed as a percentage of the estimated total workforce (the sum of the unemployed claimants, employees in employment, self-employed, HM Forces and participants on work-related Government-supported training programmes). These rates are shown in Table 5.20, while rates for ILO unemployment are shown in Table 5.21. A fuller description of these two measures and the way they relate to one another is in a booklet *How exactly is unemployment measured?* available from the Office for National Statistics.

CHAPTER 6: HOUSING

Tables 6.1 and 6.2 Dwellings

In the 1981 Census, a dwelling was defined as: structurally separate accommodation whose rooms, excluding bathrooms and WCs, are self-contained. In the 1991 Census the definition changed to: structurally separate accommodation whose rooms, including bath or shower, WC, and kitchen facilities, are self-contained. The figures in Table 6.1 include vacant dwellings and temporary dwellings occupied as a normal place of residence. Estimates of the stock in England are based on data from the 1981 and 1991 Censuses. In Scotland data from the Census is supplemented by local authority and other public sector landlords' figures. Northern Ireland stock figures are based on rating lists, Northern Ireland Housing Executive and Housing Association figures. Estimates for Table 6.2 are based on the above estimates and certain assumptions regarding the tenure distribution of gains and losses in the housing stock.

Table 6.3 Renovations

The system of grants to private owners, landlords and tenants came into operation in England and Wales in 1990. They are provided under the *Local Government and Housing Act 1989*; the previous system was provided under the *Housing Act 1985*. In Scotland, current legislation is contained in the *Housing (Scotland) Act 1987*. In Northern Ireland, all repair and improvement grants are payable under the *Housing (Northern Ireland) Order 1992*.

Table 6.4 New dwellings completed

A dwelling is defined for the purposes of this table as a building or any part of a building which forms a separate and self-contained set of premises designed to be occupied by a single family. The figures relate to new permanent dwellings only, ie dwellings with a life expectancy of 60 years or more. A dwelling is counted as completed when it becomes ready for occupation, whether actually occupied or not.

Table 6.6 Bedroom standard

This concept is used to estimate occupation density by allocating a standard number of bedrooms to each household in accordance with its age/gender/marital status composition and the relationship of the members to one another. A separate bedroom is allocated to each married couple, any other person aged 21 or over, each pair of adolescents aged 10 to 20 of the same gender, and each pair of children under 10. Any unpaired person aged 10 to 20 is paired if possible with a child under 10 of the same gender, or, if that is not possible, is given a separate room, as is any unpaired child under 10. This standard is then compared with the actual number of bedrooms (including bedsitters) available for the sole use of the household, and deficiencies or excesses are tabulated. Bedrooms converted to other uses are not counted as available unless they have been denoted as bedrooms by the informants; bedrooms not actually in use are counted unless uninhabitable.

Table 6.7 Council Tax bandings

For Council Tax purposes, dwellings were banded according to their valuation at 1 April 1991. The bands are:

	England	Wales	Scotland
Band A	up to £40,000	up to £30,000	up to £27,000
Band B	£40,001-£52,000	£30,001-£39,000	£27,001-£35,000
Band C	£52,001-£68,000	£39,001-£51,000	£35,001-£45,000
Band D	£68,001-£88,000	£51,001-£66,000	£45,001-£58,000
Band E	£88,001-£120,000	£66,001-£90,000	£58,001-£80,000
Band F	£120,001-£160,000	£90,001-£120,000	£80,001-£106,000
Band G	£160,001-£320,000	£120,001-£240,000	£106,001-£212,000
Band H	£320,001 or over	£240,001 or over	£212,001 or over

Table 6.8 Average weekly rents: by tenure

Private sector rents: rents eligible for Housing Benefit (HB) purposes, average 1995-96. Figures include any HB in payment but exclude ineligible water and other service changes paid as part of rent.

Local authority rents: show unrebated rents at April 1996. Northern Ireland Housing Executive average unrebated rent for Northern Ireland.

Housing association rents: these figures cover the whole stock at 31 March 1996, from Housing Corporation returns.

Table 6.9 Housing costs of owner occupiers

Mortgage Payments: mortgage interest plus any premiums on mortgage protection policies for loans used to purchase the property. For repayment mortgages, interest is calculated using the amount of loan outstanding and the standard interest rate at time of interview.

Endowment policies: premium on endowment policies covering the repayment of mortgages and loans used to purchase the property.

Structural insurance: includes cases where insurance cover includes furniture and contents and structural element cannot be separately identified.

Services: includes payments of ground rent, feu duties (applies in Scotland), chief rent, service charges, compulsory or regular maintenance charges, site rent (caravans) and any other regular payments in connection with accommodation.

Tables 6.10 Dwelling prices and mortgages

Figures in this table are taken from The Survey of Mortgage Lenders, a five per cent sample survey of mortgages at completion stage. Full details of the survey are given in *The New Survey of Mortgage Lenders by Bob Pannell and David Champion (Department of the Environment) in Housing Finance No.16 November 1992* published by the Council of Mortgage Lenders.

Table 6.12 County Court actions for mortgage possessions

The figures do not indicate how many houses have been repossessed through the courts; not all the orders will have resulted in the issue and execution of warrants of possession. The regional breakdown relates to the location of the court rather than the address of the property.

Actions entered: a plaintiff begins an action for an order for possession of residential property by way of a summons in a county court.

Orders made: the court, following a judicial hearing, may grant an order for possession immediately. This entitles the plaintiff to apply for a warrant to have the defendant evicted. However, even where a warrant for possession is issued, the parties can still negotiate a compromise to prevent eviction.

Suspended orders: frequently, the court grants the mortgage lender possession but suspends the operation of the order. Provided the defendant complies with the terms of the suspension, which usually require them to pay the current mortgage instalments plus some of the accrued arrears, the possession order cannot be enforced.

Table 6.13 Homeless households by reason

In England and Wales the basis for these figures is households accepted for re-housing by local authorities under the homelessness provisions of Part III of the *Housing Act 1985*. The Welsh figures, however, also include:

    i.   non-priority cases, given advice and assistance;
    ii.   intentionally homeless, priority accepted; and
    iii.   intentionally homeless, non-priority accepted.

In Northern Ireland, the *Housing (Northern Ireland) Order 1988* (Part II) defines the basis under which households (including one person households) are classified as homeless.

CHAPTER 7: HEALTH

7.3 Life expectation at birth

Estimates of life expectation are calculated on a calendar year basis nationally for life expectation at birth and at ages of 5, 20, 30, 40, 50, 60, 70 and 80. These are regularly published in the ONO publication *Population Trends*. The mortality rates which underlie the expectation of life figures are based on total deaths occurring in each year. Figures used in the chart were compiled as part of research into mortality rates and life expectation and regional and area classifications. Findings of this research were published in *Population Trends* No. 83.

Table 7.4 Limiting long-standing illness

'Long-standing illness' is measured by asking respondents if they have any long-standing illness, disability or infirmity. Long-standing means anything that has troubled the respondent over a period of time or that is likely to affect the respondent over a period of time. A limiting long-standing illness/disability/infirmity is one which limits the respondent's activities in any way.

Table 7.9 Alcohol consumption

A unit of alcohol is 8 grammes of pure alcohol, approximately equivalent to half a pint of ordinary strength beer, a glass of wine, or a pub measure of spirits.

At the time the survey was conducted, recommended sensible levels were 21 units per week for men and 14 for women. Following an inter-departmental review of medical research and scientific evidence, revised guidance was published by the Department of Health in December 1995 in the report *Sensible Drinking*. This moved away from a weekly figure for safe drinking to focus on daily consumption and to warn of the dangers of excessive drinking bouts and intoxication.

Sensible Drinking concluded that 'regular consumption of between 3 and 4 units a day by men(2 to 3 by women) will not accrue significant health risk' but that consistently drinking 4 or more units a day (3 for women) is not advised as a sensible drinking level because of the progressive health risk it carries.

7.10 Eating habits amongst adults

The questions asked in the Health Survey for England do not provide direct information on the population's diet; rather they are concerned with reported behaviour relating to a few selected healthy eating messages. More detailed information is collected through other surveys, notably the *National Food Survey*. In the 1994 survey the focus was on Cardiovascular disease and examining particular eating habits in relation to this disease. The focus of the survey in subsequent years has changed and so eating habits are not covered every year.
Similar, though not directly comparable, information for Scotland is available from the Scottish Health Survey. Information for Wales on behaviour relating to 'healthy eating' messages can be found in *Health-related behaviour in Wales, 1985-1993: Findings from the Health in Wales Surveys*, Health Promotion Wales Technical Report No. 8.

Table 7.13
Notifications of measles

Since late 1994, routine laboratory confirmation has been performed on over 50 per cent of cases of measles notified. Less than 5 per cent of cases investigated are confirmed suggesting that many notified cases are not genuine measles infections.

Tables 7.14 and 7.16
Age-adjusted mortality rates

The age-standardised rate for a particular condition is that which would have occurred if the observed age-specific rates for the condition had applied in a given standard population.

The causes of death included in Table 7.16 correspond to International Classification of Diseases (9th Revision) codes as follows: all circulatory diseases - 390-459; ischaemic heart disease - 410-414; cerebrovascular disease - 430-438; all respiratory diseases - 460-519; bronchitis et al - 490-493 +496; cancers (malignant neoplasms) - 140-208; all injuries and poisonings - 800-999; road traffic accidents - E810-E819; suicides and open verdicts - E950-E959 and E980-E989.

For England and Wales, deaths represent the number registered in each year, except for 1993 and 1994 (figures for which were published in earlier editions of *Regional Trends*) which relate to occurences in the year. Also, new procedures for coding cause of death from 1993 mean that figures for 1993 onwards may not be exactly comparable with earlier years. For most conditions these effects are small.

Table 7.14 Cervical and breast cancer screening

For cervical screening the figures are for average of the programme and are shown as a snapshot at 31 March for each year for England, Wales and Northern Ireland. For Scotland figures are at 31 December as data are collected on a calendar year basis. Scottish figures are calculated as the number of women screened divided by eligible population aged 20-59. This is not the same as uptake (number of women screened divided by number invited) nor coverage (number of women invited divided by eligible population) as data on the number of women invited is not available.

Figures for breast screening show the uptake during 1992-92, 1994-95 and 1995-96.

Table 7.18 Hospital activity

Data for England are based on Finished Consultant Episodes (FCEs). An FCE is a completed period of care of a patient using an NHS hospital bed, under one consultant within one health care provider (an NHS Trust or a Directly Managed Unit). If a patient is transferred from one consultant to another, even if this is within the same provider, the episode ends and another one begins. The transfer of a patient from one hospital to another with the same consultant and within the same provider does not end the episode. Healthy live-born babies are included. Data for Wales, Scotland and Northern Ireland are based on a system where transfers between consultants do not count as a discharge except in Scotland where figures include patients transferred from one consultant to another within the same hospital, provided there is a change of speciality. Transfers from one hospital to another, with the same consultant, however, count as a discharge. New-born babies are excluded. Deaths are included in all four countries.

A day case is a person who comes for investigation, treatment or operation under clinical supervision on a planned non-resident basis, who occupies a bed for part or all of that day, and who returns home as planned the same day.

An out-patient is defined as a person attending an out-patients' department for treatment or advice. A new out-patient is one whose first attendance of a continuous series (or single attendance where relevant) at a clinical out-patient department for the same course of treatment falls within the period under review. Each out-patient attendance of a course or series is included in the year in which the attendance occurred. Persons attending more than one department are counted in each department.

Mean duration of stay: this is calculated for any category as the total bed-days for that category divided by the number of ordinary admissions (Finished Consultant Episodes in England and Northern Ireland) for that category. An ordinary admission is one where the patient is expected to remain in hospital for at least one night. It should be noted that length of stay for mental illness specialities can be affected by the closure of long-stay wards resulting in the resettlement of a relatively small number of very long-stay patients discharged to more appropriate accommodation.

Table 7.20 Hospital and Community Health Service Staff

General Medical Practitioners (ie family GPs), General Dental Practitioners, the staff employed by the practitioners, pharmacists in General Pharmaceutical Services and staff working in other contracted out services are not included in the figures.

Medical and dental staff included are those holding permanent paid (whole-time, part-time and part-time sessional) and/or honorary appointments in NHS hospitals and Community Health Services. Figures include clinical assistants and hospital practitioners. Occasional sessional staff in Community Health Medical and Dental Services for whom no whole-time equivalent is collected are not included. The whole-time equivalent of staff holding appointments with more than one region is included in the appropriate region.

CHAPTER 8: LIFESTYLES

Comparability of earnings statistics

Earnings statistics shown in this and the labour market sections are not comparable owing to differences in the coverage of the surveys, differences in classifying individuals to regions and different levels of reliability of the regional data. The bases of the surveys differ, in that the Survey of Personal Incomes is a sample of administrative records, the Family Expenditure Survey is a sample of households and the New Earnings Survey is a sample of employees. The administrative and household surveys are classified according to regions of residence while the surveys of employees and firms are classified according to the region of work place. The reliability depends partly upon the size of the sample and response rates. Different surveys will have their own sources of bias which will affect the reliability of their results.

Tables 8.1 and 8.2 Household income

These tables contain results from the Family Expenditure Survey. The survey covers all types of private households in the United Kingdom. It is a continuous sample survey of approximately 10,350 households per year, of which around 66 per cent co-operate. The available evidence suggests that non-response tended to increase with increasing age of the head of household up to age 65. Response is lower than average in London and higher in non-metropolitan areas. Households containing 3 or more adults also tended to have lower response. Data shown in the tables for Northern Ireland are obtained from an enhanced sample, which provides detailed analyses within the region and reduces the sampling errors; however, for consolidation into UK figures, the standard FES sample is used.

Results of the FES are published annually in the report *Family Spending (The Stationery Office)*, together with a full list of definitions and items on which information is collected.

FES data are shown without adjustment for non-response, outliers or non-sampling errors. The figures are also subject to sampling errors. The sampling error (ie the precision of the figures) needs to be taken into account in any comparison of FES figures, eg comparisons between region or over time. Figures shown for particular groups of households, regions and other sub-sets of the sample are subject to larger sampling variability, and are more sensitive to possible extreme values or outliers, than are figures for the UK sample as a whole. Estimates of sampling error are shown in the FES annual report *Family Spending*.

In the FES, a household comprises one person living alone or a group of people living at the same address having common housekeeping. The members of a household are not necessarily related by blood or marriage. As the survey covers only private households, people living in hostels, hotels, boarding houses or institutions are excluded.

Gross household income is the aggregate of the gross incomes of the individual members of the household before deduction of income tax, National Insurance contributions and any other deductions at source. Income thus defined excludes: housing benefit; money received by one member from another member of the household; withdrawals of savings, receipts from maturing insurance policies, proceeds from the sale of financial and other assets (eg cars, furniture, houses, etc.); winnings from betting, lump sum gratuities and windfalls such as legacies; the value of income in kind, including the value of goods received free, of meal vouchers, and of bills paid by someone who is not a member of the household.

Some other analyses of FES data use 'equivalisation' of income, ie adjustment of household income by allowing for the different size and composition of each household. Equivalisation is not used in Tables 8.1 and 8.2.

Tables 8.3, 8.4, 8.7 and 8.12 Family Resources Survey (FRS)

The Family Resources Survey (FRS) is a continuous survey of over 26,000 private households in Great Britain. As with any survey, results are subject to sampling errors. In addition, there is the possibility of bias, firstly because not everyone approached agreed to take part, and secondly because some information may be incorrectly reported. Results are based on unweighted survey data. Results of the survey are published in the report Family Resources Survey Great Britain (published from 1994-95 by The Stationery Office). Available evidence suggests particular problems of misreporting certain types of benefit, such as the under-reporting of Income Support, where respondents have stated that all money received comes from a single benefit, eg Retirement Pension or Unemployment Benefit.

In the FRS a household comprises a single person or a group of people who have the address as their only or main residence and who either share one meal a day or share the living accommodation.

Table 8.3

The measure of income used in compiling Table 8.3 is that used in the Department of Social Security's Households Below Average Income. The income of a household is the total income of all members of the household after the deduction of income tax, National Insurance contributions, contributions to occupational pension schemes, additional voluntary contributions, contributions to personal pensions, maintenance/child support payments and Council Tax. Income includes earnings from employment and self-employment, social security benefits including Housing Benefit, occupational and private pensions, investment income, maintenance payments, educational grants, scholarships and top-up loans and some in-kind benefits such as luncheon vouchers. Income is adjusted for household size and composition by means of the McClements equivalence scale (see below). This reflects the common sense notion that a household of five will need a higher income than a single person living alone to enjoy a comparable standard of living. The total equivalised income of a household is used to represent the income level of every individual in that household; all individuals are then ranked according to this level.

McClements equivalence scale

	Before housing costs
Household member:	
First adult (head)	0.61
Spouse of head	0.39
Other second adult	0.46
Third adult	0.42
Subsequent adults	0.36
Each dependant aged:	
0-1	0.09
2-4	0.18
5-7	0.21
8-10	0.23
11-12	0.25
13-15	0.27
16 or over	0.36

Tables 8.5 and 8.6
Survey of Personal Incomes

The Survey of Personal Incomes uses a sample of around 80 thousand cases drawn from all individuals for whom income tax records are held by the Inland Revenue: not all are taxpayers -about 6 per cent do not pay tax because the operation of personal reliefs and allowances removes them from liability. The data in Table 8.5 relate to individuals whose income over the year amounted to the threshold for operation of Pay-As-You-Earn (3,445 in 1994-95) or more. Below this threshold, coverage of incomes is incomplete in tax records. A more complete description of the survey appears in Inland Revenue Statistics.

Table 8.5
Distribution of income liable to assessment for tax

The income shown is that liable to assessment in the tax year. For most incomes this is the amount earned or receivable in that year, but for business profits and professional earnings the assessments are normally based on the amount of income arising in the trading account ending in the previous year. Those types of income that were specifically exempt from tax eg certain social security benefits are excluded.

Incomes are allocated to regions according to the place of residence of the recipient, except for the self-employed, where allocation is according to the business address. For many self-employed people home address and business address are the same, and for the majority the region will correspond.

The table classifies incomes by range of total income. This is defined as gross income, whether earned or unearned, including estimates of employees' superannuation contributions, but after deducting employment expenses, losses, capital allowances, and any expenses allowable as a deduction from gross income from lettings or overseas investment income. Superannuation contributions have been estimated and distributed among earners in the Survey of Personal Incomes consistently with information about numbers contracted in or out of the State Earnings Related Pension Scheme and the proportion of their earnings contribution. The coverage of unearned income also includes estimates of that part of the investment income (whose liability to tax at basic rate has been satisfied at source) not known to tax offices.

Sampling errors need to be borne in mind when interpreting small differences in income distributions between regions.

Chart 8.6
Average income tax payable

Income tax is calculated as the liability for the income tax year, regardless of when the tax may have been paid or how it was collected.

The income tax liability shown here is calculated from the individual's total income, including tax credits on dividends, and interest received after the deduction of tax grossed up at the appropriate rate. From total income is deducted allowable reliefs etc, and personal allowances in order to calculate the tax liability, but not relief given at source on mortgage interest, which cannot be estimated with sufficient reliability at regional level.

Table 8.7 Households in receipt of benefits

See notes on Family Resources Survey above.

Income Support replaced Supplementary Benefit in April 1988. It is a non-contributory benefit payable to people working less than 16 hours a week, whose incomes are below the levels (called 'applicable amounts') laid down by Parliament. The applicable amounts generally consist of personal allowances for members of the family and premiums for families, lone parents, pensioners, the disabled and carers. Amounts for certain housing costs (mainly mortgage interest) are also included.

Housing Benefit is administered by local authorities. People are eligible only if they are liable to pay rent in respect of the dwelling they occupy as their home. Couples are treated as a single benefit unit. The amount of benefit depends on eligible rent, income, deductions in respect of any non-dependants and the applicable amount. 'Eligible rent' is the amount of a tenant's rental liability which can be met by Housing Benefit. Payments made by owner-occupiers do not count. Deductions are made for service charges in rent which relate to personal needs.

Council Tax Benefit is also administered by local authorities. Generally, it mirrors the Housing Benefit scheme in the calculation of the claimants' applicable amount, resources and deductions in respect of any non-dependants.

Unemployment Benefit (UB) was payable at the time of the survey to those who were unemployed, available for, and actively seeking employment, satisfied conditions for the receipt of UB and were free from certain grounds for disallowance or disqualification; for example, disqualification for up to 26 weeks may have been imposed if any former employment had been left voluntarily without just cause, or employment had been refused without good reason. If National Insurance contribution conditions were satisfied in full, UB was normally payable at a standard rate with additional components for dependants. On 7 October 1996 UB was replaced by the Jobseeker's Allowance.

Retirement Pensions are paid to men aged 65 or over and women aged 60 or over who have paid sufficient National Insurance contributions over their working life. A wife who cannot claim a pension in her own right may qualify on the basis of her husband's contributions. The table excludes non-contributory pensions which are paid to people aged 80 or over who did not qualify for the standard retirement pension, or whose pension was lower than the non-contributory rate.

Incapacity Benefit replaced Sickness Benefit and Invalidity Benefit from 13 April 1995. It is paid to people who are assessed as being incapable of work and who satisfy the contribution conditions for the benefit. The figures do not include people receiving Statutory Sick Pay.

Industrial injuries includes pensions, gratuities and sundry allowances for disablement and specified deaths arising from industrial causes.

Child Benefit is normally paid for children up to the age of 16. Benefit may continue up to age 19 for children in full-time education up to 'A' level standard. 16 and 17 year olds are also eligible for a short period after leaving school.

One Parent Benefit is normally paid for the eldest dependent child. Claimants must be bringing up the child/children alone, either because they are single, widowed divorced or permanently separated. The claimant does not need to be the child's parent. From April 1997 One Parent Benefit is incorporated into Child Benefit.

A brief description of the main features of the various benefits paid in Great Britain is set out in Social Security Statistics (published annually by The Stationery Office). Detailed information on benefits paid in Northern Ireland is contained in *Northern Ireland Annual Abstract of Statistics and Northern Ireland Social Security Statistics*.

Table 8.9
Household expenditure

This table contains results from the Family Expenditure Survey for 1995-96. Some details of the survey are given in the notes to Tables 8.1 and 8.2.

Expenditure excludes savings or investments (eg life assurance premiums), income tax payments, National Insurance contributions, Housing Benefit and mortgage and other payments for the purchase of, or major additions to, dwellings.

Housing expenditure of households living in owner-occupied dwellings consists of the payments by these households for Council Tax (rates in Northern Ireland), water, ground rent, etc., insurance of the structure and mortgage interest payments. Mortgage capital repayments and amounts paid for the outright purchase of the dwelling or for major structural alterations are not included as housing expenditure.

Estimates of household expenditure on a few items are below those which might be expected by comparison with other sources eg alcoholic drink, tobacco and, to a lesser extent, confectionery and ice cream.

Tables 8.10 and 8.11
National Food Survey

This is a continuous sample survey in which about 7-8,000 households per year keep a record of the type, quantity and amount spent on foods entering the home during a one week period and the amount they spend on food and drink consumed outside the home. Nutritional values are also calculated from the information collected. In 1996, the survey was extended to include Northern Ireland, but covering foods entering the home only.

Detailed survey results and definitions are published by The Stationery Office in the annual report on the *National Food Survey*.

There are three main reasons why the recorded crime figures for Scotland and the notifiable offences figures for England and Wales and Northern Ireland cannot be compared. They are as follows:

(i) Differences in *legal systems*. The legal system operating in Scotland differs from that in England and Wales and Northern Ireland.

(ii) Differences in *classification*. The offences included within the recorded crime categories and the notifiable offence categories vary significantly. For example, simple possession of a controlled drug is **included** in the Scottish figures and in those for Northern Ireland but excluded from notifiable offences figures in England and Wales.

(iii) *Counting rules*. In Scotland **each** individual offence occurring within an incident is recorded whereas in England and Wales and Northern Ireland a principal offence rule is applied (in general) ie only the main offence is counted.

Table 9.1, Tables 9.3-9.7

The figures are compiled from police returns to the Home Office and The Scottish Office Home Department and from statistics supplied by the Royal Ulster Constabulary in Northern Ireland.

In England and Wales and Northern Ireland, indictable offences cover those offences which must or may be tried by jury in the Crown Court and include the more serious offences. Summary offences are those for which a defendant would normally be tried at a magistrates' court and are generally less serious - the majority of motoring offences fall into this category. In general in Northern Ireland non-indictable offences are dealt with at a magistrates' court. Some indictable offences can also be dealt with there.

In Scotland the term 'crimes' is generally used for the more serious criminal acts (roughly equivalent to indictable offences); the less serious are termed 'offences', although the term 'offence' is also used in relation to serious breaches of criminal law. The majority of cases are tried summarily (without a jury) in the Sheriff or District Court, while the more serious cases are tried in the Sheriff Court under solemn procedure (with a jury), or in the High Court. With effect from April 1996 (the date which the relevant section of the *Criminal Procedure (Scotland) Act 1995* came into force) >offending while on bail= is no longer an offence in its own right and therefore does not appear in the recorded crime figures for Scotland. Thus, to facilitate across year comparisons, such offences have been removed from the historical recorded crime figures.

Cautions - if a person admits to committing an offence he may be given a formal police caution by, or on the instruction of, a senior police officer as an alternative to court proceedings. The figures exclude informal warnings given by the police, written warnings issued for motoring offences and warnings given by non-police bodies eg a department store in the case of shoplifting. Cautions by the police are not available in Scotland, but warnings may be given by the Procurator Fiscal.

**Tables 9.2 and 9.12
Crime Surveys**

The British Crime Survey (BCS) was conducted by the Home Office in 1982, 1984, 1992, 1994 and 1996. Each survey measured crimes experienced in the previous year, including those not reported to the police. The survey also covers other matters of Home Office interest including fear of crime, contacts with the police, and drug use. The 1996 survey had a nationally representative sample of 16,300 people aged 16 and over in England and Wales. The sample was drawn from the Postcode Address File - a listing of all postal delivery points. The response rate was 83 per cent.

Scotland participated in sweeps of the British Crime Survey in 1982 and 1988 and ran its own Scottish Crime Surveys in 1993 and 1996 based on nationally representative samples of 5,000 respondents aged 16 or over interviewed in their homes. In addition 495 young people aged between 12 and 15 completed questionnaires in 1993 and 353 completed questionnaires in the 1996 survey. Addresses were randomly generated from the Postcode Address file in 1993 and 1996. Both the 1993 and 1996 surveys had response rates of 77 per cent.

The Northern Ireland Crime Survey was commissioned by the Northern Ireland Office in 1994. The survey was conducted throughout Northern Ireland and fieldwork took place between October 1994 and January 1995. Almost 3,000 people aged 16 years and above participated in the survey. They were sampled from the rating valuation list which is the most up-to-date listing of private households in Northern Ireland. The response rate was 72 per cent.

In each of the surveys, respondents answered questions about offences against their household (such as theft or damage of household property) and about offences against them personally (such as assault or robbery). However, none of the surveys provides a complete count of crime. Many offence types cannot be covered in a household survey (eg shoplifting, fraud or drug offences). Crime surveys are also prone to various forms of error, mainly to do with the difficulty of ensuring that samples are representative, the frailty of respondents' memories, their reticence to talk about their experiences as victims, and their failure to realise an incident is relevant to the survey.

Table 9.3 Clear-up rates	In England and Wales and Northern Ireland offences recorded by the police as having been cleared up include offences for which persons have been charged, summonsed or cautioned, those admitted and taken into consideration when persons are tried for other offences, and those admitted by prisoners who have been sentenced for other offences (except in Northern Ireland). In Scotland a crime or offence is regarded as cleared up if one or more offenders is apprehended, cited, warned or traced for it.
	The clear-up rate is the ratio of offences cleared up in the year to offences recorded in the year. Some offences cleared up may relate to offences recorded in previous years. There is considerable variation between police forces in the emphasis placed on certain of the methods listed above and, as some methods are more resource intensive than others, this can have a significant effect on a force=s overall clear-up rate.
Table 9.5 Seizure of controlled drugs	The figures in this table, which are compiled from returns to the Home Office, relate to seizures made by the police and officials of HM Customs and Excise, and to drugs controlled under the *Misuse of Drugs Act 1971*. The Act divides drugs into three categories according to their harmfulness. A full list of drugs in each category is given in Schedule 2 to the *Misuse of Drugs Act 1971*, as amended by Orders in Council.
Tables 9.8 Persons found guilty of offences	The power to partly suspend certain sentences of imprisonment in England and Wales was abolished on 1 October 1992 following the implementation of Section 5 of the *Criminal Justice Act 1991*. As a result, the term 'suspended sentence' is known as 'fully suspended sentence' and 'immediate custody' includes unsuspended sentences of imprisonment and sentence to detention in a young offender institution. Fully and partly suspended sentences are not available to Scottish courts; partly suspended sentences are not available to courts in Northern Ireland.
Table 9.9 Driving etc after consuming alcohol or drugs	Driving etc includes all drink/drug-related driving offences ie driving, attempting, in charge of, failing to provide a specimen etc.

CHAPTER 10: TRANSPORT

Tables 10.4-10.6	Trunk roads. these are roads comprising the national network of through routes for which the Secretary of State for Transport, in England, and the Secretaries of State for Wales and Scotland, are the Highway Authorities.
	Non-trunk roads: roads for which local authorities (Unitary Authorities in Wales and New Councils in Scotland) are Highway Authorities.
	Major roads. motorways and A roads.
	Principal roads: important regional or local roads for which local authorities are the Highway Authorities.
	A Roads: trunk and principal roads (excluding motorways).
	Minor roads: comprise B, C and unclassified roads.
	Built-up roads: all those having a speed limit of 40 mph or less (irrespective of whether there are buildings or not).
	Non built-up roads: all those with a speed limit in excess of 40 mph.
Tables 10.6 and 10.7 Road accidents/casualties	An accident is one involving personal injury occurring on the public highway (including footways) in which a road vehicle is involved and which becomes known to the police within 30 days. The vehicle need not be moving and it need not be in collision with anything.
	Persons killed are those who sustained injuries which caused death less than 30 days after the accident.
	A serious injury is one for which a person is detained in hospital as an in-patient, or any of the following injuries whether or not they are detained in hospital: fractures, concussion, internal injuries, crushing, severe cuts and lacerations, severe general shock requiring medical treatment, injuries causing death 30 or more days after the accident.
	There are many reasons why accident rates per head of population (for all roads) and per 100 million vehicle kilometres (for major roads) vary by region. They will be influenced by the mix of pedestrian and vehicle traffic within each region, which vary as a result of the considerable differences in vehicle ownership by region.
	In addition, an area that 'imports' large numbers of visitors or commuters will have a relatively high proportion of accidents related to vehicles or drivers from outside the area. A rural area with low population density but high road mileage can be expected, other things being equal, to have lower than average accident rates.

Table 10.4 Annual average daily flow	Traffic estimates are derived from roadside traffic counts which take two forms; occasional 12 hour counts at a large number of sites to estimate the absolute level of traffic (the 'rotating' census) and frequent counts at a small number of sites (the 'core' census) to estimate changes in the amount of traffic.
Tables 10.8, 10.10 and Chart 10.9 National Travel Survey	The National Travel Survey (NTS) is the only comprehensive national source of travel information for Great Britain which links different kinds of travel with the characteristics of travellers and their families. Since July 1988, the NTS has been conducted on a small scale continuous basis. The last of the previous ad hoc surveys was carried out in 1985/86.

From about 3,300 households in Great Britain each year, every member provides personal information (eg age, gender, working status, driving licence, season ticket) and details of journeys carried out in a sample week, including purpose of journey, method of travel, time of day, length, duration, and cost of any tickets bought.

Travel included in the NTS covers all journeys by GB residents within Great Britain for personal reasons, including travel in the course of work. Travel information is recorded at two levels for multi-stage journeys: journey and stage.

A *journey* is defined as a one-way course of travel having a single main purpose. It is the basic unit of personal travel in the survey. A round trip is split into two journeys, with the first ending at a convenient point about half way round as a notional stopping point for the outward destination and return origin.

A *stage* is that portion of a journey defined by the use of a specific method of transport or of a specific ticket (a new stage being defined if either the mode or ticket changes).

The purpose of a journey is normally taken to be the activity at the destination, unless that destination is 'home' in which case the purpose is defined by the origin of the journey. The classification of journeys to 'work' are also dependent on the origin of the journey.

CHAPTER 11: ENVIROMENT

Tables 11.1, 11.2, 11.4, 11.5 and 11.6	The Environment Agency for England and Wales was formally created on 8 August 1995 by the *Environment Act 1995*. It took up its statutory duties on 1 April 1996.

The Agency brings together the functions previously carried out by the National Rivers Authority, Her Majesty's Inspectorate of Pollution, the waste regulatory functions of 83 local authorities and a small number of units from the Department of the Environment dealing with aspects of waste regulation and contaminated land. One of the key reasons for setting up the Agency was to promote a more coherent and integrated approach to environmental management.

The Agency's principal aim is to protect and improve the environment. Its business can be grouped under two broad headings: *pollution prevention and control* which includes regulating the disposal of controlled waste, protecting and improving the quality of rivers estuaries and coastal waters, and regulating major industrial processes, nuclear sites and premises authorised to dispose of radioactive waste; and, *water management* covering water resources, flood defence, fisheries, recreation, conservation and navigation.

The Agency has a budget of around £550 million per annum. About 30 per cent of this is allocated to the prevention and control of pollution; nearly 50 per cent is spent on flood defence, and the remaining 20 per cent on the Agency's other waste management functions.

Table 11.4 Chemical quality of rivers and canals	The General Quality Assessment (GQA) Scheme provides a rigorous and objective method for assessing the basic chemical quality of rivers and canals based on three determinants - dissolved oxygen, biochemical oxygen demand (BOD), and ammoniacal nitrogen. The GQA grades river stretches into six categories (A-F) of chemical quality and these in turn have been grouped into four broader groups - good (classes A and B), fair (classes C and D), poor (class E), and bad (class F).

Water quality in Northern Ireland is assessed using the four categories of the National Water Council classification system. This system is not directly comparable with the GQA system used in England and Wales.

Table 11.5 **Water pollution incidents**	The Environment Agency defines three categories of pollution incidents: Category 1 A 'major' incident involving one or more of the following: a) potential or actual persistent effect on water quality or aquatic life; b) closure of potable water, industrial or agricultural abstraction necessary; c) extensive fish kill; d) excessive breaches of consent conditions; e) extensive remedial measures necessary; f) major effect on amenity value. Category 2 A 'significant' pollution which involves one or more of the following: a) notification to abstractors necessary; b) significant fish kill; c) measurable effect on invertebrate life; d) water unfit for stock; e) bed of watercourse contaminated; f) amenity value to the public, owners or users reduced by odour or appearance. Category 3 'Minor suspected or probable' pollution which, on investigation, proves unlikely to be capable of substantiation or to have no notable effect.
Chart 11.7 Critical loads for acidity of soil vegetation and freshwaters	The risk of harmful effects on soil vegetation and freshwater ecosystems from acid deposition is assessed using a concept known as 'critical loads', which assumes that there are damage thresholds for the response of different ecosystems to acidic deposition. The critical load for a particular ecosystem-pollutant combination is defined as the highest deposition load of the pollutant that the ecosystem can stand without long-term damage occurring. The most vulnerable soil vegetation and freshwaters are generally in the upland areas of north and west Britain.
Chart 11.9 Ground level ozone levels	Ground level ozone (O_3) occurs naturally but levels can be increased when nitrogen oxides and other pollutants react with strong sunlight. Episodes in which concentrations rise substantially above background levels occur in summer heat waves when there are long hours of bright sunlight, temperatures above 20°C, and little or no winds. Once formed, O_3 can persist for several days and can be transported long distances. At ground level, O_3 can affect human health and can damage crops.
Chart 11.10 Radon affected areas	Radon accounts for half of the average overall dose of radioactivity received by the UK population. The health hazard associated with radon is from its radioactive decay products. These may be inhaled and deposited in the lungs where radiation from them can damage lung tissue, and may increase the risk of lung cancer. Parts of the United Kingdom have been designated as Radon Affected Areas, that is areas where more than 1 in 100 homes are estimated to have radon concentrations above the National Radiological Protection Board (NRPB) recommended action level of $200Bq/m^3$. Above this level, NRPB recommend that actions be taken to limit exposure of householders to high levels of radon.
Table 11.12 and Chart 11.13 Designated Protected areas	National Parks, Areas of Outstanding Natural Beauty in England and Wales and Northern Ireland, Defined Heritage Coasts in England and Wales and National Scenic Areas in Scotland are the major areas designated by legislation to protect their landscape importance. Green Belts have been designated in England, Scotland and Northern Ireland to restrict the sprawl of built-up areas onto previously undeveloped land and to preserve the character of historic towns. Other areas, such as National Nature Reserves, Special Protection Areas, Marine Nature Reserves, are protected for their value as wildlife habitat, in particular for endangered species. 'Ramsar sites' are wetland sites of international importance, particularly for water fowl, designated under the Ramsar Convention in 1971. Sites in the United Kingdom are protected by Sites of Special Scientific Interest (SSSI) status.
Table 11.14 Land changing to urban use	Land use refers to the main activity taking place on an area of land, eg agriculture, housing. Details of changes in land use are recorded for the Department of the Environment by Ordnance Survey as part of its map revision programme. Under this programme, physical development (eg housing) tends to be recorded relatively sooner than changes between other uses (eg agriculture and forestry), some of which may not be recorded for some years. Hence the statistics are best suited to analyses of changes to urban uses and recycling of land already in urban uses. Land use is classified into 24 categories which are then grouped into 'urban uses' and 'rural uses'. Urban uses include: residential; transport and utilities; industry and commerce; community services; vacant land (classified according to whether it was previously developed or within a built-up area, but not previously developed). Rural uses include: agriculture; forestry; open land and water; minerals and landfill; outdoor

CHAPTER 12: REGIONAL ACCOUNTS

The sources and methodology used to compile the regional accounts are given in a booklet in the *Studies in Official Statistics series* (HMSO), No 31, *Regional Accounts*, and more recently in the Eurostat publication *Methods used to compile regional accounts*.

Tables 12.1, 12.3, 12.4 and Chart 12.2 Gross Domestic Product (GDP)

Regional estimates of GDP are compiled as the sum of factor incomes, ie incomes earned by residents, whether corporate or individual, from the production of goods and services. This approach breaks the total down into four components: income from employment; income from self-employment; profits and surpluses; and rent (including the imputed charge for consumption of non-trading capital). Stock appreciation is deducted from the sum of total domestic income to give GDP. The figures for all regions are adjusted to sum to the national totals as published in *United Kingdom National Accounts 1996* (HMSO).

In order to accommodate the offshore oil and gas extraction industry in the regional accounts, a region known as the Continental Shelf is included. GDP for this region includes only profits and stock appreciation related to the offshore activities of UK and foreign contractors. The allocation of income from employment is not altered by the Continental Shelf region since throughout the regional accounts this is allocated according to the region of residence of the employee.

Table 12.7 Personal income

Total personal income is an estimate of the income of the personal sector including households, other individuals and non-profit-making bodies serving persons. Total personal income includes the wages and salaries of employees plus employers' contributions; self-employment income; rent, dividends, and net interest received by the personal sector; National Insurance benefits and other current grants from general government; and the imputed charge for consumption of private non-profit-making bodies. Figures are also shown of personal disposable income, which is the income remaining after deduction of taxes on income, National Insurance etc. contributions, the Community Charge or Council Tax and transfers abroad (net). The Community Charge was introduced in Scotland in April 1989 and in England and Wales in April 1990 and was superseded by the Council Tax in April 1993. However, Northern Ireland has retained domestic rates. Care should thus be taken when making comparisons between the countries of the United Kingdom, or when comparing time series, since domestic rates are not deducted when calculating personal disposable income.

Tables 12.8 and 12.9 Consumers' expenditure

Consumers' expenditure measures expenditure by households and private non-profit-making bodies resident in a region. Estimates are based mainly on the Family Expenditure Survey and are subject to sampling error and should be used with caution.

Up-to-date information on the data can be obtained from *Economic Trends*, No. 523, June 1997 (TSO).

CHAPTER 13: INDUSTRY AND AGRICULTURE

Charts 13.1, 13.3, 13.13 and 13.14

The industrial breakdown used is in accordance with the Standard Industrial Classification (SIC) Revised 1992. Agriculture, production and services are broken down as follows:

AGRICULTURE:
Section A	Agriculture, hunting and forestry
Section B	Fishing

PRODUCTION:
Section C	Mining and quarrying
Section D	Manufacturing
Section E	Utilities
Section F	Construction

SERVICES:
Section G	Wholesale and retail trade; repair of motor vehicles, motorcycles and personal and household goods
Section H	Hotels and restaurants
Section I	Transport, storage and communications
Section J	Financial intermediation
Section K	Real estate, renting and business activities
Section L	Public administration and defence; compulsory social security
Section M	Education
Section N	Health and social work
Section O	Other community, social and personal service activities

Previous editions featured manufacturing in these items; the move to production has been introduced so that the industrial coverage of these items is 100 per cent. These definitions are in line with National Accounts concepts.

Tables 13.4 and 13.5 Annual Sample Inquiry Into Production	The Annual Sample Inquiry Into Production covers UK businesses engaged in the production and construction industries: Section C to F of the SIC Revised 1992. Regional information is available only for manufacturing industry: ie. Section D of the SIC 1992.

Businesses often conduct their activities at more than one address (local unit) but it is not usually possible for them to provide the full range of inquiry data for each. For this reason only employment and capital expenditure are collected for these. Gross value added (GVA) is estimated for each local unit by apportioning the total GVA for the business in proportion to the total employment at each.

Gross value added is defined as:

The value of total sales and work done, adjusted by any changes during the year in work in progress and goods on hand for sale

Less: the value of purchases, adjusted by any changes in the stocks of material, stores and fuel etc.

Less: payments for industrial services received

Less: net duties and levies etc.

Less: the cost of non-industrial services, rates and motor vehicle licences.

GVA per head is derived by dividing the estimated GVA by the total number of people employed.

The tables include estimates for businesses not responding, or not required to respond, to the census.

Table 13.7 Government expenditure on regional preferential assistance to industry	The types of assistance included in Table 13.7 for Great Britain are: Regional Development Grants; Regional Selective Assistance; Regional Enterprise Grants; expenditure on Land and Factories by the English Industrial Estates Corporation, Scottish Enterprise, the Welsh Development Agency; and expenditure on Land and Factories and Grants by the Development Board for Rural Wales and Highlands and Islands Enterprise.

Northern Ireland has a different range of financial incentives available and so the figures have not been aggregated into a United Kingdom total. The items included are: Industrial Development Board grants and loans; expenditure on land and factories; Standard Capital Grants; and Local Enterprise Development Unit grants and loans.

All figures are gross and include payments to nationalised industries. GB payments relate only to projects situated in the Assisted Areas of Great Britain. A map showing the areas qualifying for preferential assistance to industry was included in *Regional Trends 31*.

Table 13.8 EU Structural Funds	Regions may be eligible for funding in one of three categories. 'Objective 1' funds promote the development of regions which are lagging behind the rest of the EU. To be eligible regions need to have a per capita GDP of 75 per cent or less of the EU average, although there are some exceptions to this. In these areas, emphasis is placed on creating a sound infrastructure: modernising transport and communication links, improving energy and water supplies, encouraging research and development, providing training and helping small businesses.

Areas suffering from industrial decline may be designated 'Objective 2'. These areas need help adjusting their economies to new industrial activities; they have high unemployment rates, and a high but declining share of industrial activity. EU grants may be provided to help create jobs, encourage new businesses, renovate land and buildings, promote research and development, and foster links between universities and industry.

Rural areas where economic development needs to be encouraged may be designated 'Objective 5b'. In these areas the focus is on developing jobs outside agriculture in small businesses and tourism, and improvements to transport and basic services are promoted to prevent rural depopulation.

Grants under Objectives 1, 2 and 5b are disbursed under the terms of Single Programming Documents or their equivalents, which provide a strategic framework relevant to the region concerned. The other objectives under which grants are allocated (3, 4, 5a), which cover long-term unemployment, jobs for young people and modernisation of farms, are not defined geographically. In addition the Structural Funds provide support for Community-wide Initiatives. These Initiatives account for 9 per cent of the Structural Funds budget.

A map showing the areas qualifying for EU Structural Funds under Objectives 1,2 and 5b was included in *Regional Trends 31*.

Table 13.9
Business registrations
and deregistrations

The estimates shown in Table 13.9 are the first in a new series compiled by the Department of Trade and Industry. They are based on counts of VAT registered enterprises. Estimates shown in previous editions of *Regional Trends* were based on VAT legal units. An enterprise is a legal unit, person or group of people producing goods or services under their own control and with their own legal identity. A branch or office of a larger organisation is not in itself an enterprise. There may be more than one VAT unit within an enterprise. The move to VAT-based enterprises is in line with changes in the VAT estimates published by the ONS, and allow users to compare the estimates with other enterprise based series.

The estimates are based on VAT data held by the ONS on the Inter Departmental Business Register (IDBR). They exclude firms which are not registered for VAT, either because their main activity is exempt from VAT, or because they have a turnover below the VAT threshold (currently £48,000) and have not registered on a voluntary basis. The threshold in November 1993 was £45,000; it was raised in November 1994 to £46,000, to £47,000 in November 1995 and to £48,000 in November 1996.

Tables 13.15-13.18
Agricultural census

The annual census encompasses the 245,000 main agricultural holdings in the United Kingdom in 1995. Estimates for minor holdings are included in the national totals for England, Wales and Northern Ireland; estimates are not included for Scotland or the English regions. Generally, minor holdings are characterised by a small agricultural area, low economic activity and a small labour input.

Table 13.17 Areas and yields

The figures for specific crops relate to those in the ground on the date of the June census or for which the land is being prepared for sowing at that date. In England and Wales cereal production is estimated from sample surveys held in September, November and April; oilseed rape production is estimated from a sample survey held in August. In Scotland, cereals and oilseed rape yields are estimated by local office staff in mid-September, followed by sample surveys later in the year. The Department of Agriculture for Northern Ireland estimates cereal and oilseed rape yields from a stratified sample survey of 200 farms carried out in the autumn of each year.

Table 13.19 Agricultural
gross domestic fixed
capital formation

The figures contained in this table represent gross fixed investment in agriculture net of asset sales. As well as including investments made by farmers, Plant and Machinery includes the value of new assets leased by the agricultural industry from the Banking, Insurance and Finance sector. Tractors and tractor parts are also included under this heading, but breeding livestock are excluded.

Vehicles include cars, vans and utilities used wholly or mainly in connection with the farm business. Similarly, Building and Works comprise only investments in buildings, drainage and other improvements which are wholly or mainly for agricultural purposes. More diversified investments in items such as farm shops and 'bed and breakfast' accommodation are excluded.

CHAPTERS 14-17:
SUB-REGIONAL STATISTICS

The statistics cover: counties and, where available, districts/unitary authorities in England; unitary authorities in Wales; the new council areas in Scotland; Health and Social Services Boards/Education and Library Boards/ districts as available in Northern Ireland.

Tables 14.2, 14.4, 14.6
District statistics
within England

These tables show selected statistics for individual local authority districts and the London boroughs. They complement the data shown in the other sub-regional tables and regionally in Chapters 3 to 13. A wide range of data are presented, covering population in Table 14.2, housing and households in Table 14.4, and labour market and economic statistics in Table 14.6.

Where data can be easily combined, county, regional and national totals are given to make comparison easier. However, it is sometimes the case that different sources of data or methodologies are used when disaggregating data to lower and lower geographical levels, and therefore it is not necessarily the case that data in this chapter are strictly comparable with data in other chapters. These data identify local as well as regional trends and because of the level of disaggregation more caution in interpretation is necessary.

There are specific and known problems in comparing population, employment and unemployment data at the district level. Primarily these are brought about by the fact that people will not always work or claim at an Employment Service Local Office in the district where they live. At national and regional level, unemployment is often expressed as a rate of the estimated total workforce. Such rates are calculated only for broadly self-contained labour markets and it is entirely inappropriate to calculate rates for individual districts. Table 14.6 excludes unemployment rates for this reason.

Allowing for the difficulties in interpreting such geographically disaggregated data, the figures in the relevant sub-regional tables can be used to give a broad picture of a particular district and how it compares with other districts.

The tables are intended to take a reasonably broad sweep across a range of subjects. More detailed statistics on specific topics may be readily available elsewhere. For example:

Key population and vital statistics (local and health authority areas of England and Wales)

Local Housing Statistics England and Wales (quarterly statistics by Local Authority area)

Projections of Households in England to 2016 (statistics for counties, metropolitan districts and London boroughs)

Labour Market Trends (unemployment by local authority districts and parliamentary constituency).

Tables 14.3-17.3 Education

Pupils in last year of compulsory schooling with no graded results are those who either did not attempt any GCSE, GCE, CSE or SCE examinations or did not achieve a sufficient standard to be awarded a grade.

Table 14.4 Housing starts

The housebuilding figures are complied from data provided by local authorities and by the National House-Building Council. If a local authority has not sent back statistical returns for 1995, the table shows that the data are not available. The table also shows where there has been a partial local authority response for the year. County, regional and England figures, however, include estimated figures that allow for these missing data. It is inappropriate to derive figures for any missing authorities from these estimated totals.

Figures shown for some local authorities may come from late statistical returns received after county and regional estimates were finalised. In these cases the total for individual local authorities in a county differ from the county total shown.

Tables 14.4-16.4 Council Tax

Amounts shown for Council Tax are headline Council Tax for the area of each billing authority for Band D, 2 adults, before transitional relief and benefit. The ratios of other bands are: A 6/9, B 7/9, C 8/9, E 11/9, F 13/9, G 15/9 and F 18/9.

Averages are calculated by dividing the sum of the tax requirement for each area by the tax base for the area. The taxbase is calculated by weighting each dwelling on the valuation list to take account of exemptions, discounts and disabled relief and the valuation band it falls into. It therefore represents the number of Band D equivalent (fully chargeable) dwellings.

Table 14.7 Regional accounts

Gross Domestic Product (GDP) measures the value of production of goods and services within each county of England. It does not measure the income of a county for two reasons.

Firstly, GDP excludes transfer payments such as pensions, social security, dividends and interest, which are important sources of income for residents and vary considerably between counties. Secondly, county GDP is measured on a workplace basis which means that the income from employment of commuters is attributed to the counties where they work rather than to those where they reside.

Comparisons of GDP between areas are usually in terms of GDP per head. However, in calculating GDP per head at county level, workplace estimates of GDP are divided by resident population: this results in very high estimates of GDP per head in urban counties where many workers are commuters, and low estimates for surrounding counties where these commuters reside. Thus the figures should be treated with caution.

The sources and methods used to compile county GDP are similar to those used for regional GDP although a simpler approach is sometimes necessary. A description of the methods is given in *Economic Trends*, No. 411, January 1988 (HMSO).

Tables 15.1-15.5 and 16.1-16.5 Unitary Authority/ New Council Statistics

The warnings given above on Tables 14.2, 14.4 and 14.6 apply to these tables.

Further Unitary Authority statistics can be found in *Digest of Welsh Local Area Statistics 1997* (Welsh Office) and (for Scotland) *The New Councils: Statistical Report* (The Stationery Office).

Reference years. Where a choice of years has to be made, the most recent year or a run of recent years is shown together with the past population census years (1991, 1981 etc) and sometimes the mid-points between census years (1986, etc). Other years may be added if they represent a peak or trough in the series.

Rounding of figures. In tables where figures have been rounded to the nearest final digit, there may be an apparent discrepancy between the sum of the constituent items and the total as shown.

Billion. This term is used to represent a thousand million.

Provisional and estimated data. Some data for the latest year (and occasionally for earlier years) are provisional or estimated. To keep footnotes to a minimum, these have not been indicated; source departments will be able to advise if revised data are available.

Non-calendar years.
Financial year - eg 1 April 1995-31 March 1996 would be shown as 1995-96
Academic year - eg September 1994/July 1995 would be shown as 1994/95
Data covering more than one year - eg 1993, 1994 and 1995 would be shown as 1993-1995

Units. Figures are shown in italics when they represent percentages.

Symbols. The following symbols have been used throughout *Regional Trends*:

..	*not available*
.	*not applicable*
-	*negligible (less than half the final digit shown)*
0	*nil*

Subject Index

Figures in the index refer to table or chart numbers, page numbers refer to maps. The Technical notes are not indexed.

Regional Trends 32, © Crown copyright 1997

Regional Trends 32, © Crown copyright 1997

Social Trends is essential reading for those involved in social policy work both inside and outside government. It has also become an essential book for market researchers, journalists and other commentators as well as students and the business community.

Social Trends draws together statistics from a wide range of government departments and other organisations to paint a broad picture of British society today.

13 chapters each focus on a different social policy area, described in tables, charts and explanatory text.

Available from the ONS Sales Desk on 0171-533 5678 or from The Stationery Office.

Social Trends

Published for
Office for **National Statistics** *by* The Stationery Office
Price £37.50
ISBN 0-11-620838-4

MONITOR THE LABOUR MARKET

If you need to keep tabs on the changing world of work, there's one publication you can't do without.........

Labour Market Trends (incorporating *Employment Gazette*) is ONS's monthly guide to the state of the labour market. First published in 1893, the journal contains over 100 pages of statistics and analysis of the latest trends in:

- **employment**
- **unemployment**
- **earnings**
- **vacancies**
- **hours**
- **labour disputes**
- **training**

Labour Market Trends gives latest results from national surveys like the monthly claimant count of unemployment and the Labour Force Survey, plus the most significant findings from the Government's labour market research programme. It also contains occasional statistical supplements.

Available from the ONS Sales Office on 0171-533 5678, the House of Commons Bookshop on 0171-219 3913 or from The Stationery Office.

Labour Market Trends

Published for

Office for **National Statistics** *by* The Stationery Office
Price £6.00 (individual copies); £63.50 (UK annual subscription); £89.50 (overseas annual subscription).
ISSN 1361 4819